D1587034

Blackstone's Police Manual

General Police Duties

The University of Law
14 Store Street
London
WC1E 7DE

WITHDRAWN

University of Law

A08968

Blackstone's Police Manual

Volume 4

General Police Duties

2022

Glenn Hutton

BA, MPhil, FCIPD

Elliot Gold

LLB (Hons), Barrister-at-Law

and

Paul Connor

Cert Ed (FE), PG Cert Ed (ODE), LLB

Consultant Editor: Paul Connor

OXFORD
UNIVERSITY PRESS

OXFORD

UNIVERSITY PRESS

Great Clarendon Street, Oxford, OX2 6DP,
United Kingdom

Oxford University Press is a department of the University of Oxford.
It furthers the University's objective of excellence in research, scholarship,
and education by publishing worldwide. Oxford is a registered trade mark of
Oxford University Press in the UK and in certain other countries

© Oxford University Press 2021

The moral rights of the authors have been asserted

First Edition published in 1998
Twenty-fourth Edition published in 2021

Impression: 1

All rights reserved. No part of this publication may be reproduced, stored in
a retrieval system, or transmitted, in any form or by any means, without the
prior permission in writing of Oxford University Press, or as expressly permitted
by law, by licence or under terms agreed with the appropriate reprographics
rights organization. Enquiries concerning reproduction outside the scope of the
above should be sent to the Rights Department, Oxford University Press, at the
address above

You must not circulate this work in any other form
and you must impose this same condition on any acquirer

Crown copyright material is reproduced under Class Licence
Number C01P0000148 with the permission of OPSI
and the Queen's Printer for Scotland

Published in the United States of America by Oxford University Press
198 Madison Avenue, New York, NY 10016, United States of America

British Library Cataloguing in Publication Data

Data available

ISBN 978–0–19–284845–1

DOI: 10.1093/law/9780192848451.001.0001

Printed in Great Britain by
Bell & Bain Ltd., Glasgow

Links to third party websites are provided by Oxford in good faith and
for information only. Oxford disclaims any responsibility for the materials
contained in any third party website referenced in this work.

Foreword for 2022 Blackstone's Police Manuals

The police service currently faces a series of challenges, from the changes that police forces must make to deliver savings and reduce crime, to the increasing complexity of the threats to national security, public safety and public order. Underpinning the ability of officers to deal effectively with these challenges are the knowledge and understanding of relevant law and procedure, and the skills to apply this on a daily basis. This understanding is the cornerstone in providing a professional policing service.

The College of Policing plays a vital role in the development of police officers and staff, helping them to obtain and retain the skills and knowledge they need to fight crime and protect the public. The College has a remit to develop, maintain and test standards to ensure suitability for promotion. Part of this responsibility requires the College to ensure a comprehensive and relevant syllabus is produced. As such, the College works alongside Oxford University Press to ensure these Manuals are an accurate and up-to-date source of information and that they reflect what is required by people working across policing.

The *Blackstone's Police Manuals 2022* are the definitive reference source and official study guide for the national legal examination which all candidates must successfully pass in order to be promoted to sergeant or inspector. Their content is derived from evidence gathered from operational sergeants and inspectors alongside input from the wider police service. Whilst they are primarily designed to support officers seeking to progress their careers in preparing for their promotion examinations, they also provide a reference point for officers and staff seeking to continue their professional development and maintain their knowledge as a professional in policing. If you are using these Manuals to prepare for your promotion examinations I would like to take this opportunity to wish you the very best of luck in your studies, and I hope these books will assist you in progressing your career within the police service.

Bernie O'Reilly
Interim CEO of the
College of Policing

Preface

The *Blackstone's Police Manuals* are the only official study guides for the Police Promotion Examinations—if the law is not in the Manuals, it will not be in the exams.

All the Manuals include explanatory keynotes and case law examples, providing clear and incisive analysis of important areas. They can also be used as a training resource for police probationers, special constables and PCSOs, or as an invaluable reference tool for police staff of all ranks and positions.

The 2022 edition has been edited and updated to incorporate all recent legislative changes and a number of recent criminal cases decided by the appellate courts.

The aim of this Manual is to take this shifting and growing body of law and analyse the essential elements in a practical and pragmatic context—without losing the specific meaning and applicability along the way. If we have achieved that, it is thanks to the contributions of the many police officers and staff, lawyers and practitioners who have helped in the development of this Manual, now in its twenty-third edition; if we haven't, it is not for the want of trying.

Oxford University Press are always happy to receive any useful written feedback from any reader on the content and style of the Manual, especially from those involved in or with the criminal justice system. Please email this address with any comments or queries: police@oup.com.

The law is stated as at 1 June 2021.

Acknowledgements

Blackstone's Police Manuals have become firmly established as a 'household name' in the context of police law for which they are the leading text in England and Wales. Their growth and refinement year on year is a result, not simply of Parliament and the legislators, but also of the many and varied contributions of the Manuals' wide readership.

Thanks are due to all (except perhaps the legislators) and there is never space to mention everyone individually.

In particular, thanks to the staff of the Legal Services Department of the College of Policing (CoP) and Examinations and Assessment.

Our thanks, as always, to all the staff involved in the production of the Manual in the Academic and Professional Law Department at Oxford University Press. Special thanks also to Sonal, Priya, Jayna, Selina and Rosalie for their continued support and forbearance.

Glenn Hutton, Paul Connor and Elliot Gold

Contents

Table of Cases

Table of Statutes

Table of Statutory Instruments

Table of Codes of Practice

Table of European Legislation

Table of Home Office Circulars

Table of International Treaties and Conventions

How to use this Manual

Volume numbers for the Manuals

The 2022 Blackstone's Police Manuals each have a volume number as follows:

Volume 1: *Crime*
Volume 2: *Evidence and Procedure*
Volume 3: *Road Policing*
Volume 4: *General Police Duties*

The first digit of each paragraph number in the text of the Manuals denotes the Manual number. For example, chapter 2.3 is chapter 3 of the *Evidence and Procedure* Manual and chapter 4.3 is chapter 3 of the *General Police Duties* Manual.

All index entries and references in the Tables of Legislation and the Table of Cases, etc. refer to paragraph numbers instead of page numbers, making information easier to find.

Material outside the scope of the police promotion examinations syllabus—blacklining

These Manuals contain some information which is outside the scope of the police promotion examinations. A full black line down the margin indicates that the text beside it is excluded from Inspectors' examinations.

PACE Code Chapters

The PACE Codes of Practice have been taken out of the appendices and are now incorporated within chapters in the main body of the Blackstone's Police Manuals. A thick grey line down the margin is used to denote text that is an extract of the PACE Code itself (i.e. the actual wording of the legislation) and does not form part of the general commentary of the chapter.

The PACE Codes of Practice form an important part of the police promotion examinations syllabus and are examinable for both Sergeants and Inspectors. They are not to be confused with 'blacklined' content that is excluded from the syllabus for Inspectors' examinations (see 'Material outside the scope of the police promotion examinations syllabus—blacklining').

Length of sentence for an offence

Where a length of sentence for an offence is stated in this Manual, please note that the number of months or years stated is the maximum number and will not be exceeded.

Any feedback regarding content or other editorial matters in the Manuals can be emailed to police@oup.com.

Police Promotion Examinations Rules and Syllabus Information

The rules and syllabus for the police promotion examinations system are defined within the Rules & Syllabus document published by College of Policing Selection and Assessment on behalf of the Police Promotion Examinations Board (PPEB). The Rules & Syllabus document is published annually each September, and applies to all police promotion assessments scheduled for the calendar year following its publication. For example, the September 2021 Rules & Syllabus document would apply to all police promotion assessments held during 2022.

The document provides details of the law and procedure to be tested within the National Police Promotion Framework Step 2 Legal Examination, and also outlines the rules underpinning the police promotion examination system.

All candidates who are taking a police promotion examination are strongly encouraged to familiarise themselves with the Rules & Syllabus document during their preparation. The police promotion examination rules apply to candidates undertaking the National Police Promotion Framework.

The document can be downloaded from the Development Section of the College of Policing website, which can be found at <https://www.college.police.uk>. Electronic versions are also supplied to all force examination officers.

If you have any problems obtaining the Rules & Syllabus document from the above source, please contact the Candidate Administration Team via the 'Contact us' section of the College of Policing website (see above).

Usually, no further updates to the Rules & Syllabus document will be issued during its year-long lifespan. However, in exceptional circumstances, the College of Policing (on behalf of the PPEB) reserves the right to issue an amended syllabus prior to the next scheduled annual publication date.

For example, a major change to a key area of legislation or procedure (e.g. the Codes of Practice) during the lifespan of the current Rules & Syllabus document would render a significant part of the current syllabus content obsolete. In such circumstances, it may be necessary for an update to the syllabus to be issued, which would provide guidance to candidates on any additional material which would be examinable within their police promotion examinations.

In such circumstances, an update to the Rules & Syllabus document would be made available through the College of Policing website, and would be distributed to all force examination contacts. The College of Policing will ensure that any syllabus update is distributed well in advance of the examination date, to ensure that candidates have sufficient time to familiarise themselves with any additional examinable material. Where possible, any additional study materials would be provided to candidates free of charge.

Please note that syllabus updates will only be made in *exceptional* circumstances; an update will not be made for every change to legislation included within the syllabus. For further guidance on this issue, candidates are advised to check regularly the College of Policing website, or consult their force examination officer, during their preparation period.

4.1 Stop and Search

PACE Code of Practice for the Exercise by Police Officers of Statutory Powers of Stop and Search; Police Officers and Police Staff of Requirements to Record Public Encounters (Code A)

> A thick grey line down the margin denotes text that is an extract of the PACE Code itself (i.e. the actual wording of the legislation). This material is examinable for both Sergeants and Inspectors.

4.1.1 Introduction

Code A deals with the exercise by police officers of statutory powers of stop and search and has been incorporated into this chapter with the addition of keynotes in appropriate places. This permits additional useful and explanatory detail to be presented to candidates that would not ordinarily be mentioned in any standard version of the code.

4.1.2 PACE Code of Practice for the Exercise by Police Officers of Statutory Powers of Stop and Search; Police Officers and Police Staff of Requirements to Record Public Encounters (Code A)

This code applies to any search by a police officer and the requirement to record public encounters taking place after midnight on 19 March 2015.

1.0 General

1.01 This Code of Practice must be readily available at all police stations for consultation by police officers, police staff, detained persons and members of the public.

1.02 The notes for guidance [included within the Keynotes of this chapter] are not provisions of this code, but are guidance to police officers and others about its application and interpretation. Provisions in the annexes to the code are provisions of this code.

1.03 This code governs the exercise by police officers of statutory powers to search a person or a vehicle without first making an arrest. The main stop and search powers to which this code applies are set out in Annex A, but that list should not be regarded as definitive. In addition, it covers requirements on police officers and police staff to record encounters not governed by statutory powers. This code does not apply to:

(a) the powers of stop and search under;

(i) Aviation Security Act 1982, section 27(2);

(ii) Police and Criminal Evidence Act 1984, section 6(1) (which relates specifically to powers of constables employed by statutory undertakers on the premises of the statutory undertakers).

(b) searches carried out for the purposes of examination under Schedule 7 to the Terrorism Act 2000 and to which the Code of Practice issued under paragraph 6 of Schedule 14 to the Terrorism Act 2000 applies.

(c) the powers to search persons and vehicles and to stop and search in specified locations to which the Code of Practice issued under section 47AB of the Terrorism Act 2000 applies.

4.1.3 Code A—1 Principles governing stop and search

1.1 Powers to stop and search must be used fairly, responsibly, with respect for people being searched and without unlawful discrimination. Under the Equality Act 2010, section 149, when police officers are carrying out their functions, they also have a duty to have due regard to the need to eliminate unlawful discrimination, harassment and victimisation, to advance equality of opportunity between people who share a relevant protected characteristic and people who do not share it, and to take steps to foster good relations between those persons. The Children Act 2004, section 11, also requires chief police officers and other specified persons and bodies to ensure that in the discharge of their functions they have regard to the need to safeguard and promote the welfare of all persons under the age of 18.

1.2 The intrusion on the liberty of the person stopped or searched must be brief and detention for the purposes of a search must take place at or near the location of the stop.

1.3 If these fundamental principles are not observed the use of powers to stop and search may be drawn into question. Failure to use the powers in the proper manner reduces their effectiveness. Stop and search can play an important role in the detection and prevention of crime, and using the powers fairly makes them more effective.

1.4 The primary purpose of stop and search powers is to enable officers to allay or confirm suspicions about individuals without exercising their power of arrest. Officers may be required to justify the use or authorisation of such powers, in relation both to individual searches and the overall pattern of their activity in this regard, to their supervisory officers or in court. Any misuse of the powers is likely to be harmful to policing and lead to mistrust of the police. Officers must also be able to explain their actions to the member of the public searched. The misuse of these powers can lead to disciplinary action.

1.5 An officer must not search a person, even with his or her consent, where no power to search is applicable. Even where a person is prepared to submit to a search voluntarily, the person must not be searched unless the necessary legal power exists, and the search must be in accordance with the relevant power and the provisions of this Code. The only exception, where an officer does not require a specific power, applies to searches of persons entering sports grounds or other premises carried out with their consent given as a condition of entry.

1.6 Evidence obtained from a search to which this Code applies may be open to challenge if the provisions of this Code are not observed.

4.1.4 Code A—2 Types of stop and search powers

2.1 This code applies, subject to paragraph 1.03, to powers of stop and search as follows:
(a) powers which require reasonable grounds for suspicion, before they may be exercised; that articles unlawfully obtained or possessed are being carried such as section 1 of PACE

for stolen and prohibited articles and section 23 of the Misuse of Drugs Act 1971 for controlled drugs;

(b) authorised under section 60 of the Criminal Justice and Public Order Act 1994, based upon a reasonable belief that incidents involving serious violence may take place or that people are carrying dangerous instruments or offensive weapons within any locality in the police area or that it is expedient to use the powers to find such instruments or weapons that have been used in incidents of serious violence, and

(c) *Not used.*

(d) the powers in Schedule 5 to the Terrorism Prevention and Investigation Measures (TPIM) Act 2011 to search an individual who has not been arrested, conferred by:

　(i) paragraph 6(2)(a) at the time of serving a TPIM notice;

　(ii) paragraph 8(2)(a) under a search warrant for compliance purposes; and

　(iii) paragraph 10 for public safety purposes.

See paragraph 2.18A.

(e) powers to search a person who has not been arrested in the exercise of a power to search premises (see Code B paragraph 2.4).

4.1.4.1

KEYNOTE

This Code does not affect the ability of an officer to speak to or question a person in the ordinary course of the officer's duties without detaining the person or exercising any element of compulsion. It is not the purpose of the Code to prohibit such encounters between the police and the community with the cooperation of the person concerned and neither does it affect the principle that all citizens have a duty to help police officers to prevent crime and discover offenders. This is a civic rather than a legal duty; but when a police officer is trying to discover whether, or by whom, an offence has been committed he/she may question any person from whom useful information might be obtained, subject to the restrictions imposed by Code C. A person's unwillingness to reply does not alter this entitlement, but in the absence of a power to arrest, or to detain in order to search, the person is free to leave at will and cannot be compelled to remain with the officer.

'Relevant Protected Characteristics'

The 'relevant protected characteristics' referred to in para. 1.1 include: age, disability, gender reassignment, pregnancy and maternity, race, religion or belief, sex and sexual orientation.

Application

It is important to emphasise that Code A of the PACE Codes of Practice applies to any search by a police officer, i.e. the principles and processes created by Code A must be followed in *all* searches (there are exceptions for certain powers under the Aviation Security Act 1982 and those exercised by statutory undertakers). A useful reference to the powers that Code A applies to within the syllabus material is produced in the following table.

Limited Operation of Search With Consent

Code A does not allow the routine searching of people with their consent and only permits very limited use of the power as a condition of entry (e.g. to a sports ground) (para. 1.5). This means the practice of conducting 'voluntary' searches in the street or other public places is not permitted.

Section 1 PACE 1984

There are many specific statutory authorities providing the police (and others) with powers to stop people and vehicles and search them (see Annex A of this Code at **appendix 4.1**). Perhaps the most important of these is the general power for police officers to stop and search people and vehicles under s. 1 of the Police and Criminal Evidence Act 1984 (PACE) referred to at para. 2.1(a).

Powers to Find Unlawful Articles Generally

What Power?	Who Uses It?	Where Exercisable?	What Mindset?	Why Use It?	Who/What Are You Searching?	Where in the Manuals?
Misuse of Drugs Act 1971, s. 23	Constable	Anywhere	Reasonable suspicion	To find controlled drugs	Persons and vehicles	*Crime*, para. 1.6.7.1
Firearms Act 1968, s. 47	Constable	A public place, or anywhere in the case of reasonable suspicion of offences of carrying firearms with criminal intent or trespassing with firearms	Reasonable suspicion	To find firearms/ammunition	Persons and vehicles	*Crime*, para. 1.7.13
Police and Criminal Evidence Act 1984, s. 1	Constable	Where there is public access	Reasonable suspicion	To find: Stolen goods; Articles made, adapted or intended for use in the course of or in connection with, certain offences under the Theft Act 1968, Fraud Act 2006 and Criminal Damage Act 1971; Offensive weapons, bladed or sharply pointed articles (except folding pocket knives with a bladed cutting edge not exceeding 3 inches); Fireworks: Category 4 (display grade) fireworks if possession prohibited, adult fireworks in possession of a person under 18 in a public place	Persons and vehicles	para. 4.1.4.1
Sporting events (Control of Alcohol etc.) Act 1985, s. 7	Constable	Designated sports grounds or coaches and trains travelling to or from a designated sporting event	Reasonable suspicion	To find intoxicating liquor	Persons, coaches and trains	para. 4.10.5
Criminal Justice Act 1988, s. 139B	Constable	School premises	Reasonable suspicion	Offensive weapons, bladed or sharply pointed article	Persons	para. 1.8.5.5
Other Search Powers						
Terrorism Prevention and Investigation Measures Act 2011, sch. 5, paras 6 and 8	Constable	Anywhere	No mindset required	Anything that contravenes measures specified in a TPIM notice	Persons in respect of whom a TPIM notice is being served or is in force	para. 4.1.4.14
Terrorism Prevention and Investigation Measures Act 2011, sch. 5, para. 10.	Constable	Anywhere	No mindset required	Anything that could be used to threaten or harm any person	Persons in respect of whom a TPIM notice is in force	para. 4.1.4.14
Criminal Justice and Public Order Act 1994, s. 60	Constable in uniform	Anywhere within a locality authorised under subs. (1)	No mindset required	Offensive weapons or dangerous instruments to prevent incidents of serious violence or to deal with the carrying of such items or find such items which have been used in incidents of serious violence	Persons and vehicles	para. 4.1.4.4

A summary of s. 1 of the Police and Criminal Evidence Act 1984 is that it provides a constable with the power to stop, detain and search a person and/or a vehicle (or anything in or on a vehicle) for stolen articles, prohibited articles, bladed or sharply pointed articles and for fireworks. While such a summary is useful, a more detailed analysis of the power is required.

The Police and Criminal Evidence Act 1984, s. 1 states:

(1) A constable may exercise any power conferred by this section—
    (a) in any place to which at the time when he proposes to exercise the power the public or any section of the public has access, on payment or otherwise, as of right or by virtue of express or implied permission; or
    (b) in any other place to which people have ready access at the time when he proposes to exercise the power but which is not a dwelling.

(2) Subject to subsection (3) to (5) below, a constable—
    (a) may search—
        (i) any person or vehicle;
        (ii) anything which is in or on a vehicle, for stolen or prohibited articles or any article to which subsection (8A) below applies or any firework to which subsection (8B) below applies; and
    (b) may detain a person or vehicle for the purpose of such a search.

(3) This section does not give a constable power to search a person or vehicle or anything in or on a vehicle unless he has reasonable grounds for suspecting that he will find stolen or prohibited articles or any article to which subsection (8A) below applies or any firework to which subsection (8B) below applies.

(4) If a person is in a garden or yard occupied with and used for the purposes of a dwelling or on other land so occupied and used, a constable may not search him in the exercise of the power conferred by this section unless the constable has reasonable grounds for believing—
    (a) that he does not reside in the dwelling; and
    (b) that he is not in the place in question with the express or implied permission of a person who resides in the dwelling.

(5) If a vehicle is in a garden or yard occupied with and used for the purposes of a dwelling or on other land so occupied and used, a constable may not search the vehicle or anything in or on it in the exercise of the power conferred by this section unless he has reasonable grounds for believing—
    (a) that the person in charge of the vehicle does not reside in the dwelling; and
    (b) that the vehicle is not in the place in question with the express or implied permission of a person who resides in the dwelling.

(6) If in the course of such a search a constable discovers an article which he has reasonable grounds for suspecting to be stolen or a prohibited article or an article to which subsection (8A) below applies or a firework to which subsection (8B) below applies, he may seize it.

(7) An article is prohibited for the purposes of this Part of this Act if it is—
    (a) an offensive weapon; or
    (b) an article—
        (i) made or adapted for use in the course of or in connection with an offence to which this sub-paragraph applies; or
        (ii) intended by the person having it with him for such use by him or by some other person.

(8) The offences to which subsection (7)(b)(i) above applies are—
    (a) burglary;
    (b) theft;
    (c) offences under section 12 of the Theft Act 1968 (taking motor vehicle or other conveyance without authority);
    (d) fraud (contrary to section 1 of the Fraud Act 2006); and
    (e) offences under section 1 of the Criminal Damage Act 1971 (destroying or damaging property).

(8A) This subsection applies to any article in relation to which a person has committed, or is committing or is going to commit an offence under section 139 of the Criminal Justice Act 1988.

(8B) This subsection applies to any firework which a person possesses in contravention of a prohibition imposed by fireworks regulations.

(8C) In this section—
    (a) 'firework' shall be construed in accordance with the definition of 'fireworks' in section 1(1) of the Fireworks Act 2003; and
    (b) 'fireworks regulations' has the same meaning as in that Act.

(9) In this Part of this Act 'offensive weapon' means any article—
    (a) made or adapted for use for causing injury to persons; or
    (b) intended by the person having it with him for such use by him or by some other person.

4.1.4.2

KEYNOTE

'Vehicle' and 'In Charge'

For these purposes, 'vehicle' includes vessels, aircraft and hovercraft (s. 2(10) of the 1984 Act).

For the meaning of 'in charge' of a vehicle, see *Road Policing*, chapter 3.1.

Search in a Garden, Yard or Land Connected to Dwelling

If the person to be searched is in a garden, yard or other land occupied with and used as part of a dwelling, the power to search *will not* apply unless the officer has 'reasonable grounds for *believing*' that the person does not live there and that he/she is not there with the permission (express or implied) of any person who does live there.

If the garden or yard is attached to a house that is not so 'occupied', the restriction at s. 1(4) would not appear to apply.

Similar restrictions are placed on the searching of vehicles found in such places by s. 1(5).

4.1.4.3

KEYNOTE

Prohibited Articles

'Offensive weapon' is defined as any article made or adapted for use for causing injury to the person, or intended by the person having it with him for such use or by someone else. There are three categories of offensive weapons: those made for causing injury to the person; those adapted for such a purpose; and those not so made or adapted, but carried with the intention of causing injury to the person. A firearm, as defined by s. 57 of the Firearms Act 1968, would fall within the definition of offensive weapon if any of the criteria above apply.

The power under s. 1 of the Police and Criminal Evidence Act 1984 *does not* authorise an officer in plain clothes to stop a vehicle (s. 2(9)(b)).

The power is restricted to those places set out in s. 1(1)(a) or (b) of the 1984 Act. This does not mean that the search itself must be carried out there; in fact Code A, paras 3.6 and 3.7 require certain searches to be carried out away from public view (**see para. 4.1.5**).

The power under s. 1 of PACE applies where the officer has 'reasonable grounds for suspecting' that he/she will find stolen or prohibited articles or articles falling under s. 139 of the Criminal Justice Act 1988 (bladed or sharply pointed articles; see *Crime*, chapter 1.8) or any firework to which s. 1(8B) of the 1984 Act applies (possession of a firework in contravention of a prohibition imposed by fireworks regulations.

The existence of reasonable grounds for suspicion is at the heart of the power under s. 1 and for that reason, Code A devotes considerable attention to the concept.

(a) Stop and search powers requiring reasonable grounds for suspicion—explanation

General

2.2   Reasonable grounds for suspicion is the legal test which a police officer must satisfy before they can stop and detain individuals or vehicles to search them under powers such as section 1 of PACE (to find stolen or prohibited articles) and section 23 of the Misuse of Drugs Act 1971 (to find controlled drugs). This test must be applied to the particular circumstances in each case and is in two parts:

(i) *Firstly,* the officer must have formed a *genuine suspicion* in their own mind that they will find the object for which the search power being exercised allows them to search (see Annex A, second column, for examples); and

(ii) *Secondly*, the suspicion that the object will be found must be *reasonable*. This means that there must be an *objective* basis for that suspicion based on facts, information and/or intelligence which are relevant to the likelihood that the object in question will be found, so that a reasonable person would be entitled to reach the same conclusion based on the same facts and information and/or intelligence.

Officers must therefore be able to explain the basis for their suspicion by reference to intelligence or information about, or some specific behaviour by, the person concerned (see *paragraphs 3.8(d)*, *4.6* and *5.5*).

2.2A The exercise of these stop and search powers depends on the likelihood that the person searched is in possession of an item for which they may be searched; it does not depend on the person concerned being suspected of committing an offence in relation to the object of the search. A police officer who has reasonable grounds to suspect that a person is in *innocent possession* of a stolen or prohibited article, controlled drug or other item for which the officer is empowered to search, may stop and search the person even though there would be no power of arrest. This would apply when a child under the age of criminal responsibility (10 years) is suspected of carrying any such item, even if they knew they had it.

Personal factors can never support reasonable grounds for suspicion

2.2B Reasonable suspicion can never be supported on the basis of personal factors. This means that unless the police have information or intelligence which *provides a description* of a person suspected of carrying an article for which there is a power to stop and search, the following *cannot be used*, alone or in combination with each other, or in combination with any other factor, as the reason for stopping and searching any individual, including any vehicle which they are driving or are being carried in:

(a) A person's physical appearance with regard, for example, to any of the 'relevant protected characteristics' set out in the Equality Act 2010, section 149, which are age, disability, gender reassignment, pregnancy and maternity, race, religion or belief, sex and sexual orientation (see *paragraph 1.1*), or the fact that the person is known to have a previous conviction; and

(b) Generalisations or stereotypical images that certain groups or categories of people are more likely to be involved in criminal activity.

2.3 *Not used*.

Reasonable grounds for suspicion based on information and/or intelligence

2.4 Reasonable grounds for suspicion should normally be linked to accurate and current intelligence or information, relating to articles for which there is a power to stop and search, being carried by individuals or being in vehicles in any locality. This would include reports from members of the public or other officers describing:

- a person who has been seen carrying such an article or a vehicle in which such an article has been seen.
- crimes committed in relation to which such an article would constitute relevant evidence, for example, property stolen in a theft or burglary, an offensive weapon or bladed or sharply pointed article used to assault or threaten someone or an article used to cause criminal damage to property.

2.4A Searches based on accurate and current intelligence or information are more likely to be effective. Targeting searches in a particular area at specified crime problems not only increases their effectiveness but also minimises inconvenience to law-abiding members of the public. It also helps in justifying the use of searches both to those who are searched and to the public. This does not, however, prevent stop and search powers being exercised in other locations where such powers may be exercised and reasonable suspicion exists.

2.5 *Not used.*

Reasonable grounds for suspicion and searching groups

2.6 Where there is reliable information or intelligence that members of a group or gang habitually carry knives unlawfully or weapons or controlled drugs, and wear a distinctive item of clothing or other means of identification in order to identify themselves as members of that group or gang, that distinctive item of clothing or other means of identification may provide reasonable grounds to stop and search any person believed to be a member of that group or gang.

2.6A A similar approach would apply to particular organised protest groups where there is reliable information or intelligence:
   (a) that the group in question arranges meetings and marches to which one or more members bring articles intended to be used to cause criminal damage and/or injury to others in support of the group's aims;
   (b) that at one or more *previous* meetings or marches arranged by that group, such articles have been used and resulted in damage and/or injury; and
   (c) that on the subsequent occasion in question, one or more members of the group have brought with them such articles with similar intentions.

These circumstances may provide reasonable grounds to stop and search any members of the group to find such articles. See also *paragraphs 2.12* to *2.18, 'Searches authorised under section 60 of the Criminal Justice and Public Order Act 1994'*, when serious violence is anticipated at meetings and marches.

Reasonable grounds for suspicion based on behaviour, time and location

2.6B Reasonable suspicion may also exist without specific information or intelligence and on the basis of the behaviour of a person. For example, if an officer encounters someone on the street at night who is obviously trying to hide something, the officer may (depending on the other surrounding circumstances) base such suspicion on the fact that this kind of behaviour is often linked to stolen or prohibited articles being carried. An officer who forms the opinion that a person is acting suspiciously or that they appear to be nervous must be able to explain, with reference to specific aspects of the person's behaviour or conduct which they have observed, why they formed that opinion (see *paragraphs 3.8(d)* and *5.5*). A hunch or instinct which cannot be explained or justified to an objective observer can never amount to reasonable grounds.

2.7 *Not used.*
2.8 *Not used.*

Securing public confidence and promoting community relations

2.8A All police officers must recognise that searches are more likely to be effective, legitimate and secure public confidence when their reasonable grounds for suspicion are based on a range of objective factors. The overall use of these powers is more likely to be effective when up-to-date and accurate intelligence or information is communicated to officers and they are well-informed about local crime patterns. Local senior officers have a duty to ensure that those under their command who exercise stop and search powers have access to such information, and the officers exercising the powers have a duty to acquaint themselves with that information (see *paragraphs 5.1 to 5.6*).

Questioning to decide whether to carry out a search

2.9 An officer who has reasonable grounds for suspicion may detain the person concerned in order to carry out a search. Before carrying out the search the officer may ask questions about the person's behaviour or presence in circumstances which gave rise to the suspicion. As a result of questioning the detained person, the reasonable grounds for suspicion necessary to detain that person may be confirmed or, because of a satisfactory explanation, be dispelled. Questioning may also reveal reasonable grounds to suspect the possession of a different kind of unlawful article from that originally suspected. Reasonable grounds for suspicion however cannot be provided retrospectively by such questioning during a person's detention or by refusal to answer any questions asked.

2.10 If, as a result of questioning before a search, or other circumstances which come to the attention of the officer, there cease to be reasonable grounds for suspecting that an article of a kind for which there is a power to stop and search is being carried, no search may take place. In the absence of any other lawful power to detain, the person is free to leave at will and must be so informed.

2.11 There is no power to stop or detain a person in order to find grounds for a search. Police officers have many encounters with members of the public which do not involve detaining people against their will and do not require any statutory power for an officer to speak to a person (see *paragraph 4.12*). However, if reasonable grounds for suspicion emerge during such an encounter, the officer may detain the person to search them, even though no grounds existed when the encounter began. As soon as detention begins, and before searching, the officer must inform the person that they are being detained for the purpose of a search and take action in accordance with *paragraphs 3.8 to 3.11 under 'Steps to be taken prior to a search'*.

4.1.4.4

KEYNOTE

Reasonable Grounds for Suspicion

Innocent possession (mentioned at para. 2.2A) means that the person does not have the guilty knowledge that they are carrying an unlawful item which is required before an arrest on suspicion that the person has committed an offence in respect of the item sought (if arrest is necessary—see PACE Code G) and/or a criminal prosecution can be considered. It is not uncommon for children under the age of criminal responsibility to be used by older children and adults to carry stolen property, drugs and weapons and, in some cases, firearms, for the criminal benefit of others, either:

- in the hope that police may not suspect they are being used for carrying the items; or
- knowing that if they are suspected of being couriers and are stopped and searched, they cannot be arrested or prosecuted for any criminal offence.

Stop and search powers therefore allow the police to intervene effectively to break up criminal gangs and groups that use young children to further their criminal activities.

Whenever a child under 10 is suspected of carrying unlawful items for someone else, or is found in circumstances which suggest that their welfare and safety may be at risk, the facts should be reported and actioned in accordance with established force safeguarding procedures. This will be in addition to treating the child as a potentially vulnerable or intimidated witness in respect of their status as a witness to the serious criminal offence(s) committed by those using them as couriers. Safeguarding considerations will also apply to other persons aged under 18 who are stopped and searched under any of the powers to which this Code applies. See para. 1.1 with regard to the requirement under the Children Act 2004, s. 11, for chief police officers and other specified persons and bodies to ensure that in the discharge of their functions they have regard to the need to safeguard and promote the welfare of all persons under the age of 18.

In some circumstances preparatory questioning may be unnecessary, but in general a brief conversation or exchange will be desirable not only as a means of avoiding unsuccessful searches, but to explain the grounds for the stop/search, to gain cooperation and reduce any tension there might be surrounding the stop/search process.

Where a person is lawfully detained for the purpose of a search, but no search in the event takes place, the detention will not thereby have been rendered unlawful.

The issue of when an officer has reasonable grounds for suspicion has been developed by the courts for many years. This common law development is supported by the inclusion of specific guidance on search powers that require reasonable grounds for suspicion.

'Suspicion' requires a lower degree of certainty than 'belief'. A statutory requirement for 'belief' imposes a greater degree of certainty on the officers concerned (*Baker* v *Oxford* [1980] RTR 315). Accordingly, police officers using powers that impose such an extra requirement must be prepared to justify their belief. Suspicion can be based on any evidence, even if the evidence itself would be inadmissible at trial (e.g. because it is hearsay).

The courts have accepted that reasonable grounds for suspicion can arise from information given to the officer by a colleague, an informant or even anonymously (*O'Hara* v *Chief Constable of the Royal Ulster Constabulary* [1997] AC 286).

The courts have held that it must be shown that any such grounds on which an officer acted would have been enough to give rise to that suspicion in a 'reasonable person' (*Nakkuda Ali* v *Jayaratne* [1951] AC 66).

However, the mere existence of such circumstances or evidence is not enough. The officer must actually have a 'reasonable suspicion' that the relevant articles will be found. If, in fact, the officer knows that there is little or no likelihood of finding the articles, the power could not be used (*R* v *Harrison* [1938] 3 All ER 134).

Paragraph 2.6 makes provision for the searching of members of gangs or groups who habitually carry knives unlawfully, weapons or drugs and wear a distinctive item of clothing or other means of identifying themselves with such a group, but only where there is reliable information or intelligence that members of the group or gang do so. Other means of identification might include jewellery, insignias, tattoos or other features which are known to identify members of the particular gang or group.

A decision to search individuals believed to be members of a particular group or gang must be judged on a case-by-case basis according to the circumstances applicable at the time of the proposed searches and in particular having regard to: (a) the number of items suspected of being carried; (b) the nature of those items and the risk they pose; and (c) the number of individuals to be searched. A group search will only be justified if it is a necessary and proportionate approach based on the facts and having regard to the nature of the suspicion in these cases. The extent and thoroughness of the searches must not be excessive. The size of the group and the number of individuals it is proposed to search will be a key factor and steps should be taken to identify those who are to be searched to avoid unnecessary inconvenience to unconnected members of the public who are also present. The onus is on the police to be satisfied and to demonstrate that their approach to the decision to search is in pursuit of a legitimate aim, necessary and proportionate.

Searches authorised under section 60 of the Criminal Justice and Public Order Act 1994

2.12 Authority for a constable in uniform to stop and search under section 60 of the Criminal Justice and Public Order Act 1994 may be given if the authorising officer reasonably believes:
   (a) that incidents involving serious violence may take place in any locality in the officer's police area, and it is expedient to use these powers to prevent their occurrence;
   (b) that persons are carrying dangerous instruments or offensive weapons without good reason in any locality in the officer's police area; or

(c) that an incident involving serious violence has taken place in the officer's police area, a dangerous instrument or offensive weapon used in the incident is being carried by a person in any locality in that police area, and it is expedient to use these powers to find that instrument or weapon.

2.13 An authorisation under section 60 may only be given by an officer of the rank of inspector or above and in writing, or orally if paragraph 2.12(c) applies and it is not practicable to give the authorisation in writing. The authorisation (whether written or oral) must specify the grounds on which it was given, the locality in which the powers may be exercised and the period of time for which they are in force. The period authorised shall be no longer than appears reasonably necessary to prevent, or seek to prevent incidents of serious violence, or to deal with the problem of carrying dangerous instruments or offensive weapons or to find a dangerous instrument or offensive weapon that has been used. It may not exceed 24 hours. An oral authorisation given where paragraph 2.12(c) applies must be recorded in writing as soon as practicable.

2.14 An inspector who gives an authorisation must, as soon as practicable, inform an officer of or above the rank of superintendent. This officer may direct that the authorisation shall be extended for a further 24 hours, if violence or the carrying of dangerous instruments or offensive weapons has occurred, or is suspected to have occurred, and the continued use of the powers is considered necessary to prevent or deal with further such activity or to find a dangerous instrument or offensive weapon that has been used. That direction must be given in writing unless it is not practicable to do so, in which case it must be recorded in writing as soon as practicable afterwards.

2.14A The selection of persons and vehicles under s. 60 to be stopped and, if appropriate searched should reflect an objective assessment of the nature of the incident or weapon in question and the individuals and vehicles thought likely to be associated with that incident or those weapons. The powers must not be used to stop and search persons and vehicles for reasons unconnected with the purpose of the authorisation. When selecting persons and vehicles to be stopped in response to a specific threat or incident, officers must take care not to discriminate unlawfully against anyone on the grounds of any of the protected characteristics set out in the Equality Act 2010 (see paragraph 1.1).

2.14B The driver of a vehicle which is stopped under section 60 and any person who is searched under section 60 are entitled to a written statement to that effect if they apply within twelve months from the day the vehicle was stopped or the person was searched. This statement is a record which states that the vehicle was stopped or (as the case may be) that the person was searched under s. 60 and it may form part of the search record or be supplied as a separate record.

4.1.4.5 **KEYNOTE**

Section 60 of the Criminal Justice and Public Order Act 1994

Section 60 of the 1994 Act states:

(1) If a police officer of or above the rank of inspector reasonably believes—
  (a) that incidents involving serious violence may take place in any locality in his police area, and that it is expedient to give an authorisation under this section to prevent their occurrence,
  (aa) that—
    (i) an incident involving serious violence has taken place in England and Wales in his police area;
    (ii) a dangerous instrument or offensive weapon used in the incident is being carried in any locality in his police area by a person; and
    (iii) it is expedient to give an authorisation under this section to find the instrument or weapon; or
  (b) that persons are carrying dangerous instruments or offensive weapons in any locality in his police area without good reason, he may give an authorisation that the powers conferred by this section are to be exercisable at any place within that locality for a specified period not exceeding 24 hours.

(2)   [repealed]

(3)   . . .

(3A)   . . .

(4)   This section confers on any constable in uniform power—

    (a)   to stop any pedestrian and search him or anything carried by him for offensive weapons or dangerous instruments;

    (b)   to stop any vehicle and search the vehicle, its driver and any passenger for offensive weapons or dangerous instruments.

The powers under s. 60 are *separate from* and *additional to* the normal stop and search powers which require reasonable grounds to suspect an individual of carrying an offensive weapon (or other article). Their overall purpose is to prevent serious violence and the widespread carrying of weapons which might lead to persons being seriously injured by disarming potential offenders or finding weapons that have been used in circumstances where other powers would not be sufficient. They should not therefore be used to replace or circumvent the normal powers for dealing with routine crime problems. A particular example might be an authorisation to prevent serious violence or the carrying of offensive weapons at a sports event by rival team supporters when the expected general appearance and age range of those likely to be responsible, alone, would not be sufficiently distinctive to support reasonable suspicion (see Code A, para. 2.6).

4.1.4.6

KEYNOTE

Initial Authorisation

The *reasonable belief* on the part of the officer authorising the use of the power under s. 60 must have an objective basis, for example: intelligence or relevant information such as a history of antagonism and violence between particular groups; previous incidents of violence at, or connected with, particular events or locations; a significant increase in knife-point robberies in a limited area; reports that individuals are regularly carrying weapons in a particular locality or information following an incident in which weapons were used about where the weapons might be found.

Any authorisation made under s. 60 must be made only when the officer believes it is necessary. In practice, in addition to expediency, which is explicit in the 1994 Act, the authorising officer must also have considered the authorisation necessary to prevent serious violence or to find dangerous instruments or weapons after an incident involving serious violence, or to apprehend persons carrying weapons.

It is for the authorising officer to determine the period of time during which the power may be exercised and in any event must not exceed 24 hours. The officer should set the minimum period he/she considers necessary to deal with the risk of violence, the carrying of knives or offensive weapons or to find dangerous instruments or weapons that have been used. A direction to extend the period authorised under the power may be given only once (by a superintendent or above for a further period not exceeding 24 hours). So the maximum period a s. 60 authorisation could last for would be 48 hours—thereafter further use of the powers requires a new authorisation.

It is for the authorising officer to determine the geographical area in which the use of the powers is to be authorised. In doing so the officer may wish to take into account factors such as the nature and venue of the anticipated incident or the incident which has taken place, the number of people who may be in the immediate area of that incident, their access to surrounding areas and the anticipated level of violence. The officer should not set a geographical area which is wider than he/she believes necessary for the purpose of preventing anticipated violence, the carrying of knives or offensive weapons or for finding a dangerous instrument or weapon that has been used. It is particularly important to ensure that constables exercising such powers are fully aware of where they may be used. If the area specified is smaller than the whole force area, the officer giving the authorisation should specify either the streets which form the boundary of the area or a divisional boundary within the force area. If the power is to be used in response to a threat or incident that straddles police force areas, an officer from each of the forces concerned will need to give an authorisation.

Extending the Authorisation

If it appears to an officer of or above the rank of superintendent that:

- having regard to offences that have been, or are reasonably suspected to have been, committed
- in connection with any activity falling within the authorisation, and
- it is expedient to do so

he/she may authorise the continuation of the authority to exercise the powers under s. 60(1) for a further period of 24 hours (s. 60(3) and Code A, para. 2.14).

This authorisation must be in writing, signed by the officer giving it, and must specify:

- the grounds on which it is given
- the locality in which it is to operate, and
- the period during which the powers are exercisable

and any direction for the authorisation to continue must also be given in writing at the time or reduced into writing as soon as it is practicable to do so (s. 60(9)).

4.1.4.7 **KEYNOTE**

Interpretation

'Serious violence' is not defined in the 1994 Act but, although violence could relate to property, the whole tenor of the section suggests that it is aimed at tackling violence against people. 'Dangerous instruments' are bladed or sharply pointed instruments, while offensive weapons have the same meaning as that under s. 1(9) of the Police and Criminal Evidence Act 1984. For the purposes of s. 60, 'carrying' will mean 'having in your possession' (s. 60(11A)), a much wider meaning than carrying usually conveys.

4.1.4.8 **KEYNOTE**

Powers, Offences and Entitlements

A significant difference between this power and the general powers of stop and search (which are not affected by the granting of this power (s. 60(12))), is that it does not require any grounds at all for the officer to suspect that the person/vehicle is carrying offensive weapons or dangerous instruments (s. 60(5)). However, para. 2.14A is clear in that it states that the stopping of people and/or vehicles should reflect the purpose of the authorisation and should be capable of 'objective assessment'. A further difference is that the power under s. 60 authorises *officers in uniform* to stop vehicles in order to search them and their occupants.

The power allows the stopping and searching of pedestrians, vehicles (including caravans, aircraft, vessels and hovercraft) and passengers. If a dangerous instrument or anything reasonably suspected to be an 'offensive weapon' is found during the search, the officer may seize it (s. 60(6)).

The general requirements governing searches imposed by Code A apply to this power.

Failing to stop (or to stop a vehicle) when required to do so under this power is a summary offence punishable with one month's imprisonment and/or a fine (s. 60(8)(a)).

Powers to require removal of face coverings

2.15 Section 60AA of the Criminal Justice and Public Order Act 1994 also provides a power to demand the removal of disguises. The officer exercising the power must reasonably believe that someone is wearing an item wholly or mainly for the purpose of concealing identity. There is also a power to seize such items where the officer believes that a person intends to wear them for this purpose. There is no power to stop and search for disguises. An officer may seize any such item which is discovered when exercising a power of search for something else, or which is being carried, and which the officer reasonably believes is intended to be used for concealing anyone's identity. This power can only be used if an authorisation under section 60 or an authorisation under section 60AA is in force.

2.16 Authority for a constable in uniform to require the removal of disguises and to seize them under section 60AA may be given if the authorising officer reasonably believes that activities may take place in any locality in the officer's police area that are likely to involve the commission of offences and it is expedient to use these powers to prevent or control these activities.

2.17 An authorisation under section 60AA may only be given by an officer of the rank of inspector or above, in writing, specifying the grounds on which it was given, the locality in which the powers may be exercised and the period of time for which they are in force. The period authorised shall be no longer than appears reasonably necessary to prevent, or seek to prevent the commission of offences. It may not exceed 24 hours.

2.18 If an inspector gives an authorisation, he or she must, as soon as practicable, inform an officer of or above the rank of superintendent. This officer may direct that the authorisation shall be extended for a further 24 hours, if crimes have been committed, or is suspected to have been committed, and the continued use of the powers is considered necessary to prevent or deal with further such activity. This direction must also be given in writing at the time or as soon as practicable afterwards.

4.1.4.9 **KEYNOTE**

Section 60AA of the Criminal Justice and Public Order Act 1994

The Criminal Justice and Public Order Act 1994, s. 60AA states:

(1) Where—
  (a) an authorisation under section 60 is for the time being in force in relation to any locality for any period, or
  (b) an authorisation under subsection (3) that the powers conferred by subsection (2) shall be exercisable at any place in a locality is in force for any period, those powers shall be exercisable at any place in that locality at any time in that period.

(2) This subsection confers power on any constable in uniform—
  (a) to require any person to remove any item which the constable reasonably believes that person is wearing wholly or mainly for the purpose of concealing his identity;
  (b) to seize any item which the constable reasonably believes any person intends to wear wholly or mainly for that purpose.

(3) If a police officer of or above the rank of inspector reasonably believes—
  (a) that activities may take place in any locality in his police area that are likely (if they take place) to involve the commission of offences, and
  (b) that it is expedient, in order to prevent or control the activities, to give an authorisation under this subsection, he may give an authorisation that the powers conferred by this section shall be exercisable at any place within that locality for a specified period not exceeding twenty-four hours.

The purpose of the powers under s. 60AA is to prevent those involved in intimidatory or violent protests using face coverings to conceal identity.

These provisions are wider than those under s. 60 in that they are not restricted to anticipated outbreaks of serious violence. This is not simply a preventive power and can be used where the 'activities' are already under way.

4.1.4.10 **KEYNOTE**

Initial Authorisation

The powers under s. 60AA are accessible in one of two ways:

- an authorisation is given under s. 60 of the Act—such an authorisation automatically engages the powers under s. 60AA in addition to the powers authorised under s. 60; or
- a 'stand-alone' authorisation under s. 60AA engages the s. 60AA powers.

The authorisation process closely follows that of an authorisation under s. 60 of the Act, i.e. the authorising officer reasonably believes that activities may take place in any locality in his/her police area that are likely (if they take place) to involve the commission of offences. This reasonable belief must have an objective basis, for example where the authorising officer is aware of previous incidents of crimes being committed while wearing face coverings to conceal identity. If an inspector gives an authorisation, they must, as soon as is practicable to do so, cause an officer of or above the rank of superintendent to be informed (s. 60AA(3)).

Extending the Authorisation

If it appears to an officer of or above the rank of superintendent that it is expedient to do so, having regard to offences which have been committed in connection with the activities in respect of which the authorisation was given, or are reasonably suspected to have been so committed, he/she may direct that the authorisation shall continue in force for a further 24 hours (s. 60AA(4)).

An authorisation (whether to grant the use of the power or to extend it) shall be in writing unless it is not practicable to do so. An oral authorisation will state the matters which would otherwise have been specified in a written authorisation (grounds for the search, locality and time period) and be recorded in writing as soon as it is practicable to do so.

The limitations and requirements as to the time and geographical extent of any authorisation are the same (see para. 4.1.4.9).

4.1.4.11   **KEYNOTE**

Interpretation

Any officer exercising these powers must reasonably *believe* that the person wearing the item is doing *so wholly or mainly for the purpose of concealing his/her identity or he/she intends to wear it wholly or mainly for that purpose*. Therefore if the person is a cyclist wearing a face mask to prevent the inhalation of traffic fumes, or a motorcyclist wearing a crash helmet, the fact that its *effect* is to conceal his/her identity will not be enough—concealing his/her identity has to be the whole purpose/main purpose of the wearer.

The expression 'item' is wide and would include balaclavas, scarves and crash helmets (if the officer believes that such items are being worn wholly or mainly to conceal identity). It is not specifically restricted to face coverings and extends to anything that could be worn wholly or mainly for the purpose of concealing identity (e.g. where offenders swap clothing after an offence). The purpose of the legislation is primarily to ensure that people are not allowed to commit offences anonymously in situations of public disorder.

4.1.4.12   **KEYNOTE**

Religious Sensitivities

Specific guidance in relation to religious sensitivities is provided by Code A. Many people customarily cover their heads or faces for religious reasons, e.g. Muslim women, Sikh men, Sikh or Hindu women or Rastafarian men or women. A police officer cannot order the removal of a head or face covering except where there is reason to believe that the item is being worn by the individual wholly or mainly for the purpose of disguising identity, not simply because it disguises identity. Where there may be religious sensitivities about ordering the removal of such an item, the officer should permit the item to be removed out of public view (perhaps in a police van or a police station if there is one nearby). Where practicable, the item should be removed in the presence of an officer of the same sex as the person and out of sight of anyone of the opposite sex. This approach is a general principle of Code A and would apply to all searches the Code relates to.

4.1.4.13

KEYNOTE

Powers and Offences

Unlike s. 60, there is no specific power under this section to stop vehicles but, given that this is a power for police officers in uniform, the general power under s. 163 of the Road Traffic Act 1988 could be used.

There is no power to search for face coverings etc. under this power. Clearly, if an item is found during a lawful search for other articles (say under s. 60(4)) which does not require any 'reasonable belief' by the officer, face coverings and masks could then be seized under subs. (b). The procedure to be followed in relation to the retention and disposal of items seized under s. 60 is set out in the Police (Retention and Disposal of Items Seized) Regulations 2002 (SI 2002/1372).

4.1.4.14

KEYNOTE

OFFENCE: **FAILING TO COMPLY WITH REQUIREMENT TO REMOVE ITEMS**—*Criminal Justice and Public Order Act 1994, s. 60AA(7)*

  • Triable summarily • One month's imprisonment and/or a fine

---

The Criminal Justice and Public Order Act 1994, s. 60AA states:

(7) A person who fails to remove an item worn by him when required to do so by a constable in the exercise of his power under this section shall be liable.

The wording of this offence is absolute. There is no requirement that the person failed without reasonable excuse or without good reason etc.; simply that he/she failed to remove an item worn by him/her. However, it must be shown that:

• the requirement was made (and presumably understood)
• it was made by a police officer in uniform
• in the exercise of powers authorised under s. 60

in the reasonable belief that the person was wearing the item wholly or mainly for the purpose of concealing his/her identity.

Searches under Schedule 5 to the Terrorism Prevention and Investigation Measures Act 2011

2.18A Paragraph 3 of Schedule 5 to the TPIM Act 2011 allows a constable to detain an individual to be searched under the following powers:
  (i) paragraph 6(2)(a) when a TPIM notice is being, or has just been, served on the individual for the purpose of ascertaining whether there is anything on the individual that contravenes measures specified in the notice;
  (ii) paragraph 8(2)(a) in accordance with a warrant to search the individual issued by a justice of the peace in England and Wales, a sheriff in Scotland or a lay magistrate in Northern Ireland who is satisfied that a search is necessary for the purpose of determining whether an individual in respect of whom a TPIM notice is in force is complying with measures specified in the notice (see *paragraph 2.20*); and
  (iii) paragraph 10 to ascertain whether an individual in respect of whom a TPIM notice is in force is in possession of anything that could be used to threaten or harm any person.
  See paragraph 2.1(e).

2.19 The exercise of the powers mentioned in paragraph 2.18A does not require the constable to have reasonable grounds to suspect that the individual:
  (a) has been, or is, contravening any of the measures specified in the TPIM notice; or
  (b) has on them anything which:

- in the case of the power in sub-paragraph (i), contravenes measures specified in the TPIM notice;
- in the case of the power in sub-paragraph (ii) is not complying with measures specified in the TPIM notice; or
- in the case of the power in sub-paragraph (iii), could be used to threaten or harm any person.

2.20 A search of an individual on warrant under the power mentioned in paragraph 2.18A(ii) must carried out within 28 days of the issue of the warrant and:
- the individual may be searched on one occasion only within that period;
- the search must take place at a reasonable hour unless it appears that this would frustrate the purposes of the search.

2.21 *Not used.*

2.22 *Not used.*

2.23 *Not used.*

2.24 *Not used.*

2.24A *Not used.*

2.25 *Not used.*

2.26 The powers under Schedule 5 only allow a constable to conduct a search of an individual only for specified purposes relating to a TPIM notice as set out above. However, anything found may be seized and retained if there are reasonable grounds for believing that it is or it contains evidence of any offence for use at a trial for that offence or to prevent it being concealed, lost, damaged, altered, or destroyed. However, this would not prevent a search being carried out under other search powers if, in the course of exercising these powers, the officer formed reasonable grounds for suspicion.

4.1.5 | Code A—3 Conduct of searches

3.1 All stops and searches must be carried out with courtesy, consideration and respect for the person concerned. This has a significant impact on public confidence in the police. Every reasonable effort must be made to minimise the embarrassment that a person being searched may experience.

3.2 The cooperation of the person to be searched must be sought in every case, even if the person initially objects to the search. A forcible search may be made only if it has been established that the person is unwilling to co-operate or resists. Reasonable force may be used as a last resort if necessary to conduct a search or to detain a person or vehicle for the purposes of a search.

3.3 The length of time for which a person or vehicle may be detained must be reasonable and kept to a minimum. Where the exercise of the power requires reasonable suspicion, the thoroughness and extent of a search must depend on what is suspected of being carried, and by whom. If the suspicion relates to a particular article which is seen to be slipped into a person's pocket, then, in the absence of other grounds for suspicion or an opportunity for the article to be moved elsewhere, the search must be confined to that pocket. In the case of a small article which can readily be concealed, such as a drug, and which might be concealed anywhere on the person, a more extensive search may be necessary. In the case of searches mentioned in paragraph 2.1(b) and (d), which do not require reasonable grounds for suspicion, officers may make any reasonable search to look for items for which they are empowered to search.

3.4 The search must be carried out at or near the place where the person or vehicle was first detained.

3.5 There is no power to require a person to remove any clothing in public other than an outer coat, jacket or gloves except under section 60AA of the Criminal Justice and Public Order Act 1994 (which empowers a constable to require a person to remove any item worn to conceal identity). A search in public of a person's clothing which has not been removed must be restricted to superficial examination of outer garments. This does not, however, prevent an officer from placing his or her hand inside the pockets of the outer clothing, or feeling round the inside of collars, socks and shoes if this is reasonably necessary in the circumstances to look for the object of the search or to remove and examine any item reasonably suspected to be the object of the search. For the same reasons, subject to the restrictions on the removal of headgear, a person's hair may also be searched in public (see paragraphs 3.1 and 3.3).

3.6 Where on reasonable grounds it is considered necessary to conduct a more thorough search (e.g. by requiring a person to take off a T-shirt), this must be done out of public view, for example, in a police van unless paragraph 3.7 applies, or police station if there is one nearby. Any search involving the removal of more than an outer coat, jacket, gloves, headgear or footwear, or any other item concealing identity, may only be made by an officer of the same sex as the person searched and may not be made in the presence of anyone of the opposite sex unless the person being searched specifically requests it (see Code C, Annex L).

3.7 Searches involving exposure of intimate parts of the body must not be conducted as a routine extension of a less thorough search, simply because nothing is found in the course of the initial search. Searches involving exposure of intimate parts of the body may be carried out only at a nearby police station or other nearby location which is out of public view (but not a police vehicle). These searches must be conducted in accordance with paragraph 11 of Annex A to Code C except that an intimate search mentioned in paragraph 11(f) of Annex A to Code C may not be authorised or carried out under any stop and search powers. The other provisions of Code C do not apply to the conduct and recording of searches of persons detained at police stations in the exercise of stop and search powers.

4.1.5.1

KEYNOTE

A search of a person should be completed as soon as possible.

A person may be detained under a stop and search power at a place other than where the person was first detained only if that place, be it a police station or elsewhere, is nearby. Such a place should be located within a reasonable travelling distance using whatever mode of travel (on foot or by car) is appropriate. This applies to all searches under stop and search powers, whether or not they involve the removal of clothing or exposure of intimate parts of the body (see Code A, paras 3.6 and 3.7) or take place in or out of public view. It means, for example, that a search under the stop and search power in s. 23 of the Misuse of Drugs Act 1971 which involves the compulsory removal of more than a person's outer coat, jacket or gloves cannot be carried out unless a place which is both nearby the place he/she was first detained and out of public view, is available. If a search involves exposure of intimate parts of the body and a police station is not nearby, particular care must be taken to ensure that the location is suitable in that it enables the search to be conducted in accordance with the requirements of para. 11 of Annex A to Code C.

A search in the street itself should be regarded as being in public for the purposes of paras 3.6 and 3.7, even though it may be empty at the time a search begins.

Although there is no power to require a person to do so, there is nothing to prevent an officer from asking a person *voluntarily to remove* more than an outer coat, jacket or gloves.

Steps to be taken prior to a search

3.8 Before any search of a detained person or attended vehicle takes place the officer must take reasonable steps, if not in uniform (see paragraph 3.9), to show their warrant card to the person to be searched or in charge of the vehicle to be searched and whether or not in uniform, to give that person the following information:

(a) that they are being detained for the purposes of a search;

(b) the officer's name (except in the case of enquiries linked to the investigation of terrorism, or otherwise where the officer reasonably believes that giving their name might put him or her in danger, in which case a warrant or other identification number shall be given) and the name of the police station to which the officer is attached;

 (c) the legal search power which is being exercised; and

 (d) a clear explanation of:

  (i) the object of the search in terms of the articles or articles for which there is a power to search; and

  (ii) in the case of

   • the power under section 60 of the Criminal Justice and Public Order Act 1994 (see paragraph 2.1(b)), the nature of the power, the authorisation and the fact that it has been given;

   • the powers under Schedule 5 to the Terrorism Prevention and Investigation Measures Act 2011 (see *paragraph 2.1(e)* and 2.18A):

    ~ the fact that a TPIM notice is in force or, (in the case of paragraph 6(2)(a)) that a TPIM notice is being served;

    ~ the nature of the power being exercised.

    For a search under paragraph 8 of Schedule 5, the warrant must be produced and the person be provided with a copy of it.

   • all other powers requiring reasonable suspicion (see paragraph 2.1(a)), the grounds for that suspicion. This means explaining the basis for the suspicion by reference to information and/or intelligence about, or some specific behaviour by, the person concerned (see *paragraph 2.2*).

 (e) that they are entitled to a copy of the record of the search if one is made (see section 4 below) if they ask within 3 months from the date of the search and:

  (i) if they are not arrested and taken to a police station as a result of the search and it is practicable to make a record on the spot, that immediately after the search is completed they will be given, if they request, either:

   • a copy of the record, or

   • a receipt which explains how they can obtain a copy of the full record or access to an electronic copy of the record, or

  (ii) if they are arrested and taken to a police station as a result of the search, that the record will be made at the station as part of their custody record and they will be given, if they request, a copy of their custody record which includes a record of the search as soon as practicable whilst they are at the station.

3.9 Stops and searches under the power mentioned in paragraph 2.1(b) may be undertaken only by a constable in uniform.

3.10 The person should also be given information about police powers to stop and search and the individual's rights in these circumstances.

3.11 If the person to be searched, or in charge of a vehicle to be searched, does not appear to understand what is being said, or there is any doubt about the person's ability to understand English, the officer must take reasonable steps to bring information regarding the person's rights and any relevant provisions of this Code to his or her attention. If the person is deaf or cannot understand English and is accompanied by someone, then the officer must try to establish whether that person can interpret or otherwise help the officer to give the required information.

4.1.5.2 **KEYNOTE**

This Code A requirement is mirrored by the specific requirements of s. 2 of the Police and Criminal Evidence Act 1984.

 The Police and Criminal Evidence Act 1984, s. 2 states:

(1) A constable who detains a person or vehicle in the exercise—

 (a) of the power conferred by section 1 above; or

     (b) of any other power—

         (i) to search a person without first arresting him; or

         (ii) to search a vehicle without making an arrest,

     need not conduct a search if it appears to him subsequently—

         (i) that no search is required; or

         (ii) that a search is impracticable.

(2) If a constable contemplates a search, other than a search of an unattended vehicle, in the exercise—

     (a) of the power conferred by section 1 above; or

     (b) of any other power, except the power conferred by section 6 below and the power conferred by section 27(2) of the Aviation Security Act 1982—

         (i) to search a person without first arresting him; or

         (ii) to search a vehicle without making an arrest,

     it shall be his duty, subject to subsection (4) below, to take reasonable steps before he commences the search to bring to the attention of the appropriate person—

         (i) if the constable is not in uniform, documentary evidence that he is a constable; and

         (ii) whether he is in uniform or not, the matters specified in subsection (3) below;

     and the constable shall not commence the search until he has performed that duty.

(3) The matters referred to in subsection (2)(ii) above are—

     (a) the constable's name and the name of the police station to which he is attached;

     (b) the object of the proposed search;

     (c) the constable's grounds for proposing to make it; and

     (d) the effect of section 3(7) or (8) below, as may be appropriate.

Having stopped a person for the purposes of searching him/her, there is no requirement for the officer to conduct the search if it appears that to do so is not necessary or that it is impracticable.

The officer carrying out the search must take reasonable steps to bring the matters at s. 2(3)(a)–(d) to the person's attention before starting the search. This information must be given whether it is requested or not. Whether reasonable steps have been taken to communicate information will ultimately be a question of fact for the court to decide and what is 'reasonable' will vary with the particular circumstances of each search (e.g. what is reasonable outside a busy city centre nightclub may well be different from that which is required on a rural public footpath). The courts have taken a firm position in interpreting and applying these requirements. For example, the requirements for officers to provide details of their names and police stations still apply even though that information is discernible from the officers' uniform; failure to provide the information in such circumstances will make any subsequent search unlawful and will mean that the person being searched may use reasonable force to resist it (*Osman* v *DPP* (1999) 163 JP 725). The requirement to provide the name of the officer concerned applies even if the officer conducting the search and the person who is subject to the search are well known to each other (*R (Michaels)* v *Highbury Corner Magistrates' Court* [2009] EWHC 2928 (Admin)). In a further case, the Divisional Court held that the officers conducting the stop and search had not informed the suspect of their intention to search him at an early enough stage before laying their hands on him. The suspect, who was standing with his hands in his pockets and who was suspected of drugs offences, had struggled with the officers when they took hold of him and had been arrested. The magistrates' court held that, where it was obvious that the people apprehending a suspect were police officers and where an officer was genuinely concerned for the safety of a fellow officer, it was not essential to comply with all the requirements of s. 2(3). However, the Divisional Court disagreed, quashing the conviction and holding that, where police officers contemplated a statutory search, they were required (by s. 2(2)) to comply with s. 2(3) before commencing the search (*Bonner* v *DPP* [2004] EWHC 2415 (Admin)).

The 'effect of section 3(7) or (8)' referred to in s. 2(3)(d) means the person's entitlement to a copy of any search record made.

The 'appropriate person' is the person to be searched or the person in charge of the vehicle to be searched (s. 2(5)).

Searching Unattended Vehicles

In the case of unattended vehicles, s. 2 of the Police and Criminal Evidence Act 1984 states:

(6) On completing a search of an unattended vehicle or anything in or on such a vehicle in the exercise of any such power as is mentioned in subsection (2) above a constable shall leave a notice—

     (a) stating that he has searched it;

(b) giving the name of the police station to which he is attached;

(c) stating that an application for compensation for any damage caused by the search may be made to that police station; and

(d) stating the effect of section 3(8) below.

(7) The constable shall leave the notice inside the vehicle unless it is not reasonably practicable to do so without damaging the vehicle.

4.1.6

Code A—4 Recording requirements

(a) Searches which do not result in an arrest

4.1 When an officer carries out a search in the exercise of any power to which this Code applies, and the search does not result in the person searched or person in charge of the vehicle searched being arrested and taken to a police station, a record must be made of it, electronically or on paper, unless there are exceptional circumstances which make this wholly impracticable (e.g. in situations involving public disorder or where the recording officer's presence is urgently required elsewhere). If a record is to be made, the officer carrying out the search must make the record on the spot unless this is not practicable, in which case, the officer must make the record as soon as practicable after the search is completed.

4.2 If the record is made at the time, the person who has been searched or who is in charge of the vehicle that has been searched must be asked if they want a copy and if they do, they must be given immediately, either:

- a copy of the record, or
- a receipt which explains how they can obtain a copy of the full record or access to an electronic copy of the record.

4.2A An officer is not required to provide a copy of the full record or a receipt at the time if they are called to an incident of higher priority.

(b) Searches which result in an arrest

4.2B If a search in the exercise of any power to which this Code applies results in a person being arrested and taken to a police station, the officer carrying out the search is responsible for ensuring that a record of the search is made as a part of their custody record. The custody officer must then ensure that the person is asked if they want a copy of the record and if they do, that they are given a copy as soon as practicable.

4.1.6.1

KEYNOTE

When the search results in the person searched or in charge of a vehicle which is searched being arrested, the requirement to make the record of search part of the person's custody record does not apply if the person is granted 'street bail' after arrest (s. 30A of the Police and Criminal Evidence Act 1984) to attend a police station and is not taken in custody to the police station. An arrested person's entitlement to a copy of the search record which is made as part of his/her custody record does not affect his/her entitlement to a copy of his/her custody record or any other provisions of PACE Code C, section 2 (Custody Records).

(c) Record of search

4.3 The record of a search must always include the following information:

(a) A note of the self-defined ethnicity, and if different, the ethnicity as perceived by the officer making the search, of the person searched or of the person in charge of the vehicle (as the case may be);

(b) The date, time and place the person or vehicle was searched;

(c) The object of the search in terms of the article or articles for which there is a power to search;

(d) In the case of:

- the power under section 60 of the Criminal Justice and Public Order Act 1994 (see paragraph 2.1(b)), the nature of the power, the authorisation and the fact that it has been given;
- the powers under Schedule 5 to the Terrorism Prevention and Investigation Measures Act 2011 (see paragraphs 2.1(e) and 2.18A):
  - ~ the fact that a TPIM notice is in force or, (in the case of paragraph 6(2)(a)), that a TPIM notice is being served;
  - ~ the nature of the power, and
  - ~ for a search under paragraph 8, the date the search warrant was issued, the fact that the warrant was produced and a copy of it provided and the warrant must also be endorsed by the constable executing it to state whether anything was found and whether anything was seized, and
- all other powers requiring reasonable suspicion (see paragraph 2.1(a)), the grounds for that suspicion.

(e) subject to paragraph 3.8(b), the identity of the officer carrying out the search.

4.3A For the purposes of completing the search record, there is no requirement to record the name, address and date of birth of the person searched or the person in charge of a vehicle which is searched and the person is under no obligation to provide this information.

4.4 Nothing in paragraph 4.3 requires the names of police officers to be shown on the search record or any other record required to be made under this code in the case of enquiries linked to the investigation of terrorism or otherwise where an officer reasonably believes that recording names might endanger the officers. In such cases the record must show the officers' warrant or other identification number and duty station.

4.5 A record is required for each person and each vehicle searched. However, if a person is in a vehicle and both are searched, and the object and grounds of the search are the same, only one record need be completed. If more than one person in a vehicle is searched, separate records for each search of a person must be made. If only a vehicle is searched, the self-defined ethnic background of the person in charge of the vehicle must be recorded, unless the vehicle is unattended.

4.6 The record of the grounds for making a search must, briefly but informatively, explain the reason for suspecting the person concerned, by reference to information and/or intelligence about, or some specific behaviour by, the person concerned (see *paragraph 2.2*).

4.7 Where officers detain an individual with a view to performing a search, but the need to search is eliminated as a result of questioning the person detained, a search should not be carried out and a record is not required. [See paragraph 2.10]

4.8 After searching an unattended vehicle, or anything in or on it, an officer must leave a notice in it (or on it, if things on it have been searched without opening it) recording the fact that it has been searched.

4.9 The notice must include the name of the police station to which the officer concerned is attached and state where a copy of the record of the search may be obtained and how (if applicable) an electronic copy may be accessed and where any application for compensation should be directed.

4.10 The vehicle must if practicable be left secure.

4.10A *Not used.*

4.10B *Not used.*

KEYNOTE

Recording Searches

Once again, Code A is mirrored by the requirements of s. 3 of the Police and Criminal Evidence Act 1984.

The Police and Criminal Evidence Act 1984, s. 3 states:

> (6) The record of a search of a person or a vehicle—
>   (a) shall state—
>   (i) the object of the search;
>   (ii) the grounds for making it;
>   (iii) the date and time when it was made;
>   (iv) the place where it was made;
>   (v) except in the case of a search of an unattended vehicle, the ethnic origins of the person searched or the person in charge of the vehicle searched (as the case may be); and
>   (b) shall identify the constable who carried out the search.
> (6A) The requirement in subsection (6)(a)(v) above, for a record to state a person's ethnic origins is a requirement to state –
>   (a) the ethnic origins of the person as described by the person, and
>   (b) if different, the ethnic origins of the person as perceived by the constable.

Officers should record the self-defined ethnicity of every person stopped according to the categories used in the 2001 census question listed in Annex B. The person should be asked to select one of the five main categories representing broad ethnic groups and then a more specific cultural background from within this group. The ethnic classification should be coded for recording purposes using the coding system in Annex B. An additional 'Not stated' box is available but should not be offered to respondents explicitly. Officers should be aware and explain to members of the public, especially where concerns are raised, that this information is required to obtain a true picture of stop and search activity and to help improve ethnic monitoring, tackle discriminatory practice, and promote effective use of the powers. If the person gives what appears to the officer to be an 'incorrect' answer (e.g. a person who appears to be white states that he/she is black), the officer should record the response that has been given and then record his/her own perception of the ethnic background by using the PNC classification system. If the 'Not stated' category is used the reason for this must be recorded on the form.

The requirements of s. 3 will apply to the searches of vehicles, vessels, aircraft and hovercraft (s. 3(10)).

It is important for monitoring purposes to specify if the authority for exercising a stop and search power was given under s. 60 of the Criminal Justice and Public Order Act 1994.

Where a person is lawfully detained for the purpose of a search, but no search in the event takes place, the detention will not thereby have been rendered unlawful.

It has been held that a failure to make a record of a search does not thereby render the search unlawful (*Basher* v *DPP* [1993] COD 372). However, it is not only the lawfulness of a search that is of concern to police officers and the general principles set out in Code A should be borne in mind at all times.

In situations where it is not practicable to provide a written copy of the record or immediate access to an electronic copy of the record or a receipt of the search at the time (see para. 4.2A), the officer should consider providing the person with details of the station at which the person may attend for a record. A receipt may take the form of a simple business card which includes sufficient information to locate the record should the person ask for the copy, e.g. the date and place of the search, a reference number or the name of the officer who carried out the search (unless para. 4.4 applies).

Where a stop and search is conducted by more than one officer the identity of all the officers engaged in the search must be recorded on the record. Nothing prevents an officer who is present but not directly involved in searching from completing the record during the course of the encounter.

Who is Entitled to a Copy of the Search Record?

If a record of the search under s. 1 of the Act has been made then the person who was searched shall be entitled to a copy of the record if he/she asks for one (s. 3(7)).

If a vehicle is searched and a record of the search has been made, then the owner of the vehicle which was searched or the person who was in charge of the vehicle at the time when it was searched is entitled to a copy of the record of search if they ask for one (s. 3(8)).

In both of the above cases, the entitlement to a copy of the search record will run for three months beginning on the date on which the search was made (s. 3(9)).

Recording of encounters not governed by Statutory Powers

4.11 *Not used.*

4.12 There is no national requirement for an officer who requests a person in a public place to account for themselves, i.e. their actions, behaviour, presence in an area or possession of anything, to make a record of the encounter or to give the person a receipt (see paragraph 2.11).

4.12A *Not used.*

4.13 *Not used.*

4.14 *Not used.*

4.15 *Not used.*

4.16 *Not used.*

4.17 *Not used.*

4.18 *Not used.*

4.19 *Not used.*

4.20 *Not used.*

4.1.6.3

KEYNOTE

Where there are concerns which make it necessary to monitor any local disproportionality, forces have discretion to direct officers to record the self-defined ethnicity of persons they request to account for themselves in a public place or who they detain with a view to searching but do not search. Guidance should be provided locally and efforts made to minimise the bureaucracy involved. Records should be closely monitored and supervised in line with paras 5.1 to 5.4 and forces can suspend or reinstate recording of these encounters as appropriate.

A person who is asked to account for him/herself should, if he/she requests, be given information about how to report his/her dissatisfaction about how he/she has been treated.

4.1.7

Code A—5 Monitoring and supervising the use of stop and search powers

General

5.1 Any misuse of stop and search powers is likely to be harmful to policing and lead to mistrust of the police by the local community and by the public in general. Supervising officers must monitor the use of stop and search powers and should consider in particular whether there is any evidence that they are being exercised on the basis of stereotyped images or inappropriate generalisations. Supervising officers must satisfy themselves that the practice of officers under their supervision in stopping, searching and recording is fully in accordance with this Code. Supervisors must also examine whether the records reveal any trends or patterns which give cause for concern and, if so, take appropriate action to address this. (See *paragraph 2.8A*.)

5.2 Senior officers with area or force-wide responsibilities must also monitor the broader use of stop and search powers and, where necessary, take action at the relevant level.

5.3 Supervision and monitoring must be supported by the compilation of comprehensive statistical records of stops and searches at force, area and local level. Any apparently disproportionate use of the powers by particular officers or groups of officers or in relation to specific sections of the community should be identified and investigated.

5.4 In order to promote public confidence in the use of the powers, forces in consultation with police and crime commissioners must make arrangements for the records to be scrutinised by representatives of the community, and to explain the use of the powers at a local level.

Suspected misuse of powers by individual officers

5.5 Police supervisors must monitor the use of stop and search powers by individual officers to ensure that they are being applied appropriately and lawfully. Monitoring takes many forms, such as direct supervision of the exercise of the powers, examining stop and search records (particularly examining the officer's documented reasonable grounds for suspicion) and asking the officer to account for the way in which they conducted and recorded particular searches or through complaints about a stop and search that an officer has carried out.

5.6 Where a supervisor identifies issues with the way that an officer has used a stop and search power, the facts of the case will determine whether the standards of professional behaviour as set out in the Code of Ethics [<https://www.college.police.uk/What-we-do/Ethics/Ethics-home/Pages/Code-of-Ethics.aspx>] have been breached and which formal action is pursued. Improper use might be a result of poor performance or a conduct matter, which will require the supervisor to take appropriate action such as performance or misconduct procedures. It is imperative that supervisors take both timely and appropriate action to deal with all such cases that come to their notice.

4.1.7.1

KEYNOTE

Arrangements for public scrutiny of records should take account of the right to confidentiality of those stopped and searched. Anonymised forms and/or statistics generated from records should be the focus of the examinations by members of the public.

4.2 Entry, Search and Seizure

PACE Code of Practice for Searches of Premises by Police Officers and the Seizure of Property found by Police Officers on Persons or Premises (Code B)

A thick grey line down the margin denotes text that is an extract of the PACE Code itself (i.e. the actual wording of the legislation). This material is examinable for both Sergeants and Inspectors.

4.2.1 Introduction

The main police powers dealing with entry to premises, searching them and seizing evidence from them, are contained within the Police and Criminal Evidence Act 1984; Code B of the Codes of Practice provides detailed guidance in relation to these features.

There are many other statutes that allow such processes to take place. However, only one common law power of entry without warrant exists—to deal with a breach of the peace (see chapter 4.8).

A general point worth remembering is that where police officers enter premises *lawfully* (including where they are there by invitation), they are on the premises for *all* lawful purposes (*Foster* v *Attard* [1986] Crim LR 627). This means that they can carry out any lawful functions while on the premises, even if that was not the original purpose for entry. For instance, if officers entered under a lawful power provided by the Misuse of Drugs Act 1971, they may carry out other lawful functions such as enforcing the provisions of the Gaming Act 1968. If officers are invited onto premises by someone entitled to do so, they are lawfully there unless and until that invitation is withdrawn. Once the invitation is withdrawn, the officers will become trespassers unless they have a power to be there, and the person may remove them by force (*Robson* v *Hallett* [1967] 2 QB 939). If that invitation is terminated, the person needs to communicate that clearly to the officer; merely telling officers to 'fuck off' is not necessarily sufficient (*Snook* v *Mannion* [1982] RTR 321).

The above issues are of significance to police officers but the features of the Police and Criminal Evidence Act 1984 and Code B remain the most important for the purposes of operational policing and that is the focus of this chapter.

4.2.2 PACE Code of Practice for Searches of Premises by Police Officers and the Seizure of Property found by Police Officers on Persons or Premises (Code B)

This Code applies to applications for warrants made after midnight 6 March 2011 and to searches and seizures taking place after midnight on 27 October 2013.

1 Introduction

1.1 This Code of Practice deals with police powers to:

- search premises
- seize and retain property found on premises and persons

1.1A These powers may be used to find:

- property and material relating to a crime
- wanted persons
- children who abscond from local authority accommodation where they have been remanded or committed by a court

1.2 A justice of the peace may issue a search warrant granting powers of entry, search and seizure, e.g. warrants to search for stolen property, drugs, firearms and evidence of serious offences. Police also have powers without a search warrant. The main ones provided by the Police and Criminal Evidence Act 1984 (PACE) include powers to search premises:

- to make an arrest
- after an arrest

1.3 The right to privacy and respect for personal property are key principles of the Human Rights Act 1998. Powers of entry, search and seizure should be fully and clearly justified before use because they may significantly interfere with the occupier's privacy. Officers should consider if the necessary objectives can be met by less intrusive means.

1.3A Powers to search and seize must be used fairly, responsibly, with respect for people who occupy premises being searched or are in charge of property being seized and without unlawful discrimination. Under the Equality Act 2010, section 149, when police officers are carrying out their functions, they also have a duty to have due regard to the need to eliminate unlawful discrimination, harassment and victimisation, to advance equality of opportunity between people who share a relevant protected characteristic and people who do not share it, and to take steps to foster good relations.

1.4 In all cases, police should therefore:

- exercise their powers courteously and with respect for persons and property
- only use reasonable force when this is considered necessary and proportionate to the circumstances.

1.5 If the provisions of PACE and this Code are not observed, evidence obtained from a search may be open to question.

KEYNOTE

In para. 1.3A, 'relevant protected characteristic' includes: age, disability, gender reassignment, pregnancy and maternity, race, religion or belief, sex and sexual orientation.

4.2.3

Code B—2 General

2.1 This Code must be readily available at all police stations for consultation by:

- police officers
- police staff
- detained persons
- members of the public

2.2 The *Notes for Guidance* [incorporated within Keynotes of this Manual] are not provisions of this Code.

2.3 This Code applies to searches of premises:

(a) by police for the purposes of an investigation into an alleged offence, with the occupier's consent, other than:

- routine scene of crime searches;
- calls to a fire or burglary made by or on behalf of an occupier or searches following the activation of fire or burglar alarms or discovery of insecure premises;
- searches when *paragraph 5.4* applies;
- bomb threat calls;

(b) under powers conferred on police officers by PACE, sections 17, 18 and 32;

(c) undertaken in pursuance of search warrants issued to and executed by constables in accordance with PACE, sections 15 and 16;

(d) subject to *paragraph 2.6*, under any other power given to police to enter premises with or without a search warrant for any purpose connected with the investigation into an alleged or suspected offence.

For the purposes of this Code, 'premises' as defined in PACE, section 23, includes any place, vehicle, vessel, aircraft, hovercraft, tent or movable structure and any offshore installation as defined in the Mineral Workings (Offshore Installations) Act 1971, section 1.

2.4 A person who has not been arrested but is searched during a search of premises should be searched in accordance with Code A.

2.5 This Code does not apply to the exercise of a statutory power to enter premises or to inspect goods, equipment or procedures if the exercise of that power is not dependent on the existence of grounds for suspecting that an offence may have been committed and the person exercising the power has no reasonable grounds for such suspicion.

2.6 This Code does not affect any directions or requirements of a search warrant, order or other power to search and seize lawfully exercised in England or Wales that any item or evidence seized under that warrant, order or power be handed over to a police force, court, tribunal, or other authority outside England or Wales. For example, warrants and orders issued in Scotland or Northern Ireland, and search warrants and powers provided for in sections 14 to 17 of the Crime (International Co-operation) Act 2003.

2.7 When this Code requires the prior authority or agreement of an officer of at least inspector or superintendent rank, that authority may be given by a sergeant or chief inspector authorised to perform the functions of the higher rank under PACE, section 107.

2.8 Written records required under this Code not made in the search record shall, unless otherwise specified, be made:
- in the recording officer's pocket book ('pocket book' includes any official report book issued to police officers) or
- on forms provided for the purpose.

2.9 Nothing in this Code requires the identity of officers, or anyone accompanying them during a search of premises, to be recorded or disclosed:

(a) in the case of enquiries linked to the investigation of terrorism; or

(b) if officers reasonably believe recording or disclosing their names might put them in danger.

In these cases officers should use warrant or other identification numbers and the name of their police station. Police staff should use any identification number provided to them by the police force.

2.10 The 'officer in charge of the search' means the officer assigned specific duties and responsibilities under this Code. Whenever there is a search of premises to which this Code applies one officer must act as the officer in charge of the search.

2.11 In this Code:

(a) 'designated person' means a person other than a police officer, designated under the Police Reform Act 2002, Part 4 who has specified powers and duties of police officers conferred or imposed on them;

(b) any reference to a police officer includes a designated person acting in the exercise or performance of the powers and duties conferred or imposed on them by their designation;

(c) a person authorised to accompany police officers or designated persons in the execution of a warrant has the same powers as a constable in the execution of the warrant and the search and seizure of anything related to the warrant. These powers must be exercised in the company and under the supervision of a police officer.

2.12 If a power conferred on a designated person:

(a) allows reasonable force to be used when exercised by a police officer, a designated person exercising that power has the same entitlement to use force;

(b) includes power to use force to enter any premises, that power is not exercisable by that designated person except:

(i) in the company and under the supervision of a police officer; or

(ii) for the purpose of:
- saving life or limb; or
- preventing serious damage to property.

2.13 Designated persons must have regard to any relevant provisions of the Codes of Practice.

4.2.3.1

KEYNOTE

The purpose of para. 2.9(b) of Code B is to protect those involved in serious organised crime investigations or arrests of particularly violent suspects when there is reliable information that those arrested or their associates may threaten or cause harm to the officers or anyone accompanying them during a search of premises. In cases of doubt, an officer of inspector rank or above should be consulted.

For the purposes of para. 2.10, the officer in charge of the search should normally be the most senior officer present. Some exceptions are:

(a) a supervising officer who attends or assists at the scene of a premises search may appoint an officer of lower rank as officer in charge of the search if that officer is:
- more conversant with the facts;
- a more appropriate officer to be in charge of the search;

(b) when all officers in a premises search are the same rank. The supervising officer if available must make sure one of them is appointed officer in charge of the search, otherwise the officers themselves must nominate one of their number as the officer in charge;

(c) a senior officer assisting in a specialist role. This officer need not be regarded as having a general supervisory role over the conduct of the search or be appointed or expected to act as the officer in charge of the search.

Except in (c), nothing in this keynote diminishes the role and responsibilities of a supervisory officer who is present at the search or knows of a search taking place.

An officer of the rank of inspector or above may direct a designated investigating officer not to wear a uniform for the purposes of a specific operation.

4.2.3.2

KEYNOTE

Application for Warrant—s. 15 PACE

The Police and Criminal Evidence Act 1984, s. 15 states:

(1) This section and section 16 below have effect in relation to the issue to constables under any enactment, including an enactment contained in an Act passed after this Act, of warrants to enter and search premises; and an entry on or search of premises under a warrant is unlawful unless it complies with this section and section 16 below.

(2) Where a constable applies for any such warrant, it shall be his duty—

(a) to state—

(i) the ground on which he makes the application;

(ii) the enactment under which the warrant would be issued; and

(iii) if the application is for a warrant authorising entry and search on more than one occasion, the ground on which he applies for such a warrant, and whether he seeks a warrant authorising an unlimited number of entries, or (if not) the maximum number of entries desired;

    (b) to specify the matters set out in subsection (2A) below; and

    (c) to identify, so far as is practicable, the articles or persons to be sought.

(2A) The matters which must be specified pursuant to subsection (2)(b) above are—

    (a) if the application relates to one or more sets of premises specified in the application each set of premises which it is desired to enter and search; and

    (b) if the application relates to any premises occupied or controlled by a person specified in the application—

        (i) as many sets of premises which it is desired to enter and search as it is reasonably practicable to specify;

        (ii) the person who is in occupation or control of those premises and any others which it is desired to enter and search;

        (iii) why it is necessary to search more premises than those specified under sub-paragraph (i); and

        (iv) why it is not reasonably practicable to specify all the premises which it is desired to enter and search.

(3) An application for such a warrant shall be made ex parte and supported by information in writing.

(4) The constable shall answer on oath any question that the justice of the peace or judge hearing the application asks him.

(5) A warrant shall authorise an entry on one occasion only unless it specifies that it authorises multiple entries.

(5A) If it specifies that it authorises multiple entries, it must also specify whether the number of entries authorised is unlimited, or limited to a specified maximum.

(6) A warrant—

    (a) shall specify—

        (i) the name of the person who applies for it;

        (ii) the date on which it is issued;

        (iii) the enactment under which it is issued;

        (iv) each set of premises to be searched, or (in the case of an all premises warrant) the person who is in occupation or control of premises to be searched, together with any premises under his occupation or control which can be specified and which are to be searched; and

    (b) shall identify, so far as is practicable, the articles or persons to be sought.

(7) Two copies shall be made of a warrant (see section 8(1A)(a) above) which specifies only one set of premises and does not authorise multiple entries; and as many copies as are reasonably required may be made of any other kind of warrant.

(8) The copies shall be clearly certified as copies.

4.2.3.3

KEYNOTE

Execution of a Warrant—s. 16 PACE

The Police and Criminal Evidence Act 1984, s. 16 states:

(1) A warrant to enter and search premises may be executed by any constable.

(2) Such a warrant may authorise persons to accompany any constable who is executing it.

(2A) A person so authorised has the same powers as the constable whom he accompanies in respect of—

    (a) the execution of the warrant, and

    (b) the seizure of anything to which the warrant relates.

(2B) But he may exercise those powers only in the company, and under the supervision, of a constable.

(3) Entry and search under a warrant must be within three months from the date of its issue.

(3A) If the warrant is an all premises warrant, no premises which are not specified in it may be entered or searched unless a police officer of at least the rank of inspector has in writing authorised them to be entered.

(3B) No premises may be entered or searched for the second or any subsequent time under a warrant which authorises multiple entries unless a police officer of at least the rank of inspector has in writing authorised that entry to those premises.

(4) Entry and search under a warrant must be at a reasonable hour unless it appears to the constable executing it that the purpose of a search may be frustrated on an entry at a reasonable hour.

(5) Where the occupier of premises which are to be entered and searched is present at the time when a constable seeks to execute a warrant to enter and search them, the constable—

    (a) shall identify himself to the occupier and, if not in uniform, shall produce to him documentary evidence that he is a constable;

    (b) shall produce the warrant to him; and

    (c) shall supply him with a copy of it.

(6) Where—

    (a) the occupier of such premises is not present at the time when a constable seeks to execute such a warrant; but

(b) some other person who appears to the constable to be in charge of the premises is present, Subsection (5) above shall have effect as if any reference to the occupier were a reference to that other person.

(7) If there is no person present who appears to the constable to be in charge of the premises, he shall leave a copy of the warrant in a prominent place on the premises.

(8) A search under a warrant may only be a search to the extent required for the purpose for which the warrant was issued.

(9) A constable executing the warrant shall make an endorsement on it stating—

(a) whether the articles or persons sought were found; and

(b) whether any articles were seized, other than articles which were sought; and

unless the warrant is a warrant specifying one set of premises only, he shall do so separately in respect of each set of premises entered and searched, which he shall in each case state in the endorsement.

(10) A warrant shall be returned to the appropriate person mentioned in subsection (10A) below—

(a) when it has been executed; or

(b) in the case of a specific premises warrant which has not been executed, or an all premises warrant, or any warrant authorising multiple entries, upon the expiry of the period of three months referred to in subsection (3) above or sooner.

(10A) The appropriate person is—

(a) if the warrant was issued by a justice of the peace, the designated officer for the local justice area in which the justice was acting when he issued the warrant;

(b) if it was issued by a judge, the appropriate officer of the court from which he issued it.

(11) A warrant which is returned under subsection (10) above shall be retained for 12 months from its return—

(a) by the designated officer for the local justice area, if it was returned under paragraph (i) of that subsection; and

(b) by the appropriate officer, if it was returned under paragraph (ii).

(12) If during the period for which a warrant is to be retained the occupier of premises to which it relates asks to inspect it, he shall be allowed to do so.

4.2.3.4

KEYNOTE

General Points

If an application for a warrant is refused, no further application can be made unless it is supported by additional grounds.

'Premises' include any place, and in particular, (a) any vehicle, vessel, aircraft or hovercraft; (b) any offshore installation; (c) any renewable energy installation; (d) any tent or moveable structure (s. 23 of the 1984 Act).

The details of the extent of the proposed search should be made clear in the application and the officer swearing the warrant out must be prepared to answer *any* questions put to him/her on oath under s. 15(4). Courts will go into background detail about the particular premises, or part of the premises, and who is likely to be present on the premises at the time the warrant is executed (e.g. children).

4.2.3.5

KEYNOTE

Examples

Sections 15 and 16 of the 1984 Act apply to all search warrants issued to and executed by constables under any enactment, e.g. search warrants issued by:

(a) a justice of the peace under:

- Theft Act 1968, s. 26—stolen property;
- Misuse of Drugs Act 1971, s. 23—controlled drugs;
- PACE, s. 8—evidence of an indictable offence;
- Terrorism Act 2000, sch. 5, para. 1;
- Terrorism Prevention and Investigation Measures Act 2011, sch. 5, para. 8(2)(b)—search of premises for compliance purposes.

(b) a Circuit judge under:

- PACE, sch. 1;
- Terrorism Act 2000, sch. 5, para. 11.

Examples of the other powers in para. 2.3(d) include:

(a) Road Traffic Act 1988, s. 6E(1) giving police power to enter premises under s. 6E(1) to:
  - require a person to provide a specimen of breath; or
  - arrest a person following
    — a positive breath test;
    — failure to provide a specimen of breath;
(b) Transport and Works Act 1992, s. 30(4) giving police powers to enter premises mirroring the powers in (a) in relation to specified persons working on transport systems to which the Act applies;
(c) Criminal Justice Act 1988, s. 139B giving police power to enter and search school premises for offensive weapons, bladed or pointed articles;
(d) Terrorism Act 2000, sch. 5, paras 3 and 15 empowering a superintendent in urgent cases to give written authority for police to enter and search premises for the purposes of a terrorist investigation;
(e) Explosives Act 1875, s. 73(b) empowering a superintendent to give written authority for police to enter premises, examine and search them for explosives;
(f) search warrants and production orders or the equivalent issued in Scotland or Northern Ireland endorsed under the Summary Jurisdiction (Process) Act 1881 or the Petty Sessions (Ireland) Act 1851 respectively for execution in England and Wales.
(g) Terrorism Prevention and Investigation Measures Act 2011, sch. 5, paras 5(1), 6(2)(b) and 7(2), searches relating to TPIM notices (see para. 10.1).

Searching Persons

The Criminal Justice Act 1988, s. 139B provides that a constable who has reasonable grounds for suspecting that an offence under the Criminal Justice Act 1988, s. 139A or 139AA has been or is being committed may enter school premises and search the premises and any persons on the premises for any bladed or pointed article or offensive weapon. Persons may be searched under a warrant issued under the Misuse of Drugs Act 1971, s. 23(3) to search premises for drugs or documents only if the warrant specifically authorises the search of persons on the premises. Powers to search premises under certain terrorism provisions also authorise the search of persons on the premises, e.g. under paras 1, 2, 11 and 15 of sch. 5 to the Terrorism Act 2000 and s. 52 of the Anti-terrorism, Crime and Security Act 2001.

Immigration Act 1971

The Immigration Act 1971, part III and sch. 2 gives immigration officers powers to enter and search premises, seize and retain property, with and without a search warrant. These are similar to the powers available to police under search warrants issued by a justice of the peace and without a warrant under ss. 17, 18, 19 and 32 of the 1984 Act except they only apply to specified offences under the Immigration Act 1971 and immigration control powers. For certain types of investigations and enquiries these powers avoid the need for the Immigration Service to rely on police officers becoming directly involved. When exercising these powers, immigration officers are required by the Immigration and Asylum Act 1999, s. 145 to have regard to this Code's corresponding provisions. When immigration officers are dealing with persons or property at police stations, police officers should give appropriate assistance to help them discharge their specific duties and responsibilities.

4.2.3.6   **KEYNOTE**

Exclusion of Evidence

If the provisions of these sections are not fully complied with, any entry and search made under a warrant will be unlawful. Although the officers executing the warrant may have some protection from personal liability where there has been a defect in the *procedure* by which the warrant was issued, failure to follow the requirements of ss. 15 and 16 may result in the exclusion of any evidence obtained under the warrant. Therefore, where officers failed to provide the occupier of the searched premises with a copy of the warrant (under s.16(5)(c)), they were obliged to return the property seized during the search (*R* v *Chief Constable of Lancashire, ex parte Parker* [1993] QB 577).

If a warrant itself is invalid for some reason, any entry and subsequent seizure made under it are unlawful (*R* v *Central Criminal Court and British Railways Board, ex parte AJD Holdings Ltd* [1992] Crim LR 669).

Very minor departures from the letter of the warrant, however, will not render any search unlawful (*Attorney-General of Jamaica* v *Williams* [1998] AC 351).

4.2.3.7

KEYNOTE

Search Warrants for Indictable Offences—s. 8 PACE

The Police and Criminal Evidence Act 1984, s. 8 states:

(1) If on an application made by a constable a justice of the peace is satisfied that there are reasonable grounds for believing—
 (a) that an indictable offence has been committed; and
 (b) that there is material on premises mentioned in subsection (1A) below which is likely to be of substantial value (whether by itself or together with other material) to the investigation of the offence; and
 (c) that the material is likely to be relevant evidence; and
 (d) that it does not consist of or include items subject to legal privilege, excluded material or special procedure material; and
 (e) that any of the conditions specified in subsection (3) below applies in relation to each set of premises specified in the application

 he may issue a warrant authorising a constable to enter and search the premises.

(1A) The premises referred to in subsection (1)(b) above are—
 (a) one or more sets of premises specified in the application (in which case the application is for a 'specific premises warrant'); or
 (b) any premises occupied or controlled by a person specified in the application, including such sets of premises as are so specified (in which case the application is for an 'all premises warrant').

(1B) If the application is for an all premises warrant, the justice of the peace must also be satisfied—
 (a) that because of the particulars of the offence referred to in paragraph (a) of subsection (1) above, there are reasonable grounds for believing that it is necessary to search premises occupied or controlled by the person in question which are not specified in the application in order to find the material referred to in paragraph (b) of that subsection; and
 (b) that it is not reasonably practicable to specify in the application all the premises which he occupies or controls and which might need to be searched.

(1C) The warrant may authorise entry to and search of premises on more than one occasion if, on the application, the justice of the peace is satisfied that it is necessary to authorise multiple entries in order to achieve the purpose for which he issues the warrant.

(1D) If it authorises multiple entries, the number of entries authorised may be unlimited, or limited to a maximum.

(2) A constable may seize and retain anything for which a search has been authorised under subsection (1) above.

(3) The conditions mentioned in subsection (1)(e) above are—
 (a) that it is not practicable to communicate with any person entitled to grant entry to the premises;
 (b) that it is practicable to communicate with a person entitled to grant entry to the premises but it is not practicable to communicate with any person entitled to grant access to the evidence;
 (c) that entry to the premises will not be granted unless a warrant is produced;
 (d) that the purpose of a search may be frustrated or seriously prejudiced unless a constable arriving at the premises can secure immediate entry to them.

(4) In this Act 'relevant evidence', in relation to an offence, means anything that would be admissible in evidence at a trial for the offence.

(5) The power to issue a warrant conferred by this section is in addition to any such power otherwise conferred.

This section provides that a constable can apply for two different types of search warrant: a 'specific premises warrant' for the search of one set of premises; and an 'all premises warrant' when it is necessary to search all premises occupied or controlled by an individual, but where it is not reasonably practicable to specify all such premises at the time of applying for the warrant. The warrant allows access to all premises occupied or controlled by that person, both those which are specified on the application, and those which are not. Note that s. 8(1C) and (1D) provide that a warrant (either an 'all premises warrant' or a 'specific premises warrant') may authorise access on more than one occasion, and if multiple entries are authorised these may be unlimited or limited to a maximum.

The officer applying for a warrant under s. 8 must have reasonable grounds for believing that material which is likely *to be of substantial value to the investigation of the offence* is on the premises specified. Therefore, when executing such a warrant, the officer must be able to show that any material seized thereunder fell within that description (*R* v *Chief Constable of the Warwickshire Constabulary, ex parte Fitzpatrick* [1999] 1 WLR 564). Possession of a warrant under s. 8 does not authorise police officers to seize all material found on the relevant premises to be taken away and 'sifted' somewhere else (*R* v *Chesterfield Justices, ex parte Bramley* [2000] QB 576) (see s. 50 of the Criminal Justice and Police Act 2001 for the power to 'seize and sift'). This means that material which is solely of value for *intelligence* purposes may not be seized under a s. 8 warrant.

The power to apply for and execute a warrant under s. 8 and to carry out the actions under s. 8(2) are among those powers that can be conferred on a person designated as an Investigating Officer under sch. 4 to the Police Reform Act 2002.

The conditions set out under s. 8(1)(e) are part of the *application* process, not part of the general execution process (which is set out at s. 16 above). Therefore the officer swearing out a s. 8 warrant will have to satisfy the court that any of those conditions apply.

4.2.3.8
KEYNOTE
Legally Privileged Material

Material which falls within the definition in s. 10 of the 1984 Act is subject to legal privilege which means that it cannot be searched for or seized.

The Police and Criminal Evidence Act 1984, s. 10 states:

(1) Subject to subsection (2) below, in this Act 'items subject to legal privilege' means—
  (a) communications between a professional legal adviser and his client or any person representing his client made in connection with the giving of legal advice to the client;
  (b) communications between a professional legal adviser and his client or any person representing his client or between such an adviser or his client or any such representative and any other person made in connection with or in contemplation of legal proceedings and for the purposes of such proceedings; and
  (c) items enclosed with or referred to in such communications and made—
    (i) in connection with the giving of legal advice; or
    (ii) in connection with or in contemplation of legal proceedings and for the purposes of such proceedings,
  when they are in the possession of a person who is entitled to possession of them.

Items held with the intention of furthering a criminal purpose are not subject to this privilege (s. 10(2)). When making an application for a warrant to search for and seize such material the procedure under sch. 1 should be used. Occasions where this will happen are rare and would include instances where a solicitor's firm is the subject of a criminal investigation (*R* v *Leeds Crown Court, ex parte Switalski* [1991] Crim LR 559). However, it may be possible during a search to ascertain which material is subject to legal privilege and which might be lawfully seized under the warrant being executed. Therefore, although a warrant cannot authorise a search for legally privileged material, the fact that such material is inadvertently seized in the course of a search authorised by a proper warrant does not render the search unlawful (*R* v *HM Customs and Excise, ex parte Popely* [2000] Crim LR 388).

4.2.3.9
KEYNOTE
Excluded Material

Access to 'excluded material' can generally only be gained by applying to a judge for a production order under the procedure set out in s. 9 of, and sch. 1 to, the 1984 Act and PACE Code B. That strict statutory procedure also applies to the application for and execution of warrants by Investigating Officers designated under sch. 4 to the Police Reform Act 2002.

The Police and Criminal Evidence Act 1984, s. 11 states:

(1) Subject to the following provisions of this section, in this Act 'excluded material' means—
  (a) personal records which a person has acquired or created in the course of any trade, business, profession or other occupation or for the purposes of any paid or unpaid office and which he holds in confidence;
  (b) human tissue or tissue fluid which has been taken for the purposes of diagnosis or medical treatment and which a person holds in confidence;
  (c) journalistic material which a person holds in confidence and which consists—
    (i) of documents; or
    (ii) of records other than documents.
(2) A person holds material other than journalistic material in confidence for the purposes of this section if he holds it subject—
  (a) to an express or implied undertaking to hold it in confidence; or
  (b) to a restriction on disclosure or an obligation of secrecy contained in any enactment, including an enactment contained in an Act passed after this Act.
(3) A person holds journalistic material in confidence for the purposes of this section if—
  (a) he holds it subject to such an undertaking, restriction or obligation; and
  (b) it has been continuously held (by one or more persons) subject to such an undertaking, restriction or obligation since it was first acquired or created for the purposes of journalism.

Medical records and dental records would fall into this category, as might records made by priests or religious advisers.

'Personal records' are defined under s. 12 of the 1984 Act and include records relating to the physical or mental health, counselling or assistance given to an individual who can be identified by those records.

'Journalistic material' is defined under s. 13 as material acquired or created for the purposes of journalism.

4.2.3.10

KEYNOTE

Special Procedure Material

Special procedure material can be gained by applying for a search warrant or a production order under sch. 1 to the 1984 Act.

The Police and Criminal Evidence Act 1984, s. 14 states:

(1) In this Act 'special procedure material' means—
  (a) material to which subsection (2) below applies; and
  (b) journalistic material, other than excluded material.
(2) Subject to the following provisions of this section, this subsection applies to material, other than items subject to legal privilege and excluded material, in the possession of a person who—
  (a) acquired or created it in the course of any trade, business, profession or other occupation or for the purpose of any paid or unpaid office; and
  (b) holds it subject—
    (i) to an express or implied undertaking to hold it in confidence; or
    (ii) to a restriction or obligation such as is mentioned in section 11(2)(b) above.

For items subject to 'legal privilege' and 'excluded material', see para. 4.2.3.8.

The person believed to be in possession of the material must have come by it under the circumstances set out at s. 14(2)(a) *and* must hold it under the undertakings or obligations set out at s. 14(2)(b).

4.2.4

Code B—3 Search warrants and production orders

(a) Before making an application

3.1 When information appears to justify an application, the officer must take reasonable steps to check the information is accurate, recent and not provided maliciously or irresponsibly. An application may not be made on the basis of information from an anonymous source if corroboration has not been sought.

3.2 The officer shall ascertain as specifically as possible the nature of the articles concerned and their location.

3.3 The officer shall make reasonable enquiries to:

(i) establish if:
- anything is known about the likely occupier of the premises and the nature of the premises themselves;
- the premises have been searched previously and how recently;

(ii) obtain any other relevant information.

3.4 An application:

(a) to a justice of the peace for a search warrant or to a Circuit judge for a search warrant or production order under PACE, Schedule 1 must be supported by a signed written authority from an officer of inspector rank or above:

Note: *If the case is an urgent application to a justice of the peace and an inspector or above is not readily available, the next most senior officer on duty can give the written authority.*

(b) to a circuit judge under the Terrorism Act 2000, Schedule 5 for
- a production order;
- search warrant; or
- an order requiring an explanation of material seized or produced under such a warrant or production order

must be supported by a signed written authority from an officer of superintendent rank or above.

3.5 Except in a case of urgency, if there is reason to believe a search might have an adverse effect on relations between the police and the community, the officer in charge shall consult the local police/community liaison officer:
- before the search; or
- in urgent cases, as soon as practicable after the search.

(b) Making an application

3.6 A search warrant application must be supported in writing, specifying:

(a) the enactment under which the application is made;

(b)

    (i) whether the warrant is to authorise entry and search of:
- one set of premises; or
- if the application is under PACE section 8, or Schedule 1, paragraph 12, more than one set of specified premises or all premises occupied or controlled by a specified person; and

    (ii) the premises to be searched;

(c) the object of the search;

(d) the grounds for the application, including, when the purpose of the proposed search is to find evidence of an alleged offence, an indication of how the evidence relates to the investigation;

(da) where the application is under PACE section 8, or Schedule 1, paragraph 12 for a single warrant to enter and search:

    (i) more than one set of specified premises, the officer must specify each set of premises which it is desired to enter and search

    (ii) all premises occupied or controlled by a specified person, the officer must specify:
- as many sets of premises which it is desired to enter and search as it is reasonably practicable to specify;

- the person who is in occupation or control of those premises and any others which it is desired to search;
- why it is necessary to search more premises than those which can be specified;
- why it is not reasonably practicable to specify all the premises which it is desired to enter and search;

(db) whether an application under PACE section 8 is for a warrant authorising entry and search on more than one occasion, and if so, the officer must state the grounds for this and whether the desired number of entries authorised is unlimited or a specified maximum;

(e) there are no reasonable grounds to believe the material to be sought, when making application to a:

(i) justice of the peace or a Circuit judge consists of or includes items subject to legal privilege;

(ii) justice of the peace, consists of or includes excluded material or special procedure material;

Note: *this does not affect the additional powers of seizure in the Criminal Justice and Police Act 2001, Part 2 covered in paragraph 7.7;*

(f) if applicable, a request for the warrant to authorise a person or persons to accompany the officer who executes the warrant.

3.7 A search warrant application under PACE, Schedule 1, paragraph 12(a), shall if appropriate indicate why it is believed service of notice of an application for a production order may seriously prejudice the investigation. Applications for search warrants under the Terrorism Act 2000, Schedule 5, paragraph 11 must indicate why a production order would not be appropriate.

3.8 If a search warrant application is refused, a further application may not be made for those premises unless supported by additional grounds.

4.2.4.1 **KEYNOTE**

The identity of an informant need not be disclosed when making an application, but the officer should be prepared to answer any questions the magistrate or judge may have about:

- the accuracy of previous information from that source
- any other related matters.

Under s. 16(2) of the 1984 Act, a search warrant may authorise persons other than police officers to accompany the constable who executes the warrant. This includes, for example, any suitably qualified or skilled person or an expert in a particular field whose presence is needed to help accurately identify the material sought or to advise where certain evidence is most likely to be found and how it should be dealt with. It does not give them any right to force entry, but it gives them the right to be on the premises during the search and to search for or seize property without the occupier's permission.

The information supporting a search warrant application should be as specific as possible, particularly in relation to the articles or persons being sought and where in the premises it is suspected they may be found.

4.2.5 **Code B—4 Entry without warrant—particular powers**

(a) Making an arrest etc.

4.1 The conditions under which an officer may enter and search premises without a warrant are set out in PACE, section 17. It should be noted that this section does not create or confer any powers of arrest.

4.2.5.1 **KEYNOTE**

Power of Entry—s.17 PACE

The Police and Criminal Evidence Act 1984, s. 17 states:

(1) Subject to the following provisions of this section, and without prejudice to any other enactment, a constable may enter and search any premises for the purpose—

    (a) of executing—

        (i) a warrant of arrest issued in connection with or arising out of criminal proceedings; or

        (ii) a warrant of commitment issued under section 76 of the Magistrates' Courts Act 1980;

    (b) of arresting a person for an indictable offence;

    (c) of arresting a person for an offence under—

        (i) section 1 (prohibition of uniforms in connection with political objectives) of the Public Order Act 1936;

        (ii) any enactment contained in sections 6 to 8 or 10 of the Criminal Law Act 1977 (offences relating to entering and remaining on property);

        (iii) section 4 of the Public Order Act 1986 (fear or provocation of violence);

        (iiia) section 4 (driving etc. when under influence of drink or drugs) or 163 (failure to stop when required to do so by constable in uniform) of the Road Traffic Act 1988;

        (iiib) section 27 of the Transport and Works Act 1992 (which relates to offences involving drink or drugs);

        (iv) section 76 of the Criminal Justice and Public Order Act 1994 (failure to comply with interim possession order);

        (v) any of sections 4, 5, 6(1) and (2), 7 and 8(1) and (2) of the Animal Welfare Act 2006 (offences relating to the prevention of harm to animals);

        (vi) section 144 of the Legal Aid, Sentencing and Punishment of Offenders Act 2012 (squatting in a residential building);

    (ca) of arresting, in pursuance of section 32(1A) of the Children and Young Persons Act 1969, any child or young person who has been remanded or committed to local authority accommodation or youth detention accommodation under section 91 of the Legal Aid, Sentencing and Punishment of Offenders Act 2012;

    (caa) of arresting a person for an offence to which section 61 of the Animal Health Act 1981 applies;

    (cab) of arresting a person under any of the following provisions—

        (i) section 30D(1) or (2A);

        (ii) section 46A(1) or (1A);

        (iii) section 5B(7) of the Bail Act 1976 (arrest where a person fails to surrender to custody in accordance with a court order);

        (iv) section 7(3) of the Bail Act 1976 (arrest where a person is not likely to surrender to custody etc.);

        (v) section 97(1) of the Legal Aid, Sentencing and Punishment of Offenders Act 2012 (arrest where a child is suspected of breaking conditions of remand);

    (cb) of recapturing any person who is, or is deemed for any purpose to be, unlawfully at large while liable to be detained—

        (i) in a prison, remand centre, young offender institution or secure training centre, or

        (ii) in pursuance of section 92 of the Powers of Criminal Courts (Sentencing) Act 2000 (dealing with children and young persons guilty of grave crimes), in any other place;

    (d) of recapturing any person whatever who is unlawfully at large and whom he is pursuing; or

    (e) of saving life or limb or preventing serious damage to property.

(2) Except for the purpose specified in paragraph (e) of subsection (1) above, the powers of entry and search conferred by this section—

    (a) are only exercisable if the constable has reasonable grounds for believing that the person whom he is seeking is on the premises; and

    (b) are limited, in relation to premises consisting of two or more separate dwellings, to powers to enter and search—

        (i) any parts of the premises which the occupiers of any dwelling comprised in the premises use in common with the occupiers of any other such dwelling; and

        (ii) any such dwelling in which the constable has reasonable grounds for believing that the person whom he is seeking may be.

(3) The powers of entry and search conferred by this section are only exercisable for the purposes specified in subsection (1)(c)(ii), (iv) or (vi) above by a constable in uniform.

(4) The power of search conferred by this section is only a power to search to the extent that is reasonably required for the purpose for which the power of entry is exercised.

(5) Subject to subsection (6) below, all the rules of common law under which a constable has power to enter premises without a warrant are hereby abolished.

(6) Nothing in subsection (5) above affects any power of entry to deal with or prevent a breach of the peace.

38 | Code B—4 Entry without warrant—particular powers 4.2.5

Force may be used in exercising the power of entry where it is necessary to do so. Generally, the officer should first attempt to communicate with the occupier of the premises, explaining by what authority and for what purpose entry is to be made, before making a forcible entry. Clearly though, there will be occasions where such communication is impossible, impracticable or unnecessary; in those cases there is no need for the officer to enter into such an explanation (*O'Loughlin* v *Chief Constable of Essex* [1998] 1 WLR 374).

In a case where police had been called to an address by an abandoned 999 call, the officers had to move a man away from the front door in order to gain entry under s. 17. It was held that the officers had the power to use reasonable force in order to do so under s. 117 of the Police and Criminal Evidence Act 1984 (*Smith (Peter John)* v *DPP* [2001] EWHC Admin 55).

'Unlawfully at large' does not have a particular statutory meaning and can apply to someone who is subject to an order under the Mental Health Act 1983 or someone who has escaped from custody. The pursuit of the person who is unlawfully at large must be 'fresh' and entry must effectively be contemporaneous with that pursuit (the power will only be available while the officer is actually 'pursuing' the person concerned (*D'Souza* v *DPP* [1992] 1 WLR 1073)).

The officer must have reasonable grounds to *believe* that the person is on the premises in all cases except saving life and limb at s. 17(1)(e).

The power to enter and search any premises in the relevant police area for the purpose of saving life or limb or preventing serious damage to property above is among those that can be conferred on a designated person under sch. 4 to the Police Reform Act 2002.

(b) Search of premises where arrest takes place or the arrested person was immediately before arrest

4.2 When a person has been arrested for an indictable offence, a police officer has power under PACE, section 32 to search the premises where the person was arrested or where the person was immediately before being arrested.

KEYNOTE

Power to Search after Arrest—s. 32 PACE

The Police and Criminal Evidence Act 1984, s. 32 states:

(1) A constable may search an arrested person, in any case where the person to be searched has been arrested at a place other than a police station, if the constable has reasonable grounds for believing that the arrested person may present a danger to himself or others.

(2) Subject to subsections (3) to (5) below, a constable shall also have power in any such case—
   (a) to search the arrested person for anything—
      (i) which he might use to assist him to escape from lawful custody; or
      (ii) which might be evidence relating to an offence; and
   (b) if the offence for which he has been arrested is an indictable offence, to enter and search any premises in which he was when arrested or immediately before he was arrested for evidence relating to the offence.

(3) The power to search conferred by subsection (2) above is only a power to search to the extent that is reasonably required for the purpose of discovering any such thing or any such evidence.

(4) The powers conferred by this section to search a person are not to be construed as authorising a constable to require a person to remove any of his clothing in public other than an outer coat, jacket or gloves but they do authorise a search of a person's mouth.

(5) A constable may not search a person in the exercise of the power conferred by subsection (2)(a) above unless he has reasonable grounds for believing that the person to be searched may have concealed on him anything for which a search is permitted under that paragraph.

The power to search the arrested person under s. 32(1) is a general one relating to safety.

The House of Lords have confirmed that the police have a common law power to search for and seize property after a lawful arrest (*R* v *Governor of Pentonville Prison, ex parte Osman* [1990] 1 WLR 277). This decision was confirmed by the House of Lords in *R (On the Application of Rottman)* v *Commissioner of Police of the Metropolis* [2002] UKHL 20. In *Rottman* it was held that it was a well-established principle of the common law that an arresting officer had the power to search a room in which a person had been arrested (per *Ghani* v *Jones* [1970] 1 QB 693). This extended power is not limited to purely 'domestic' offences, but also applies to cases involving extradition offences.

Section 32 also states:

(6) A constable may not search premises in the exercise of the power conferred by subsection (2)(b) above unless he has reasonable grounds for believing that there is evidence for which a search is permitted under that paragraph on the premises.

(7) In so far as the power of search conferred by subsection (2)(b) above relates to premises consisting of two or more separate dwellings, it is limited to a power to search—

(a) any dwelling in which the arrest took place or in which the person arrested was immediately before his arrest; and

(b) any parts of the premises which the occupier of any such dwelling uses in common with the occupiers of any other dwellings comprised in the premises.

(8) A constable searching a person in the exercise of the power conferred by subsection (1) above may seize and retain anything he finds, if he has reasonable grounds for believing that the person searched might use it to cause physical injury to himself or to any other person.

(9) A constable searching a person in the exercise of the power conferred by subsection (2)(a) above may seize and retain anything he finds, other than an item subject to legal privilege, if he has reasonable grounds for believing—

(a) that he might use it to assist him to escape from lawful custody; or

(b) that it is evidence of an offence or has been obtained in consequence of the commission of an offence.

(10) Nothing in this section shall be taken to affect the power conferred by section 43 of the Terrorism Act 2000.

Both 'reasonable grounds' and 'immediately' are questions of fact for a court to determine. It has been held that the power under s. 32(2)(b) is one for use at the time of arrest and should not be used to return to the relevant premises some time after the arrest in the way that s. 18 of the 1984 Act may be used (*R* v *Badham* [1987] Crim LR 202).

Officers exercising their power to enter and search under s. 32 must have a *genuine belief* that there is evidence on the premises; it is not a licence for a general fishing expedition (*R* v *Beckford* [1992] 94 Cr App R 43).

The Divisional Court has refused to allow s. 32 to be used in a situation where the arrested person had not been in the relevant premises (where he did not live) for a period of over two hours preceding his arrest and where there were no reasonable grounds for believing that he presented a danger to himself or others (*Hewitson* v *Chief Constable of Dorset Police* [2003] EWHC 3296 (QB)).

(c) Search of premises occupied or controlled by the arrested person

4.3 The specific powers to search premises which <u>are</u> occupied or controlled by a person arrested for an indictable offence are set out in PACE, section 18. They may not be exercised, except if section 18(5) applies, unless an officer of inspector rank or above has given written authority. That authority should only be given when the authorising officer is satisfied that the premises <u>are</u> occupied or controlled by the arrested person and that the necessary grounds exist. If possible the authorising officer should record the authority on the Notice of Powers and Rights and, subject to *paragraph 2.9*, sign the Notice. The record of the grounds for the search and the nature of the evidence sought as required by section 18(7) of the Act should be made in:

• the custody record if there is one, otherwise

• the officer's pocket book, or

• the search record.

KEYNOTE

Power to Search after Arrest for Indictable Offence—s.18 PACE

The Police and Criminal Evidence Act 1984, s. 18 states:

(1) Subject to the following provisions of this section, a constable may enter and search any premises occupied or controlled by a person who is under arrest for an indictable offence, if he has reasonable grounds for suspecting that there is on the premises evidence, other than items subject to legal privilege, that relates—

   (a) to that offence; or

   (b) to some other indictable offence which is connected with or similar to that offence.

(2) A constable may seize and retain anything for which he may search under subsection (1) above.

(3) The power to search conferred by subsection (1) above is only a power to search to the extent that is reasonably required for the purpose of discovering such evidence.

(4) Subject to subsection (5) below, the powers conferred by this section may not be exercised unless an officer of the rank of inspector or above has authorised them in writing.

(5) A constable may conduct a search under subsection (1)—

   (a) before the person is taken to a police station or released on bail under section 30A; and

   (b) without obtaining an authorisation under subsection (4), if the condition in subsection (5A) is satisfied.

(5A) The condition is that the presence of the person at a place (other than a police station) is necessary for the effective investigation of the offence.

(6) If a constable conducts a search by virtue of subsection (5) above, he shall inform an officer of the rank of inspector or above that he has made the search as soon as practicable after he has made it.

(7) An officer who—

   (a) authorises a search; or

   (b) is informed of a search under subsection (6) above, shall make a record in writing—

      (i) of the grounds for the search; and

      (ii) of the nature of the evidence that was sought.

(8) If the person who was in occupation or control of the premises at the time of the search is in police detention at the time the record is to be made, the officer shall make the record as part of his custody record.

The power under s. 18 only applies to premises which are occupied and controlled by a person under arrest for an indictable offence; reasonable *suspicion* that the person occupies or controls the premises is *not sufficient*. A short stay may be sufficient to amount to 'occupation', but it must be such as to support the belief that it will have caused or contributed to the evidence sought being on the premises (*R (AB and CD) v Huddersfield Magistrates' Court and Chief Constable of West Yorkshire Police* [2014] 2 Cr App R 409 (25)).

The search is limited to evidence relating to the indictable offence for which the person has been arrested or another indictable offence which is similar or connected; it does not authorise a general search for anything that might be of use for other purposes (e.g. for intelligence reports). The extent of the search is limited by s. 18(3). If you are looking for a stolen fridge-freezer, you would not be empowered to search through drawers or small cupboards. You would be able to, however, if you were looking for packaging, receipts or other documents relating to the fridge-freezer.

That authority is for a search which is lawful *in all other respects*, that is, the other conditions imposed by s. 18 must be met. An inspector cannot make an otherwise unlawful entry and search lawful simply by authorising it (*Krohn* v *DPP* [1997] COD 345).

Where officers carry out a search under s. 18 they must, so far as is possible in the circumstances, explain to the occupier(s) the reason for it. If officers attempt to carry out an authorised search under s. 18 without attempting to explain to an occupier the reason, it may mean that the officers are not acting in the execution of their duty and their entry may be lawfully resisted (*Lineham* v *DPP* [2000] Crim LR 861).

The provision under s. 18(5) relates to cases where the presence of the person *is in fact necessary* for the effective investigation of the offence. If such a search is made, the searching officer must inform an inspector (or above) as soon as practicable after the search.

If the person is in police detention after the arrest, the facts concerning the search must be recorded in the custody record. Where a person is re-arrested under s. 31 of the 1984 Act for an indictable offence, the powers to search under s. 18 begin again, that is, a new power to search is created in respect of each indictable offence.

Code B—5 Search with consent

5.1 Subject to *paragraph 5.4*, if it is proposed to search premises with the consent of a person entitled to grant entry the consent must, if practicable, be given in writing on the Notice of Powers and Rights before the search. The officer must make any necessary enquiries to be satisfied the person is in a position to give such consent.

5.2 Before seeking consent the officer in charge of the search shall state the purpose of the proposed search and its extent. This information must be as specific as possible, particularly regarding the articles or persons being sought and the parts of the premises to be searched. The person concerned must be clearly informed they are not obliged to consent, that any consent can be withdrawn at any time, including before the search starts or while it is underway and anything seized may be produced in evidence. If at the time the person is not suspected of an offence, the officer shall say this when stating the purpose of the search.

5.3 An officer cannot enter and search or continue to search premises under *paragraph 5.1* if consent is given under duress or withdrawn before the search is completed.

5.4 It is unnecessary to seek consent under *paragraphs 5.1* and *5.2* if this would cause disproportionate inconvenience to the person concerned.

KEYNOTE

In a lodging house or similar accommodation, every reasonable effort should be made to obtain the consent of the tenant, lodger or occupier. A search should not be made solely on the basis of the landlord's consent.

If the intention is to search premises under the authority of a warrant or a power of entry and search without warrant, and the occupier of the premises cooperates in accordance with para. 6.4, there is no need to obtain written consent.

Paragraph 5.4 is intended to apply when it is reasonable to assume innocent occupiers would agree to, and expect, police to take the proposed action, e.g. if:

- a suspect has fled the scene of a crime or to evade arrest and it is necessary quickly to check surrounding gardens and readily accessible places to see if the suspect is hiding or;
- police have arrested someone in the night after a pursuit and it is necessary to make a brief check of gardens along the pursuit route to see if stolen or incriminating articles have been discarded.

Code B—6 Searching premises—general considerations

(a) Time of searches

6.1 Searches made under warrant must be made within three calendar months of the date of the warrant is issued or within the period specified in the enactment under which the warrant is issued if this is shorter.

6.2 Searches must be made at a reasonable hour unless this might frustrate the purpose of the search.

6.3 When the extent or complexity of a search mean it is likely to take a long time, the officer in charge of the search may consider using the seize and sift powers referred to in *section 7*.

6.3A A warrant under PACE, section 8 may authorise entry to and search of premises on more than one occasion if, on the application, the justice of the peace is satisfied that it is necessary to authorise multiple entries in order to achieve the purpose for which the warrant is issued. No premises may be entered or searched on any subsequent occasions without the prior written authority of an officer of the rank of inspector who is not involved in the investigation. All other warrants authorise entry on one occasion only.

6.3B Where a warrant under PACE section 8, or Schedule 1, paragraph 12 authorises entry to and search of all premises occupied or controlled by a specified person, no premises which are not specified in the warrant may be entered and searched without the prior written authority of an officer of the rank of inspector who is not involved in the investigation.

(b) Entry other than with consent

6.4 The officer in charge of the search shall first try to communicate with the occupier, or any other person entitled to grant access to the premises, explain the authority under which entry is sought and ask the occupier to allow entry, unless:
   (i) the search premises are unoccupied;
   (ii) the occupier and any other person entitled to grant access are absent;
   (iii) there are reasonable grounds for believing that alerting the occupier or any other person entitled to grant access would frustrate the object of the search or endanger officers or other people.

6.5 Unless *sub-paragraph 6.4(iii)* applies, if the premises are occupied the officer, subject to *paragraph 2.9*, shall, before the search begins:
   (i) identify him or herself, show their warrant card (if not in uniform) and state the purpose of, and grounds for, the search, and
   (ii) identify and introduce any person accompanying the officer on the search (such persons should carry identification for production on request) and briefly describe that person's role in the process.

6.6 Reasonable and proportionate force may be used if necessary to enter premises if the officer in charge of the search is satisfied the premises are those specified in any warrant, or in exercise of the powers described in *paragraphs 4.1* to *4.3*, and if:
   (i) the occupier or any other person entitled to grant access has refused entry;
   (ii) it is impossible to communicate with the occupier or any other person entitled to grant access; or
   (iii) any of the provisions of *paragraph 6.4* apply.

(c) Notice of Powers and Rights

6.7 If an officer conducts a search to which this Code applies the officer shall, unless it is impracticable to do so, provide the occupier with a copy of a Notice in a standard format:
   (i) specifying if the search is made under warrant, with consent, or in the exercise of the powers described in *paragraphs 4.1* to *4.3*. Note: the notice format shall provide for authority or consent to be indicated, see *paragraphs 4.3* and *5.1*;
   (ii) summarising the extent of the powers of search and seizure conferred by PACE and other relevant legislation as appropriate;
   (iii) explaining the rights of the occupier, and the owner of the property seized;
   (iv) explaining compensation may be payable in appropriate cases for damages caused entering and searching premises, and giving the address to send a compensation application, and
   (v) stating this Code is available at any police station.

6.8 If the occupier is:
   • present, copies of the Notice and warrant shall, if practicable, be given to them before the search begins, unless the officer in charge of the search reasonably believes this would frustrate the object of the search or endanger officers or other people
   • not present, copies of the Notice and warrant shall be left in a prominent place on the premises or appropriate part of the premises and endorsed, subject to *paragraph 2.9* with the name of the officer in charge of the search, the date and time of the search
   the warrant shall be endorsed to show this has been done.

(d) Conduct of searches

6.9 Premises may be searched only to the extent necessary to achieve the object of the search, having regard to the size and nature of whatever is sought.

6.9A A search may not continue under:
- a warrant's authority once all the things specified in that warrant have been found
- any other power once the object of that search has been achieved.

6.9B No search may continue once the officer in charge of the search is satisfied whatever is being sought is not on the premises. This does not prevent a further search of the same premises if additional grounds come to light supporting a further application for a search warrant or exercise or further exercise of another power. For example, when, as a result of new information, it is believed articles previously not found or additional articles are on the premises.

6.10 Searches must be conducted with due consideration for the property and privacy of the occupier and with no more disturbance than necessary. Reasonable force may be used only when necessary and proportionate because the cooperation of the occupier cannot be obtained or is insufficient for the purpose.

6.11 A friend, neighbour or other person must be allowed to witness the search if the occupier wishes unless the officer in charge of the search has reasonable grounds for believing the presence of the person asked for would seriously hinder the investigation or endanger officers or other people. A search need not be unreasonably delayed for this purpose. A record of the action taken should be made on the premises search record including the grounds for refusing the occupier's request.

6.12 A person is not required to be cautioned prior to being asked questions that are solely necessary for the purpose of furthering the proper and effective conduct of a search, see Code C, *paragraph 10.1(c)*. For example, questions to discover the occupier of specified premises, to find a key to open a locked drawer or cupboard or to otherwise seek cooperation during the search or to determine if a particular item is liable to be seized.

6.12A If questioning goes beyond what is necessary for the purpose of the exemption in Code C, the exchange is likely to constitute an interview as defined by Code C, *paragraph 11.1A* and would require the associated safeguards included in Code C, *section 10*.

(e) Leaving premises

6.13 If premises have been entered by force, before leaving the officer in charge of the search must make sure they are secure by:
- arranging for the occupier or their agent to be present
- any other appropriate means.

(f) Searches under PACE Schedule 1 or the Terrorism Act 2000, Schedule 5

6.14 An officer shall be appointed as the officer in charge of the search, see *paragraph 2.10*, in respect of any search made under a warrant issued under PACE Act 1984, Schedule 1 or the Terrorism Act 2000, Schedule 5. They are responsible for making sure the search is conducted with discretion and in a manner that causes the least possible disruption to any business or other activities carried out on the premises.

6.15 Once the officer in charge of the search is satisfied material may not be taken from the premises without their knowledge, they shall ask for the documents or other records concerned. The officer in charge of the search may also ask to see the index to files held on the premises, and the officers conducting the search may inspect any files which, according to the index, appear to contain the material sought. A more extensive search of the premises may be made only if:

- the person responsible for them refuses to:
  - produce the material sought, or
  - allow access to the index
- it appears the index is:
  - inaccurate, or
  - incomplete
  - for any other reason the officer in charge of the search has reasonable grounds for believing such a search is necessary in order to find the material sought.

4.2.7.1

KEYNOTE

Whether compensation is appropriate depends on the circumstances in each case. Compensation for damage caused when effecting entry is unlikely to be appropriate if the search was lawful, and the force used can be shown to be reasonable, proportionate and necessary to effect entry. If the wrong premises are searched by mistake everything possible should be done at the earliest opportunity to allay any sense of grievance and there should normally be a strong presumption in favour of paying compensation.

It is important that, when possible, all those involved in a search are fully briefed about any powers to be exercised and the extent and limits within which it should be conducted.

In all cases the number of officers and other persons involved in executing the warrant should be determined by what is reasonable and necessary according to the particular circumstances.

4.2.8

Code B—7 Seizure and retention of property

(a) Seizure

7.1 Subject to *paragraph 7.2*, an officer who is searching any person or premises under any statutory power or with the consent of the occupier may seize anything:
  (a) covered by a warrant
  (b) the officer has reasonable grounds for believing is evidence of an offence or has been obtained in consequence of the commission of an offence but only if seizure is necessary to prevent the items being concealed, lost, disposed of, altered, damaged, destroyed or tampered with
  (c) covered by the powers in the Criminal Justice and Police Act 2001, Part 2 allowing an officer to seize property from persons or premises and retain it for sifting or examination elsewhere.

7.2 No item may be seized which an officer has reasonable grounds for believing to be subject to legal privilege, as defined in PACE, section 10, other than under the Criminal Justice and Police Act 2001, Part 2.

7.3 Officers must be aware of the provisions in the Criminal Justice and Police Act 2001, section 59, allowing for applications to a judicial authority for the return of property seized and the subsequent duty to secure in section 60, see *paragraph 7.12(iii)*.

7.4 An officer may decide it is not appropriate to seize property because of an explanation from the person holding it but may nevertheless have reasonable grounds for believing it was obtained in consequence of an offence by some person. In these circumstances, the officer should identify the property to the holder, inform the holder of their suspicions and explain the holder may be liable to civil or criminal proceedings if they dispose of, alter or destroy the property.

7.5 An officer may arrange to photograph, image or copy, any document or other article they have the power to seize in accordance with *paragraph 7.1*. This is subject to specific restrictions on the examination, imaging or copying of certain property seized under the Criminal Justice and

Police Act 2001, Part 2. An officer must have regard to their statutory obligation to retain an original document or other article only when a photograph or copy is not sufficient.

7.6 If an officer considers information stored in any electronic form and accessible from the premises could be used in evidence, they may require the information to be produced in a form:

- which can be taken away and in which it is visible and legible; or
- from which it can readily be produced in a visible and legible form.

4.2.8.1 **KEYNOTE**

General Powers of Seizure—s.19 PACE

The Police and Criminal Evidence Act 1984, s. 19 states:

(1) The powers conferred by subsections (2), (3) and (4) below are exercisable by a constable who is lawfully on any premises.

(2) The constable may seize anything which is on the premises if he has reasonable grounds for believing—

(a) that it has been obtained in consequence of the commission of an offence; and

(b) that it is necessary to seize it in order to prevent it being concealed, lost, damaged, altered or destroyed.

(3) The constable may seize anything which is on the premises if he has reasonable grounds for believing—

(a) that it is evidence in relation to an offence which he is investigating or any other offence; and

(b) that it is necessary to seize it in order to prevent the evidence being concealed, lost, altered or destroyed.

(4) The constable may require any information which is stored in any electronic form and is accessible from the premises to be produced in a form in which it can be taken away and in which it is visible and legible or from which it can readily be produced in a visible and legible form if he has reasonable grounds for believing—

(a) that—

(i) it is evidence in relation to an offence which he is investigating or any other offence; or

(ii) it has been obtained in consequence of the commission of an offence; and

(b) that it is necessary to do so in order to prevent it being concealed, lost, or destroyed.

(5) The powers conferred by this section are in addition to any power otherwise conferred.

(6) No power of seizure conferred on a constable under any enactment (including an enactment contained in an Act passed after this Act) is to be taken to authorise the seizure of an item which the constable exercising the power has reasonable grounds for believing to be subject to legal privilege.

For this power to apply, the officers concerned must be on the premises lawfully. If the officers are on the premises only with the consent of the occupier, they become trespassers once that consent has been withdrawn. Once the officers are told to leave, they are no longer 'lawfully' on the premises. They must be given a reasonable opportunity to leave and cannot then seize any property that they may find. For this reason, it is far safer to exercise a power where one exists, albeit that the *cooperation* of the relevant person should be sought.

Where the 'premises' searched is a vehicle (s. 23), the vehicle (the 'premises') can itself be seized (*Cowan* v *Commissioner of Police for the Metropolis* [2000] 1 WLR 254). In *Cowan* it was held that the power to seize 'premises', where it was appropriate and practical to do so, was embodied in both ss. 18 and 19 and also at common law. Therefore, the powers of seizure conferred by ss. 18(2) and 19(3) of the Police and Criminal Evidence Act 1984 extend to the seizure of the whole premises when it is physically possible to seize and retain the premises in their totality and practical considerations make seizure desirable. The police may remove premises such as tents, vehicles or caravans to a police station for the purpose of preserving evidence. However, it does not extend to seizing things that are not on the premises, such as a car parked in a car park adjacent to the premises (*Wood* v *North Avon Magistrates' Court* [2009] EWHC 3614 (Admin)).

Unless the elements above are satisfied, the power under s. 19 will not apply. Therefore, the power does not authorise the seizure of property purely for intelligence purposes.

Section 19(5) expressly preserves any common law power of search and seizure; however, in *R (On the Application of Rottman)* v *Commissioner of Police for the Metropolis* [2002] UKHL 20, it was held that s. 19 was confined to 'domestic' offences (and did not extend to extradition offences). The same applies to powers under s. 18 of the Police and Criminal Evidence Act 1984.

If the warrant under which entry or seizure was made is invalid, the officers will not be on the premises lawfully.

The power of seizure under s. 19(1), along with the power to require information stored in any electronic form to be made accessible under s. 19(4), are among those that can be conferred on an Investigating Officer designated under sch. 4 to the Police Reform Act 2002. The safeguards provided by s. 19(6) in relation to privileged material also apply to the exercise of these powers by designated Investigating Officers.

4.2.8.2

KEYNOTE

Powers of Seizure and Information in Electronic Form

The Police and Criminal Evidence Act 1984, s. 20 states:

(1) Every power of seizure which is conferred by an enactment to which this section applies on a constable who has entered premises in the exercise of a power conferred by an enactment shall be construed as including a power to require any information stored in any electronic form and accessible from the premises to be produced in a form in which it can be taken away and in which it is visible and legible or from which it can readily be produced in a visible and legible form.

(2) This section applies—
   (a) to any enactment contained in an Act passed before this Act;
   (b) to sections 8 and 18 above;
   (c) to paragraph 13 of Schedule 1 to this Act; and
   (d) to any enactment contained in an Act passed after this Act.

This provision applies to:

- powers conferred under pre-PACE statutes;
- powers exercised under a s. 8 warrant (for 'indictable offences');
- powers exercised under s. 18 (following arrest for an indictable offence);
- powers under sch. 1 ('excluded' or 'special procedure material');
- powers exercised under s. 19 (officers lawfully on premises);
- powers of seizure exercised by Investigating Officers designated under sch. 4 to the Police Reform Act 2002.

4.2.8.3

KEYNOTE

Supply of Copies of Seized Material

Section 21 of the 1984 Act makes provision for the supplying of copies of records of seizure to certain people after property has been seized. If requested by the person who had custody or control of the seized property immediately before it was seized, the officer in charge of the investigation must allow that person access to it under police supervision. The officer must also make provisions to allow for the property to be photographed or copied by that person or to supply the person with photographs/copies of it within a reasonable time. Such a request need not be complied with if there are reasonable grounds to believe that to do so would prejudice any related investigation or criminal proceedings (s. 21(8)).

4.2.8.4

KEYNOTE

Retention of Seized Material

The provisions for accessing and copying of seized material as set out in ss. 21 and 22 of the Police and Criminal Evidence Act 1984 also apply to powers of seizure exercised by Investigating Officers designated under sch. 4 to the Police Reform Act 2002.

Section 22 of the 1984 Act makes provision for the retention of seized property. Section 22(1) provides that anything seized may be retained for as long as necessary in all the circumstances. However, s. 22(2) allows for property to be retained for use as evidence in a trial, forensic examination or further investigation *unless a photograph or copy would suffice*. Seized property may be retained in order to establish its lawful owner (s. 22(2)(b)). Once this power to retain property is exhausted, a person claiming it can rely on his/her right to possession at the time the property was seized as giving sufficient title to recover the property from the police. This situation was confirmed by the Court of Appeal in a case where the purchaser of a stolen car was allowed to rely upon his possession of the car at the time it was seized. As it could not be established that anyone else was entitled to the vehicle, the court allowed the claimant's action for return of the car to him (*Costello* v *Chief Constable of Derbyshire Constabulary* [2001] EWCA Civ 381). Clearly any claim based on previous possession where it would be unlawful for the police to return the property (e.g. a controlled drug) could not be enforced. There is no specific provision under s. 22 for the retention of property for purely intelligence purposes.

The importance of police officers being able to point clearly to the need for retaining property either in order to establish its owner or as a necessary part of the investigative or law enforcement process when relying on the above powers, was highlighted by the Court of Appeal in *Gough* v *Chief Constable of the West Midlands Police* [2004] EWCA Civ 206. In that case it was clear that neither of these purposes was being served and therefore the officers could not rely on the statutory power for retaining the property.

Property seized simply to prevent an arrested person from using it to escape or to cause injury, damage etc. cannot be retained for those purposes once the person has been released (s. 22(3)). This includes car keys belonging to someone who is released from police detention having been detained under the relevant drink driving legislation.

4.2.8.5 **KEYNOTE**

Prohibitions on Re-use of Information Seized

Information gained as a result of a lawful search may be passed on to other individuals and organisations for purposes of investigation and prosecution. It must not be used for private purposes (*Marcel* v *Commissioner of Police for the Metropolis* [1992] Ch 225).

4.2.8.6 **KEYNOTE**

Disposal of Property in Police Possession

Any person claiming property seized by the police may apply to a magistrates' court under the Police (Property) Act 1897 for its possession and should, if appropriate, be advised of this procedure.

(b) Criminal Justice and Police Act 2001: Specific procedures for seize and sift powers

7.7 The Criminal Justice and Police Act 2001, Part 2 gives officers limited powers to seize property from premises or persons so they can sift or examine it elsewhere. Officers must be careful they only exercise these powers when it is essential and they do not remove any more material than necessary. The removal of large volumes of material, much of which may not ultimately be retainable, may have serious implications for the owners, particularly when they are involved in business or activities such as journalism or the provision of medical services. Officers must carefully consider if removing copies or images of relevant material or data would be a satisfactory alternative to removing originals. When originals are taken, officers must be prepared to facilitate the provision of copies or images for the owners when reasonably practicable.

7.8 Property seized under the Criminal Justice and Police Act 2001, sections 50 or 51 must be kept securely and separately from any material seized under other powers. An examination under section 53 to determine which elements may be retained must be carried out at the earliest practicable time, having due regard to the desirability of allowing the person from whom the property was seized, or a person with an interest in the property, an opportunity of being present or represented at the examination.

7.8A All reasonable steps should be taken to accommodate an interested person's request to be present, provided the request is reasonable and subject to the need to prevent harm to, interference with, or unreasonable delay to the investigatory process. If an examination proceeds in the absence of an interested person who asked to attend or their representative, the officer who exercised the relevant seizure power must give that person a written notice of why the examination was carried out in those circumstances. If it is necessary for security reasons or to maintain confidentiality officers may exclude interested persons from decryption or other processes which facilitate the examination but do not form part of it.

7.9 It is the responsibility of the officer in charge of the investigation to make sure property is returned in accordance with sections 53 to 55. Material which there is no power to retain must be:

- separated from the rest of the seized property
- returned as soon as reasonably practicable after examination of all the seized property.

7.9A Delay is only warranted if very clear and compelling reasons exist, e.g. the:

- unavailability of the person to whom the material is to be returned
- need to agree a convenient time to return a large volume of material.

7.9B Legally privileged, excluded or special procedure material which cannot be retained must be returned:

- as soon as reasonably practicable
- without waiting for the whole examination.

7.9C As set out in section 58, material must be returned to the person from whom it was seized, except when it is clear some other person has a better right to it.

7.10 When an officer involved in the investigation has reasonable grounds to believe a person with a relevant interest in property seized under section 50 or 51 intends to make an application under section 59 for the return of any legally privileged, special procedure or excluded material, the officer in charge of the investigation should be informed as soon as practicable and the material seized should be kept secure in accordance with section 61.

7.11 The officer in charge of the investigation is responsible for making sure property is properly secured. Securing involves making sure the property is not examined, copied, imaged or put to any other use except at the request, or with the consent, of the applicant or in accordance with the directions of the appropriate judicial authority. Any request, consent or directions must be recorded in writing and signed by both the initiator and the officer in charge of the investigation.

7.12 When an officer exercises a power of seizure conferred by sections 50 or 51 they shall provide the occupier of the premises or the person from whom the property is being seized with a written notice:

(i)   specifying what has been seized under the powers conferred by that section;

(ii) specifying the grounds for those powers;

(iii) setting out the effect of sections 59 to 61 covering the grounds for a person with a relevant interest in seized property to apply to a judicial authority for its return and the duty of officers to secure property in certain circumstances when an application is made;

(iv) specifying the name and address of the person to whom:

- notice of an application to the appropriate judicial authority in respect of any of the seized property must be given;
- an application may be made to allow attendance at the initial examination of the property.

7.13 If the occupier is not present but there is someone in charge of the premises, the notice shall be given to them. If no suitable person is available, so the notice will easily be found it should either be:

- left in a prominent place on the premises
- attached to the exterior of the premises.

KEYNOTE

Seize and Sift Powers

The Criminal Justice and Police Act 2001 powers allow officers to remove materials from the premises being searched where there are real practical difficulties in not doing so.

These seize and sift powers only extend the scope of *some other existing power*. They do not provide free-standing powers to seize property—rather, they supplement other powers of search and seizure where the relevant conditions and circumstances apply. The full list of these powers is set out in sch. 1 to the Act and includes all the relevant powers under the Police and Criminal Evidence Act 1984, along with those under other key statutes such as the Firearms Act 1968 and the Misuse of Drugs Act 1971. If there is no existing power of seizure other than the Criminal Justice and Police Act 2001, then there is no power.

Section 50 of the 2001 Act provides the extended powers to seize material where it is not reasonably practicable to sort through it at the scene of the search. The factors that can be taken into account in considering whether or not it is reasonably practicable for something to be determined, or for relevant material to be separated from other materials, are set out in s. 50(3); these include the length of time and number of people that would be required to carry out the determination or separation on those premises within a reasonable period, whether that would involve damage to property, any apparatus or equipment that would be needed and (in the case of separation of materials) whether the separation would be likely to prejudice the use of some or all of the separated seizable property. Section 50 also allows for the seizure of material that is reasonably believed to be legally privileged where it is not reasonably practicable to separate it. In some cases, the power to 'seize' will be read as a power to take copies (s. 63).

Section 51 provides for extended seizure of materials in the same vein as above but where the material is found on people who are being lawfully searched.

Initial Examination

Where any property has been seized under ss. 50 or 51, the officer in possession of it is under a duty to make sure that a number of things are done (s. 53). These include ensuring that an initial examination of the property is carried out *as soon as reasonably practicable* after the seizure. In determining the earliest practicable time to carry out an initial examination of the seized property, due regard must be had to the desirability of allowing the person from whom it was seized (or a person with an interest in it) an opportunity of being present, or of being represented, at the examination (s. 53(4)). Officers should consider reaching agreement with owners and/or other interested parties on the procedures for examining a specific set of property, rather than awaiting the judicial authority's determination. Agreement can sometimes give a quicker and more satisfactory route for all concerned and minimise costs and legal complexities. What constitutes a relevant interest in specific material may depend on the nature of that material and the circumstances in which it is seized. Anyone with a reasonable claim to ownership of the material and anyone entrusted with its safe keeping by the owner should be considered.

The officer must also ensure that any such examination is confined to whatever is *necessary* for determining how much of the property:

- is property for which the person seizing it had power to search when making the seizure but is not property that has to be returned (by s. 54—see Protected Material, below);
- is property authorised to be retained (by s. 56—**see para. 4.2.8.9**); or
- is something which, in all the circumstances, it will not be reasonably practicable, following the examination, to separate from the property above (see generally s. 53(3)).

The officer must ensure that anything found not to fall within the categories above is separated from the rest of the seized property and *is returned as soon as reasonably practicable* after the examination of all the seized property. That officer is also under a duty to ensure that, until the initial examination of all the seized property has been completed and anything which does not fall within the categories above has been returned, the seized property is kept separate from anything seized under any other power.

Protected Material

If, at any time, after a seizure of anything has been made in exercise of *any statutory power of seizure*, it appears that the property is subject to legal privilege (or it has such an item comprised in it), s. 54 imposes a general duty on the officer in possession of the property to ensure that the item is returned as soon as reasonably practicable after the seizure. This general duty is subject to some exceptions (e.g. where in all the circumstances it is not reasonably practicable for that item to be separated from the rest of that property without prejudicing the use of the rest of that property—see s. 54(2)) but is otherwise very wide-ranging and absolutely clear. A similar duty is generally imposed in relation to property that appears to be excluded material or special procedure material (s. 55).

4.2.8.8   (c) Retention

7.14 Subject to *paragraph 7.15*, anything seized in accordance with the above provisions may be retained only for as long as is necessary. It may be retained, among other purposes:

  (i)   for use as evidence at a trial for an offence;

  (ii) to facilitate the use in any investigation or proceedings of anything to which it is inextricably linked;

  (iii) for forensic examination or other investigation in connection with an offence;

  (iv) in order to establish its lawful owner when there are reasonable grounds for believing it has been stolen or obtained by the commission of an offence.

7.15 Property shall not be retained under *paragraph 7.14(i)*, *(ii)* or *(iii)* if a copy or image would be sufficient.

4.2.8.9   KEYNOTE

Retention of Property

The Act authorises the retention of certain seized property by the police. In order to be retained, the property must have been seized on any premises by a constable who was lawfully on the premises, by a person authorised under a relevant statute (s. 56(5)) who was on the premises accompanied by a constable, or by a constable carrying out a lawful search of any person (s. 56). Generally property so seized will fall within these categories if there are reasonable grounds for believing:

- that it is property obtained in consequence of the commission of an offence; or
- that it is evidence in relation to any offence; *and* (in either case)
- that it is necessary for it to be retained in order to prevent its being concealed, lost, altered or destroyed

(for full details see s. 56(2) and (3)). Note, so far as s. 56(2) is concerned, property may be retained if it is necessary to prevent it being 'damaged', in addition to the other factors listed.

    These are fairly wide provisions and, if the property fits the above description, it may be retained even if it was not being searched for. Section 57 goes on to make certain provisions for the retention of property under other statutes such as s. 5(4) of the Knives Act 1997, para. 7(2) of sch. 9 to the Data Protection Act 1998, and sch. 5 to the Human Tissue Act 2004.

Inextricably Linked Material

Paragraph 7.14(ii) applies if inextricably linked material is seized under the Criminal Justice and Police Act 2001, s. 50 or 51. Inextricably linked material is material it is not reasonably practicable to separate from other linked material without prejudicing the use of that other material in any investigation or proceedings. For example, it may not be possible to separate items of data held on computer disk without damaging their evidential integrity. There are very strict limits on what use can be made of this material—it must not be examined, imaged, copied or used for any purpose other than for proving the source and/or integrity of the linked material (s. 62).

4.2.8.10

(d) Rights of owners etc.

7.16 If property is retained, the person who had custody or control of it immediately before seizure must, on request, be provided with a list or description of the property within a reasonable time.

7.17 That person or their representative must be allowed supervised access to the property to examine it or have it photographed or copied, or must be provided with a photograph or copy, in either case within a reasonable time of any request and at their own expense, unless the officer in charge of an investigation has reasonable grounds for believing this would:

(i) prejudice the investigation of any offence or criminal proceedings; or

(ii) lead to the commission of an offence by providing access to unlawful material such as pornography.

A record of the grounds shall be made when access is denied.

4.2.8.11

KEYNOTE

Notice

Where a person exercises a power of seizure conferred by ss. 50 or 51, that person will be under a duty, on doing so, to give the occupier or person from whom property is seized a written notice (s. 52). That notice will specify:

- what has been seized and the grounds on which the powers have been exercised;
- the effect of the safeguards and rights to apply to a judicial authority for the return of the property (see Return of Property Seized, below);
- the name and address of the person to whom notice of an application to a judge and an application to be allowed to attend the initial examination should be sent.

Where it appears to the officer exercising a power of seizure under s. 50 that the occupier of the premises is not present at the time of the exercise of the power, but there is some other person present who is in charge of the premises, the officer may give the notice to that other person (s. 52(2)). Where it appears that there is no one present on the premises to whom a notice can be given, the officer must, before leaving the premises, attach a notice in a prominent place to the premises (s. 52(3)).

Return of Property Seized

There are specific obligations on the police to return property seized under these powers—particularly where the property includes legally privileged, excluded or special procedure material. The general rule is that any extraneous property initially seized under these provisions must be returned—usually—to the person from whom it was seized unless the investigating officer considers that someone else has a better claim to it (ss. 53 to 58).

Any person with a relevant interest in the seized property may apply to the appropriate judicial authority, on one or more of the grounds in s. 59(3) for the return of the whole or a part of the seized property. Generally those grounds are that there was no power to make the seizure or that the seized property did not fall into one of the permitted categories (s. 59). Where a person makes such an application, the police must secure the property in accordance with s. 61 (e.g. in a way that prevents investigators from looking at or copying it until the matter has been considered by a judge). There are other occasions where protected material is involved that will also give rise to the duty to secure the property under s. 61. The mechanics of securing property vary according to the circumstances; 'bagging up', i.e. placing material in sealed bags or containers and strict subsequent control of access, is the appropriate procedure in many cases. The 'judicial authority' (at least a Crown Court judge) will be able to make a number of wide-ranging orders in relation to the treatment of the seized property, including its return or examination by a third party. Failure to comply with any such order will amount to a contempt of court (s. 59(9)). Requirements to secure and return property apply equally to all copies, images or other material created because of seizure of the original property.

When material is seized under the powers of seizure conferred by the Police and Criminal Evidence Act 1984, the duty to retain it under the Code of Practice issued under the Criminal Procedure and Investigations Act 1996 is subject to the provisions on retention of seized material in s. 22 of the 1984 Act.

4.2.9 Code B—8 Action after searches

8.1 If premises are searched in circumstances where this Code applies, unless the exceptions in *paragraph 2.3(a)* apply, on arrival at a police station the officer in charge of the search shall make or have made a record of the search, to include:

    (i) the address of the searched premises;

    (ii) the date, time and duration of the search;

    (iii) the authority used for the search:

- if the search was made in exercise of a statutory power to search premises without warrant, the power which was used for the search:
- if the search was made under a warrant or with written consent;
  - a copy of the warrant and the written authority to apply for it, see paragraph 3.4; or
  - the written consent;

shall be appended to the record or the record shall show the location of the copy warrant or consent.

    (iv) subject to paragraph 2.9, the names of:

- the officer(s) in charge of the search;
- all other officers and any authorised persons who conducted the search;

    (v) the names of any people on the premises if they are known;

    (vi) any grounds for refusing the occupier's request to have someone present during the search, see *paragraph 6.11*;

    (vii) a list of any articles seized or the location of a list and, if not covered by a warrant, the grounds for their seizure;

    (viii) whether force was used, and the reason;

    (ix) details of any damage caused during the search, and the circumstances;

    (x) if applicable, the reason it was not practicable:

      (a) to give the occupier a copy of the Notice of Powers and Rights, see *paragraph 6.7*;

      (b) before the search to give the occupier a copy of the Notice, see *paragraph 6.8*;

    (xi) when the occupier was not present, the place where copies of the Notice of Powers and Rights and search warrant were left on the premises, *see paragraph 6.8*.

8.2 On each occasion when premises are searched under warrant, the warrant authorising the search on that occasion shall be endorsed to show:

    (i) if any articles specified in the warrant were found and the address where found;

    (ii) if any other articles were seized;

    (iii) the date and time it was executed and if present, the name of the occupier or if the occupier is not present the name of the person in charge of the premises;

    (iv) subject to paragraph 2.9, the names of the officers who executed it and any authorised persons who accompanied them;

    (v) if a copy, together with a copy of the Notice of Powers and Rights was:

- handed to the occupier; or
- endorsed as required by paragraph 6.8; and left on the premises and where.

8.3 Any warrant shall be returned within three calendar months of its issue or sooner on completion of the search(es) authorised by that warrant, if it was issued by a:

- justice of the peace, to the designated officer for the local justice area in which the justice was acting when issuing the warrant; or
- judge, to the appropriate officer of the court concerned.

4.2.10 Code B—9 Search registers

9.1 A search register will be maintained at each sub-divisional or equivalent police station. All search records required under *paragraph 8.1* shall be made, copied, or referred to in the register.

Paragraph 9.1 also applies to search records made by immigration officers. In these cases, a search register must also be maintained at an immigration office.

4.2.11   Code B—10 Searches under Schedule 5 to the Terrorism Prevention and Investigation Measures Act 2011

10.1 This Code applies to the powers of constables under Schedule 5 to the Terrorism Prevention and Investigation Measures Act 2011 relating to TPIM notices to enter and search premises subject to the modifications in the following paragraphs.

10.2 In paragraph 2.3(d), the reference to the investigation into an alleged or suspected offence include the enforcement of terrorism prevention and investigation measures which may be imposed on an individual by a TPIM notice in accordance with the Terrorism Prevention and Investigation Measures Act 2011.

10.3 References to the purpose and object of the entry and search of premises, the nature of articles sought and what may be seized and retained include (as appropriate):

(a) in relation to the power to search *without a search warrant in paragraph 5* (for purposes of serving TPIM notice), finding the individual on whom the notice is to be served.

(b) in relation to the power to search *without a search warrant in paragraph 6* (at time of serving TPIM notice), ascertaining whether there is anything in the premises, that contravenes measures specified in the notice.

(c) in relation to the power to search *without a search warrant under paragraph 7* (suspected absconding), ascertaining whether a person has absconded or if there is anything on the premises which will assist in the pursuit or arrest of an individual in respect of whom a TPIM notice is in force who is reasonably suspected of having absconded.

(d) in relation to the power to search *under a search warrant* issued under *paragraph 8* (for compliance purposes), determining whether an individual in respect of whom a TPIM notice is in force is complying with measures specified in the notice.

KEYNOTE

Searches of individuals under sch. 5, paras 6(2)(a) (at time of serving TPIM notice) and 8(2)(a) (for compliance purposes) must be conducted and recorded in accordance with Code A. See Code A, para. 2.18A for details.

Powers of Arrest

PACE Code of Practice for the Statutory Power of Arrest by Police Officers (Code G)

> A thick grey line down the margin denotes text that is an extract of the PACE Code itself (i.e. the actual wording of the legislation). This material is examinable for both Sergeants and Inspectors.

4.3.1 Introduction

This chapter scrutinises a number of key features that are relevant to powers of arrest and introduces certain shared points regarding arrest procedures before examining specific powers in detail (and consequently, Code G of the Codes of Practice).

4.3.2 Article 5—The Right to Liberty and Security

Arresting a person amounts to a deprivation of liberty and security and therefore engages Article 5 of the European Convention on Human Rights. Of course, a person may be deprived of their liberty for a number of legitimate and lawful reasons.

Article 5 of the Convention states:

1. Everyone has the right to liberty and security of person. No one shall be deprived of his liberty save in the following cases and in accordance with a procedure prescribed by law:
   (a) the lawful detention of a person after conviction by a competent court;
   (b) the lawful arrest or detention of a person for non-compliance with the lawful order of a court or in order to secure the fulfilment of any obligation prescribed by law;
   (c) the lawful arrest or detention of a person effected for the purpose of bringing him before the competent legal authority on reasonable suspicion of having committed an offence or when it is reasonably considered necessary to prevent his committing an offence or fleeing after having done so;
   (d) the detention of a minor by lawful order for the purpose of educational supervision or his lawful detention for the purpose of bringing him before the competent legal authority;
   (e) the lawful detention of persons for the prevention of the spreading of infectious diseases, of persons of unsound mind, alcoholics or drug addicts or vagrants;
   (f) the lawful arrest or detention of a person to prevent his effecting an unauthorised entry into the country or of a person against whom action is being taken with a view to deportation or extradition.

KEYNOTE

Article 5 does not provide any power to arrest or detain; it simply sets out certain circumstances where the general right to liberty may be interfered with by some existing lawful means.

A person can only be deprived of his/her general right to liberty under one of the conditions set out on the permitted grounds in Article 5(1)(a)–(f), and even then that deprivation must be carried out in accordance with *a procedure prescribed by law*. The 'procedure' must be set out in the domestic law of the country and be recorded in such a way that people can appreciate the possible consequences of their actions and adapt their behaviour accordingly. If the legal authority used to deprive a person of his/her liberty is ambiguous or unclear, that may well provide grounds for challenge under Article 5.

Even if a lawful power is sufficiently clear and well established, the list of permitted grounds in Article 5(1) (a)–(f) will have to be construed narrowly by the courts (*Winterwerp* v *Netherlands* (1979–80) 2 EHRR 387).

Lawful Detention after Conviction

This exception allows a person to be detained after their conviction by a 'competent court', i.e. a court having the jurisdiction to try that particular case. People who have been so convicted may be detained in accordance with the order of the court. Clearly, if the court does not have the power to pass the relevant order, the exception at Article 5(1)(a) will not apply and any detention will potentially amount to a violation of Article 5.

Lawful Arrest or Detention for Non-compliance

The exception under Article 5(1)(b) allows for the detention or arrest of a person who has failed to comply with the *lawful* order of a court. Failing to pay a fine or to observe the conditions of an injunction would be examples of such non-compliance. The exception also extends to the arrest or detention in order to secure the fulfilment of any obligation prescribed by law. Such an obligation might include an obligation to provide a roadside breath specimen or to surrender documents relating to a vehicle. The circumstances of any arrest or detention will be examined by the courts which will need to consider whether the person was given a reasonable opportunity to comply with the order/obligation and whether the arrest or detention was a reasonable way to make sure that the order/obligation was met.

Lawful Arrest/Detention in Relation to an Offence

There are several aspects to the permitted grounds under Article 5(1)(c). The arrest/detention must first be lawful in itself. Any arrest/detention that is later shown to have been *unlawful* cannot be saved under any of the other headings. Even a lawful arrest/detention will only meet the requirements of Article 5(1)(c) if it can be shown to have been:

- effected for the purpose of bringing the person before the relevant 'competent legal authority' (i.e. a judge or magistrate) on reasonable suspicion that the person had committed an offence; or
- reasonably considered necessary to prevent the person committing an offence or from fleeing afterwards.

Where a person has been lawfully arrested for the purpose of bringing him/her before a competent legal authority, it is not necessary to show that he/she actually *was brought* before that authority (*Brogan* v *United Kingdom* (1989) 11 EHRR 117). It is the *purpose* of the arrest at the time that is relevant as opposed to its ultimate achievement. This accords with the provisions of s. 30(7) of the Police and Criminal Evidence Act 1984 which require an arrested person to be released if the grounds for detaining him/her cease to exist (see para. 4.5.12). Given the statutory status of a custody officer, he/she would probably not be a 'competent legal authority' for this purpose, which seems to be judicial in nature and requiring a degree of independence from the arresting authorities. However, it is hard to see how the expression 'competent legal authority' can be limited to judges and magistrates because Article 5(3) goes on to use a more restrictive expression (*judge or other officer authorised by law to exercise judicial power*) to define just such people. The lack of fit here between the wording and our own police and judicial roles is caused partly by the fact that those roles are different in nature from those in many other European Union countries.

'Reasonable suspicion' here will be assessed objectively and the court will look for 'the existence of facts or information which would satisfy an objective observer that the person may have committed the offence' (*Fox* v *United Kingdom* (1991) 13 EHRR 157).

Lawful Detention of Minors

This ground refers solely to 'detention' rather than arrest, although Article 5 seems to use the two expressions interchangeably in places (e.g. Article 5(4) in the following section). The initial detention must be lawful. A minor for these purposes is a person who has not attained the age of 18.

Lawful Detention of Others

Article 5(1)(e) also refers to 'detention' of certain people, in this case those who have various physical or mental ailments. It also extends to 'vagrants'. The reasoning behind Article 5(1)(e) is that the people described may need to be detained in their own interests. The permitted grounds set out here appear to allow the detention of people under the Mental Health Act 1983. Although there is a power under s. 34 of the Criminal Justice Act 1972 for a person to be taken after arrest to an approved alcohol treatment centre, it is unlikely that Article 5(1)(e) would apply as there is no further power to *detain* such a person once he/she arrives at the centre. In such cases, the permitted grounds under Article 5(1)(c) would be more appropriate.

Whatever its extent, Article 5(1)(e) is likely to be narrowly applied by the courts and the mere fact that an individual has, for example, an infectious disease, will not of itself justify his/her 'detention'.

Lawful Arrest/Detention for Deportation or Extradition

Article 5(1)(f) does not require the detention to be *necessary* in order to be justified (*R (On the Application of Saadi)* v *Secretary of State for the Home Department* [2002] UKHL 41). In that case it was held that the temporary detention of asylum seekers pending their application to remain in the United Kingdom was not unlawful simply by reason of it not being strictly necessary.

4.3.2.1 Procedure

Article 5 goes on to state:

2. Everyone who is arrested shall be informed promptly, in a language which he understands, of the reasons for his arrest and of any charge against him.
3. Everyone arrested or detained in accordance with the provisions of paragraph 1(c) of this Article shall be brought promptly before a judge or other officer authorised by law to exercise judicial power and shall be entitled to trial within a reasonable time or to release pending trial. Release may be conditioned by guarantees to appear for trial.
4. Everyone who is deprived of his liberty by arrest or detention shall be entitled to take proceedings by which the lawfulness of his detention shall be decided speedily by a court and his release ordered if the detention is not lawful.
5. Everyone who has been the victim of arrest or detention in contravention of the provisions of this Article shall have an enforceable right to compensation.

KEYNOTE

The right to be informed of the reason for arrest already exists under s. 28 of the Police and Criminal Evidence Act 1984 (see para. 4.5.3.1). The wording of Article 5(2) strengthens that requirement by specifying that the information must be given in a language that the person understands.

The reason for requiring this information to be given would appear to be to allow the arrested person to challenge the arrest and subsequent detention (*X* v *United Kingdom* (1982) 4 EHRR 188). The ability to challenge the lawfulness of that detention (and presumably, the arrest) is itself a Convention right under Article 5(4).

Article 5(5) gives a person who is the 'victim' of an arrest or detention in contravention of the rest of the Article an enforceable right to compensation.

Where a person was being extradited to Spain, the hearing was entitled to conclude that a delay of over five years between an individual's arrest and his extradition did not render the extradition unjust or oppressive (*Owalabi* v *Court Number Four at the High Court of Justice in Spain* [2005] EWHC 2849 (Admin)).

4.3.3 Powers of Arrest—Common Points

An arrest involves depriving a person of his/her liberty to go where he/she pleases (*Lewis* v *Chief Constable of South Wales Constabulary* [1991] 1 All ER 206). In a criminal context an arrest will usually be to answer an alleged charge, but occasionally an arrest may be preventive (such as where a person is arrested in connection with a breach of the peace), it may be to take samples or fingerprints, to return someone to prison or bring him/her before a court.

While the courts may issue warrants ordering the arrest of certain individuals on occasions, police officers are not under any general duty to arrest without warrant and should always consider the use of alternative methods of dealing with the incident or matter.

The source of a power of arrest may come from:

- the conditions at the time (e.g. allowing an arrest under s. 24 of the Police and Criminal Evidence Act 1984);
- the provisions of the particular Act (e.g. s. 7 of the Bail Act 1976, absconding from bail; see *Evidence and Procedure*, **para. 2.2.11**);
- the provisions of an order (e.g. a court order or warrant; see *Evidence and Procedure*, **para. 2.1.6**);
- common law (e.g. breach of the peace; see **para. 4.8.2**).

An arrest begins at the time when the arresting officer informs the person of it or when his/her words or actions suggest that the person is under arrest (*Murray* v *Ministry of Defence* [1988] 1 WLR 692).

Where a power of arrest exists, any lawful arrest must be made for a proper purpose. In the past the courts have allowed the police some latitude in what amounts to a proper purpose, including bringing the person to a police station (*Holgate-Mohammed* v *Duke* [1984] AC 437) and to obtain a confession even after a complainant has withdrawn his/her initial complaint (*Plange* v *Chief Constable of Humberside* (1992) *The Times*, 23 March). The courts have even accepted an arrest based on force policy (*Al Fayed* v *Commissioner of Police of the Metropolis* [2004] EWCA Civ 1579).

The practice of arresting someone on a 'holding' offence was accepted by the Court of Appeal in *R* v *Chalkley* [1998] QB 848, provided the arresting officers had reasonable grounds for suspecting that the person had actually committed that offence. If that suspicion is present, then the fact that the officers making the arrest are doing so with the intention of investigating another, more serious offence does not render the arrest unlawful. If, however, there are no such grounds to suspect that the person had in fact committed the offence, or the officers know at the time of the arrest that there is no possibility of the person actually being charged with it, the arrest will be unlawful.

Section 30(7) of the Police and Criminal Evidence Act 1984 (in keeping with common law) requires that, if the grounds for detaining a person cease to exist before reaching a police station, the person must be released (see **para. 4.3.12**).

4.3.3.1 Information to be Given and Recorded on Arrest

When a person is arrested, it does not matter what power is being used or what the reason for arrest is, s. 28 of the Police and Criminal Evidence Act 1984 makes clear provision for the information that *must* be given to a person on arrest. Section 28 states:

(1) Subject to subsection (5) below, where a person is arrested, otherwise than by being informed that he is under arrest, the arrest is not lawful unless the person arrested is informed that he is under arrest as soon as is practicable after his arrest.

(2) Where a person is arrested by a constable, subsection (1) above applies regardless of whether the fact of the arrest is obvious.

(3) Subject to subsection (5) below, no arrest is lawful unless the person arrested is informed of the ground for the arrest at the time of, or as soon as is practicable after, the arrest.

(4) Where a person is arrested by a constable, subsection (3) above applies regardless of whether the ground for the arrest is obvious.

(5) Nothing in this section is to be taken to require a person to be informed—
  (a) that he is under arrest; or
  (b) of the ground for the arrest,
  if it was not reasonably practicable for him to be so informed by reason of his having escaped from arrest before the information could be given.

KEYNOTE

The formula used in determining whether this has been properly carried out is taken from *Fox* v *United Kingdom* (1991) 13 EHRR 157, which stated:

> Any person arrested must be told, in simple, non-technical language that he can understand, the essential legal and factual grounds for his arrest, so as to be able, if he sees fit, to apply to a court to challenge its lawfulness.

Therefore the key reason for requiring this information to be given is to allow the arrested person to challenge the arrest and subsequent detention.

Code C of the Police and Criminal Evidence Act 1984 also imposes requirements in this area.

The reality is that for certain types of offence (particularly those involving violence or disorder), it will be impractical to give each person arrested detailed particulars of the case against him/her. Whether or not the information actually given to a person on arrest was adequate for the purposes of the above legislation will have to be assessed objectively, *having regard to the information that was reasonably available to the arresting officer* (*Taylor* v *Chief Constable of Thames Valley* [2004] EWCA Civ 858). It might suffice in some cases, such as the violent disorder in *Taylor*, for the police officer to tell the person he/she is being arrested on suspicion of taking part in violent disorder at a certain time and place.

Section 28 makes provision for situations when the person cannot be told or would not be capable of understanding the information. However, as the failure to comply with s. 28 makes any arrest unlawful (*Dawes* v *DPP* [1995] 1 Cr App R 65), it is perhaps better to 'err on the side of caution'.

In relation to the requirement at s. 28(2) and (3), care should be taken when giving a suspect details of exactly why he/she is being arrested. It has been held that it was unfair and unlawful for an arresting officer to withhold facts which had led him to arrest the suspect on suspicion of having committed an offence (*Wilson* v *Chief Constable of Lancashire Constabulary* (2000) Po LR 367). In that case it was held that an arresting officer's minimum obligation was to give a suspect 'sufficient information as to the nature of an arrest to allow the suspect sufficient opportunity to respond'.

The reasons given for the arrest must be the *real* reasons in the officer's mind at the time (*Christie* v *Leachinsky* [1947] AC 573) and he/she must clearly indicate to the person the fact that he/she is being arrested.

In *R* v *Fiak* [2005] EWCA Crim 2381 it was held that an arrest had not been rendered unlawful by the police officer's failure to use the word 'arrest'—this requirement might be met by using a colloquialism, provided that the person is familiar with it and understands its meaning (e.g. 'you're locked up' or 'you're nicked' (*Christie* v *Leachinsky*)). It does not matter that the words describe more than one offence (e.g. 'burglary' or 'fraud'), provided that they adequately describe the offence for which the person has been arrested (*Abbassy* v *Metropolitan Police Commissioner* [1990] 1 WLR 385).

4.3.3.2 Caution

The Police and Criminal Evidence Act 1984 Code of Practice, Code C, para. 10, requires that a person must be cautioned on arrest or further arrest (**see para. 4.3.6**).

There will be occasions where those involved with the custody and care of prisoners will overhear remarks by a defendant or will have comments made to them, which may be of relevance to the case in which the defendant is prosecuted. While such people may not be under a strict duty to administer the caution in the same way as police officers, the admissibility of the evidence will be tested against the general requirements of fairness and it might be appropriate to give a caution and/or to make a record of such comments as soon as possible (*R* v *Ristic* [2004] EWCA Crim 2107—prison officer giving evidence of incriminating remarks overheard by a defendant).

Where police officers are themselves being interviewed or investigated, the caution used in such cases will follow the general criminal one from Code C, with the inclusion of an element relating to a failure to make a written statement.

4.3.3.3　Use of Force

Section 117 of the Police and Criminal Evidence Act 1984 allows the use of reasonable force when making an arrest. Section 3 of the Criminal Law Act 1967 also allows the use of such force as is reasonably necessary in the arrest of people and the prevention of crime.

Whether any force used is 'reasonable' will be determined in the light of all the circumstances, including the circumstances as the arresting officer believed them to be at the time. Such force may even be lethal to the defendant. Where serious harm is caused by an arrest, the courts will consider the time that was available to the officer to reflect on his/her actions and whether or not he/she believed that the danger presented to others by failing to arrest the person outweighed the harm caused to the person by the arrest (*Attorney-General for Northern Ireland's Reference (No. 1 of 1975)* [1977] AC 105).

Use of excessive force, while amounting to possible misconduct and assault, does not render an otherwise lawful arrest unlawful (*Simpson* v *Chief Constable of South Yorkshire* (1991) 135 SJ 383).

4.3.4　PACE Code of Practice for the Statutory Power of Arrest by Police Officers (Code G)

This Code applies to any arrest made by a police officer after midnight on 12 November 2012.

1　Introduction

1.1　This Code of Practice deals with statutory power of police to arrest a person who is involved, or suspected of being involved, in a criminal offence. The power of arrest must be used fairly, responsibly, with respect for people suspected of committing offences and without unlawful discrimination. The Equality Act 2010 makes it unlawful for police officers to discriminate against, harass or victimise any person on the grounds of the 'protected characteristics' of age, disability, gender reassignment, race, religion or belief, sex and sexual orientation, marriage and civil partnership, pregnancy and maternity when using their powers. When police forces are carrying out their functions they also have a duty to have regard to the need to eliminate unlawful discrimination, harassment and victimisation and to take steps to foster good relations.

1.2　The exercise of the power of arrest represents an obvious and significant interference with the Right to Liberty and Security under Article 5 of the European Convention on Human Rights set out in Part I of Schedule 1 to the Human Rights Act 1998.

1.3　The use of the power must be fully justified and officers exercising the power should consider if the necessary objectives can be met by other, less intrusive means. Absence of justification for exercising the powers of arrest may lead to challenges should the case proceed to court. It could also lead to civil claims against the police for unlawful arrest and false imprisonment. When the power of arrest is exercised it is essential that it is exercised in a non-discriminatory and proportionate manner which is compatible with the Right to Liberty under Article 5.

1.4　Section 24 of the Police and Criminal Evidence Act 1984 (as substituted by section 110 of the Serious Organised Crime and Police Act 2005) provides the statutory power for a constable to arrest without warrant for all offences. If the provisions of the Act and this Code are not observed, both the arrest and the conduct of any subsequent investigation may be open to question.

1.5　This Code of Practice must be readily available at all police stations for consultation by police officers and police staff, detained persons and members of the public.

4.3.4.1
KEYNOTE

Code G points out that juveniles should not be arrested at their place of education unless this is unavoidable. When a juvenile is arrested at their place of education, the principal or their nominee must be informed.

4.3.5

Code G—2 Elements of Arrest under section 24 PACE

2.1 A lawful arrest requires two elements:

A person's involvement or suspected involvement or attempted involvement in the commission of a criminal offence;

AND

Reasonable grounds for *believing* that the person's arrest is necessary.
- both elements must be satisfied, and
- it can never be necessary to arrest a person unless there are reasonable grounds to suspect them of committing an offence.

2.2 The arrested person must be informed that they have been arrested, even if this fact is obvious, and of the relevant circumstances of the arrest in relation to both the above elements. The custody officer must be informed of these matters on arrival at the police station. See Code C paragraph 3.4.

(a) Involvement 'in the commission of an offence'

2.3 A constable may arrest without warrant in relation to any offence anyone:
- who is about to commit an offence or is in the act of committing an offence
- whom the officer has reasonable grounds for suspecting is about to commit an offence or to be committing an offence
- whom the officer has reasonable grounds to suspect of being guilty of an offence which he or she has reasonable grounds for suspecting has been committed
- anyone who is guilty of an offence which has been committed or anyone whom the officer has reasonable grounds for suspecting to be guilty of that offence.

2.3A There must be some reasonable, objective grounds for the suspicion, based on known facts and information which are relevant to the likelihood the offence has been committed and the person liable to arrest committed it.

4.3.5.1

KEYNOTE

For the purposes of this Code, 'offence' means any statutory or common law offence for which a person may be tried by a magistrates' court or the Crown Court and punished if convicted.

This Code does not apply to powers of arrest conferred on constables under any arrest warrant, for example, a warrant issued under the Magistrates' Courts Act 1980, ss. 1 or 13, or the Bail Act 1976, s. 7(1), or to the powers of constables to arrest without warrant other than under s. 24 of PACE for an offence. These other powers to arrest without warrant do not depend on the arrested person committing any specific offence and include:

- PACE, s. 46A, arrest of person who fails to answer police bail to attend police station or is suspected of breaching any condition of that bail for the custody officer to decide whether they should be kept in police detention which applies whether or not the person commits an offence under s. 6 of the Bail Act 1976 (e.g. failing without reasonable cause to surrender to custody);
- Bail Act 1976, s. 7(3), arrest of person bailed to attend court who is suspected of breaching, or is believed likely to breach, any condition of bail to take them to court for bail to be reconsidered;

- Children and Young Persons Act 1969, s. 32(1A) (absconding)—arrest to return the person to the place where they are required to reside;
- Immigration Act 1971, sch. 2, to arrest a person liable to examination to determine their right to remain in the United Kingdom;
- Mental Health Act 1983, s. 136, to remove person suffering from a mental disorder to place of safety for assessment;
- Prison Act 1952, s. 49, arrest to return person unlawfully at large to the prison etc. where they are liable to be detained;
- Road Traffic Act 1988, s. 6D, arrest of driver following the outcome of a preliminary roadside test requirement to enable the driver to be required to provide an evidential sample;
- common law power to stop or prevent a breach of the peace—after arrest a person aged 18 or over may be brought before a justice of the peace court to show cause why they should not be bound over to keep the peace—not criminal proceedings.

4.3.5.2 Reasonable Grounds to Suspect

Central to the criteria set out in s. 24 is the concept of 'reasonable grounds for suspecting'. The wording of s. 24 has yet to be developed by the courts, however the interpretation of and approach to the pre-existing legislation are helpful in understanding the concepts involved.

Tests of 'reasonableness' impose an element of objectivity and the courts will consider whether, in the circumstances, a reasonable and sober person might have formed a similar view to that of the officer. Failing to follow up an obvious line of inquiry (e.g. as to the ownership of property found in the possession of the defendant) may well provide grounds for challenging the exercise of a power of arrest (*Castorina* v *Chief Constable of Surrey*, **see para. 4.3.5.3**).

4.3.5.3 The *Castorina* test

The key test for establishing the lawfulness of an arrest without warrant is set out in *Castorina* v *Chief Constable of Surrey* (1996) 160 LG Rev 241.

The *Castorina* test effectively has three stages:

(1) Did the arresting officer suspect that the person who was arrested was guilty of the offence (or about to commit etc.)?
(2) If so, was there reasonable cause (i.e. reasonable grounds) for the arresting officer's suspicion?
(3) If the answer to the two previous questions is in the affirmative, then the officer has a discretion which entitles him/her to make an arrest—was the arresting officer's exercise of his/her discretion reasonable in all the circumstances?

The first stage in the *Castorina* test is a subjective one in that it depends entirely on what was in the officer's mind at the time.

The second stage of the *Castorina* test is a purely objective one to be determined by the judge on facts found by the jury/court. This element means that it is not enough for the officer to claim reasonable suspicion in his/her own mind. A court will go on to look at whether there were reasonable grounds to suspect that an offence had been committed and that the person had committed it.

It is not uncommon for police officers to be called to a situation where, while there might be only one or two people responsible for an offence, it is unclear which of a group of people is the culprit. The Court of Appeal has confirmed that where an offence has been committed and one of only a small number of people could have committed it, there is no reason why each member or all the group members cannot be arrested (*Cumming* v *Chief*

Constable of Northumbria Police [2003] EWCA Civ 1844). In the absence of any information that could or should enable the police to reduce the number further, the fact that a person is in a small group, one of whom must have committed the offence, can amount to reasonable grounds for suspecting him/her.

Where only one person had the opportunity to commit the offence that 'opportunity' alone is enough to justify reasonable grounds for suspicion (*Al Fayed* v *Commissioner of Police for the Metropolis* [2004] EWCA Civ 1579). Indeed, in some circumstances opportunity may be sufficient to found a conviction.

However, merely being told to arrest someone by a more senior officer is not a reasonable ground for doing so (*O'Hara* v *Chief Constable of the Royal Ulster Constabulary* [1997] AC 286).

Facts and information relevant to a person's suspected involvement in an offence should not be confined to those which tend to indicate the person has committed or attempted to commit the offence. Before making a decision to arrest, a constable should take account of any facts and information that are available, including claims of innocence made by the person, which might dispel the suspicion. There is no need, however, for the officer to discount every possible defence or to seek complete proof of the relevant facts or circumstances before effecting an arrest (*Ward* v *Chief Constable of Avon and Somerset Constabulary* (1986) *The Times*, 26 June).

Examples of facts and information which might point to a person's innocence and dispel suspicion include those which relate to the statutory defence provided by the Criminal Law Act 1967, s. 3(1) which allows the use of reasonable force in the prevention of crime or making an arrest and the common law of self-defence. This may be relevant when a person appears, or claims, to have been acting reasonably in defence of themselves or others or to prevent their property or the property of others from being stolen, destroyed or damaged, particularly if the offence alleged is based on the use of unlawful force, e.g. a criminal assault.

When investigating allegations involving the use of force by school staff, the power given to all school staff under the Education and Inspections Act 2006, s. 93, to use reasonable force to prevent their pupils from committing any offence, injuring persons, damaging property or prejudicing the maintenance of good order and discipline may be similarly relevant. ACPO and the CPS have published joint guidance to help the public understand the meaning of reasonable force and what to expect from the police and CPS in cases which involve claims of self-defence. Separate advice for school staff on their powers to use reasonable force is available from the Department for Education.

(b) Necessity criteria

2.4 The power of arrest is only exercisable if the constable has reasonable grounds for **believing** that it is necessary to arrest the person. The statutory criteria for what may constitute necessity are set out in paragraph 2.9 and it remains an operational decision at the discretion of the constable as to:

- which one or more of the necessity criteria (if any) applies to the individual; and
- if any of the criteria do apply, whether to arrest, grant street bail after arrest, report for summons or for charging by post, issue a fixed penalty notice or take any other action that is open to the officer.

2.5 In applying the criteria, the arresting officer has to be satisfied that at least one of the reasons supporting the need for arrest is satisfied.

2.6 Extending the power of arrest to all offences provides a constable with the ability to use that power to deal with any situation. However applying the necessity criteria requires the constable to examine and justify the reason or reasons why a person needs to be arrested or (as the case may be) further arrested, for an offence for the custody officer to decide whether to authorise their detention for that offence.

4.3.5.4

KEYNOTE

For a constable to have reasonable grounds for *believing* it *necessary* to arrest, he/she is not required to be satisfied that there is no viable alternative to arrest. However, it does mean that in all cases, the officer should consider that arrest is the practical, sensible and proportionate option in all the circumstances at the time the decision is made. This applies to a person in police detention after being arrested for an offence who is suspected of involvement in a further offence and where the necessity to arrest them for that further offence is being considered.

2.7 The criteria in paragraph 2.9 below which are set out in section 24 of PACE as substituted by section 110 of the Serious Organised Crime and Police Act 2005 **are** exhaustive. However, the circumstances that may satisfy those criteria remain a matter for the operational discretion of individual officers. Some examples are given to illustrate what those circumstances may be and what officers might consider when deciding whether an arrest is necessary.

2.8 In considering the individual circumstances, the constable must take into account the situation of the victim, the nature of the offence, the circumstances of the suspect and the needs of the investigative process.

2.9 When it is practicable to tell a person why their arrest is necessary (as required by paragraphs 2.2 and 3.3), the constable should outline the facts, information and other circumstances which provide the grounds for believing that their arrest is necessary and which the officer considers satisfy one or more of the statutory criteria in sub-paragraphs (a) to (f) namely:

(a) to enable the name of the person in question to be ascertained (in the case where the constable does not know, and cannot readily ascertain, the person's name, or has reasonable grounds for doubting whether a name given by the person as his name is his real name):

An officer might decide that a person's name cannot be readily ascertained if they fail or refuse to give it when asked, particularly after being warned that failure or refusal is likely to make their arrest necessary. Grounds to doubt a name given may arise if the person appears reluctant or hesitant when asked to give their name or to verify the name they have given.

Where mobile fingerprinting is available and the suspect's name cannot be ascertained or is doubted, the officer should consider using the power under section 61(6A) of PACE (see Code D paragraph 4.3(e)) to take and check the fingerprints of a suspect as this may avoid the need to arrest solely to enable their name to be ascertained.

(b) correspondingly as regards the person's address:

An officer might decide that a person's address cannot be readily ascertained if they fail or refuse to give it when asked, particularly after being warned that such a failure or refusal is likely to make their arrest necessary. Grounds to doubt an address given may arise if the person appears reluctant or hesitant when asked to give their address or is unable to provide verifiable details of the locality they claim to live in.

When considering reporting to consider summons or charging by post as alternatives to arrest, an address would be satisfactory if the person will be at it for a sufficiently long period for it to be possible to serve them with the summons or requisition and charge; or, that some other person at that address specified by the person will accept service on their behalf. When considering issuing a penalty notice, the address should be one where the person will be in the event of enforcement action if the person does not pay the penalty or is convicted and fined after a court hearing.

(c) to prevent the person in question—

(i) causing physical injury to himself or any other person;

This might apply where the suspect has already used or threatened violence against others and it is thought likely that they may assault others if they are not arrested.

(ii) suffering physical injury;

This might apply where the suspect's behaviour and actions are believed likely to provoke, or have provoked, others to want to assault the suspect unless the suspect is arrested for their own protection.

(iii) causing loss or damage to property;

This might apply where the suspect is a known persistent offender with a history of serial offending against property (theft and criminal damage) and it is thought likely that they may continue offending if they are not arrested.

(iv) committing an offence against public decency (only applies where members of the public going about their normal business cannot reasonably be expected to avoid the person in question);

This might apply when an offence against public decency is being committed in a place to which the public have access and is likely to be repeated in that or some other public place at a time when the public are likely to encounter the suspect.

(v) causing an unlawful obstruction of the highway;

This might apply to any offence where its commission causes an unlawful obstruction which it is believed may continue or be repeated if the person is not arrested, particularly if the person has been warned that they are causing an obstruction.

(d) to protect a child or other vulnerable person from the person in question.

This might apply when the health (physical or mental) or welfare of a child or vulnerable person is likely to be harmed or is at risk of being harmed, if the person is not arrested in cases where it is not practicable and appropriate to make alternative arrangements to prevent the suspect from having any harmful or potentially harmful contact with the child or vulnerable person.

(e) to allow the prompt and effective investigation of the offence or of the conduct of the person in question.

This may arise when it is thought likely that unless the person is arrested and then either taken in custody to the police station or granted 'street bail' to attend the station later, further action considered necessary to properly investigate their involvement in the offence would be frustrated, unreasonably delayed or otherwise hindered and therefore be impracticable. Examples of such actions include:

(i) interviewing the suspect on occasions when the person's voluntary attendance is not considered to be a practicable alternative to arrest, because for example:

- it is thought unlikely that the person would attend the police station voluntarily to be interviewed.
- it is necessary to interview the suspect about the outcome of other investigative action for which their arrest is necessary, see (ii) to (v) below.
- arrest would enable the special warning to be given in accordance with Code C paragraphs 10.10 and 10.11 when the suspect is found:
  ~ in possession of incriminating objects, or at a place where such objects are found;
  ~ at or near the scene of the crime at or about the time it was committed.
- the person has made false statements and/or presented false evidence;
- it is thought likely that the person:
  ~ may steal or destroy evidence;
  ~ may collude or make contact with, co-suspects or conspirators;
  ~ may intimidate or threaten or make contact with, witnesses.

(ii) when considering arrest in connection with the investigation of an indictable offence, there is a need:

- to enter and search without a search warrant any premises occupied or controlled by the arrested person or where the person was when arrested or immediately before arrest;

- to prevent the arrested person from having contact with others;
- to detain the arrested person for more than 24 hours before charge.

   (iii) when considering arrest in connection with any recordable offence and it is necessary to secure or preserve evidence of that offence by taking fingerprints, footwear impressions or samples from the suspect for evidential comparison or matching with other material relating to that offence, for example, from the crime scene.

   (iv) when considering arrest in connection with any offence and it is necessary to search, examine or photograph the person to obtain evidence.

   (v) when considering arrest in connection with an offence to which the statutory Class A drug testing requirements in Code C section 17 apply, to enable testing when it is thought that drug misuse might have caused or contributed to the offence.

(f) to prevent any prosecution for the offence from being hindered by the disappearance of the person in question.

This may arise when it is thought that:

- if the person is not arrested they are unlikely to attend court if they are prosecuted;
- the address given is not a satisfactory address for service of a summons or a written charge and requisition to appear at court because the person will not be at it for a sufficiently long period for the summons or charge and requisition to be served and no other person at that specified address will accept service on their behalf.

4.3.5.5

KEYNOTE

Arrested persons must be given sufficient information to enable them to understand they have been deprived of their liberty and the reason they have been arrested, as soon as practicable after the arrest, e.g. when persons are arrested on suspicion of committing an offence they must be informed of the nature of the suspected offence and when and where it was committed. Suspects must also be informed of the reason or reasons why arrest is considered necessary. Vague or technical language should be avoided. When explaining why one or more of the arrest criteria apply, it is not necessary to disclose any specific details that might undermine or otherwise adversely affect any investigative processes. For example, the conduct of a formal interview when prior disclosure of such details might give the suspect an opportunity to fabricate an innocent explanation or to otherwise conceal lies from the interviewer.

4.3.5.6   **Paragraph 2.9(a), (b) and (c)**

Although a warning is not expressly required, officers should, if practicable, consider whether to issue a warning which points out the person's offending behaviour, and explains why, if the person does not stop, the resulting consequences may make his/her arrest necessary. Such a warning might:

- if heeded, avoid the need to arrest, or
- if ignored, support the need to arrest and also help prove the mental element of certain offences, e.g. the person's intent or awareness, or help to rebut a defence that he/she was acting reasonably.

A person who is warned that he/she may be liable to arrest if his/her real name and address cannot be ascertained, should be given a reasonable opportunity to establish his/her real name and address before deciding that either or both are unknown and cannot be readily ascertained or that there are reasonable grounds to doubt that a name and address the person has given is his/her real name and address. He/she should be told why his/her name is not known and cannot be readily ascertained and (as the case may be) of the grounds for doubting that a name and address he/she has given is his/her real name and address, including, for example, the reason why a particular document the person has produced to verify his/her real name and/or address is not sufficient.

4.3.5.7   Paragraph 2.9(e)

The meaning of 'prompt' should be considered on a case-by-case basis taking account of all the circumstances. It indicates that the progress of the investigation should not be delayed to the extent that it would adversely affect the effectiveness of the investigation. The arresting officer also has discretion to release the arrested person on 'street bail' as an alternative to taking the person directly to the station. Having determined that the necessity criteria have been met and having made the arrest, the officer can then consider the use of street bail on the basis of the effective and efficient progress of the investigation of the offence in question. It gives the officer discretion to compel the person to attend a police station at a date/time that best suits the overall needs of the particular investigation. Its use is not confined to dealing with child care issues or allowing officers to attend to more urgent operational duties, and granting street bail does not retrospectively negate the need to arrest.

4.3.5.8   Paragraph 2.9(e)(i)

An officer who believes that it is necessary to interview the person suspected of committing the offence must then consider whether his/her arrest is necessary in order to carry out the interview. The officer is not required to interrogate the suspect to determine whether he/she will attend a police station voluntarily to be interviewed but the officer must consider whether the suspect's voluntary attendance is a practicable alternative for carrying out the interview. If it is, then arrest would not be necessary. Conversely, an officer who considers this option but is not satisfied that it is a practicable alternative, may have reasonable grounds for deciding that the arrest is necessary at the outset 'on the street'. Without such considerations, the officer would not be able to establish that arrest was necessary in order to interview.

Circumstances which suggest that a person's arrest 'on the street' would not be necessary to interview him/her might be where the officer:

* is satisfied as to the person's identity and address and that he/she will attend the police station voluntarily to be interviewed, either immediately or by arrangement at a future date and time; and
* is not aware of any other circumstances which indicate that voluntary attendance would not be a practicable alternative. See para. 2.9(e)(i)–(v).

When making arrangements for the person's voluntary attendance, the officer should tell the person:

* that to properly investigate his/her suspected involvement in the offence he/she must be interviewed under caution at the police station, but in the circumstances his/her arrest for this purpose will not be necessary if he/she attends the police station voluntarily to be interviewed;
* that if he/she attends voluntarily, he/she will be entitled to free legal advice before, and to have a solicitor present at, the interview;
* that the date and time of the interview will take account of the person's circumstances and the needs of the investigation; and
* that if the person does not agree to attend voluntarily at a time which meets the needs of the investigation, or having so agreed, fails to attend, or having attended, fails to remain for the interview to be completed, his/her arrest will be necessary to enable him/her to be interviewed.

When the person attends the police station voluntarily for interview by arrangement (as above), his/her arrest on arrival at the station prior to interview would only be justified if:

* new information coming to light after the arrangements were made indicates that, from that time, voluntary attendance ceased to be a practicable alternative and the person's arrest became necessary; and

- it was not reasonably practicable for the person to be arrested before he/she attended the station.
- If a person who attends the police station voluntarily to be interviewed decides to leave before the interview is complete, the police would at that point be entitled to consider whether the person's arrest was necessary to carry out the interview. The possibility that the person might decide to leave during the interview is therefore not a valid reason for arresting him/her before the interview has commenced. See Code C, para. 3.21.

4.3.5.9 Paragraph 2.9(e)(ii)

It should be remembered that certain powers available as the result of an arrest (e.g. entry and search of premises, detention without charge beyond 24 hours, holding a person incommunicado and delaying access to legal advice) only apply in respect of indictable offences and are subject to the specific requirements on authorisation as set out in PACE and the relevant Code of Practice.

4.3.5.10 Paragraph 2.9(e)(iii) and (iv)

The necessity criteria do not permit arrest solely to enable the routine taking, checking (speculative searching) and retention of fingerprints, samples, footwear impressions and photographs when there are no prior grounds to believe that checking and comparing the fingerprints etc. or taking a photograph would provide relevant evidence of the person's involvement in the offence concerned or would help to ascertain or verify his/her real identity.

The necessity criteria do not permit arrest for an offence solely because it happens to be one of the statutory drug testing 'trigger offences' when there is no suspicion that Class A drug misuse might have caused or contributed to the offence (para. 2.9(e)(v)).

4.3.6 Code G—3 Information to be given on Arrest

(a) Cautions—when a caution must be given

3.1 Code C paragraphs 10.1 and 10.2 set out the requirement for a person whom there are grounds to suspect of an offence to be cautioned before being questioned or further questioned about an offence.

3.2 *Not used.*

3.3 A person who is arrested, or further arrested, must be informed at the time if practicable, or if not, as soon as it becomes practicable thereafter, that they are under arrest and the grounds and reasons for their arrest.

3.4 A person who is arrested, or further arrested, must also be cautioned unless:
   (a) it is impracticable to do so by reason of their condition or behaviour at the time;
   (b) they have already been cautioned immediately prior to arrest as in paragraph 3.1.

3.5 The caution, which must be given on arrest, should be in the following terms:
   'You do not have to say anything. But it may harm your defence if you do not mention when questioned something which you later rely on in Court. Anything you do say may be given in evidence.'
   Where the use of the Welsh Language is appropriate, a constable may provide the caution directly in Welsh in the following terms:
   'Does dim rhaid i chi ddweud dim byd. Ond gall niweidio eich amddiffyniad os na fyddwch chi'n sôn, wrth gael eich holi, am rywbeth y byddwch chi'n dibynnu arno nes ymlaen yn y Llys. Gall unrhyw beth yr ydych yn ei ddweud gael ei roi fel tystiolaeth.'

3.6 Minor deviations from the words of any caution given in accordance with this Code do not constitute a breach of this Code, provided the sense of the relevant caution is preserved.

3.7 *Not used.*

KEYNOTE

The Caution

Nothing in this Code requires a caution to be given or repeated when informing a person not under arrest that he/she may be prosecuted for an offence. However, a court will not be able to draw any inferences under the Criminal Justice and Public Order Act 1994, s. 34, if the person was not cautioned.

If it appears a person does not understand the caution, the people giving it should explain it in their own words.

In addition to the caution being given on arrest, Code C, para. 10.5 states that a caution must be given on all other occasions before a person is charged or informed they may be prosecuted (see *Evidence and Procedure*, para. 2.9.2.2).

4.3.7 | Code G—4 Records of Arrest

(a) General

4.1 The arresting officer is required to record in his pocket book or by other methods used for recording information:
- the nature and circumstances of the offence leading to the arrest
- the reason or reasons why arrest was necessary
- the giving of the caution
- anything said by the person at the time of arrest.

4.2 Such a record should be made at the time of the arrest unless impracticable to do. If not made at that time, the record should then be completed as soon as possible thereafter.

4.3 On arrival at the police station or after being first arrested at the police station, the arrested person must be brought before the custody officer as soon as practicable and a custody record must be opened in accordance with section 2 of Code C. The information given by the arresting officer on the circumstances and reason or reasons for arrest shall be recorded as part of the custody record. Alternatively, a copy of the record made by the officer in accordance with paragraph 4.1 above shall be attached as part of the custody record. See *paragraph 2.2* and *Code C paragraphs 3.4 and 10.3.*

4.4 The custody record will serve as a record of the arrest. Copies of the custody record will be provided in accordance with paragraphs 2.4 and 2.4A of Code C and access for inspection of the original record in accordance with paragraph 2.5 of Code C.

(b) Interviews and arrests

4.5 Records of interview, significant statements or silences will be treated in the same way as set out in sections 11 and 12 of Code C and in Codes E and F (audio and visual recording of interviews).

4.3.8 | Arrest without Warrant—Arrest by Others

The Police and Criminal Evidence Act 1984 makes provision for the so-called citizen's arrest powers. Far narrower than the police powers, these powers of arrest are set out in s. 24A, which states:

(1) A person other than a constable may arrest without a warrant—
   (a) anyone who is in the act of committing an indictable offence;
   (b) anyone whom he has reasonable grounds for suspecting to be committing an indictable offence.

(2) Where an indictable offence has been committed, a person other than a constable may arrest without a warrant—

    (a) anyone who is guilty of the offence;

    (b) anyone whom he has reasonable grounds for suspecting to be guilty of it.

(3) But the power of summary arrest conferred by subsection (1) or (2) is exercisable only if—

    (a) the person making the arrest has reasonable grounds for believing that for any of the reasons mentioned in subsection (4) it is necessary to arrest the person in question; and

    (b) it appears to the person making the arrest that it is not reasonably practicable for a constable to make it instead.

(4) The reasons are to prevent the person in question:

    (a) causing physical injury to himself or any other person;

    (b) suffering physical injury;

    (c) causing loss of or damage to property; or

    (d) making off before a constable can assume responsibility for him.

(5) This section does not apply in relation to an offence under Part 3 or 3A of the Public Order Act 1986.

KEYNOTE

Unlike the powers of arrest available to police officers (which apply to any and every offence), the citizen's power of arrest only applies where the relevant offence is *indictable*. This power is available to police staff and others such as Police Community Support Officers.

Under s. 24A(2), an indictable offence must have been committed; it is not enough to suspect or even believe that such an offence has been committed, even if there are very good grounds for that suspicion or belief. This can cause difficulties for the person carrying out the arrest if the 'offender' is subsequently acquitted at court (*R* v *Self* [1992] 1 WLR 657).

'Summary arrest', in this context, means an arrest without warrant (regardless of whether the offence in question is a summary, either way or indictable only offence).

Racial and religious hatred offences provided by the Racial and Religious Hatred Act 2006 do not apply to this section (s. 24A(5)).

4.3.9   Arrest without Warrant—Other Powers of Arrest

Apart from the general power of arrest under s. 24 of the Police and Criminal Evidence Act 1984, several other powers of arrest exist.

4.3.9.1   Preserved Powers of Arrest

Section 26 of the Police and Criminal Evidence Act 1984 repealed all other powers of arrest without warrant which existed before the 1984 Act except those listed in sch. 2.

The common law power of arrest for breach of the peace has been preserved by s. 26 of the 1984 Act (*DPP* v *Orum* [1989] 1 WLR 88).

4.3.9.2   Fingerprinting

The Police and Criminal Evidence Act 1984, s. 27 provides a power of arrest to take a person's fingerprints.

4.3.9.3   Failure to Answer Police Bail

Section 46A of the Police and Criminal Evidence Act 1984 provides a power of arrest when a person fails to answer police bail—this is discussed in detail in **Evidence and Procedure, chapter 2.2.**

4.3.9.4 Arrest to Take Samples

Section 63A of the Police and Criminal Evidence Act 1984 provides a power of arrest without warrant in respect of people:

- who have been charged with/reported for a recordable offence and who have not had a sample taken or the sample was unsuitable/insufficient for analysis;
- who have been convicted of a recordable offence and have not had a sample taken since conviction;
- who have been so convicted and have had a sample taken before or since conviction but the sample was unsuitable/insufficient for analysis.

This is simply a summary of s. 63A and reference should be made to the 1984 Act for the exact wording.

4.3.9.5 Cross-border Arrest without Warrant

The Criminal Justice and Public Order Act 1994 (ss. 136 to 140) makes provision for officers from one part of the United Kingdom to go into another part of the United Kingdom to arrest someone there in connection with an offence committed within their jurisdiction and gives them powers to search on arrest.

Under the 1994 Act an officer from a police service in England and Wales may arrest a person in Scotland where it appears to the officer that it would have been lawful for him/her to have exercised his/her powers had the suspected person been in England and Wales or where it would be impracticable to serve a summons for the same reasons which would justify an arrest in England and Wales.

A Scottish officer may arrest someone suspected of committing an offence in Scotland who is found in England, Wales or Northern Ireland if it would have been lawful to arrest that person had he/she been found in Scotland. In such a case the officer must take the person to a designated police station in Scotland or to the nearest designated police station in England or Wales (s. 137(7)).

The 1994 Act sets out where a person arrested outside the relevant country should be taken on arrest (s. 137(7)). The Act also provides wide powers of search in connection with arrests (s. 139).

4.3.10 Arrest under Warrant

Arrest warrants may be issued by magistrates (generally under s. 1 of the Magistrates' Courts Act 1980) and the Crown Court (under the Senior Courts Act 1981, s. 80(2)) where the statute in question, together with the powers of the court allow. Warrants of arrest may also be issued to secure the attendance of witnesses (s. 97 of the Magistrates' Courts Act 1980 and s. 4 of the Criminal Procedure (Attendance of Witnesses) Act 1965).

The police owe defendants a duty of care when drawing up and enforcing the contents of warrants. Therefore, where officers put the wrong date on an arrest warrant issued by a magistrates' court and, as a result, the defendant was not released by the Prison Service when he should have been, the police were liable in damages for the defendant's unlawful imprisonment (*Clarke* v *Chief Constable of Northamptonshire Police* (1999) *The Times*, 14 June). Though not employed by the police, civilian enforcement officers (CEOs) and approved enforcement agencies (AEAs) are nevertheless empowered to execute arrest warrants in certain circumstances. The details of these specific provisions are beyond the scope of this Manual.

Warrants issued in relation to an offence may be backed for bail, in which case the person is then granted bail in accordance with the conditions on the warrant. If not backed for bail, the warrant will specify where the person is to be brought (i.e. before the next sitting of the court).

Warrants issued in England, Wales, Scotland or Northern Ireland may be executed by officers from the country where they are issued or in the country where the person is arrested (s. 136 of the Criminal Justice and Public Order Act 1994).

Warrants from the Republic of Ireland (provided they are not issued for political offences) may be executed in England and Wales if so endorsed (s. 125 of the Magistrates' Courts Act 1980), as, indeed, may warrants issued in the Isle of Man or the Channel Islands if so endorsed (s. 13 of the Indictable Offences Act 1848).

Warrants issued in connection with 'an offence' do not need to be in the possession of the officer executing them at the time. The majority of warrants issued for the arrest of a person in England and Wales arise from matters such as failure to appear at court, breaching bail conditions or failing to pay fines. All of these were once a significant source of policing activity, but they are now enforceable by civilian enforcement officers and approved enforcement agencies.

The procedure dealing with European Arrest Warrants is outside the scope of this Manual.

4.3.11   Voluntary Attendance at a Police Station

There are a variety of situations where a person attends at a police station in a voluntary capacity. For example, where the person is a suspect, by pre-arrangement with the officers in the case or where the person learns that the police want to speak to him/her or perhaps where a person has elected to accompany a Police Community Support Officer to a police station rather than awaiting the arrival of a constable.

There is no distinction between a person being arrested at a police station after attending voluntarily, and a person arrested elsewhere, provided the arresting officers acted appropriately and reasonably (*Al Fayed*).

However, there are certain statutory provisions with regard to the entitlements and treatment of people who are 'voluntary attendees' and these are set out below.

The Police and Criminal Evidence Act 1984, s. 29 states:

> Where for the purpose of assisting with an investigation a person attends voluntarily at a police station or at any other place where a constable is present or accompanies a constable to a police station or any such other place without having been arrested—
> (a) he shall be entitled to leave at will unless he is placed under arrest;
> (b) he shall be informed at once that he is under arrest if a decision is taken by a constable to prevent him from leaving at will.

KEYNOTE

The person's attendance at a police station or other place must be for the purpose of 'assisting with an investigation', which would, on a strict interpretation, encompass witnesses and victims. The principle behind s. 29 (and see also Code C, para. 3.2.1) is to avoid the situation where people find themselves at a police station (or any other place where there is a police officer present) and feel compelled to remain there but without the attendant procedural protection that follows a formal arrest. Section 29(b) is unusual in that it (along with s. 31 below) imposes an obligation on a police officer to make an arrest, an activity that is usually entirely within his/her discretion. The time when the need to arrest the person arises is when the officer takes the decision to prevent the person from leaving (e.g. the time when the officer decides him/herself). It is not the time when the person is actually prevented from leaving or even when he/she is told of the decision.

If such a person is cautioned (under PACE Code C, para. 10), he/she must also be told that he/she is free to leave the police station. Although not in police detention (s. 118), voluntary attendees should be given the opportunity to seek legal advice if they wish and should be given the appropriate notice (see Code C).

The Police and Criminal Evidence Act 1984, s. 31 states:

Where—
(a) a person—
    (i) has been arrested for an offence; and
    (ii) is at a police station in consequence of that arrest; and
(b) it appears to a constable that, if he were released from that arrest, he would be liable to arrest for some other offence, he shall be arrested for that other offence.

Like s. 29, this section also imposes an obligation to make an arrest under certain circumstances. The purpose of the s. 31 requirement is to prevent the release and immediate re-arrest of an offender. Therefore, s. 31 does not prevent any further arrest from being delayed until the release of the prisoner for the initial arrest is imminent (*R* v *Samuel* [1988] QB 615). It has been held that, where officers who had arrested a man for a breach of the peace failed to arrest him formally for the further offence of assault on the police, their omission did not impact on the magistrates' decision that there was a case to answer in respect of the assault charge (*Blench* v *DPP* [2004] EWHC 2717 (Admin)).

The power (though not, on the strict wording, the *obligation*) to arrest a person at a police station for a further offence under s. 31 is among those that can be conferred on an Investigating Officer designated under sch. 4 to the Police Reform Act 2002. Where this power is exercised by a designated Investigating Officer, the provisions of s. 36 of the Criminal Justice and Public Order Act 1994 (failing to account for objects etc.) will apply.

Where a person is re-arrested under this provision, the powers of search under s. 18 of the Police and Criminal Evidence Act 1984 apply (see para. 4.2.5.3).

4.3.12 After Arrest

The Police and Criminal Evidence Act 1984, s. 30 provides for the procedure to be adopted after a person has been arrested. Section 30 states:

(1) Subsection (1A) applies where a person is, at any place other than a police station—
    (a) arrested by a constable for an offence, or
    (b) taken into custody by a constable after being arrested for an offence by a person other than a constable.

(1A) The person must be taken by a constable to a police station as soon as practicable after the arrest.

(1B) Subsection (1A) has effect subject to section 30A (release on bail) and subsection (7) (release without bail).

(2) Subject to subsections (3) and (5) below, the police station to which an arrested person is taken under subsection (1A) above shall be a designated police station.

(3) A constable to whom this subsection applies may take an arrested person to any police station unless it appears to the constable that it may be necessary to keep the arrested person in police detention for more than six hours.

(4) Subsection (3) above applies—
    (a) to a constable who is working in a locality covered by a police station which is not a designated police station; and
    (b) to a constable belonging to a body of constables maintained by an authority other than a police authority.

(5) Any constable may take an arrested person to any police station if—
    (a) either of the following conditions is satisfied—
        (i) the constable has arrested him without the assistance of any other constable and no other constable is available to assist him;
        (ii) the constable has taken him into custody from a person other than a constable without the assistance of any other constable and no other constable is available to assist him; and

(b) it appears to the constable that he will be unable to take the arrested person to a designated police station without the arrested person injuring himself, the constable or some other person.

(6) If the first police station to which an arrested person is taken after his arrest is not a designated police station, he shall be taken to a designated police station not more than six hours after his arrival at the first police station unless he is released previously.

(7) A person arrested by a constable at any place other than a police station must be released without bail if the condition in subsection (7A) is satisfied.

(7A) The condition is that, at any time before the person arrested reaches a police station, a constable is satisfied that there are no grounds for keeping him under arrest or releasing him on bail under section 30A.

KEYNOTE

When arrested at a place other than a police station, the person must be taken to a designated police station unless the conditions under s. 30(5) and (6) apply.

Under s. 30(7) and (7A), the officer *must* de-arrest a person if he/she is satisfied, before reaching the police station, that there are no grounds for detaining that person. This may happen where the person has been arrested under one of the general arrest conditions and the particular condition has ceased to apply (e.g. the person gives a suitable name and address having originally failed to do so). An officer who releases a prisoner under s. 30(7) and (7A) must record the fact that he/she has done so and must make that record as soon as practicable after the release (s. 30(8) and (9)).

Section 30(10) allows the officer to delay taking the arrested person to a police station where his/her presence elsewhere is *necessary in order to carry out such investigations as it is reasonable to carry out immediately*. Where there is such a delay, the reasons for it must be recorded when the person first arrives at the police station (s. 30(11)). The delay permitted under s. 30(10) and (11) will only apply if the matter requires *immediate* investigation; if it can wait, the exception will not apply and the person must be taken straight to a police station (*R* v *Kerawalla* [1991] Crim LR 451).

Taking an arrested person to check out an alibi before going to a police station may be justified in some circumstances (*Dallison* v *Caffery* [1965] 1 QB 348).

Escort Officers designated under sch. 4 to the Police Reform Act 2002 may be authorised to take people who have been arrested by a constable in the relevant police area to a police station under the provisions of s. 30(1). The provisions for taking a prisoner to a non-designated police station (s. 30(3) and 4(a)), and also the provisions allowing a delay in taking the prisoner to a police station (s. 30(10)) will also apply to any exercise of the powers by a designated Escort Officer (Police Reform Act 2002, sch. 4, part 4). Other exceptions in the application of s. 30(1) to terrorism and immigration are made by s. 30(12).

4.4 Protection of People Suffering from Mental Disorders

4.4.1 Introduction

The Mental Health Act 1983, as amended by the Policing and Crime Act 2017, provides for the care and treatment of people suffering from mental disorders and supplies powers for enforcing some of its provisions. If those powers are executed in good faith, the 1983 Act also provides some protection against criminal and civil liability for the police officers and care workers who use them (s. 139). The 1983 Act is supported by a Code of Practice that sets out guidance for the police and other agencies when dealing with people suffering from mental disorders.

4.4.2 Removal etc. of Mentally Disordered Persons Without a Warrant

Section 136 of the Mental Health Act 1983 creates a power for police officers to remove a person who appears to be suffering from a mental disorder under certain conditions.
Section 136 states:

(1) If a person appears to a constable to be suffering from mental disorder and to be in immediate need of care or control, the constable may, if he thinks it necessary to do so in the interests of that person or for the protection of other persons—
(a) remove the person to a place of safety within the meaning of section 135, or
(b) if the person is already at a place of safety within the meaning of that section, keep the person at that place or remove the person to another place of safety.

(1A) The power of a constable under subsection (1) may be exercised where the mentally disordered person is at any place, other than—
(a) any house, flat or room where that person, or any other person, is living, or
(b) any yard, garden, garage or outhouse that is used in connection with the house, flat or room, other than one that is also used in connection with one or more other houses, flats or rooms.

(1B) For the purpose of exercising the power under subsection (1), a constable may enter any place where the power may be exercised, if need be by force.

(1C) Before deciding to remove a person to, or to keep a person at, a place of safety under subsection (1), the constable must, if it is practicable to do so, consult—
(a) a registered medical practitioner,
(b) a registered nurse,
(c) an approved mental health professional, or
(d) a person of a description specified in regulations made by the Secretary of State.

(2) A person removed to, or kept at a place of safety under this section may be detained there for the permitted period of detention for the purpose of enabling him to be examined by a registered medical practitioner and to be interviewed by an approved mental health professional and of making any necessary arrangements for his treatment or care.

(2A) In subsection (2), 'the permitted period of detention' means—
(a) the period of 24 hours beginning with—
(i) in a case where the person is removed to a place of safety, the time when the person arrives at that place;

(ii) in a case where the person is kept at a place of safety, the time when the constable decides to keep the person at that place; or

(b) where an authorisation is given in relation to the person under section 136B, that period of 24 hours and such further period as is specified in the authorisation.

(3) A constable, an approved mental health professional or a person authorised by either of them for the purposes of this subsection may, before the end of the period of the permitted period of detention mentioned in subsection (2) above, take a person detained in a place of safety under that subsection to one or more other places of safety.

(4) A person taken to a place of safety under subsection (3) above may be detained there for a purpose mentioned in subsection (2) above for a period ending no later than at the end of the period of the permitted period of detention mentioned in that subsection.

(5) This section is subject to section 136A which makes provision about the removal and taking of persons to a police station, and the keeping of persons at a police station, under this section.

KEYNOTE

The power places a lot of responsibility and latitude on the officer who must decide whether:

- the person is suffering from mental disorder (see below),
- the person is in immediate need of care or control, and
- it is necessary in the person's interest or for someone else's protection that he/she be removed to a place of safety,

before the power is applicable.

For the purposes of this Act 'mental disorder' means any disorder or disability of the mind; and 'mentally disordered' shall be construed accordingly (s. 1(2)).

Section 135(6) defines a 'place of safety' as:

- residential accommodation provided by a local social services authority;
- a hospital;
- a police station;
- an independent hospital or care home for mentally disordered persons; or
- any other suitable place the occupier of which is willing temporarily to receive the patient.

For the purpose of subs. (6) a house, flat or room where a person is living may not be regarded as a suitable place unless the person believed to be suffering from a mental disorder is the sole occupier of the place, and that person agrees to the use of the place as a place of safety, or any other occupier or person responsible for the management of the property agrees to such use (s. 135(7)).

The use of police stations as places of safety is subject to s. 136A of the Act. This provides that a child (a person aged under 18) may not be removed to, kept at or taken to, a place of safety that is a police station (subs. (1A)).

However, an adult may be removed to, kept at or taken to a place of safety that is a police station but only in circumstances specified in the Mental Health Act 1983 (Places of Safety) Regulations 2017 (SI 2017/1036). Regulation 2 provides that a police station can only be used as a place of safety for an adult where the person exercising, or authorising the exercise of, the power under s. 135 or s. 136 is satisfied that:

(a) the behaviour of the adult presents an imminent risk of serious injury or death to that adult or to others;

(b) as a result, no other place of safety in the police area in which the adult is located can reasonably be expected to detain them; and

(c) the adult will have access to a health care professional, so far as is reasonably practicable, throughout the period during which they are detained at the police station.

Regulation 2 further provides that, where the person considering using a police station as a place of safety is a police officer, they must, if reasonably practicable, consult with a registered medical practitioner, a registered nurse, an approved mental health professional, an occupational therapist or a paramedic, before making the decision.

The decision to use a police station as a place of safety must be authorised by an officer of the rank of inspector or above.

Regulations 4 to 7 set out how adults detained at a police station must be treated during the period that they are detained (see *Evidence and Procedure*, para. 2.7.7).

Any person being conveyed to a place of safety or detained at such a place will be deemed to be in legal custody (s. 137(1)). Such a person will not be in 'police detention' for the purposes of s. 118 of the Police and Criminal Evidence Act 1984 even where the place of safety is a police station.

The registered medical practitioner who is responsible for the examination of a person detained, at any time before the expiry of the period of 24 hours, may authorise the detention of the person for a further period not exceeding 12 hours (beginning immediately at the end of the period of 24 hours). This authorisation may be given only if the registered medical practitioner considers that the extension is necessary because the condition of the person detained is such that it would not be practicable for the assessment of the person to be carried out before the end of the period of 24 hours (s. 136B).

Where a person is detained under s. 136(2) or (4), a constable may search the person, at any time while the person is so detained, if the constable has reasonable grounds for believing that the person may present a danger to himself or herself or to others and is concealing on his or her person an item that could be used to cause physical injury to himself or herself or to others. The power to search is only a power to search to the extent that is reasonably required for the purpose of discovering the item that the constable believes the person to be concealing. It does not authorise a constable to require a person to remove any of his or her clothing other than an outer coat, jacket or gloves, but does authorise a search of a person's mouth (s. 136C).

4.4.3 Warrant to Search for and Remove Patients

Where there is reasonable cause to suspect that a person believed to be suffering from mental disorder has been, or is being, ill-treated, neglected or kept otherwise than under proper control, or being unable to care for himself, is living alone, a warrant may be issued by a magistrate (s. 135(1)).

The warrant authorises any constable to enter, if need be by force, any premises specified in the warrant in which that person is believed to be, and, if thought fit, to remove him or her to a place of safety. The constable must be accompanied by an approved mental health professional and by a registered medical practitioner (s. 135(4)). Where the premises specified in the warrant are a place of safety, the constable executing the warrant may, instead of removing the person to another place of safety, keep the person at those premises for the purpose mentioned in subs. (1) (s. 135(1A)).

A warrant may also be issued in respect of a patient ordered to be detained by a court (s. 135(2)). The constable executing the warrant must be accompanied by a registered medical practitioner, or any person authorised by or under the Act to take or retake the patient (s. 135(4)).

Where a warrant is issued under s. 135, a constable may search the person to whom the warrant relates if the constable has reasonable grounds for believing that the person may present a danger to himself or herself or to others, and is concealing on his or her person an item that could be used to cause physical injury to himself or herself or to others. The power to search may be exercised at any time during the period beginning with the time when a constable enters the premises specified in the warrant and ending when the person ceases to be detained under s. 135, or at any time while the person is being removed under the authority of the warrant (s. 136C).

4.4.4 Power to Retake Escaped Patients

Section 138 of the 1983 Act provides a power to retake people who have been legally detained.

Where a person escapes while being removed to a place of safety in the execution of a warrant under s. 135(1) or under s. 136(1), they shall not be retaken after the end of the period of 24 hours beginning with the escape (s. 138(3)(a)). In the case of a person where further detention has been authorised under s. 136B, they shall not be retaken after the end of the period of 36 hours (s. 138(3)(b)).

Section 18 of the Act deals with the return and readmission of patients absent without leave. This provides occasions where a constable may take a person into custody and return them to hospital where they are a patient subject of a hospital order authorising their detention.

It is an offence to assist someone to absent themselves without leave or assist someone removed under s. 136 to escape (s. 128). A person guilty of an offence under this section shall be liable on summary conviction to imprisonment for a term not exceeding six months and/or a fine; on conviction on indictment, to imprisonment for a term not exceeding two years and/or a fine.

Additionally, a court may issue a warrant for the arrest of a convicted mental patient who is unlawfully at large (Criminal Justice Act 1967, s. 72(3)).

4.4.5 Ambit of the Mental Health Act 1983

The ambit of the Mental Health Act 1983 was reviewed in *St George's Healthcare NHS Trust v S* [1999] Fam 26, by the Court of Appeal. There it was held that:

- The 1983 Act should not be invoked to overrule the decision of a patient concerning medical treatment simply because that decision appears to be irrational.
- A person detained under the 1983 Act should not be forced to receive medical treatment which is not connected with his/her mental condition unless his/her capacity to give consent is seriously diminished.

4.4.6 Mental Health Units (Use of Force): Police Body Cameras

The Mental Health Units (Use of Force) Act 2018, s. 12 states:

(1) If a police officer is going to a mental health unit on duty that involves assisting staff who work in that unit, the officer must take a body camera if reasonably practicable.

(2) While in a mental health unit on duty that involves assisting staff who work in that unit, a police officer who has a body camera there must wear it and keep it operating at all times when reasonably practicable.

(3) Subsection (2) does not apply if there are special circumstances at the time that justify not wearing the camera or keeping it operating.

(4) A failure by a police officer to comply with the requirements of subsection (1) or (2) does not of itself make the officer liable to criminal or civil proceedings.

(5) But if those requirements appear to the court or tribunal to be relevant to any question arising in criminal or civil proceedings, they must be taken into account in determining that question.

KEYNOTE

This Act was introduced to require mental health inpatient units to comply with requirements around use of force policies, training and data collection.

In this section 'body camera' means a device that operates so as to make a continuous audio and video recording while being worn (s. 12(6)).

'Mental health unit' means a health service hospital in England providing inpatient mental health care, or an independent hospital providing such treatment on behalf of the NHS (s. 1(3)).

4.5 | Offences Relating to Land and Premises

4.5.1 Criminal Trespass

'Criminal' trespass can generally be categorised as:

- trespassing with the intention of disrupting or obstructing a lawful activity, or intimidating those engaged in it;
- two or more people trespassing with the purpose of residing on the land;
- residing in vehicles on land.

This chapter also includes the legislation dealing with 'criminal' trespass in relation to residential, educational and protected premises.

4.5.2 Aggravated Trespass

OFFENCE: **Trespass Intending to Obstruct, Disrupt or Intimidate—**
Criminal Justice and Public Order Act 1994, s. 68

- Triable summarily • Three months' imprisonment and/or a fine

The Criminal Justice and Public Order Act 1994, s. 68 states:

(1) A person commits the offence of aggravated trespass if he trespasses on land and, in relation to any lawful activity which persons are engaging in or are about to engage in on that or adjoining land, does there anything which is intended by him to have the effect—
   (a) of intimidating those persons or any of them so as to deter them or any of them from engaging in that activity,
   (b) of obstructing that activity, or
   (c) of disrupting that activity.
(2) Activity on any occasion on the part of a person or persons on land is 'lawful' for the purposes of this section if he or they may engage in the activity on the land on that occasion without committing an offence or trespassing on the land.

KEYNOTE

Examples of the sort of conduct envisaged would be environmental activists disrupting a building programme or disrupting the planting of genetically modified crops (*DPP* v *Bayer* [2003] EWHC 2567 (Admin)).

It must be shown that the defendant intended to bring about the effects set out at s. 68(1)(a)–(c). There is no need to specify which of the intended activities (i.e. deterring, obstructing or disrupting) in any charge and use of all three expressions is not bad for duplicity (*Nelder* v *DPP* (1988) *The Times*, 11 June). However, proof is required of both the trespassing on land *and* of some overt act, other than the trespassing, which was intended to have the effects set out at s. 68(1)(a)–(c) (*DPP* v *Barnard* [2000] Crim LR 371; *Peppersharp* v *DPP* [2012] EWHC 474 (Admin)).

In *Bauer* v *DPP* [2013] EWHC 634 (Admin) it was held that a large group of protesters, known as 'UK Uncut', protesting against tax avoidance, who occupied Fortnum and Mason's store in London for a period of nearly two and a half hours were guilty of aggravated trespass by virtue of their presence which had the intention to intimidate staff and customers within the store. It was also held that if the facts showed that people were part of the group which had committed the aggravated trespass then they were as guilty as the rest as a joint principal.

Under s. 68(5) land does not include land forming part of a highway unless it is:

- a footpath, bridleway or byway open to all traffic or road used as a public path (as defined by s. 54 of the Wildlife and Countryside Act 1981) or
- a cycle track under the Highways Act 1980 or the Cycle Tracks Act 1984.

Lawful activity is defined at s. 68(2) and is a very wide concept. This point has been determined in the context of anti-war protestors where it was argued that the war against Iraq was illegal and therefore the activities carried out by staff at airbases were also unlawful. The House of Lords determined that for the purposes of s. 68(2), an act of aggression against another State or a general crime against peace did not constitute an offence contrary to the law of England and Wales (*R* v *Jones* [2006] UKHL 16; *Ayliffe* v *DPP* [2005] EWHC 684 (Admin); *Nero* v *DPP* [2012] EWHC 1238 (Admin); *Richardson* v *DPP* [2014] UKSC 8).

4.5.2.1   Aggravated Trespass: Power to Remove Persons

The Criminal Justice and Public Order Act 1994, s. 69 states:

(1) If the senior police officer present at the scene reasonably believes—
  (a) that a person is committing, has committed or intends to commit the offence of aggravated trespass on land; or
  (b) that two or more persons are trespassing on land and are present there with the common purpose of intimidating persons so as to deter them from engaging in a lawful activity or of obstructing or disrupting a lawful activity,
  he may direct that person or (as the case may be) those persons (or any of them) to leave the land.
(2) A direction under subsection (1) above, if not communicated to the persons referred to in subsection (1) by the police officer giving the direction, may be communicated to them by any constable at the scene.

KEYNOTE

Although this power requires the senior officer present at the scene to have a reasonable *belief* as to the circumstances set out at s. 69(1)(a) or (b), the power is available as a preventive measure and as a means of dealing with the incident after it has happened.

The direction to leave the land may be communicated to the relevant people by any police officer at the scene and there is no requirement for either officer to be in uniform.

4.5.2.2   Failure to Leave Land or Re-entry to Land when Directed to Leave

OFFENCE: **Failure to Leave or Re-entry when Directed to Leave—*Criminal Justice and Public Order Act 1994, s. 69(3)***
  • Triable summarily • Three months' imprisonment and/or a fine

The Criminal Justice and Public Order Act 1994, s. 69 states:

(3) If a person knowing that a direction under subsection (1) above has been given which applies to him—
  (a) fails to leave the land as soon as practicable, or
  (b) having left again enters the land as a trespasser within the period of three months beginning with the day on which the direction was given,
  he commits an offence ...

KEYNOTE

In order to prove this offence it must be shown that the person knew of the direction and that it applied to him/her. Clearly the easiest way of ensuring both elements would be to serve a written notice on the person at the same time as communicating the direction to leave and to record any response.

It is a defence for the accused to show that he/she was not trespassing on the land, or had a reasonable excuse for failing to leave the land as soon as practicable or for again entering the land as a trespasser (s. 69(4)).

In *Nero* v *DPP* [2012] EWHC 1238 (Admin), the court quashed the appellants' convictions for failing to leave the premises as soon as practicable when so directed by the police because they were physically unable to move until they had been unchained, and had left as soon as this was done. What they did was designed to disrupt the shop's trade, not to frustrate the operation of s. 69: the fact that they had voluntarily (and deliberately) placed themselves in a situation in which they could not leave when directed was held to be irrelevant. Likewise, in *Richardson* v *DPP* [2012] EWHC 1238 (Admin), it was held that protesters tying themselves together who could not leave until untied left 'as soon as practicable'.

4.5.3 Trespassing for Purpose of Residence: Police Direction to Leave

The Criminal Justice and Public Order Act 1994, s. 61 states:

(1) If the senior police officer present at the scene reasonably believes that two or more persons are trespassing on land and are present there with the common purpose of residing there for any period, that reasonable steps have been taken by or on behalf of the occupier to ask them to leave and—

    (a) that any of those persons has caused damage to the land or to property on the land or used threatening, abusive or insulting words or behaviour towards the occupier, a member of his family or an employee or agent of his, or

    (b) that those persons have between them six or more vehicles on the land,

    he may direct those persons, or any of them, to leave the land and to remove any vehicles or other property they have with them on the land.

(2) Where the persons in question are reasonably believed by the senior police officer to be persons who were not originally trespassers but have become trespassers on the land, the officer must reasonably believe that the other conditions specified in subsection (1) are satisfied after those persons became trespassers before he can exercise the power conferred by that subsection.

(3) A direction under subsection (1) above, if not communicated to the persons referred to in subsection (1) by the police officer giving the direction, may be communicated to them by any constable at the scene.

KEYNOTE

The key features of this section can be broken down into two parts. First, the senior officer present at the scene must have a reasonable belief that:

- at least two people *are trespassing* on land *and*
- that they are there with the common purpose of residing there *and*
- that reasonable (though not *all* reasonable) steps have been taken by/on behalf of the occupier to ask them to leave.

If this is the case, the senior officer must also have a reasonable belief that:

- *any* of those people have caused damage to the land or to property on the land *or*
- *any* of those people have used threatening, abusive or insulting words or behaviour towards the occupier or a member of the occupier's family or staff or one of his/her agents *or*
- those people have between them six or more vehicles on the land.

If all the conditions under the first heading, together with any of the conditions under the second are met, the officer may direct the people to leave the land and to take their vehicles and other property with them.

Most of the terms used in this section are defined under s. 61(9). 'Land' does not include buildings other than agricultural buildings or scheduled monuments. It also has the same restrictions in relation to highways as those set out under s. 68 (see para. 4.5.2).

Under s. 61(4) a person commits a summary offence who, if knowing that a direction under subs. (1) has been given which applies to him/her, fails to leave the land as soon as reasonably practicable or, having left, again enters the land as a trespasser within the period of three months beginning with the day on which the direction was given. It is a defence for the accused to show that he/she was not trespassing on the land or had a reasonable excuse for failing to leave as soon as reasonably practicable or for re-entering the land as a trespasser (s. 61(6)).

4.5.4 Trespassing for Purpose of Residence with Vehicle(s) when Alternative Site Available: Police Direction to Leave

Section 62A of the Criminal Justice and Public Order Act 1994 creates a power for a senior police officer to direct people to leave land and remove any vehicle or other property with them on that land.

Section 62A states:

(1) If the senior police officer present at a scene reasonably believes that the conditions in subsection (2) are satisfied in relation to a person and land, he may direct the person—
   (a) to leave the land;
   (b) to remove any vehicle and other property he has with him on the land.
(2) The conditions are—
   (a) that the person and one or more others ('the trespassers') are trespassing on the land;
   (b) that the trespassers have between them at least one vehicle on the land;
   (c) that the trespassers are present on the land with the common purpose of residing there for any period;
   (d) if it appears to the officer that the person has one or more caravans in his possession or under his control on the land, that there is a suitable pitch on a relevant caravan site for that caravan or each of those caravans;
   (e) that the occupier of the land or a person acting on his behalf has asked the police to remove the trespassers from the land.

KEYNOTE

This effectively creates two situations in which the power can be exercised—*one excluding the element at s. 62(2)(d) and one including it*. The below table illustrates the relevant circumstances; in order for a direction to be given under s. 62A, the senior officer present at the scene must have a reasonable belief that:

Situation 1	Situation 2
at least two people are trespassing on the land; and ↓	at least two people are trespassing on the land; ↓
that they have at least one vehicle between them; and ↓	that they have at least one vehicle between them; and ↓
that they are there with the common purpose of residing there for any period; and	that they are there with the common purpose of residing there for any period; and ↓
	it appears to the officer that the person has one or more caravans in his possession or under his control on the land that there are relevant caravan sites with suitable pitches available for the trespassers to move to; and ↓
that the occupier (or person acting on the occupier's behalf) has asked the police to remove the trespassers from the land.	that the occupier (or person acting on the occupier's behalf) has asked the police to remove the trespassers from the land.

A person commits an offence if he or she knows that a direction has been given and he or she fails to leave the land as soon as reasonably practicable or enters any land in the area of the relevant local authority as a trespasser before the end of the relevant period with the intention of residing there (s. 62B). The relevant period is the period of three months starting with the day on which the direction is given (s.62B(2)).

The Criminal Justice and Public Order Act 1994, s. 77, also provides local authorities with the power to give a direction to unauthorised campers. This section provides that if it appears to a local authority that persons are for the time being residing in a vehicle or vehicles within that authority's area on any land forming part of a highway; on any other unoccupied land; or on any occupied land without the consent of the occupier, the authority may give a direction that those persons and any others with them are to leave the land and remove the vehicle or vehicles and any other property they have with them on the land.

4.5.5 Squatting in a Residential Building

OFFENCE: **Squatting in a Residential Building—*Legal Aid, Sentencing and Punishment of Offenders Act 2012, s. 144***

- Six months' imprisonment and/or a fine summarily

The Legal Aid, Sentencing and Punishment of Offenders Act 2012, s. 144 states:

(1) A person commits an offence if—
  (a) the person is in a residential building as a trespasser having entered it as a trespasser,
  (b) the person knows or ought to know that he or she is a trespasser, and
  (c) the person is living in the building or intends to live there for any period.
(2) The offence is not committed by a person holding over after the end of a lease or licence (even if the person leaves and re-enters the building).

KEYNOTE

'Building' includes any structure or part of a structure (including a temporary or moveable structure), and a building is 'residential' if it is designed or adapted, before the time of entry, for use as a place to live (s. 144(3)).

For the purposes of this section the fact that a person derives title from a trespasser, or has the permission of a trespasser, does not prevent the person from being a trespasser (s. 144(4)).

Section 17 of the Police and Criminal Evidence Act 1984 gives police officers the power to enter and search premises for the purpose of arresting a person for the offence of squatting in a residential building.

4.5.6 Nuisance on Educational Premises

In relation to nuisances on educational premises, the Education Act 1996 applies to premises that provide primary or secondary education (or both) and which are maintained by a local education authority or are grant-maintained.

OFFENCE: **Causing or Permitting Nuisance—*Education Act 1996, s. 547(1)***

- Triable summarily • Fine

The Education Act 1996, s. 547 states:

(1) Any person who without lawful authority is present on premises to which this section applies and causes or permits nuisance or disturbance to the annoyance of persons who lawfully use those premises (whether or not any such persons are present at the time) is guilty of an offence.

KEYNOTE

This offence is designed to deal with many types of nuisance, from using school playing fields inappropriately (this provision applies to playing fields and other premises for outdoor recreation of the relevant institution including playgrounds (s. 547(2)), to interrupting lessons and lectures.

To be guilty of the above offence the defendant must be on the relevant premises without lawful authority and have caused (been directly responsible for bringing about) or permitted a nuisance or disturbance.

If a police constable, or a person whom the appropriate authority has authorised to exercise the power conferred by this section, has reasonable cause to suspect that any person is committing or has committed an offence under this section they may remove them from the premises in question.

4.5.7 Causing Nuisance or Disturbance on NHS Premises

OFFENCE: **Causing a Nuisance or Disturbance on NHS Premises—*Criminal Justice and Immigration Act 2008, s. 119***

- Triable summarily

The Criminal Justice and Immigration Act 2008, s. 119 states:

(1) A person commits an offence if—
   (a) the person causes, without reasonable excuse and while on NHS premises, a nuisance or disturbance to an NHS staff member who is working there or otherwise there in connection with work,
   (b) the person refuses, without reasonable excuse, to leave the NHS premises when asked to do so by a constable or an NHS staff member, and
   (c) the person is not on the NHS premises for the purpose of obtaining medical advice, treatment or care for himself or herself.

KEYNOTE

A person ceases to be on NHS premises for the purpose of obtaining medical advice, treatment or care for him/herself once the person has received the advice, treatment or care. Also, a person is not on NHS premises for the purpose of obtaining medical advice, treatment or care for him/herself if the person has been refused the advice, treatment or care during the last eight hours (s. 119(3)).

If a constable reasonably suspects that a person is committing or has committed an offence under s. 119, the constable may remove the person from the NHS premises concerned (s. 120(1)).

If an authorised officer reasonably suspects that a person is committing or has committed an offence, he/she may remove the person from the NHS premises concerned, or authorise an appropriate NHS staff member to do so (s. 120(2)).

Any person removing another person from NHS premises under this section may, if necessary, use reasonable force (s. 120(3)).

An authorised officer cannot remove the person or authorise another person to do so if it is reasonably believed he/she is in need of medical advice, etc. or that such removal would endanger his/her mental or physical health (s. 120(4)). An authorised officer is a duly authorised NHS staff member (s. 120(5)).

It will be a defence for a person to show they had a reasonable excuse for causing a nuisance or disturbance or refusing to leave the premises, for instance where a person's behaviour was consequent upon a bereavement.

Licensing and Offences Relating to Alcohol

4.6.1 Introduction

The sale, supply and consumption of alcohol, along with the proper control and management of relevant premises, is a significant part of everyday policing.

This chapter only provides a brief overview of these matters and concentrates on the specific offences and police powers contained within the relevant legislation.

4.6.2 Licensable Activities

The Licensing Act 2003, s. 1 states:

(1) For the purposes of this Act the following are licensable activities—
   (a) the sale by retail of alcohol,
   (b) the supply of alcohol by or on behalf of a club to, or to the order of, a member of the club,
   (c) the provision of regulated entertainment, and
   (d) the provision of late night refreshment.

> **KEYNOTE**
>
> A licensable activity may be carried on under a premises licence or in circumstances where the activity is a permitted temporary activity (s. 2(1)).
>
> There is a raft of exemptions to licensable activities which include aircraft, vessels, hovercraft, ports, railway vehicles, premises occupied by the armed forces and premises exempt for national security purposes (ss. 173 to 175).
>
> In the Act, 'alcohol' means spirits, wine, beer, cider or any other fermented, distilled or spirituous liquor (in any state) (s. 191(1)).
>
> In relation to s. (1)(1)(d) the provision of late night refreshment means the supply of hot food or hot drink for consumption on or off the premises between 11.00pm and 5.00am.

4.6.3 Licensing Objectives

The purpose of the system of licensing for licensable activities is to promote four fundamental objectives—the licensing objectives (s. 4(2)). These objectives are:

(a) the prevention of crime and disorder;
(b) public safety;
(c) the prevention of public nuisance; and
(d) the protection of children from harm.

> **KEYNOTE**
>
> The aim of the licensing objectives is to ensure that carrying on licensable activities on or from premises is done in the public interest. The third objective, the prevention of public nuisance, will not extend to every

activity where annoyance may be caused to other people but will cover behaviour which, when balanced against the public interest, is found to be unacceptable. The fourth objective is concerned with the harm to children beyond matters relating to physical safety.

4.6.4 The Licensing System

The 2003 Act sets out a single licensing system that governs all premises used for licensable activities. The system is administered by licensing authorities that include councils of a district, county or borough within England and Wales (s. 3(1)).

The key licensing authorisations that may be issued are:

- Premises Licence
- Personal Licence
- Club Premises Certificate
- Temporary Event Notice.

Carrying on a licensable activity other than in accordance with a premises licence, club premises certificate or temporary event notice is an offence (s. 136).

4.6.4.1 Premises Licence

A premises licence authorises the use of any premises including a vehicle, vessel or moveable structure or any place or a part of any premises for licensable activities as defined in s. 1 of the 2003 Act (s. 11).

The premises licence will name a designated premises supervisor who holds a valid personal licence (see below).

A constable or an authorised person may require production of a premises licence or a certified copy of it (s. 57(5)), and a person who fails, without reasonable excuse, to produce the licence, or certified copy, commits a summary offence (s. 57(7)).

A premises licence may be reviewed by a licensing authority where it is considered a licensee is failing to take sufficient measures to prevent public nuisance, or where the police consider that measures put in place to prevent crime and disorder are not being effective.

4.6.4.2 Personal Licences

The supply of alcohol is regulated generally by the granting of a personal licence to an individual that authorises that individual to supply alcohol, or authorise the supply of alcohol in accordance with a premises licence (s. 111(1)).

A personal licence must be held by the designated premises supervisor and more than one individual at the licensed premises may hold a personal licence. It is not necessary for all staff to be licensed, but all supplies of alcohol under a premises licence must be made by or under the authority of a personal licence holder.

A constable or an authorised person may require production of a personal licence (s. 135(2)), and a person who fails without reasonable excuse to produce the licence commits a summary offence (s. 135(4)).

4.6.4.3 Club Premises Certificate

Members' clubs can operate under club premises certificates, granted by a licensing authority, instead of premises licences. This means, for example, that they are not required to have a designated premises supervisor, and sales of alcohol do not need to be authorised by a personal licence holder.

A constable or authorised person may require production of a club premises certificate or any list of mandatory conditions (s. 94(7)). Failure to produce a certificate or conditions without reasonable excuse is a summary offence (s. 94(9)).

A constable may enter and search the club premises where they have reasonable cause to believe that an offence under s. 4(3)(a), (b) or (c) of the Misuse of Drugs Act 1971 (supplying or offering to supply, or being concerned in supplying or making an offer to supply, a controlled drug) or an offence under s. 5(1) or (2) of the Psychoactive Substances Act 2016 (supplying or offering to supply a psychoactive substance), has been, is being, or is about to be committed there, or there is likely to be a breach of the peace there (s. 97(1)). The constable may use reasonable force if necessary (s. 97(2)).

4.6.4.4 Temporary Event Notice

A temporary event notice, issued by the licensing authority, is required where a person (the premises user) intends to carry out a licensable activity on unlicensed premises or wishes to operate outside the terms of their existing premises licence or club premises licence (s. 100).

A temporary event is a relatively small-scale event attracting fewer than 500 people and lasting no more than 168 hours.

Where the police consider the temporary event notice would undermine the 'crime prevention objective' they must notify the premises user and licensing authority of their objection. The licensing authority may withdraw the temporary event notice or it may be modified so that it no longer undermines the objective (s. 104).

At any reasonable time, a constable or an authorised person may enter premises to which a temporary event notice relates to assess the likely effect of the notice on the promotion of the crime prevention objective (s. 108(1)). Obstructing a constable or authorised officer is an offence (s. 108(3)).

On the day of the event a copy of the temporary event notice and any statement of conditions attached to it following an objection, must be prominently displayed at the premises or be in possession of the premises user or their nominated representative. Failure to comply with these requirements is an offence (s. 109(4)) and failure to produce a temporary event notice or statement of conditions when required by a constable or authorised person is also an offence (s. 109(8)).

4.6.5 Power of Entry to Investigate Licensable Activities or Offences

Where a constable or an authorised person has reason to believe that any premises are being, or are about to be, used for a licensable activity, he may enter the premises with a view to seeing whether the activity is being, or is to be, carried on under and in accordance with an authorisation (s. 179(1)). An authorised person exercising the power must, if so requested, produce evidence of his authority to exercise the power (s. 179(2)).

A person exercising the power conferred by this section may, if necessary, use reasonable force (s. 179(3)), and a person commits an offence if he intentionally obstructs an authorised person exercising a power conferred by this section (s. 179(4)).

A constable may enter and search any premises in respect of which he has reason to believe that an offence under this Act has been, is being or is about to be committed (s. 180(1)), and may, if necessary, use reasonable force (s. 180(2)).

4.6.6 Regulated Entertainment

Regulated entertainment is a licensable activity and must be authorised by a premises licence, club premises certificate or a temporary event notice unless it falls under any of the exemptions. The descriptions of regulated entertainment include such activities as the performance of a play, exhibition or a film, an indoor sporting event, boxing or wrestling entertainment, performance of live music or dance, etc.

To be regulated entertainment, the entertainment must take place in the presence of an audience and be provided for the purpose of entertaining that audience, and the entertainment must be provided for the public or a section of the public, or members and their guests of a club. Otherwise the entertainment must be provided with a view to profit.

Schedule 1 of the 2003 Act provides a number of exemptions to regulated entertainment, for example, entertainment at a garden fete, Morris dancing (or dancing of a similar nature), and entertainment provided on vehicles in motion.

4.6.7   Premises—Offences under the Licensing Act 2003

The Licensing Act 2003 makes provision for offences and breaches of the regulatory framework in relation to premises. In summary, the key offences under the 2003 Act are:

Unauthorised licensable activities (s. 136). A person who carries on or attempts to carry on a licensable activity on or from any premises otherwise than under and in accordance with an authorisation or the person knowingly allows a licensable activity to be carried on.

Exposing alcohol for unauthorised sale (s. 137). A person, on any premises, exposes for sale by retail any alcohol in circumstances where the sale by retail of that alcohol on those premises would be an unauthorised licensable activity.

Keeping alcohol on premises for unauthorised sale (s. 138). A person has in their possession or under their control alcohol which they intend to sell by retail or supply in circumstances where that activity would be an unauthorised licensable activity.

Allowing disorderly conduct on licensed premises (s. 140). A person who works at relevant or licensed premises in a capacity whether paid or unpaid knowingly allows disorderly conduct on those premises.

Sale of alcohol to a person who is drunk (s. 141). A person who works in a capacity whether paid or unpaid on relevant or licensed premises knowingly sells or attempts to sell alcohol to a person who is drunk or allows alcohol to be sold to such a person.

Obtaining alcohol for a person who is drunk (s. 142). This section has no associated Explanatory Notes. A person who on relevant premises knowingly obtains or attempts to obtain alcohol for consumption on those premises by a person who is drunk.

Failure to leave licensed premises (s. 143). A person who is drunk or disorderly, without reasonable excuse, fails to leave relevant premises when requested to do so by an authorised person or enters or attempts to enter relevant premises after an authorised person has requested them not to enter. An authorised person includes a constable and any person who works at the premises in a capacity, whether paid or unpaid, which authorises them to make such a request. When requested to do so, a police officer is under a duty (rather than simply having a power) to help authorised persons at licensed premises to expel anyone who is drunk and disorderly. In assisting the removal of an individual, a police officer is entitled to use force (*Semple v Luton and South Bedfordshire Magistrates' Court* [2009] EWHC 3241 (Admin)).

4.6.8   Drunk and Disorderly

OFFENCE: **Drunk and Disorderly—*Criminal Justice Act 1967, s. 91(1)***
   • Triable summarily • Fine

The Criminal Justice Act 1967, s. 91 states:

(1) Any person who in any public place is guilty, while drunk, of disorderly behaviour shall be liable ...

KEYNOTE

In *Carroll* v *DPP* [2009] EWHC 554 (Admin) the court stated that drunk and disorderly was one of the most basic of offences and that it required proof of three elements: the accused was drunk; he/she was in a public place; and he/she was guilty of disorderly behaviour.

The drunkenness must be as a result of excessive consumption of alcohol; if the person's state is caused by some other intoxicant (e.g. glue solvents), the offence is not made out (*Neale* v *R.M.I.E. (a minor)* (1985) 80 Cr App R 20). The same ruling applies to a person 'found drunk' in a public place (*Lanham* v *Rickwood* (1984) 148 JP 737).

'Drunkenness' here means where the defendant has taken intoxicating liquor (alcohol) to an extent that affects his/her steady self-control (per Goff LJ in *Neale*).

Where there are several causes of a person's incapacitated state, one of which is alcohol, a court can find that the person was in fact 'drunk', even though some additional intoxicant had an exacerbating effect on his/her loss of 'steady self-control'.

In *McMillan* v *CPS* [2008] EWHC 1457 (Admin), it was held that where a police officer took hold of a drunken person by the arm to steady her for her own safety it was not an arrest. The circumstances entailed the officer leading the drunken person from a private garden to a public place. It was then legitimate for the officer to arrest for this offence where the accused displayed disorderly behaviour. However, this offence is not committed where a person did not commit any disorderly act until after the arrest (*H* v *DPP* [2005] EWHC 2459 (Admin)).

This offence is a 'penalty offence' for the purposes of s. 1 of the Criminal Justice and Police Act 2001. Note that a penalty notice for s. 91(1) cannot be given to a person aged under 18, and a constable giving a notice to a person other than at a police station does not need to be in uniform (Legal Aid, Sentencing and Punishment of Offenders Act 2012 (Consequential Amendments) Regulations 2013 (SI 2013/903)).

Where a person is arrested for committing this offence, under the powers contained within s. 24 of the Police and Criminal Evidence Act 1984, a constable may take him/her to an approved treatment centre for alcoholism (a 'detoxification' centre) and he/she will be treated as being in lawful custody for the purposes of that journey (see s. 34(1) of the Criminal Justice Act 1972). This course of action does not preclude the person being charged with any offence (s. 34(2)).

The conduct of passengers who are drunk on an aircraft has a potential impact on the safety of the aircraft and the people therein, therefore they can be dealt with under s. 61 of the Civil Aviation Act 1982 and the relevant regulations made thereunder (*R* v *Tagg* [2001] EWCA Crim 1230 and Air Navigation Order 2009 (SI 2009/3015, part 19) made under the Civil Aviation Act 1982 and the Airports Act 1986).

4.6.9 Found Drunk

OFFENCE: **Being Found Drunk—*Licensing Act 1872, s. 12***

- Triable summarily • Fine

The Licensing Act 1872, s. 12 states:

> Every person found drunk in any highway or other public place, whether a building or not, or on any licensed premises, shall be liable ...
>
> Every person who is drunk while in charge on any highway or other public place of any carriage, horse, cattle, or steam engine, or who is drunk when in possession of any loaded firearms, shall be liable to a penalty not exceeding level 1 on the standard scale or in the discretion of the court to imprisonment for any term not exceeding one month.

KEYNOTE

This offence is committed if a person is on the highway or public place and shown to be drunk. It does not matter that the person is there only briefly or of his/her own volition.

'Other public place' will include all places to which the public have access (whether on payment or otherwise).

The offence has been held to apply to the licensee when found drunk on the licensed premises, even when those premises were not open to the public (*Evans* v *Fletcher* (1926) 135 LT 153).

This offence is a 'penalty offence' for the purposes of s. 1 of the Criminal Justice and Police Act 2001.

On arresting a person for this offence, under the powers contained in s. 24 of the Police and Criminal Evidence Act 1984, a police officer may, if he/she thinks fit, take the person to an approved treatment centre under s. 34 of the Criminal Justice Act 1972. During the journey to such a treatment centre the person will be deemed to be in lawful custody. Section 34 does not allow a person to be detained at the centre and does not preclude any charge being brought in relation to the offence.

4.6.10   Children—Offences under the Licensing Act 2003

The Licensing Act 2003 makes provision for offences and breaches of the regulatory framework with the protection of children as one of its primary objectives. In summary, the key offences under the 2003 Act are:

Unaccompanied children prohibited from certain premises (s. 145). Allowing an unaccompanied child, aged under 16, on relevant premises at a time when they are open for the purposes of being used for the supply of alcohol for consumption on the premises.

Sale of alcohol to children (s. 146). The 'selling' of alcohol to a person aged under 18 *anywhere* (not just on licensed premises). It is a defence where the person charged believed that the individual was 18 or over, had taken all reasonable steps to establish the individual's age, or nobody could reasonably have suspected from the individual's appearance that they were aged under 18.

Allowing the sale of alcohol to children (s. 147). Where a person, who works at relevant premises in a paid or unpaid capacity which authorises them to prevent the sale, knowingly allows the sale of alcohol on the premises to an individual under 18.

Persistently selling alcohol to children (s. 147A). If on two or more different occasions within a period of three consecutive months alcohol is unlawfully sold on the same premises to an individual aged under 18. It is 'unlawfully sold' if the person making the sale believed the individual to be under 18 or did not have reasonable grounds for believing them to be 18 or over.

Purchase of alcohol by or on behalf of children (s. 149). This covers all forms of under-18s buying (or trying to buy) alcohol or someone else doing it on their behalf.

Consumption of alcohol by children (s. 150). A person aged under 18 knowingly consumes alcohol on relevant premises and a person working at the premises knowingly allows the consumption of alcohol. However, no offences are committed where the individual is aged 16 or 17, the alcohol is beer, wine or cider, the consumption is at a table meal and the individual is accompanied by an person aged 18 or over.

Delivering alcohol to children (s. 151). A person working on relevant premises knowingly delivering alcohol sold on the premises to a person aged under 18. For example, circumstances where a child takes delivery of a consignment of alcohol bought by a parent from an off-licence.

Sending a child to obtain alcohol (s. 152). A person knowingly sending an individual aged under 18 to obtain alcohol that is sold on relevant premises, for consumption off the premises. For example, where a parent sends their child to an off-licence to collect some alcohol which had been bought over the telephone. The offence will be committed regardless of whether the child is sent to the actual premises from where the alcohol is sold or supplied, or whether the child is sent to other premises to which the alcohol has been sent.

Prohibition of unsupervised sales by children (s. 153). A premises licence holder, designated premises supervisor or someone over 18 authorised by them, to knowingly allow an individual aged under 18 to make on the relevant premises any sale of alcohol, or in the case of a club, any supply of alcohol to members of the club. This does not apply to the sale or supply of alcohol to persons having table meals.

KEYNOTE

All of the offences listed above are triable summarily and punishable by a fine.

In relation to *allowing the sale of alcohol to children* (s. 147), *purchase of alcohol by or on behalf of children* (s. 149) and *sending a child to obtain alcohol* (s. 152), an offence will not be committed where the individual buys or attempts to buy the alcohol at the request of a constable or a weights and measures inspector who is acting in the course of his/her duty.

With the exceptions of ss. 146, 147A and 149, all the other offences listed refer to the offence occurring on 'relevant premises'. This means premises that are exclusively or primarily used for the supply of alcohol for consumption on the premises and include premises operating with a temporary event notice.

4.6.11   Children—Other Offences

In addition to the offences outlined above, other legislation creates specific offences in relation to children.

4.6.11.1   Being Drunk While in Charge of Child

OFFENCE: **Being Drunk While in Charge of Child—*Licensing Act 1902, s. 2***

- One months' imprisonment and/or a fine summarily

The Licensing Act 1902, s. 2 states:

(1) If any person is found drunk in any highway or other public place, whether a building or not, or on any licensed premises, while having the charge of a child apparently under the age of seven years, he shall, if the child is under that age, be liable ...

(2) If the child appears to the court to be under the age of seven, the child shall, for the purposes of this section, be deemed to be under that age unless the contrary is proved.

KEYNOTE

This is used for its specific purpose, i.e. the safety of young children *(R (On the Application of A)* v *Lowestoft Magistrates' Court* [2013] EWHC 659 (Admin)).

4.6.11.2   Persistently Possessing Alcohol in a Public Place

OFFENCE: **Persistently Possessing Alcohol in a Public Place—*Policing and Crime Act 2009, s. 30***

- Triable summarily • Fine

The Policing and Crime Act 2009, s. 30 states:

(1) A person under the age of 18 is guilty of an offence if, without reasonable excuse, the person is in possession of alcohol in any relevant place on 3 or more occasions within a period of 12 consecutive months.

(2) 'Relevant place', in relation to a person, means—
  (a) any public place, other than excluded premises, or
  (b) any place, other than a public place, to which the person has unlawfully gained access.
  ...

(4) For the purposes of subsection (2) a place is a public place if at the material time the public or any section of the public has access to it, on payment or otherwise, as of right or by virtue of express or implied permission.

KEYNOTE

In relation to s. 30(2)(a), 'excluded premises' means premises with a premises licence or permitted temporary activity used for the supply of alcohol, and premises with a club premises certificate used for the supply of alcohol to members or guests.

The original Home Office guidance set out the steps to be taken to deter young people from drinking and possessing alcohol in public places, including engagement with their parents or guardians. It was intended that this offence be used in conjunction with s. 1 of the Confiscation of Alcohol (Young Persons) Act 1997 (see para. 4.6.11.3), to enable a constable to confiscate alcohol from those under 18 years of age, and to ensure that the young person was required to give his/her name and address to the constable.

4.6.11.3 Confiscation of Intoxicating Liquor

The Confiscation of Alcohol (Young Persons) Act 1997, s. 1 states:

(1) Where a constable reasonably suspects that a person in a relevant place is in possession of alcohol, and that either—
   (a) he is under the age of 18; or
   (b) he intends that any of the alcohol should be consumed by a person under the age of 18 in that or any other relevant place; or
   (c) a person under the age of 18 who is, or has recently been, with him has recently consumed alcohol in that or any other relevant place,
   the constable may require him to surrender anything in his possession which is, or which the constable reasonably believes to be, alcohol or a container for alcohol.

(1AA) A constable who imposes a requirement on a person under subsection (1) shall also require the person to state the person's name and address.

(1AB) A constable who imposes a requirement on a person under subsection (1) may, if the constable reasonably suspects that the person is under the age of 16, remove the person to the person's place of residence or a place of safety.

KEYNOTE

A 'relevant place' is: any public place, other than licensed premises; or any place, other than a public place, to which that person has unlawfully gained access (s. 1(6)).

The power may be exercised in any public place where the public have access on payment or otherwise but this does not include licensed premises.

This is a discretionary power for police officers to exercise as they deem fit.

It is unusual that the wording of the section says 'either', then goes on to give *three* instances where the power will be available. However, if one of the instances at s. 1(1)(a)–(c) applies, the police officer may require the person concerned to surrender anything that is, or that the officer reasonably *believes* to be, alcohol or a container for such alcohol.

Subsection (1AA) states the constable *shall* require the person to state his/her name and address. Although a 'place of safety' is not defined, this may be a relative or friend, or where necessary, a police station or social services accommodation.

There is no requirement for the officer to be in uniform.

Under s. 1(2), the officer may dispose of *anything* surrendered to him/her in answer to the making of such a requirement.

It is a summary offence for a person to fail without reasonable excuse to comply with a requirement imposed under subs. (1) or (1AA) (s. 1(3)). A constable may arrest without warrant a person who fails to comply with a requirement imposed on him under subs. (1) (s. 1(5)).

4.6.11.4 Closure Notices for Persistently Selling Alcohol to Children

Section 169A of the Licensing Act 2003, provides that a senior police officer (of the rank of superintendent or higher), or an inspector of weights and measures, may give a closure notice where there is evidence that a person has committed the offence of persistently selling alcohol to children at the premises in question, and he/she considers that the evidence is such that there would be a realistic prospect of conviction if the offender was prosecuted for it. A closure notice can only be given within three months of the last offence (s. 169A(9)).

A closure notice will propose a prohibition on sales of alcohol at the premises in question for at least 48 hours but not more than 336 hours (s. 169A(4)), and will offer the opportunity to discharge all criminal liability in respect of the alleged offence by the acceptance of the prohibition proposed in the notice (s. 169A(2)). The premises licence holder will have 14 days to decide whether or not to accept the proposed prohibition or to elect to be tried for the offence (s. 169A(4)). Where the licence holder decides to accept the prohibition, it must take effect not less than 14 days after the date on which the notice was served at a time specified in the closure notice (s. 169A(5)).

A closure notice may be served on the premises to which it applies only by being handed by a constable or trading standards officer to a person on the premises who appears to the constable or trading standards officer to have control of or responsibility for the premises (s. 169A(7)). The closure notice can only be served at a time when licensable activities are being carried on at the premises.

4.6.12 Public Spaces Protection Order: Alcohol Prohibition

The power to make a Public Spaces Protection Order is contained in s. 59 of the Anti-social Behaviour, Crime and Policing Act 2014. It provides for an order to be made prohibiting the consumption of alcohol in designated public places, as well as dealing with any other particular nuisance or problem in a particular area.

4.6.12.1 Power to Make Orders

The Anti-social Behaviour, Crime and Policing Act 2014, s. 59 states:

(1) A local authority may make a public spaces protection order if satisfied on reasonable grounds that two conditions are met.
(2) The first condition is that—
    (a) activities carried on in a public place within the authority's area have had a detrimental effect on the quality of life of those in the locality, or
    (b) it is likely that activities will be carried on in a public place within that area and that they will have such an effect.
(3) The second condition is that the effect, or likely effect, of the activities—
    (a) is, or is likely to be, of a persistent or continuing nature,
    (b) is, or is likely to be, such as to make the activities unreasonable, and
    (c) justifies the restrictions imposed by the notice.
(4) A public spaces protection order is an order that identifies the public place referred to in subsection (2) ('the restricted area') and—
    (a) prohibits specified things being done in the restricted area,
    (b) requires specified things to be done by persons carrying on specified activities in that area, or
    (c) does both of those things.

KEYNOTE

The breach of an order prohibiting the consumption of alcohol is an offence when an individual does not cease drinking or surrender alcoholic drinks when challenged by an enforcement officer, which includes a constable, PCSO or local authority officer (s. 63(6)).

Persons breaching an order prohibiting the consumption of alcohol (s. 63) or failing to comply with an order (s. 67) may be subject to a Fixed Penalty Notice or prosecution (s. 68).

A constable or an authorised person may dispose of anything surrendered in whatever way he/she thinks appropriate (s. 63(5)).

4.6.13 Orders to Close Premises in Area Experiencing Disorder

The Licensing Act 2003, s.160 states:

(1) Where there is or is expected to be disorder in any local justice area, a magistrates' court acting in the area may make an order requiring all premises—
  (a) which are situated at or near the place of the disorder or expected disorder, and
  (b) in respect of which a premises licence or a temporary event notice has effect, to be closed for a period, not exceeding 24 hours, specified in the order.

(2) A magistrates' court may make an order under this section only on the application of a police officer who is of the rank of superintendent or above.

(3) A magistrates' court may not make such an order unless it is satisfied that it is necessary to prevent disorder.

KEYNOTE

This provision can be used where disorder is taking place in an area or where it is expected to take place.

A constable may use such force as may be necessary for the purpose of closing premises ordered to be closed under this section (s. 160(7)).

Where an order is made under this section, any manager of the premises, holder of a premises licence in respect of the premises, and the designated premises supervisor (if any) under such a licence, and the premises user in relation to a temporary event notice, commits an offence if they knowingly allow the premises to be kept open (s. 160(4) and (5)).

4.6.14 Closure Notices for Unlicensed Premises

The Criminal Justice and Police Act 2001, s. 19 states:

(1) Where a constable is satisfied that any premises are being, or within the last 24 hours have been, used for the unauthorised sale of alcohol for consumption on, or in the vicinity of, the premises, he may serve under subsection (3) a notice in respect of the premises.

(2) Where a local authority is satisfied that any premises in the area of the authority are being, or within the last 24 hours have been, used for the unauthorised sale of alcohol for consumption on, or in the vicinity of, the premises, the authority may serve under subsection (3) a notice in respect of the premises.

(3) A notice under subsection (1) or (2) ('a closure notice') shall be served by the constable or local authority concerned on a person having control of, or responsibility for, the activities carried on at the premises.

(4) A closure notice shall also be served by the constable or local authority concerned on any person occupying another part of any building or other structure of which the premises form part if the constable or (as the case may be) the local authority concerned reasonably believes, at the time of serving notice under subsection (3), that the person's access to the other part of the building or other structure would be impeded if an order under section 21 providing for the closure of the premises were made.

(5) A closure notice may also be served by a constable or the local authority concerned on—
  (a) any other person having control of, or responsibility for, the activities carried on at the premises;
  (b) any person who has an interest in the premises.

KEYNOTE

The power provided by this section is available to any police officer irrespective of rank.

The closure notice must specify the alleged use of the premises, the grounds on which it has been issued, the steps that are required to be taken to ensure that the alleged use of the premises ceases or does not recur, and state the effects of s. 20 (s. 19(6)).

Where a closure notice has been served under s. 19(3), a constable or the local authority concerned may make a complaint to a justice of the peace for a closure order (s. 20(1)). The complaint must be made not less than seven days, and not more than six months, after the service of the closure notice (s. 20(2)). However, a complaint cannot be made under this subsection if the constable or the local authority is satisfied that the use of the premises for the unauthorised sale of alcohol for consumption on, or in the vicinity of, the premises has ceased, and there is no reasonable likelihood that the premises will be so used in the future (s. 20(3)).

Where a closure order is made by the court a constable or authorised person may enter the premises, if necessary using reasonable force, at any reasonable time to do anything necessary to secure compliance with the order (s. 25(1)). The constable or authorised person must produce identification if so required by the owner, occupier or person in charge of the premises (s. 25(2)). Intentionally obstructing a constable or authorised person is a summary offence (s. 25(3)). Permitting premises to be open in contravention of the order is an offence (s. 25(4), as is failing to comply with a closure order generally (s. 25(5)).

Closure Orders and Closure Notices must be 'policeable' in the sense that they must be clear and comprehensible to the defendant, the police and the public (*R* v *Maguire* [2019] EWCA Crim 1193).

4.7 Protecting Citizens and the Community: Injunctions, Orders and Police Powers

4.7.1 Introduction

This chapter covers a variety of preventative and protective measures available under the Policing and Crime Act 2009, the Anti-social Behaviour, Crime and Policing Act 2014 and the Crime and Disorder Act 1998.

4.7.2 Injunctions to Prevent Gang-related Violence and Drug Dealing Activity

The Policing and Crime Act 2009 provides courts with the power to grant injunctions to prevent gang-related violence and drug dealing activity.

Section 34 of the 2009 Act, as amended, states:

(1) A court may grant an injunction under this section against a respondent aged 14 or over if the first and second conditions are met.

(2) The first condition is that the court is satisfied on the balance of probabilities that the respondent has engaged in or has encouraged or assisted—
 (a) gang-related violence, or
 (b) gang-related drug-dealing activity.

(3) The second condition is that the court thinks it is necessary to grant the injunction for either or both of the following purposes—
 (a) to prevent the respondent from engaging in, or encouraging or assisting, gang-related violence or gang-related drug-dealing activity;
 (b) to protect the respondent from gang-related violence or gang-related drug-dealing activity.

(4) An injunction under this section may (for either or both of those purposes)—
 (a) prohibit the respondent from doing anything described in the injunction;
 (b) require the respondent to do anything described in the injunction.

(5) For the purposes of this section, something is 'gang-related' if it occurs in the course of, or is otherwise related to, the activities of a group that—
 (a) consists of at least three people, and
 (b) has one or more characteristics that enable its members to be identified by others as a group.

(6) In this section 'violence' includes a threat of violence.

(7) In this Part 'drug-dealing activity' means—
 (a) the unlawful production, supply, importation or exportation of a controlled drug, or
 (b) the unlawful production, supply, importation or exportation of a psychoactive substance.

KEYNOTE

These injunctions are a civil tool allowing the police or local authority to apply to the High Court, a county court or, in the case of juveniles, a youth court (sitting in a civil capacity), for an injunction against an individual who has been involved in gang-related violence or drug dealing activity. A range of prohibitions and requirements on the behaviour and activities of a person can be included in an injunction, such as prohibiting someone from being in a particular place or requiring them to participate in rehabilitative activities (s. 35).

The court may attach a power of arrest in relation to (a) any prohibition in the injunction, or (b) any requirement in the injunction other than one which has the effect of requiring the respondent to participate in particular activities (s. 36). Where a power of arrest is attached to a provision, a constable may arrest without warrant a person whom the constable has reasonable cause to suspect to be in breach of the provision. The constable must inform the person who applied for the injunction of the arrest, and the person arrested must be brought before a judge of the court that granted the injunction within 24 hours of the arrest (s. 43).

In relation to subs. (7)(a), 'controlled drug' has the meaning given by s. 37(1) of the Misuse of Drugs Act 1971, and for subs. (7)(b) 'psychoactive substance' has the meaning given by s. 59 of the Psychoactive Substances Act 2016.

4.7.3 Injunctions under the Anti-social Behaviour, Crime and Policing Act 2014

Part 1 of the 2014 Act provides a regime of injunctions for dealing with anti-social behaviour. Section 1 of the 2014 Act deals with the power to grant injunctions detailed in subsections (1) to (7) below:

(1) A court may grant an injunction under this section against a person aged 10 or over ('the respondent') if two conditions are met.

(2) The first condition is that the court is satisfied, on the balance of probabilities, that the respondent has engaged or threatens to engage in anti-social behaviour.

(3) The second condition is that the court considers it just and convenient to grant the injunction for the purpose of preventing the respondent from engaging in anti-social behaviour.

(4) An injunction under this section may for the purpose of preventing the respondent from engaging in anti-social behaviour—

    (a) prohibit the respondent from doing anything described in the injunction;

    (b) require the respondent to do anything described in the injunction.

(5) Prohibitions and requirements in an injunction under this section must, so far as practicable, be such as to avoid—

    (a) any interference with the times, if any, at which the respondent normally works or attends school or any other educational establishment;

    (b) any conflict with the requirements of any other court order or injunction to which the respondent may be subject.

(6) An injunction under this section must—

    (a) specify the period for which it has effect, or

    (b) state that it has effect until further order.

    In the case of an injunction granted before the respondent has reached the age of 18, a period must be specified and it must be no more than 12 months.

(7) An injunction under this section may specify periods for which particular prohibitions or requirements have effect.

4.7.3.1 The Injunction

The injunction is a purely civil injunction available in the county court for adults and in the youth court for those under the age of 18.

4.7.3.2 Anti-social Behaviour

Section 2(1) defines 'anti-social behaviour' for this purpose:

(1) In this Part 'anti-social behaviour' means—

    (a) conduct that has caused, or is likely to cause, harassment, alarm or distress to any person,

    (b) conduct capable of causing nuisance or annoyance to a person in relation to that person's occupation of residential premises, or

    (c) conduct capable of causing housing-related nuisance or annoyance to any person.

4.7.3.3 Prohibitions or Requirements

The injunction could include prohibitions or requirements that assist in the prevention of future anti-social behaviour (s. 1(3)). Such prohibitions may include, for example, not being in possession of a can of spray paint in a public place, not entering a particular area, or not being drunk in a public place. Requirements would be designed to deal with the underlying causes of an individual's anti-social behaviour and could include, for example, attendance at an alcohol or drugs misuse course or dog training in the case of irresponsible dog owners.

Where an injunction imposes requirements on the respondent, it must specify the person (an individual or an organisation) who is responsible for supervising compliance (s. 3). The court must receive evidence on the suitability and enforceability of a requirement from this person. Such individuals or organisations could include the local authority, youth offending teams, recognised providers of substance misuse recovery or dog training providers for irresponsible dog owners.

4.7.3.4 Time Limits

There is no minimum or maximum term for the injunction for adults, so the court may decide that the injunction should be for a specified period or an indefinite period. However, in the case of injunctions against under-18s, the maximum term is 12 months (s. 1(6)). The duration of any prohibitions or requirements may be shorter than the duration of the injunction itself.

4.7.3.5 Power of Arrest

Section 4 provides officers with a power of arrest in certain circumstances:

(1) A court granting an injunction under section 1 may attach a power of arrest to a prohibition or requirement of the injunction if the court thinks that—
   (a) the anti-social behaviour in which the respondent has engaged or threatens to engage consists of or includes the use or threatened use of violence against other persons, or
   (b) there is a significant risk of harm to other persons from the respondent.
   'Requirement' here does not include one that has the effect of requiring the respondent to participate in particular activities.
(2) If the court attaches a power of arrest, the injunction may specify a period for which the power is to have effect which is shorter than that of the prohibition or requirement to which it relates.

A power of arrest attached to an injunction allows a police officer to arrest the respondent without a warrant if the respondent breached a condition in the injunction, that is, a prohibition or a requirement (s. 9). Where no power of arrest is attached to the injunction, the applicant may apply to the court to issue a warrant of arrest of a respondent if the applicant thinks that the respondent has breached the injunction (s. 10). Section 11 and sch. 1 make provision for the remand, whether on bail or in custody, of a person arrested for breach of an injunction.

4.7.3.6 Applying for an Injunction

There is a formal requirement for the applicant to consult with the local youth offending team (YOT) before making an application, if an injunction is against someone under the age of 18. The consultation requirement does not give a veto power to the local YOT. The applicant must also inform any other body or individual about the application that they think appropriate (s. 14), again before making an application. This could include a social landlord (when an application is made by another body against one of their tenants) or mental health team.

Applications for an injunction would normally be made to the county court or High Court where the respondent is an adult, or to the youth court where the respondent is under

18. However, s. 18(2) makes provision for cases involving multiple respondents where one (or more) of them is aged 18 or over and one (or more) is under that age. In such a case, an applicant may apply at the time of the application to the youth court for permission for the application in respect of the adult(s) to be heard in that court. The youth court would be able to grant the application if it was in the interest of justice. Sections 8(2)(b), 9(3)(b) and 10(2)(b) ensure that while an application in respect of an under-18 will be heard by the youth court, subsequent proceedings against a defendant who has attained the age of 18 since the injunction was made would take place in the appropriate adult court.

Injunction applications would normally be made following the giving of notice to the respondent; however, s. 6 allows an application for an injunction to be made without notice. Without notice applications would, in practice, only be made in exceptional or urgent circumstances and the applicant would need to produce evidence to the court as to why a without notice hearing was necessary. Where a without notice application is made, the court would be able to grant an interim injunction pending a full hearing following the giving of notice to the respondent (ss. 6 and 7). The consultation requirements in s. 14 do not apply to without notice applications.

4.7.3.7 Breaching an Injunction

Breach of an injunction by an adult will be contempt of court, punishable in the usual way by the county court by a term of imprisonment of up to two years or an unlimited fine. Breach of an injunction by someone aged under 18 could result in the youth court imposing a supervision order or a detention order. A detention order can be made for breaching the injunction or for breaching a supervision order that was imposed for breaching the injunction. The court may revoke the supervision order and impose a new one or it may revoke the supervision order and make a detention order. The court can only impose a detention order where it considers that the severity or extent of the behaviour warrants it and that no other sanction available to it is appropriate. The court must be satisfied beyond reasonable doubt that the under-18 has, without reasonable excuse, breached the injunction or breached a supervision order that was imposed for breaching the injunction before it can make the detention order. The court must also consider any representations from the YOT specified in the supervision order before imposing a detention order. The maximum duration of a detention order is three months and it cannot be imposed on under-14s (s. 12 and sch. 2). A supervision order may contain one or more of the following requirements: a supervision requirement, an activity requirement or a curfew requirement. An electronic monitoring requirement may be attached to a curfew requirement in order to monitor compliance.

4.7.3.8 Special Measures

Section 16 enables the court to give a special measures direction to protect vulnerable or intimidated witnesses in injunction proceedings. Such measures may include giving evidence behind a screen or by video link or in private.

4.7.4 Criminal Behaviour Orders

A Criminal Behaviour Order (CBO) can be issued under part 2 of the Anti-social Behaviour, Crime and Policing Act 2014.

4.7.4.1 The Order

An order may only be made against an offender when he/she has been sentenced for the offence or given a conditional discharge (s. 22(6)). No order may be made where the offender has been given an absolute discharge or has only been bound over to keep the peace. The order is aimed at tackling the most serious and persistent offenders where their behaviour has brought them before a criminal court. A court is able to make a CBO against an offender only if the prosecutor applies for it, on the advice of the police or the local authority.

4.7.4.2 Granting an Order

Section 22 sets out a two-part test for granting an order. An order may be made against a person over the age of 10 if the court is satisfied that the offender has engaged in behaviour that caused, or was likely to cause, harassment, alarm or distress to any person; and the court considers that making the order will assist in preventing the offender from engaging in such behaviour. The standard of proof is the criminal standard, that is, 'beyond reasonable doubt' (s. 22(3)).

4.7.4.3 Prohibitions and/or Requirements

The order can include prohibitions and/or positive requirements that assist in preventing the offender from engaging in behaviour that could cause harassment, alarm or distress in the future (s. 22(5)). Such prohibitions are similar to those mentioned in relation to injunctions (**see para. 4.7.3.3**), for example, they could include not being in possession of a can of spray paint in a public place, not entering a particular area, or not being drunk in a public place. The requirements in an order could include attendance at a course to educate offenders on alcohol and its effects.

4.7.4.4 Consultation Requirements

The only formal consultation requirement applies where an offender is under 18 years of age. In those cases, the prosecution must find out the views of the local YOT before applying for the CBO. The views of the YOT must be included in the file of evidence forwarded to the prosecution. In practice, the consultation with the YOT must be carried out by the organisation preparing the application for the CBO, namely the council or police force.

The legislation keeps formal consultation requirements to a minimum, to enable agencies to act quickly where needed to protect victims and communities. However, in most cases it is likely there would be a number of agencies the police or local council would wish to consult with. This could include local organisations that have come into contact with the individual, such as schools and colleges of further education, providers of probation services, social services, mental health services, housing providers or others.

4.7.4.5 Time Limits and Reviews

The terms of the CBO must include the duration of the order. For adults this is a minimum of two years up to an indefinite period. For under-18s the order must be between one and three years. Reviews must be held every 12 months for offenders under the age of 18 (s. 28). The 12-month period starts from the date the order was made, or from the date it was subsequently varied. The review must consider the offender's compliance with the order and the support provided to help him or her comply with it, and give consideration to whether an application should be made to vary or discharge the order. The review should be carried out by the police with the local authority and any other relevant person or body (s. 29).

4.7.4.6 Special Measures

In any proceedings in relation to a CBO it is open to the court to make a special measures direction in relation to vulnerable and intimidated witnesses. Such measures may include the physical screening of a witness, enabling evidence to be given in private or the use of a video-recorded interview.

4.7.4.7 Offences and Penalties

It is a criminal offence if an offender fails to comply, without reasonable excuse, with either the requirements or prohibitions in the CBO. Failure to comply with a prohibition or requirement should be notified to the police. The court has the power to impose serious penalties on conviction, including:

- on summary conviction in the magistrates' court: a maximum of six months in prison or a fine or both;
- on conviction on indictment in the Crown Court: a maximum of five years in prison or a fine or both.

Hearings for those under 18 will take place in the youth court where the maximum sentence is a two year detention and training order.

4.7.4.8 Publicising a CBO

Making the public aware of the offender and the terms of the order is an important part of the process in dealing with anti-social behaviour. It provides reassurance to communities that action is being taken when they report anti-social behaviour. It also provides the information local people need to identify and report breaches. The decision to publicise a CBO will be taken by the police or council unless the court has made a s. 39 order (Children and Young Persons Act 1933) prohibiting publication. When deciding whether to publicise a CBO, public authorities (including the courts) must consider that it is necessary and proportionate to interfere with the young person's right to privacy, and the likely impact on a young person's behaviour. This will need to be balanced against the need to provide reassurance to the victims and the wider community as well as providing them with information so that they can report any breaches. Each case should be decided carefully on its own facts.

4.7.5 Dispersal Powers

Part 3 of the Anti-social Behaviour, Crime and Policing Act 2014 provides a dispersal power enabling officers (constables in uniform and police community support officers (PCSOs)) to direct a person who has committed, or is likely to commit, anti-social behaviour to leave a specified area and not return for a specified period of up to 48 hours.

The test is that the officer is satisfied on reasonable grounds that the person's behaviour is contributing, or is likely to contribute to anti-social behaviour or crime or disorder in the area and that the direction is necessary to prevent the same (s. 35(2) and (3)). Police officers have access to all elements of the power, and PCSOs have access to some or all elements of the power at the discretion of the chief constable (s. 40).

4.7.5.1 Authorising the Power

The dispersal power can only be used where an officer of at least the rank of inspector has authorised its use in a specified locality (s. 34(1)). The authorisation can last a maximum of 48 hours. That authorisation can only be given where the police officer of or above the rank of inspector reasonably believes that, in respect of any locality within their police area, the exercise of the dispersal powers in part 3 of the Act may be required in order to remove or reduce the likelihood of the anti-social behaviour occurring. For instance, the inspector may have intelligence to indicate that there is likely to be anti-social behaviour on a particular housing estate during the weekend and authorise the use of the dispersal for 48 hours. Alternatively, in a situation where an officer needs to use the dispersal power in an area that has not been authorised, the officer can contact an inspector for an authorisation and describe the circumstances to him/her.

Before authorising the use of the dispersal power in a specified area, the authorising police officer must have particular regard to the rights of freedom of expression and freedom of assembly and association (s. 34(3)). A similar duty is placed on a constable before issuing a dispersal direction (s. 36(5)).

The direction would in most instances be given in writing to ensure that those individuals being dispersed are clear where they are being dispersed from. Where this is not reasonably practicable, the direction could be given orally (s. 35(5)(a)) and the officer would keep a written record of the direction (s. 38). Any constable can vary or withdraw a direction and must do this in writing to the person originally issued with the order unless not reasonably practicable (s. 35(8) and (9)).

4.7.5.2 Powers and Offences

The officer must specify the area from which the person is excluded, and may specify when and by which route they must leave the area (s. 35(5)(b) and (c)). Where the officer believes an individual is under the age of 16, an officer can remove that individual to a place where he/she lives or to a place of safety (s. 35(7)).

Failure to comply with the direction would be a criminal offence and is punishable by a fine and/or three months' imprisonment (s. 39).

An officer would also be able to require an individual to hand over items causing, or likely to cause, anti-social behaviour—for instance, alcohol or a can of spray paint (s. 37). Failure to comply with the requirement is a criminal offence punishable by a fine (s. 39(4)).

However, the officer does not have power under this provision to retain any seized item indefinitely. The officer must give the person information in writing about how and when they can recover the item, which must not be returned before the exclusion period is over. If the person is under 16 the officer can require that person to be accompanied by an adult when collecting the item.

4.7.6 Community Protection Notices

Community Protection Notices (CPN) are provided for under part 4 of the Anti-social, Crime and Policing Act 2014. The notice is intended to deal with unreasonable, ongoing problems or nuisances which negatively affect the community's quality of life by targeting the person responsible (s. 43(1)). The notice can direct any individual over the age of 16, business or organisation responsible to stop causing the problem and it could also require the person responsible to take reasonable steps to ensure that it does not occur again (s. 43(3)).

4.7.6.1 Issuing a CPN

The test is broad and focuses on the impact anti-social behaviour has on victims and communities. A CPN can be issued if on reasonable grounds the issuer is satisfied that the conduct of the individual, business or organisation:

- is having a detrimental effect on the quality of life of those in the locality;
- is persistent or continuing in nature; and
- is unreasonable.

In many areas, councils take the lead in dealing with these kinds of issues but the power to issue a notice is also available to the police and PCSOs, if designated by the chief constable (s. 53(5); under s. 53(6) a PCSO will also be able to issue a fixed penalty notice for the offence of breaching a community protection notice, if designated for that).

The notice should be issued to someone who can be held responsible for the anti-social behaviour (s. 44). For instance, if a small shop were allowing litter to be deposited outside the property and not dealing with the issue, a notice could be issued to the business owner, whereas if a large national supermarket were to cause a similar issue, the company itself or the store manager could be issued with a notice.

Before issuing a notice, an authorised person is required to inform whatever agencies or persons he/she considered appropriate (e.g. the landlord of the person in question, or the local authority), partly in order to avoid duplication (s. 43(6)). The person would also have to have issued a written warning in advance and allowed an appropriate amount of time to pass (s. 43(5)). This is to ensure that the perpetrator is aware of their behaviour and allows them time to rectify the situation. It will be for the person issuing the written warning to decide how long is appropriate before serving a notice. In the example where a dog owner's fence needs to be fixed, this could be days or weeks, in order to allow the individual to address the problem. However, it could be minutes or hours in a case where, for example, someone was persistently playing loud music in a park.

Wherever possible, the notice should be issued in person. However, where this is not possible, it can be posted or left at the proper address (s. 55(1)). In the case of the latter when it relates to a business, the address may be different from the location of the anti-social behaviour.

Breach of any requirement in the notice, without reasonable excuse, is a criminal offence, subject to a fixed penalty notice (which attracts a penalty of £100) (s. 52) or prosecution. On summary conviction, an individual or company would be liable to a fine. On conviction, the magistrates' court would have the power to order forfeiture and destruction of any item used in the commission of the offence—for instance, noise equipment (s. 50). Where necessary, the court can also issue a warrant allowing a constable or local authority to seize such items (s. 51).

A remedial order may also require the defendant to carry out specified work (this could set out the original CPN requirements) or to allow work to be carried out by, or on behalf of, a specified local authority.

4.7.7 Closure of Premises Associated with Nuisance or Disorder

The Anti-social, Behaviour, Crime and Policing Act 2014 provides the police and local authorities with powers to close premises associated with nuisance or disorder. Closing premises has two stages:

- the closure notice; and
- the closure order.

4.7.7.1 The Closure Notice

A police officer of at least the rank of inspector, or the local authority, may issue a closure notice that lasts up to 24 hours if satisfied on reasonable grounds that there is, or is likely soon to be, a public nuisance or there is, or is likely soon to be, disorder in the vicinity of, and related to, the premises and that a closure notice is necessary for preventing the continuation or occurrence or reoccurrence of such disorder or behaviour (s. 76(1)). For example, closing a nightclub where police have intelligence to suggest that disorder is likely in the immediate vicinity on a specific night or over a specific period. A notice cannot prohibit access by the owner of the premises or people who habitually live on the premises (s. 76(4)). The notice can be designed to prohibit access to particular people at particular times. For example, where a property is closed in anticipation of a party publicised through social media, the family who lived there would not be prohibited, and additional people could also be exempted (such as other family members) where appropriate.

A notice can be issued for, or extended up to, a maximum of 48 hours if agreed by a police officer of at least the rank of superintendent or someone designated by the chief executive officer of a local authority. In total, the period for which such an out-of-court closure notice is in place cannot exceed 48 hours (s. 77(2) and (4)). If a closure notice is no longer required, the police or local authority that issued the notice must cancel the closure notice with a cancellation notice (s. 78(2)).

4.7.7.2 The Closure Order

When a closure notice is issued, the police or local authority must apply to the magistrates' court for a closure order (s. 80(1)). The magistrates' court must hear the application for the closure order within 48 hours of the closure notice being issued (excluding Christmas Day) unless the closure notice has been cancelled by a cancellation notice (s. 80(3)). The court can make a closure order for a maximum period of three months (s. 80(6)) if it is satisfied that: a person has engaged in disorder, anti-social or criminal behaviour on the premises (or that such behaviour is likely if the order is not made) or the use of the premises is associated with the occurrence of disorder or serious nuisance to members of the public (or that such disorder or serious nuisance is likely if the order is not made); and that the order is necessary to prevent the continuation or occurrence or reoccurrence of such disorder or behaviour (s. 80(5)). Unlike the closure notice, a closure order can prohibit access to anyone, including the landlord, owner or habitual residents (s. 80(7)).

4.7.7.3 Breaching the Closure Notice or Order

Breach of the notice or the order, without reasonable excuse, is a criminal offence (s. 86). On summary conviction, a person would be liable to an unlimited fine and/or up to three months' imprisonment if in breach of a notice and up to six months' imprisonment if in breach of an order. Organisations and businesses would be subject to an unlimited fine. A person guilty of obstructing an officer in the process of closing a property also commits an offence and is liable to a fine and/or up to three months' imprisonment.

4.7.8 Orders Against Parents

These orders are about influencing parental responsibility and control. The orders are designed to give parents more help and support to change the criminal and/or anti-social behaviour of their children in providing a framework where parents participate in their child's supervision. The strategy here is one of prevention in attempting to dissuade a recurrence of criminality or truancy.

4.7.8.1 Parenting Orders

Parenting orders are provided by the Crime and Disorder Act 1998, s. 8 of which states:

(1) This section applies where, in any court proceedings—
   (a) a child safety order is made in respect of a child, or the court determines on an application under section 12(6) below that a child has failed to comply with any requirement included in such an order;
   (aa) a parental compensation order is made in relation to a child's behaviour;
   (b) an injunction is granted under section 1 of the Anti-social Behaviour, Crime and Policing Act 2014, an order is made under section 22 of that Act or a sexual harm prevention order is made in respect of a child or young person;
   (c) a child or young person is convicted of an offence; or

(d) a person is convicted of an offence under section 443 (failure to comply with a school attendance order) or section 444 (failure to secure regular attendance at a school of registered pupil) of the Education Act 1996.

(2) Subject to subsection (3) and section 9(1) below, if in the proceedings the court is satisfied that the relevant condition is fulfilled, it may make a parenting order in respect of a person who is a parent or guardian of the child or young person or, as the case may be, the person convicted of the offence under section 443 or 444 ('the parent').

(3) ...

(4) A parenting order is an order which requires the parent—

(a) to comply, for a period not exceeding twelve months, with such requirements as are specified in the order; and

(b) subject to subsection (5) below, to attend, for a concurrent period not exceeding three months and not more than once in any week, such counselling or guidance sessions as may be specified in directions given by the responsible officer.

KEYNOTE

In relation to s. 8(1)(b), the order under s. 22 of the 2014 Act is a criminal behaviour order, and a sexual harm prevention order means an order under s. 103A of the Sexual Offences Act 2003.

A parenting order may be made against one or both biological parents (this would include an order against a father who may not be married to the mother), and a person who is a guardian. Guardians are defined as any person who, in the opinion of the court, has for the time being the care of a child or young person (s. 117(1)).

A parent or guardian commits a summary offence if without reasonable excuse they fail to comply with any requirement included within a parenting order (s. 9(7)).

4.7.8.2 Binding Over of Parent or Guardian

The Powers of Criminal Courts (Sentencing) Act 2000, s. 150 provides for the binding over of a parent or guardian and states:

(1) Where a child or young person (that is to say, any person aged under 18) is convicted of an offence, the powers conferred by this section shall be exercisable by the court by which he is sentenced for that offence, and where the offender is aged under 16 when sentenced it shall be the duty of the court—

(a) to exercise those powers if it is satisfied, having regard to the circumstances of the case, that their exercise would be desirable in the interests of preventing the commission by him of further offences; and

(b) if it does not exercise them, to state in open court that it is not satisfied as mentioned in paragraph (a) above and why it is not so satisfied;

but this subsection has effect subject to section 19(5) above and paragraph 13(5) of Schedule 1 to this Act (cases where referral orders made or extended).

(2) The powers conferred by this section are as follows—

(a) with the consent of the offender's parent or guardian, to order the parent or guardian to enter into a recognizance to take proper care of him and exercise proper control over him; and

(b) if the parent or guardian refuses consent and the court considers the refusal unreasonable, to order the parent or guardian to pay a fine not exceeding £1,000;

and where the court has passed on the offender a sentence which consists of or includes a youth rehabilitation order, it may include in the recognizance provision that the offender's parent or guardian ensure that the offender complies with the requirements of that sentence.

KEYNOTE

The recognizance can be imposed on the parent or guardian for up to three years or until the offender is aged 18, whichever is the shorter (s. 150(4)).

For the purposes of s. 150, taking 'care' of a person includes giving him/her protection and guidance, and 'control' includes discipline (s. 150(11)).

4.7.9　Child Safety Orders

These orders are designed to help prevent children under 10 from turning to crime. Such orders are concerned with the child's potential offending behaviour and in practice are likely to be used in conjunction with parenting orders under s. 8 of the Crime and Disorder Act 1998.

The Crime and Disorder Act 1998, s. 11 states:

(1) Subject to subsection (2) below, if the family court, on the application of a local authority, is satisfied that one or more of the conditions specified in subsection (3) below are fulfilled with respect to a child under the age of 10, it may make an order (a 'child safety order') which—
    (a) places the child, for a period (not exceeding the permitted maximum) specified in the order, under the supervision of the responsible officer; and
    (b) requires the child to comply with such requirements as are so specified.
(2) …
(3) The conditions are—
    (a) that the child has committed an act which, if he had been aged 10 or over, would have constituted an offence;
    (b) that a child safety order is necessary for the purpose of preventing the commission by the child of such an act as is mentioned in paragraph (a) above;
    (c) …
    (d) that the child has acted in a manner that caused or was likely to cause harassment, alarm or distress to one or more persons not of the same household as himself.
(4) The maximum period permitted for the purposes of subsection (1)(a) above is twelve months.
(5) The requirements that may be specified under subsection (1)(b) above are those which the court considers desirable in the interests of—
    (a) securing that the child receives appropriate care, protection and support and is subject to proper control; or
    (b) preventing any repetition of the kind of behaviour which led to the child safety order being made.

KEYNOTE

Section 12(6) states that where a child safety order is in force and it is proved to the satisfaction of the court that a child has failed to comply with any requirement included in the order, the court may make an order:

(i) by cancelling any provision included in it; or
(ii) by inserting in it (either in addition to or in substitution for any of its provisions) any provision that could have been included in the order if the court had then had power to make it and were exercising the power.

4.7.10　Removal of Truants and Excluded Pupils to Designated Premises, etc.

The Crime and Disorder Act 1998, s. 16 states:

(1) This section applies where a local authority—
    (a) designates premises in a police area ('designated premises') as premises to which children and young persons of compulsory school age may be removed under this section; and
    (b) notifies the chief officer of police for that area of the designation.
(2) A police officer of or above the rank of superintendent may direct that the powers conferred on a constable by subsection (3) and (3ZA) below—
    (a) shall be exercisable as respects any area falling within the police area and specified in the direction; and
    (b) shall be so exercisable during a period specified;
    and references in each of those subsections to a specified area and a specified period shall be construed accordingly.

(3) If a constable has reasonable cause to believe that a child or young person found by him in a public place in a specified area during a specified period—

    (a) is of compulsory school age; and

    (b) is absent from school without lawful authority,

    the constable may remove the child or young person to designated premises, or to the school from which he is so absent.

(3ZA) If a constable has reasonable cause to believe that a child or young person found by him in a public place in a specified area during a specified period and during school hours—

    (a) is of compulsory school age;

    (b) has been excluded on disciplinary grounds from a relevant school for a fixed period or permanently;

    (c) remains excluded from that school;

    (d) has not subsequently been admitted as a pupil to any other school; and

    (e) has no reasonable justification for being in the public place;

    the constable may remove the child or young person to designated premises.

KEYNOTE

'Designated premises' are not defined but will generally be a child's own school. 'Public place' means any highway, or any place to which at the material time the public or any section of the public has access, on payment or otherwise (Public Order Act 1986, s. 16).

'Without lawful authority' is qualified by s. 16(4) in that lawful authority will be that which falls within s. 444 of the Education Act 1996—leave, sickness, unavoidable cause or day set apart for religious observation.

The power of a constable to remove a child or young person to 'designated premises' is not an arrest in the traditional sense of detention, and statutory powers relating to arrests will not apply. However, the duty to explain the reason for a person's 'seizure' may well apply in such cases.

As with the powers conferred in relation to curfew notices, it appears probable that the common law rule entitling a constable to use reasonable force would apply. The requirement for the officer to have 'reasonable cause to believe' that the person meets the criteria at (a) and (b) is more stringent than mere suspicion.

The Education Act 1996 provides that penalty notices can be issued to parents or guardians who fail to ensure the regular attendance of their child of compulsory school age (5–16) who is registered at a state school, or fail to ensure that their excluded child is not found in a public place during school hours without a justifiable reason. If a child is found in such circumstances, designated local authority officers, headteachers (and authorised deputy headteachers and assistant headteachers), police officers and community support officers can issue a fixed penalty notice (ss. 444A and 444B).

The penalty to be paid will be £60 for those who pay within 21 days and £120 for those who pay within 28 days (Education (Penalty Notices) (England) (Amendment) Regulations 2013 (SI 2013/757) and Education (Penalty Notices) (Wales) Regulations 2013 (SI 2013/1983) (W. 193)).

Processions and Assemblies

4.8.1 Introduction

The law controlling processions and assemblies is primarily contained in the Public Order Act 1986. The European Convention on Human Rights has a significant impact on a number of the areas concerned within this chapter and especially Article 10 (Freedom of Expression) and Article 11 (Freedom of Assembly and Association). These two Articles are discussed in the following paragraphs.

4.8.2 Article 10—Freedom of Expression

Article 10 of the Convention states:

1. Everyone has the right to freedom of expression. This right shall include freedom to hold opinions and to receive and impart information and ideas without interference by public authority and regardless of frontiers. This Article shall not prevent States from requiring the licensing of broadcasting, television or cinema enterprises.
2. The exercise of these freedoms, since it carries with it duties and responsibilities, may be subject to such formalities, conditions, restrictions or penalties as are prescribed by law and are necessary in a democratic society, in the interests of national security, territorial integrity or public safety, for the prevention of disorder or crime, for the protection of health or morals, for the protection of the reputation or rights of others, for preventing the disclosure of information received in confidence, or for maintaining the authority and impartiality of the judiciary.

KEYNOTE

Article 10 protects the freedom:

- of expression,
- to hold opinions, and
- to receive and impart information and ideas,

in each case without interference by a public authority.

'Expression' here includes the creation of pictures and images (*Stevens* v *United Kingdom* (1986) 46 DR 245).

Although not providing a general 'right to freedom of information', Article 10 has been used in a number of different settings including the protection of artistic, political and economic expression. It has been used to protect journalists' sources (*Goodwin* v *United Kingdom* (1996) 22 EHRR 123).

As the right to express freely has to be balanced against the rights of others and the needs of democratic society generally, this area of Convention rights has generated some considerable problems and is often intermingled with issues of freedom of thought, conscience and religion (under Article 9).

In a case where the defendant damaged the perimeter fence of a Trident defence base, the Divisional Court held that her acts could be characterised as an expression of her opinion under Article 10 but that the Convention required the expression of that opinion to be proportionate. There were other ways in which the defendant could have expressed her opinion without committing a crime and therefore her conviction for criminal damage was upheld (*Hutchinson* v *DPP* (2000) *The Independent*, 20 November).

Article 10(1) is drafted to allow for State licensing of broadcasts, television and cinema performances but, as you might expect, the courts will be unlikely to tolerate interference with the freedom of expression

---

without compelling reasons. Once again, the courts will look for a 'pressing social need' and, indeed, one of the main cases setting out the requirement for proportionality (*Handyside* v *United Kingdom* (1979–80) 1 EHRR 737) involved an action under Article 10.

Article 10(2) clearly allows for an individual's freedom of expression to be curtailed under a number of circumstances including the prevention of disorder or crime and the protection of morals. Balancing these competing needs is one area where the European Court of Human Rights has allowed a reasonable 'margin of appreciation'. Nevertheless, any restrictions on an individual's freedom of expression will be narrowly construed and closely scrutinised. It has been held that the exercise of the right to free speech could fall within the concept of harassment for the purposes of the Protection from Harassment Act 1997 where the ingredients for the offence were present (*Howlett* v *Harding* [2006] EWHC 41 (QB)).

4.8.3 Article 11—Freedom of Assembly and Association

Article 11 of the Convention states:

1. Everyone has the right to freedom of peaceful assembly and to freedom of association with others, including the right to form and to join trade unions for the protection of his interests.
2. No restrictions shall be placed on the exercise of these rights other than such as are prescribed by law and are necessary in a democratic society in the interests of national security or public safety, for the prevention of disorder or crime, for the protection of health or morals or for the protection of the rights and freedoms of others. This Article shall not prevent the imposition of lawful restrictions on the exercise of these rights by members of the armed forces, of the police or of the administration of the State.

KEYNOTE

Article 11 is closely related to Article 10 and is often raised in conjunction with it, particularly in situations involving the arrest of demonstrators and protestors. In addition to refraining from interference with the individual's right to peaceful assembly, the State is also under a positive duty to prevent others from doing so. The assembly must, however, be *peaceful* and any intention to use violence or to cause disorder may take the individual's actions outside the protection of Article 11.

As with Article 10, there are allowances for reducing rights of assembly etc. under certain conditions including the prevention of disorder and crime and the interests of national security and public safety.

The right to freedom of association and to join trade unions means, among other things, that trade unions may be victims for the purposes of bringing an action under this Article. The State can impose 'lawful restrictions' on the exercise of these rights.

4.8.4 Public Processions and Assemblies

Chief officers, 'senior police officers' and constables have powers in respect of processions and assemblies.

4.8.4.1 Advance Notice of Public Processions

The Public Order Act 1986, s. 11 states:

(1) Written notice shall be given in accordance with this section of any proposal to hold a public procession intended—
   (a) to demonstrate support for or opposition to the views or actions of any person or body of persons,
   (b) to publicise a cause or campaign, or

(c) to mark or commemorate an event,

unless it is not reasonably practicable to give any advance notice of the procession.

(2) Subsection (1) does not apply where the procession is one commonly or customarily held in the police area (or areas) in which it is proposed to be held or is a funeral procession organised by a funeral director acting in the normal course of his business.

(3) The notice must specify the date when it is intended to hold the procession, the time when it is intended to start it, its proposed route, and the name and address of the person (or of one of the persons) proposing to organise it.

(4) Notice must be delivered to a police station—

(a) in the police area in which it is proposed the procession will start, or

(b) where it is proposed the procession will start in Scotland and cross into England, in the first police area in England on the proposed route.

KEYNOTE

In relation to s. 11(2) it was held that an organised cycle ride that started at the same time and place on the last Friday of every month, even though there was no fixed, settled or predetermined route, end-time or destination, was a commonly or customarily held procession (*R (On the Application of Kay)* v *Commissioner of Police of the Metropolis* [2008] UKHL 69).

If the notice is delivered not less than six clear days before the date when the procession is intended to be held, the notice may be delivered by post by the recorded delivery service (s. 11(5)). Otherwise, the notice must be delivered by hand not less than six clear days before the date when the procession is intended to be held or, if that is not reasonably practicable, as soon as delivery is reasonably practicable (s. 11(6)).

Where a public procession is held, each of the persons organising it is guilty of an offence if the requirements of this section as to notice have not been satisfied, or the date when it is held, the time when it starts, or its route, differs from the date, time or route specified in the notice (s. 11(7)).

It is a defence for the accused to prove that he/she did not know of, and neither suspected nor had reason to suspect, the failure to satisfy the requirements or (as the case may be) the difference of date, time or route (s. 11(8)). To the extent that an alleged offence turns on a difference of date, time or route, it is a defence for the accused to prove that the difference arose from circumstances beyond his/her control or from something done with the agreement of a police officer or by the officer's direction (s. 11(9)).

4.8.4.2 Imposing Conditions on Public Processions

The Public Order Act 1986, s. 12 states:

(1) If the senior police officer, having regard to the time or place at which and the circumstances in which any public procession is being held or is intended to be held and to its route or proposed route, reasonably believes that—

(a) it may result in serious public disorder, serious damage to property or serious disruption to the life of the community, or

(b) the purpose of the persons organising it is the intimidation of others with a view to compelling them not to do an act they have a right to do, or to do an act they have a right not to do,

he may give directions imposing on the persons organising or taking part in the procession such conditions as appear to him necessary to prevent such disorder, damage, disruption or intimidation, including conditions as to the route of the procession or prohibiting it from entering any public place specified in the directions.

KEYNOTE

This section may also apply to a commonly or customarily held procession as described in s. 11(2) **(see para. 4.8.4.1)**. It enables a senior police officer, who reasonably believes that a procession may result in serious disruption to the life of the community, to give such directions imposing conditions as to the route of the procession as appear to him necessary to prevent such disruption. This can be done days before the procession, or at the point of assembly or during the procession itself. The giving of directions is a preventive measure whenever given (*Powlesland* v *DPP* [2013] EWHC 3846 (Admin)).

In relation to a procession being held, or to a procession intended to be held in a case where persons are assembling with a view to taking part in it, the 'senior police officer' is the most senior in rank of the police officers present at the scene (s. 12(2)(a)). For any other intended procession it is the chief officer of police (s. 12(2)(b)), whose direction must be given in writing (s. 12(3)).

A person who organises a public procession and knowingly fails to comply with a condition imposed under this section is guilty of a summary offence, but it is a defence to prove that the failure arose from circumstances beyond his/her control (s. 12(4)).

A person who takes part in a public procession and knowingly fails to comply with a condition imposed under this section is guilty of a summary offence, but it is a defence to prove that the failure arose from circumstances beyond his/her control (s. 12(5)). Those participating in a public procession are entitled to leave it, but they are not entitled to move from the route of the procession while they remain as participants in it (*Jukes* v *DPP* [2013] EWHC 195 (Admin)).

A person who incites another to commit a summary offence under s. 12(5) is guilty of an offence (s. 12(6)).

4.8.4.3 Prohibiting Public Processions

The Public Order Act 1986, s. 13 states:

(1) If at any time the chief officer of police reasonably believes that, because of particular circumstances existing in any district or part of a district, the powers under section 12 will not be sufficient to prevent the holding of public processions in that district or part from resulting in serious public disorder, he shall apply to the council of the district for an order prohibiting for such period not exceeding 3 months as may be specified in the application the holding of all public processions (or of any class of public procession so specified) in the district or part concerned.

(2) On receiving such an application, a council may with the consent of the Secretary of State make an order either in the terms of the application or with such modifications as may be approved by the Secretary of State.

(3) Subsection (1) does not apply in the City of London or the metropolitan police district.

KEYNOTE

A person who organises a public procession the holding of which he/she knows is prohibited by virtue of an order under this section is guilty of a summary offence (s. 13(7)). A person who takes part in a public procession the holding of which he/she knows is prohibited by virtue of an order under this section is guilty of a summary offence (s. 13(8)), and a person who incites another to commit an offence under s. 13(8) is guilty of a summary offence (s. 13(9)).

4.8.4.4 Imposing Conditions on Public Assemblies

The Public Order Act 1986, s. 14 states:

(1) If the senior police officer, having regard to the time or place at which and the circumstances in which any public assembly is being held or is intended to be held, reasonably believes that—
  (a) it may result in serious public disorder, serious damage to property or serious disruption to the life of the community, or
  (b) the purpose of the persons organising it is the intimidation of others with a view to compelling them not to do an act they have a right to do, or to do an act they have a right not to do,
  he may give directions imposing on the persons organising or taking part in the assembly such conditions as to the place at which the assembly may be (or continue to be) held, its maximum duration, or the maximum number of persons who may constitute it, as appear to him necessary to prevent such disorder, damage, disruption or intimidation.

(2) In subsection (1) 'the senior police officer' means—
  (a) in relation to an assembly being held, the most senior in rank of the police officers present at the scene, and
  (b) in relation to an assembly intended to be held, the chief officer of police.

(3) A direction given by a chief officer of police by virtue of subsection (2)(b) shall be given in writing.

KEYNOTE

In *Jones* v *The Commissioner of Police for the Metropolis* [2019] EWHC 2026 (QB), it was held that separate gatherings of Extinction Rebellion protesters, separated both in time and by many miles, even if coordinated under the umbrella of one body, was not a public assembly under the meaning of s. 14(1).

Where a chief officer gives a direction he/she must identify what limb of s. 14(1) was being relied upon and in sufficient detail to enable demonstrators to understand why the decision was made and for a court to understand if a decision was reasonable or not (*R (On the Application of Brehony)* v *Chief Constable of Greater Manchester Police* [2005] EWHC 640 (Admin)).

A direction under this section was lawful where a senior police officer imposed a condition that a Climate Camp protest against the G20 Summit in London must stop. The demonstration had lasted the best part of 12 hours—quite long enough for the protestors to take advantage of their human rights under Article 10 (Freedom of Expression) and Article 11 (Freedom of Assembly and Association)—and those wishing to remain were intent on continuing to block the highway, the main thoroughfare into and out of the City. There was no justification to prolong the demonstration and its continuation would cause serious disturbances and disruption to traffic and pedestrians wishing to use the highway. The police had a duty to clear the highway that could not be done without removing the protestors by force if necessary (*R (On the Application of Moos)* v *Commissioner of Police of the Metropolis* [2011] EWHC 957 (Admin)).

In *R* v *Lucas* (2014) 17 April, unreported, an assembly was already taking place and the notice under s. 14 was signed by a chief officer who was not present at the scene. It was held that the notice was invalid as the police officer giving it was not the authorised officer as required by s. 2(a).

The necessity for imposing a condition must genuinely appear to the relevant senior police officer and must be proportional to the circumstances in which the public assembly is being held (*James* v *DPP* [2015] EWHC 3296 (Admin)).

A person who organises a public assembly and knowingly fails to comply with a condition imposed under this section is guilty of a summary offence, but it is a defence to prove that the failure arose from circumstances beyond his/her control (s. 14(4)). A person who takes part in a public assembly and knowingly fails to comply with a condition imposed under this section is guilty of a summary offence, but it is a defence to prove that the failure arose from circumstances beyond his/her control (s. 14(5)). A person who incites another to commit an offence under s. 14(5) is guilty of a summary offence (s. 14(6)).

The distinction between this section and s. 12 concerns the conditions that may be imposed under each section. In *DPP* v *Jones* [2002] EWHC 110 (Admin) demonstrators against the Huntingdon Life Sciences Centre were prosecuted for failing to comply with a condition set out in a police notice issued under s. 14. It was held that some of the conditions imposed were more properly concerned with a public procession and therefore were beyond the police powers under s. 14. The offending parts of the police notice were 'severed' leaving the enforceable parts intact. However it may be safer for the police to issue two separate notices, in appropriate circumstances, one relating to the conditions to be observed by participants in the 'procession' element of an operation and the other imposing conditions on the 'assembly' element.

4.8.4.5 Prohibiting Trespassory Assemblies

The provisions of s. 14 (**see para. 4.8.4.4**) apply to public assemblies. However, occasions have arisen where the assembly has been *trespassory*, that is, on land which is either private or where there is only a limited right of public access and the permission of the relevant landowner has not been granted. In such instances, s. 14A of the Public Order Act 1986 provides the police with certain powers.

The Public Order Act 1986, s. 14A states:

(1) If at any time the chief officer of police reasonably believes that an assembly is intended to be held in any district at a place on land to which the public has no right of access or only a limited right of access and that the assembly—

(a) is likely to be held without the permission of the occupier of the land or to conduct itself in such a way as to exceed the limits of any permission of his or the limits of the public's right of access, and

(b) may result—

(i) in serious disruption to the life of the community, or

(ii) where the land, or a building or monument on it, is of historical, architectural, archaeological or scientific importance, in significant damage to the land, building or monument,

he may apply to the council of the district for an order prohibiting for a specified period the holding of all trespassory assemblies in the district or a part of it, as specified.

KEYNOTE

An 'assembly' for the purpose of this section means 20 or more people, 'land' means land in the open air, and 'public' includes a section of the public (s. 14A(9)).

A classic example of a trespassory assembly might be found at sites such as Stonehenge.

On receiving an application from a chief officer the council may make an order either in the terms of the application, or with modifications, either of which must be approved by the Secretary of State (s. 14A(2)(a)), and the order must be in writing or reduced to writing as soon as practicable after being made (s. 14A(8)).

An order must not last for more than four days, nor must it apply to an area beyond a radius of five miles from a specified centre (s. 14A(6)).

A person who organises an assembly the holding of which he/she knows is prohibited by an order under s. 14A is guilty of a summary offence (s. 14B(1)). A person who takes part in an assembly which he/she knows is prohibited by an order under s. 14A is guilty of a summary offence (s. 14B(2)), and a person who incites another to commit an offence under s. 14B(2) is guilty of a summary offence (s. 14B(3)). Even where an order has been made, there will be a need to show that the assembly was obstructive of the highway or at least that it exceeded the public's general right of access (*DPP* v *Jones* [1999] 2 AC 240).

4.8.4.6 Trespassory Assemblies Police Powers

The Public Order Act 1986, s. 14C states:

(1) If a constable in uniform reasonably believes that a person is on his way to an assembly within the area to which an order under section 14A applies which the constable reasonably believes is likely to be an assembly which is prohibited by that order, he may, subject to subsection (2) below—

(a) stop that person, and

(b) direct him not to proceed in the direction of the assembly.

(2) The power conferred by subsection (1) may only be exercised within the area to which the order applies.

(3) A person who fails to comply with a direction under subsection (1) which he knows has been given to him is guilty of an offence.

KEYNOTE

This power allows officers to stop people, though not, it would seem, vehicles (in which case the general power under s. 163 of the Road Traffic Act 1988 must be used).

4.8.5 Public Meetings

It is an offence to attempt to break up a public meeting.

OFFENCE: **Trying to Break up a Public Meeting—*Public Meeting Act 1908, s. 1***
- Triable summarily
- Six months' imprisonment and/or a fine *(No specific power of arrest)*

The Public Meeting Act 1908, s. 1 states:

(1) Any person who at a lawful public meeting acts in a disorderly manner for the purpose of preventing the transaction of the business for which the meeting was called together shall be guilty of an offence …

(2) Any person who incites others to commit an offence under this section shall be guilty of a like offence.

KEYNOTE

'Public meeting' is not defined in the 1908 Act. There appears to be no requirement for the meeting to be lawfully assembled.

This offence does not apply to meetings held in relation to s. 97 of the Representation of the People Act 1983 (meetings concerned with public elections) (s. 1(4)). In the case of people acting or inciting others to act in a disorderly way at such meetings, there is a specific summary offence under s. 97(1) of the 1983 Act.

If a constable reasonably suspects any person of committing this offence, he/she may, *if requested by the person chairing the meeting*, require the offender to declare his/her name and address immediately. Failing to comply with such a request or giving false details is a summary offence (s. 1(3)).

4.9 Public Order Offences

4.9.1 Introduction

The principal piece of legislation dealing with public order is the Public Order Act 1986. While this chapter examines some of the more well-known elements of this legislation, it also looks at the common law offence of breach of the peace.

4.9.2 Breach of the Peace

A breach of the peace is defined specifically in *R v Howell* [1982] QB 416. A breach of the peace generally occurs when an act is done, or threatened to be done:

- which harms a person or, in his/her presence, his/her property; or
- which is likely to cause such harm; or
- which puts someone in fear of such harm.

The common law provides a power of arrest and also the power to intervene and/or detain by force, in order to prevent any action likely to result in a breach of the peace in either public or private places.

Breach of the peace is dealt with by way of complaint and is not a criminal offence (*R v County of London Quarter Sessions Appeals Committee, ex parte Metropolitan Police Commissioner* [1948] 1 KB 670). Although not a criminal offence in domestic law, it may be treated as such for the purposes of the European Convention on Human Rights (*Steel v UK* (1999) 28 EHRR 603). In *Williamson v Chief Constable of West Midlands Police* [2003] EWCA Civ 337 the Court of Appeal held that a person arrested for a breach of the peace is not, strictly speaking, in police detention for the purposes of s. 118 of the Police and Criminal Evidence Act 1984 and the provisions in relation to bail do not apply. A person may be detained and placed before the next available court, or detained until there is no further likelihood of a reoccurrence of the breach of the peace. In *Williamson* it was considered good practice for people arrested and detained for breach of the peace to be treated in accordance with the provisions of PACE, and that they should also be cautioned.

4.9.2.1 Breach of the Peace on Private Premises

A breach of the peace may take place on private premises as well as in public places (*R v Chief Constable of Devon and Cornwall, ex parte Central Electricity Generating Board* [1982] QB 458). The police are entitled to enter premises to prevent a breach of the peace and to remain there in order to do so (*Thomas v Sawkins* [1935] 2 KB 249). This power has not been affected by the general powers of entry provided by the Police and Criminal Evidence Act 1984 (**see chapter 4.2** and s. 17(6) of the 1984 Act).

Where a breach of the peace takes place on private property, there is no requirement to show that the resulting disturbance affected members of the public outside that property—*McQuade v Chief Constable of Humberside Police* [2001] EWCA Civ 1330. The presence of a member (or members) of the public is, however, a highly relevant factor when dealing with a breach of the peace (*McConnell v Chief Constable of Greater Manchester Police* [1990] 1 WLR 364).

4.9.2.2 Police Powers are Discretionary

Although the police have a general duty to preserve the Queen's peace, and enjoy common law powers to carry out that duty, they also have a wide discretion as to how they go about that function. The common law powers of the police allow them, where appropriate, to prevent people from travelling to certain locations (e.g. striking miners heading for a working coalfield where their presence would give reasonable grounds to apprehend a breach of the peace (*Moss* v *McLachlan* [1985] IRLR 76)). Such an 'anticipatory' power is, however, exceptional (*Foulkes* v *Chief Constable of Merseyside Police* [1998] 3 All ER 705) and requires a balancing of the individual rights of the people involved against the wider interests of public safety, the maintenance of public order and the prevention of crime. Such exceptional powers to impose anticipatory restrictions on the movement of individuals, falling short of arrest, only arise if there is an imminent threat to public order.

The practicalities involved in this balancing exercise were considered in *R (On the Application of Laporte)* v *Chief Constable of Gloucestershire* [2006] UKHL 55. In *Laporte* a lawful assembly had been arranged under the provisions of ss. 12 and 14 of the Public Order Act 1986 in connection with protests against the war in Iraq. As the result of a stop and search order made under s. 60 of the Criminal Justice and Public Order Act 1994 (**see para. 4.1.4**) the police stopped a number of coaches en route to the lawful assembly at Fairford US Air Force base, and then escorted them back to London. Intelligence had been received that the passengers would cause disorder at the base. The House of Lords ruled that the police had acted unlawfully because a breach of the peace was not imminent when the coaches were stopped. This action interfered with the passengers' rights under Articles 10 and 11 of the European Convention on Human Rights and was disproportionate.

4.9.2.3 Which Parties are Likely to Present Actual Threat?

When exercising discretionary powers to prevent disorder, police officers will be expected to focus their attention on those who are likely to present the actual threat of violence or disorder. In *Redmond-Bate* v *DPP* [1999] Crim LR 998, people preaching on the steps of a church were warned by police that they were antagonising passers-by. Despite the warning, the preachers continued and, as there was an imminent likelihood of a recently gathered crowd attacking them, the preachers were arrested. The Divisional Court felt that the approach taken by the police was incompatible with Article 10 of the European Convention on Human Rights and that the officers' attention should have been directed at the crowd from whom the threat to the 'peace' was emanating. The individuals preaching were simply exercising their right to freedom of expression. It was the crowd who, in the court's view, ought to have received the warning and who should have been arrested in the event of their continuing to represent a threat to public order.

However, it will not always be practicable to separate those who are directly and individually presenting a threat to the peace and those who are part of a larger crowd. In *Austin* v *Commissioner of Police of the Metropolis* [2009] UKHL 5 it was held that in extreme and exceptional circumstances it would be lawful for the police to contain demonstrators and members of the public caught up in that demonstration, even though they themselves did not appear to be about to commit a breach of the peace. This would be the case where it was necessary to prevent an imminent breach of the peace by others, and no other means would achieve that. In *Austin* v *United Kingdom* (2012) 55 EHRR 14 the European Court of Human Rights decided, by a majority, that there had been no violation of Article 5 (right to liberty and security) of the European Convention on Human Rights. *Austin* [2009] was followed in *R (On the Application of Moos)* v *Commissioner of Police of the Metropolis* [2011] EWHC 957 (Admin) which related to a Climate Camp protest against the G20 Summit in London. It is only when the police reasonably believe that there is no other means whatsoever to prevent an imminent breach of the peace that they can as a matter of necessity curtail the lawful exercise of their rights of freedom of expression by third parties. The test of necessity is met only in truly extreme and exceptional circumstances. The action taken has to be both reasonably necessary and proportionate and taken in good faith. In *R (On the Application of McClure) v Commissioner of Police of the Metropolis* [2012] EWCA Civ 12, the Court of Appeal concluded that a decision to contain a substantial crowd of demonstrators whose behaviour, though at times unruly and somewhat violent, did not of itself justify containment was, however, justifiable on the ground that containment was the least drastic way of preventing what the police officer responsible for the decision reasonably apprehended would be imminent and serious breaches of the peace.

Where demonstrators were contained in a police pen, in a demonstration against Israel and its Head of State, it was held that the police may deploy reasonable force to prevent a breach of the peace that they reasonably apprehend as imminent (*Wright v Commissioner of Police for the Metropolis* [2013] EWHC 2739 (QB)).

Where officers were directed by senior officers to arrest persons for breach of the peace, it was held to be lawful where those senior officers had good reason to believe that had those persons been allowed to proceed to a nearby demonstration point there would have been a strong likelihood of a breach of the peace occurring (*R (On the Application of Hicks) v Commissioner of Police of the Metropolis* [2014] EWCA Civ 3; see also *Eiseman-Renyard v United Kingdom* (Application no. 57884/17, ECtHR, 5 March 2019)).

Guidance on 'immediacy' in relation to conduct in a domestic setting is contained in *Wragg v DPP* [2005] EWHC 1389 (Admin). Police officers attending a domestic dispute found one of the parties, who had been in a heated argument with a relative also living in the house, to have consumed a large amount of alcohol. In relation to the immediacy or imminence test the police officers believed that a breach of the peace could take place in the house after they departed that night in so far as the other household member was at risk of immediate assault while the accused was still in drink. The arrest of the accused was held to be lawful. In *Demetriou v DPP* [2012] EWHC 2443 (Admin) it was also held that an arrest was lawful if a person willing to leave premises but who an officer believed would return to cause violence gave rise to a reasonable basis for fearing imminent violence.

4.9.2.4 Power of Arrest

Any person, whether constable or civilian, has a common law power of arrest where:

(a) a breach of the peace is committed in his/her presence,
(b) the person effecting the arrest reasonably believes that such a breach will be committed in the immediate future by the person arrested, or
(c) a breach of the peace has been committed or the person effecting the arrest reasonably believes that a breach of the peace has occurred and that a further breach is threatened.

KEYNOTE

In order to comply with Article 5(1)(c) of the European Convention on Human Rights (right to liberty), an arrest must be for the purpose of bringing the person before a competent legal authority. However, in *R (On the Application of Hicks) v Metropolitan Police Commissioner* [2017] UKSC 9 it was held that an arrest is lawful notwithstanding that the person is released before he/she could practically be brought before a court.

There is an element of pre-emptive risk assessment involved in application of the test as to whether or not a breach of the peace is actually occurring even before moving on to consider whether such a breach, if not occurring, is imminent (*Laporte v Commissioner of Police of the Metropolis* [2014] EWHC 3574 (QB)).

This power of arrest may be exercised on private premises, even where there is no other member of the public present (*R v Howell* [1982] QB 416).

In *Bibby* v *Chief Constable of Essex Police* (2000) 164 JP 297, the Court of Appeal held that the power of arrest for breach of the peace was wholly exceptional and set out the conditions that must be met before this power should be used. These conditions are:

- there must be the clearest of circumstances and a real and present threat to the peace to justify the arrest
- the threat must be coming from the person who is ultimately arrested
- his/her conduct must be clearly interfering with the rights of another
- that conduct must be unreasonable.

In *Howell* it was held that where a breach of the peace has not yet occurred it is sufficient that a constable uses the wording and sets out the conditions that must be met before this power should be used.

4.9.3 Riot

OFFENCE: **Riot—*Public Order Act 1986, s. 1***

> • Triable on indictment • 10 years' imprisonment and/or a fine

The Public Order Act 1986, s. 1 states:

(1) Where 12 or more persons who are present together use or threaten unlawful violence for a common purpose and the conduct of them (taken together) is such as would cause a person of reasonable firmness present at the scene to fear for his personal safety, each of the persons using unlawful violence for the common purpose is guilty of riot.

(2) It is immaterial whether or not the 12 or more use or threaten unlawful violence simultaneously.

(3) The common purpose may be inferred from conduct.

(4) No person of reasonable firmness need actually be, or be likely to be, present at the scene.

(5) Riot may be committed in private as well as in public places.

KEYNOTE

This offence requires the consent of the DPP before a prosecution can be brought.

It is not necessary that all 12 people concerned use or threaten unlawful violence at the same time. However, the courts have held that each defendant must be shown to have *used* unlawful violence and not merely threatened to do so (*R* v *Jefferson* [1994] 1 All ER 270). A defendant must be shown to have *intended* to use/threaten violence or to have been aware that his/her conduct may have been violent (s. 6(1)).

Although there must be a common purpose, this need not be part of a pre-determined plan, nor be unlawful in itself. A common purpose to get into a rock concert or even the January sales at a high street store could therefore be enough, provided all other elements are present.

4.9.3.1 Unlawful Violence

The Public Order Act 1986, s. 8 states:

'violence' means any violent conduct, so that—

(a) except in the context of affray, it includes violent conduct towards property as well as violent conduct towards persons, and

(b) it is not restricted to conduct causing or intended to cause injury or damage but includes any other violent conduct (for example, throwing at or towards a person a missile of a kind capable of causing injury which does not hit or falls short).

KEYNOTE

The term 'unlawful' was included in the Act to allow for the general defences such as self-defence to be applicable (*R* v *Rothwell* [1993] Crim LR 626).

4.9.3.2 Drunkenness

Parliament has specifically catered for self-induced intoxication, not just for the offence of riot, but in relation to other offences under the 1986 Act, by s. 6 which states:

(5) For the purposes of this section a person whose awareness is impaired by intoxication shall be taken to be aware of that of which he would be aware if not intoxicated, unless he shows either that his intoxication was not self-induced or that it was caused solely by the taking or administration of a substance in the course of medical treatment.

(6) In subsection (5) 'intoxication' means any intoxication, whether caused by drink, drugs or other means, or by a combination of means.

4.9.4 Violent Disorder

OFFENCE: **Violent Disorder—*Public Order Act 1986, s. 2***

- Triable either way • Five years' imprisonment and/or a fine on indictment
- Six months' imprisonment and/or a fine summarily

The Public Order Act 1986, s. 2 states:

(1) Where 3 or more persons who are present together use or threaten unlawful violence and the conduct of them (taken together) is such as would cause a person of reasonable firmness present at the scene to fear for his personal safety, each of the persons using or threatening unlawful violence is guilty of violent disorder.

(2) It is immaterial whether or not the 3 or more use or threaten unlawful violence simultaneously.

(3) No person of reasonable firmness need actually be, or be likely to be, present at the scene.

(4) Violent disorder may be committed in private as well as in public places.

KEYNOTE

In order to convict a defendant of this offence, you must show that there were three or more people using or threatening unlawful violence. However, while three or more persons must have been present and used or threatened unlawful violence, it is not necessary that three or more persons should actually be charged or prosecuted with the offence. Further, where there are three defendants and two are acquitted of the charge, the remaining defendant can still be convicted of violent disorder (*R* v *Mahroof* (1989) 88 Cr App R 317) as long as *it can be proved that there were three or more people using or threatening violence* (perhaps from CCTV evidence of the incident). If it cannot be proved that there were three or more people using or threatening unlawful violence the court should acquit each defendant (*R* v *McGuigan* [1991] Crim LR 719).

In *R* v *NW* [2010] EWCA Crim 404, the circumstances of the case were that a person was violently resisting arrest by a police officer, during which time a crowd gathered and various members of the crowd used or threatened violence. The Court of Appeal held that for the purposes of this section it was not necessary for a person to act deliberately in combination with at least two other people present at the scene, but that it is sufficient that at least three people be present, each separately using or threatening unlawful violence. The court's view was that the phrase, 'where 3 or more persons who are present together use or threaten violence ...' consists of ordinary words which must be given their ordinary meaning.

There is no requirement to prove a common purpose.

Again, a defendant must be shown to have *intended* to use/threaten violence or to have *been aware* that his/her conduct may have been violent (s. 6(2)). 'Violence' for these purposes can include violent conduct towards property (s. 8).

4.9.5 Affray

OFFENCE: **Affray—*Public Order Act 1986, s. 3***

- Triable either way • Three years' imprisonment and/or a fine on indictment
- Six months' imprisonment and/or a fine summarily

The Public Order Act 1986, s. 3 states:

(1) A person is guilty of affray if he uses or threatens unlawful violence towards another and his conduct is such as would cause a person of reasonable firmness present at the scene to fear for his personal safety.

(2) Where 2 or more persons use or threaten the unlawful violence, it is the conduct of them taken together that must be considered for the purposes of subsection (1).

(3) For the purposes of this section a threat cannot be made by the use of words alone.

(4) No person of reasonable firmness need actually be, or be likely to be, present at the scene.

(5) Affray may be committed in private as well as in public places.

KEYNOTE

The House of Lords held that, in order to prove the offence of affray, the threat of unlawful violence has to be towards a person(s) present at the scene (*I* v *DPP* [2001] UKHL 10). Once this element has been proved, it will be necessary to prove the second element, namely, whether the defendant's conduct would have caused a hypothetical person present at the scene to fear for his/her personal safety (*R* v *Sanchez* (1996) 160 JP 321 and *R* v *Carey* [2006] EWCA Crim 17). However, where the likelihood of a hypothetical person of reasonable firmness being present was low this element of the offence was not satisfied. In *R (On the Application of Leeson)* v *DPP* [2010] EWHC 994 (Admin) a woman had issued a drunken threat to kill her long-term partner while holding a knife, in a bathroom, in an otherwise unoccupied house. In these circumstances the court held that there was no possibility of hypothetical bystanders fearing for their safety.

Where the accused is one of a number of people who use or threaten unlawful violence, in deciding whether the person of reasonable firmness present at the scene would be caused to fear for his personal safety, it is the conduct of the entire group taken as a whole that counts and so there is no need in such a situation for the court to attribute individual roles to the participants (*Dragjoshi* v *Croydon Magistrates' Court* [2017] EWHC 2840 (QB)).

The threat cannot be made by words alone (s. 3(3)), therefore there must be some action by the defendant—even if that 'action' consists of utilising something else such as a dog to threaten the violence (*R* v *Dixon* [1993] Crim LR 579).

The effect of s. 3(4) is that it is not necessary to show that the defendant's behaviour either was or could have been seen by someone at the time.

Although violence is 'not restricted to conduct causing or intended to cause injury or damage but includes any other violent conduct' (s. 8), the expression does not include conduct towards property as it does with the offences under ss. 1 and 2.

Once more, a defendant must be shown to have *intended* to use/threaten violence or to have *been aware* that his/her conduct may have been violent (s. 6(2)).

4.9.6 Fear or Provocation of Violence

OFFENCE: **Fear or Provocation of Violence—*Public Order Act 1986, s. 4***
- Triable summarily • Six months' imprisonment and/or a fine

OFFENCE: **Racially or Religiously Aggravated—*Crime and Disorder Act 1998, s. 31(1)(a)***
- Triable either way • Two years' imprisonment and/or a fine on indictment
- Six months' imprisonment and/or a fine summarily

The Public Order Act 1986, s. 4 states:

(1) A person is guilty of an offence if he—
   (a) uses towards another person threatening, abusive or insulting words or behaviour, or
   (b) distributes or displays to another person any writing, sign or other visible representation which is threatening, abusive or insulting,

with intent to cause that person to believe that immediate unlawful violence will be used against him or another by any person, or to provoke the immediate use of unlawful violence by that person or another, or whereby that person is likely to believe that such violence will be used or it is likely that such violence will be provoked.

(2) An offence under this section may be committed in a public or a private place, except that no offence is committed where the words or behaviour are used, or the writing, sign or other visible representation is distributed or displayed, by a person inside a dwelling and the other person is also inside that or another dwelling.

KEYNOTE

The meaning of 'racially or religiously aggravated' in relation to s. 31(1)(a) of the 1998 Act is discussed in *Crime*, chapter 1.9.

'Immediate' unlawful violence does not have to be instantaneous but it must be shown that the defendant's conduct was likely to lead to more than some form of violence at some later date. 'Immediate' here requires some close proximity between the acts of the defendant and the apprehended violence, with no intervening occurrence.

There are a number of ways in which this offence can be committed (see below). In all of these, however, there must be the use of threatening/abusive/insulting words or behaviour (or distribution/display of writing, signs, etc.). This must be carried out with the requisite state of mind set out at s. 6(3) which states:

(3) A person is guilty of an offence under section 4 only if he intends his words or behaviour, or the writing, sign or other visible representation, to be threatening, abusive or insulting, or is aware that it may be threatening, abusive or insulting.

In addition, it must be shown that the person further *intended* to bring about the consequences set out below (at (a) and (b)) or that the consequences (at (c) and (d)) were likely.

In relation to s. 4(1)(b), 'writing' includes typing, printing, lithography, photography and other modes of presenting or reproducing words in a visible form (Interpretation Act 1978, s. 5 and sch. 1).

The offence was broken down into four component parts in *Winn* v *DPP* (1992) 156 JP 881. For each of these parts it must be shown:

(a) that the defendant:
- intended the person against whom the conduct was directed
- to believe
- that immediate unlawful violence would be used
- either against him/her or against anyone else
- by the defendant or anyone else; *or*

(b) that he/she:
- intended to provoke the immediate use of unlawful violence
- by that person or anyone else; *or*

(c) that:
- the person against whom the words or behaviour (or distribution/display of writing etc.) were directed
- was likely to believe
- that immediate unlawful violence would be used; *or*

(d) that it was likely that immediate unlawful violence would be provoked.

In the case at (a) above, it does not have to be shown that the other person *actually believed* that immediate violence would be used; it has to be shown that the defendant *intended to cause* him/her to believe it (*Swanston* v *DPP* (1997) 161 JP 203).

The person in whom the defendant intends to create that belief must be the same person at whom the conduct is directed (*Loade* v *DPP* [1990] 1 QB 1052).

Section 4(2) provides that this offence cannot be committed by persons inside a dwelling. 'Dwelling' is defined as any structure or part of a structure occupied as a person's home or as other living accommodation (whether the occupation is separate or shared with others) but does not include any part not so occupied, and for this purpose 'structure' includes a tent, caravan, vehicle, vessel or other temporary movable structure (s. 8). A person who shouted a racially aggravated comment from her garden at a person in a neighbouring garden had not been 'inside a dwelling' (*DPP* v *Distill* [2017] EWHC 2244 (Admin)).

4.9.7 Intentional Harassment, Alarm or Distress

OFFENCE: **Intentionally Causing Harassment, Alarm or Distress—*Public Order Act 1986, s. 4A***

> • Triable summarily • Six months' imprisonment and/or a fine

OFFENCE: **Racially or Religiously Aggravated—*Crime and Disorder Act 1998, s. 31(1)(b)***

> • Triable either way • Two years' imprisonment and/or a fine on indictment
> • Six months' imprisonment and/or a fine summarily

The Public Order Act 1986, s. 4A states:

> (1) A person is guilty of an offence if, with intent to cause a person harassment, alarm or distress, he—
>
>   (a) uses threatening or abusive or insulting words or behaviour, or disorderly behaviour, or
>
>   (b) displays any writing, sign or other visible representation which is threatening, abusive or insulting,
>
> thereby causing that or another person harassment, alarm or distress.

KEYNOTE

For the purpose of the racially or religiously aggravated form of causing fear or provocation of violence, any words used by the defendant have to be construed within the meaning that they are given in England and Wales. In construing those words, the courts should not have any regard to the *defendant's* own racial, national or ethnic origins—or presumably their religious beliefs or lack of such (*R v White (Anthony Delroy)* [2001] EWCA Crim 216).

In order to prove this offence you must show that the defendant intended to cause harassment, alarm or distress and, it seems, that by so doing, the defendant actually caused some harassment, alarm or distress. In *Steele* v *DPP* [2008] EWHC 438 (Admin) the defendant took a digital photograph of the complainant and posted it on the internet with a speech bubble and text alleging the complainant had previous convictions for violence. It was several months later that the photograph was shown to the complainant by the police and the Divisional Court held that the time and the circumstances in which it had been brought fully to the attention of the complainant were immaterial.

Harassment, alarm or distress are not defined and it would appear that they are to be given their ordinary everyday meaning. A police officer can be caused such harassment, alarm or distress (*DPP* v *Orum* [1989] 1 WLR 88), and can also be the victim of the racially aggravated form of the offence (*R* v *Jacobs* [2001] 2 Cr App R(S) 38), and he/she can feel that harassment, alarm or distress for someone else present (e.g. a child (*Lodge* v *DPP* [1989] COD 179)). Police officers are expected to display a degree of fortitude and, for an officer to be caused harassment, alarm or distress, the conduct complained of must go beyond that which he/she would regularly come across in the ordinary course of police duties.

Whether the use of a particular phrase, in the context and circumstances in which it was used, was intended to cause harassment, alarm or distress for the offences above is a question of fact for the relevant magistrate/jury to decide (*DPP* v *Weeks* (2000) *The Independent*, 17 July). Consequently, in that case where the defendant was alleged to have called the victim a 'black bastard' during a heated argument over a business transaction, the magistrates were still entitled to find him not guilty of the aggravated s. 4A offence if they were satisfied that the relevant intention was not present.

In *R* v *Valentine* [2017] EWCA Crim 207 the Court of Appeal held that where racial hostility was directed at someone who was not the victim, the elements of 'racially aggravated' were not made out.

Posting a threatening, abusive or insulting letter through someone's letter box is not an offence under this section (*Chappell* v *DPP* (1989) 89 Cr App R 82). It may, however, amount to an offence under the Malicious Communications Act 1988 (see para. **4.12.5**).

It is a defence for a person to prove that he was inside a dwelling and had no reason to believe that the words or behaviour used, or the writing, sign or other visible representation displayed, would be heard or

---

seen by a person outside that or any other building or that his conduct was reasonable (s. 4A(3)). For the definition of dwelling, **see para. 4.9.6.**

It is for the defendant to prove that one of the elements existed at the time of the offence. The standard of proof here will be that of the balance of probabilities, i.e. that it was more likely than not.

4.9.8 Harassment, Alarm or Distress

OFFENCE: **Harassment, Alarm or Distress—*Public Order Act 1986, s. 5***

- Triable summarily • Fine

OFFENCE: **Racially or Religiously Aggravated—*Crime and Disorder Act 1998, s. 31(1)(c)***

- Triable summarily • Fine

The Public Order Act 1986, s. 5 states:

(1) A person is guilty of an offence if he—
    (a) uses threatening or abusive words or behaviour, or disorderly behaviour, or
    (b) displays any writing, sign or other visible representation which is threatening or abusive,
    within the hearing or sight of a person likely to be caused harassment, alarm or distress thereby.

KEYNOTE

Unlike the other racially or religiously aggravated forms of public order offences, the offence under s. 5 remains triable summarily, even if aggravated by the conditions set out in s. 28 of the Crime and Disorder Act 1998 (s. 31(5)).

In a case where the defendant used the words 'You're fucking Islam' in an aggressive manner towards a Sikh police officer of Asian appearance, the Divisional Court held that the expression itself was almost undeniably abusive if not insulting (*R (On the Application of DPP)* v *Humphrey* [2005] EWHC 822 (Admin)). In *Kendall* v *DPP* [2008] EWHC 1848 (Admin), British National Party posters showing a photograph of three black men with the caption 'Illegal Immigrant Murder Scum' were found to be threatening, abusive and insulting and racially aggravated. In *Abdul* v *DPP* [2011] EWHC 247 (Admin), it was held that a prosecution under this section was a proportionate response to a group of protesters carrying placards and chanting slogans such as 'British soldiers burn in hell' and calling the soldiers murderers, rapists and baby killers, during a parade to celebrate soldiers returning from Afghanistan.

Note that 'disorderly' is not defined and ought to be given its ordinary everyday meaning. It need not be shown that the disorderly behaviour is itself threatening, abusive or insulting, nor that it brought about any feelings of apprehension in the person to whom it was directed (*Chambers and Edwards* v *DPP* [1995] Crim LR 896). The wording of s. 5 is not limited to rowdy behaviour and will extend to any behaviour that could be construed as threatening or abusive.

There must be evidence that there was someone present who could see or hear what the accused was doing, though there was no requirement for the prosecution to call evidence to this effect (*Taylor* v *DPP* [2006] EWHC 1202 (Admin)).

As with the offence under s. 4A (**see para. 4.9.7**), there is nothing to stop the person likely to have felt harassment, alarm or distress from being a police officer acting in the course of his or her duty, but of course one has to be cautious about making such a finding, because police officers are expected to show a certain degree of resilience (*Williams* v *CPS* [2018] EWHC 2869 (Admin)).

A person is only guilty of an offence under this section if he intends his words or behaviour, or the writing, sign or other visible representation, to be threatening or abusive, or is aware that it may be threatening or abusive or (as the case may be) he intends his behaviour to be or is aware that it may be disorderly (s. 6(4)).

This offence is a 'penalty offence' for the purposes of s. 1 of the Criminal Justice and Police Act 2001.

This offence can be committed in a public or private place but not where the words or behaviour are used by a person inside a dwelling and the other person is inside that or another dwelling (s. 5(2)). For the definition of dwelling, see para. 4.9.6.

4.9.8.1 Defences

The Public Order Act 1986, s. 5 states:

(3) It is a defence for the accused to prove—

    (a) that he had no reason to believe that there was any person within hearing or sight who was likely to be caused harassment, alarm or distress, or

    (b) that he was inside a dwelling and had no reason to believe that the words or behaviour used, or the writing sign or other visible representation displayed, would be heard or seen by a person outside that or any other dwelling, or

    (c) that his conduct was reasonable.

KEYNOTE

It is for the defendant to prove that one of the elements existed at the time of the offence. The standard of proof here will be that of the balance of probabilities, i.e. that it was more likely than not.

In deciding whether a defendant's conduct was reasonable under s. 5(3)(c) an objective test will be applied (*DPP* v *Clarke* (1992) 94 Cr App R 359).

The relationship between the Public Order Act 1986, s. 5(1), Article 10 of the European Convention on Human Rights and the supposed 'right' to go naked in public was considered in the 'naked rambler' case, *Gough* v *DPP* [2013] EWHC 3267 (Admin). It was held that the appellant foresaw the consequence of his voluntary decision to walk naked through a town centre and was at least aware that his behaviour may have been threatening, abusive, insulting or disorderly. Thus the intent required by the legislation was proved.

4.10 Sporting Events

4.10.1 Introduction

There are several offences and statutory measures which are specifically aimed at tackling disorder and anti-social behaviour at sporting events.

4.10.2 Designated and Regulated Football Matches

Many of the offences and powers relating to football fixtures apply to 'designated' or 'regulated' football matches. Generally, this will relate to association football matches in which one or both of the participating teams represent a club which is for the time being a member (whether a full or associate member) of the Football League, the Football Association Premier League, the Football Conference National Division, the Scottish Football League or Welsh Premier League, or represents a country or territory (Football (Offences) (Designation of Football Matches) Order 2004 (SI 2004/2410)).

4.10.3 The Football (Offences) Act 1991

OFFENCE: **Misbehaviour at Designated Football Match—*Football (Offences) Act 1991, ss. 2, 3 and 4***
  - • Triable summarily • Fine

The Football (Offences) Act 1991 states:

2. **Throwing of missiles**
   It is an offence for a person at a designated football match to throw anything at or towards—
   (a) the playing area, or any area adjacent to the playing area to which spectators are not generally admitted, or
   (b) any area in which spectators or other persons are or may be present,
   without lawful authority or lawful excuse (which shall be for him to prove).
3. **Indecent or racialist chanting**
   (1) It is an offence to engage or take part in chanting of an indecent or racialist nature at a designated football match.
   (2) For this purpose—
       (a) 'chanting' means the repeated uttering of any words or sounds (whether alone or in concert with one or more others); and
       (b) 'of a racialist' nature means consisting of or including matter which is threatening, abusive or insulting to a person by reason of his colour, race, nationality (including citizenship) or ethnic or national origins.
4. **Going onto the playing area**
   It is an offence for a person at a designated football match to go onto the playing area, or any area adjacent to the playing area to which spectators are not generally admitted, without lawful authority or lawful excuse (which shall be for him to prove).

KEYNOTE

Section 1(2) of the 1991 Act provides that references to things done at a 'designated football match' include anything done at the ground:

- within the period beginning two hours before the start of the match or (if earlier) two hours before the time at which it is advertised to start and ending one hour after the end of the match;
- where the match is advertised to start at a particular time on a particular day but does not take place, within the period beginning two hours before and ending one hour after the advertised starting time.

These offences can be separated into those affecting the playing area and adjacent parts of the ground (ss. 2 and 4) and the offence of indecent or racialist chanting (s. 3).

In the case of the first offence (s. 2), throwing anything at or towards the playing area etc., there is a defence of having lawful authority or lawful excuse (which presumably would cover returning the ball to the field of play). Generally there seem to be few occasions on which a defendant would have lawful authority/reasonable excuse for the behaviour prohibited by s. 2.

Section 4 makes the same savings in relation to lawful authority/reasonable excuse and, in both cases, the burden of proof falls on the defendant. (The *standard* of proof will be that of the balance of probabilities.)

For the offence under s. 3, the defendant must be shown to have *repeated* the words or sounds before it can be classed as 'chanting'.

The wording of s. 3(2)(b) requires that the chanting *is*, rather than, *might be*, threatening, abusive or insulting. Although not expressly required, the best way to prove this element of the offence would be the evidence of a person who was threatened, abused or insulted. In relation to chants 'of a racialist' nature, shouting 'You're just a town full of Pakis' at supporters from Oldham fell squarely within the definition (*DPP v Stoke on Trent Magistrates' Court* [2003] EWHC 1593 (Admin)).

'Indecent' is not defined and will be a question of fact for the court to decide in all the circumstances.

4.10.4 Banning Orders and Detention

The Football Spectators Act 1989 contains the powers to impose banning orders that exclude offenders from attendance at regulated football matches in England, Wales, Scotland and Northern Ireland and international football matches.

There are two ways in which a banning order can be made, first where a person is convicted of a relevant offence (s. 14A), and secondly, by way of complaint by the relevant chief officer, or the DPP (s. 14B(1)).

4.10.4.1 Convicted of Relevant Offences

The relevant offences are set out in sch. 1 to the 1989 Act and include offences relating to drunkenness, violence or threats of violence, or public order offences committed at or in connection with a football match or when travelling to or from a football match (whether or not the match was actually attended by the offender). The offence of affray did not qualify merely because it related to football matches. It would only qualify if it related to a specific football match. In this case it was held that the behaviour of the participants in the affray related to the England v Panama match that ended a few minutes earlier that afternoon (*R v Jelf* [2020] EWCA Crim 631).

Rather than simply having the power to make such orders, courts are under a statutory duty to pass such orders if they are satisfied that there are reasonable grounds to believe that the orders would help prevent violence or disorder. Violence here includes violence towards property, and disorder includes stirring up racial hatred (1989 Act, s. 14C). Where these criteria are established, there is no discretion not to make an order (*R* v *Allen* [2011] EWCA Crim 3076).

KEYNOTE

Banning orders made under s. 14A of the 1989 Act (on conviction of a relevant offence) in addition to an immediate sentence of imprisonment will have a minimum of six and a maximum of 10 years' duration (s. 14F(3)). Other banning orders made under s. 14A (i.e. where they do not accompany a sentence of immediate imprisonment) have a minimum of three and a maximum of five years' duration (s. 14F(4)).

4.10.4.2 Complaint by Chief Officer or DPP

On such an application a magistrates' court can make an order if the person has at any time caused or contributed to any violence or disorder in the United Kingdom or elsewhere. The court may impose conditions on banning orders and must require the surrender of the person's passport in connection with regulated football matches outside the United Kingdom (s. 14E(3)). Where proceedings are adjourned, as with the first way of obtaining a banning order, the offender may be remanded and, where bailed, be required to surrender his/her passport (s. 14B(5)). Again, where the magistrates have failed to make a banning order, the prosecution have a right of appeal to the Crown Court (s. 14D(1A)).

The effect of a banning order, unless a person is detained in legal custody, is that he/she must initially report to a specified police station in England, Wales, Scotland or Northern Ireland, within five days of the order being made (s. 14E(2)). He/she must also notify the enforcing authority of specified changes to his/her personal circumstances within seven days of the occurrence of any such changes (s. 14E(2B) and (2C)).

KEYNOTE

Banning orders made under s. 14B (on complaint by a chief officer of police) have a minimum of three and a maximum of five years' duration (s. 14F(5)).

4.10.4.3 Failing to Comply with Banning Order

OFFENCE: **Failing to Comply with Banning Order—*Football Spectators Act 1989, s. 14J***

 • Triable summarily • Six months' imprisonment and/or a fine

The Football Spectators Act 1989, s. 14J states:

  (1) A person subject to a banning order who fails to comply with—
   (a) any requirement imposed by the order, or
   (b) any requirement imposed under section 19(2B) or (2C) below is guilty of an offence.

KEYNOTE

The reference to s. 19(2B) and (2C) is to the power for the enforcing authority to issue written notices requiring individuals to report to a police station in England, Wales, Scotland or Northern Ireland and, where relevant, to surrender their passports, in advance of certain matches.

A number of exemptions are provided for under s. 20. These allow, among other things, for the person on whom an order has been passed to apply for exemption from the duties of the order under special circumstances.

4.10.4.4 Summary Measures: Detention

The Football Spectators Act 1989, s. 21A states:

(1) This section and section 21B below apply during any control period in relation to a regulated football match outside the United Kingdom or an external tournament if a constable in uniform—

    (a) has reasonable grounds for suspecting that the condition in section 14B(2) above is met in the case of a person present before him, and

    (b) has reasonable grounds to believe that making a banning order in his case would help to prevent violence or disorder at or in connection with any regulated football matches.

(2) The constable may detain the person in his custody (whether there or elsewhere)until he has decided whether or not to issue a notice under section 21B below, and shall give the person his reasons for detaining him in writing.

    This is without prejudice to any power of the constable apart from this section to arrest the person.

(3) A person may not be detained under subsection (2) above for more than four hours or, with the authority of an officer of at least the rank of inspector, six hours.

KEYNOTE

'Control period' means, in relation to a regulated football match outside the United Kingdom, the period:

(a) beginning five days before the day of the match, and

(b) ending when the match is finished or cancelled

and in relation to an external tournament, means any period described in an order made by the Secretary of State:

(a) beginning five days before the day of the first football match outside the United Kingdom which is included in the tournament, and

(b) ending when the last football match outside the United Kingdom which is included in the tournament is finished or cancelled,

but, for the purposes of para. (a), any football match included in the qualifying or pre-qualifying stages of the tournament is to be ignored (s. 14(5) and (6)). An example of a specified 'control period' is the Football Spectators (2018 World Cup Control Period) Order 2017 (SI 2017/1257), which commenced 10 days before the first match in the tournament, and ended when the last match in the tournament was finished or cancelled.

The power under s. 21A requires the police officer to be in uniform and may be exercised only in relation to a person who is a British citizen (see s. 21C(1)).

The initial period of detention allowed is a *maximum* of four hours, extendable to a further *maximum* of six hours by an inspector. There is no requirement under this section that the inspector be either present or in uniform. The purpose of the detention is for the officer to decide whether or not to issue a notice (**see para. 4.10.4.5**).

The condition under s. 14B(2) referred to is that the person has at any time caused or contributed to any violence or disorder in the United Kingdom or elsewhere.

References to football matches include matches intended to be played (s. 14(7)). A person who has been detained under s. 21A(2) may only be further detained under that subsection in the same control period in reliance on information which was not available to the constable who previously detained him/her; and a person on whom a notice has been served under s. 21B(2) may not be detained under s. 21A(2) in the same control period (s. 21A(4)).

4.10.4.5 Summary Measures: Reference to a Court

The Football Spectators Act 1989, s. 21B states:

(1) A constable in uniform may exercise the power in subsection (2) below if authorised to do so by an officer of at least the rank of inspector.

(2) The constable may give the person a notice in writing requiring him—
  (a) to appear before a magistrates' court at a time, or between the times, specified in the notice,
  (b) not to leave England and Wales before that time (or the later of those times), and
  (c) if the control period relates to a regulated football match outside the United Kingdom or to an external tournament which includes such matches, to surrender his passport to the constable

and stating the grounds referred to in section 21A(1) above.

(3) The times for appearance before the magistrates' court must be within the period of 24 hours beginning with—
  (a) the giving of the notice, or
  (b) the person's detention under section 21A(2) above, whichever is the earlier.

KEYNOTE

The power applies during any control period in relation to a regulated football match outside England and Wales or an external tournament (as to which, **see para. 4.10.4.4, Keynote**).

A constable may arrest a person to whom he/she is giving a notice if he/she has reasonable grounds to believe that it is *necessary* to do so in order to ensure that the person complies with the notice (s. 21B(5)).

For the purposes of s. 14B, the notice is to be treated as an application for a banning order made by complaint (s. 21B(4)).

As with the provision for detention under s. 21A, the powers conferred by s. 21B may be exercised only in relation to a person who is a British citizen (s. 21C(1)).

A person who fails to comply with a notice given under s. 21B is guilty of an offence and liable on summary conviction to imprisonment for a term not exceeding six months, or a fine or both (s. 21C(2)).

4.10.5 The Sporting Events (Control of Alcohol etc.) Act 1985

This Act applies to sports grounds and sporting events designated by the Secretary of State. Only football grounds and football matches have been designated at this time. The classes of football matches differ slightly from those contained in the Football Spectators Act 1989 and are contained in the Sports Grounds and Sporting Events (Designation) Order 2005 (SI 2005/3204). The 1985 Act creates a number of offences that are outlined below.

4.10.5.1 Offences in Connection with Alcohol on Coaches and Trains

OFFENCE: **Alcohol on Coaches and Trains—*Sporting Events (Control of Alcohol etc.) Act 1985, s. 1***

  • Triable summarily • Three months' imprisonment and/or a fine (s. 1(3))
  • Fine (s. 1(2) and (4))

The Sporting Events (Control of Alcohol etc.) Act 1985, s. 1 states:

(1) This section applies to a vehicle which—
  (a) is a public service vehicle or railway passenger vehicle, and
  (b) is being used for the principal purpose of carrying passengers for the whole or part of a journey to or from a designated sporting event.
(2) A person who knowingly causes or permits alcohol to be carried on a vehicle to which the section applies is guilty of an offence—
  (a) if the vehicle is a public service vehicle and he is the operator of the vehicle or the servant or agent of the operator, or
  (b) if the vehicle is a hired vehicle and he is the person to whom it is hired or the servant or agent of that person.
(3) A person who has alcohol in his possession while on a vehicle to which this section applies is guilty of an offence.
(4) A person who is drunk on a vehicle to which this section applies is guilty of an offence.

KEYNOTE

Section 1 creates a number of offences in relation to public service vehicles and trains being used principally (though not exclusively) to carry passengers for the whole or part of a journey, to or from a designated sporting event.

The offences can be committed by the vehicle operator/hirer or his/her servant or agent provided there is evidence of *knowingly* causing or permitting the carrying of alcohol.

The other offences are committed by people who have alcohol in their 'possession' and by people who are drunk on a relevant vehicle. Generally, any mature and competent witness may give evidence as to drunkenness.

Section 7(3) provides a power for a police officer to stop a public service vehicle in order to search it where he/she has reasonable grounds to suspect that an offence under this section *is being or has been committed* in respect of that vehicle. It also provides a power to search a railway carriage (though not to stop the train) under the same circumstances. The power to search people in those vehicles comes from s. 7(2). The PACE Code of Practice for the Exercise by Police Officers of Statutory Powers of Stop and Search (Code A) (2014) (see para. 4.1.4) applies to searches under s. 7, i.e. searches of persons, coaches and trains at designated sports grounds or coaches and trains travelling to or from a designated sporting event.

The Licensing Act 2003, s. 157, provides that a magistrates' court may make an order to prohibit the sale of alcohol on trains where it is satisfied that the order is necessary to prevent disorder where an application has been made to the court by a police officer of, or above, the rank of inspector. There is no specific restriction on the period over which such an order may be made. It is a summary offence to knowingly sell, attempt to sell or allow the sale of alcohol in contravention of an order (s. 157(5)).

4.10.5.2 Alcohol on Certain Other Vehicles

OFFENCE: **Alcohol on Other Vehicles—*Sporting Events (Control of Alcohol etc.) Act 1985, s. 1A***

- Triable summarily • Three months' imprisonment and/or a fine (s. 1A(3))
- Fine (s. 1A(2) and (4))

The Sporting Events (Control of Alcohol etc.) Act 1985, s. 1A states:

(1) This section applies to a motor vehicle which—
   (a) is not a public service vehicle but is adapted to carry more than 8 passengers, and
   (b) is being used for the principal purpose of carrying two or more passengers for the whole or part of a journey to or from a designated sporting event.
(2) A person who knowingly causes or permits alcohol to be carried on a motor vehicle to which this section applies is guilty of an offence—
   (a) if he is its driver, or
   (b) if he is not its driver but is its keeper, the servant or agent of its keeper, a person to whom it is made available (by hire, loan or otherwise) by its keeper or the keeper's servant or agent, or the servant or agent of a person to whom it is so made available.
(3) A person who has alcohol in his possession while on a motor vehicle to which this section applies is guilty of an offence.
(4) A person who is drunk on a motor vehicle to which this section applies is guilty of an offence.

KEYNOTE

This section creates similar offences to those set out under s. 1 but these relate to mechanically propelled vehicles that are intended or adapted for use on roads and that are adapted to carry more than eight passengers (not being PSVs).

For the purposes of the above offences, a vehicle's 'keeper' is the person having the duty to take out a vehicle excise licence for it (s. 1A(5)).

The power to stop and search vehicles and their occupants under s. 7(3) above also applies to an offence under this section.

4.10.5.3   **Offences in Connection with Alcohol, Containers etc. at Sports Grounds**

OFFENCE: **Alcohol at Sports Grounds—*Sporting Events (Control of Alcohol etc.)***
Act 1985, s. 2

> • Triable summarily • Three months' imprisonment and/or a fine (s. 2(1))
>
> • Fine (s. 2(2))

The Sporting Events (Control of Alcohol etc.) Act 1985, s. 2 states:

(1)   A person who has alcohol or an article to which this section applies in his possession—

    (a) at any time during the period of a designated sporting event when he is in any area of a designated sports ground from which the event may be directly viewed, or

    (b) while entering or trying to enter a designated sports ground at any time during the period of a designated sporting event at that ground, is guilty of an offence.

(1A) Subsection (1)(a) above has effect subject to section 5A(1) of this Act.

(2)   A person who is drunk in a designated sports ground at any time during the period of a designated sporting event at that ground or is drunk while entering or trying to enter such a ground at any time during the period of a designated sporting event at that ground is guilty of an offence.

KEYNOTE

The articles to which s. 2 applies are:

- articles capable of causing injury to a person struck by them, being
- bottles, cans or other portable containers (including ones that are crushed or broken), which
- are for holding any drink, and
- are of a kind which are normally discarded or returned to/left to be recovered by the supplier when empty,

and include parts of those articles. Any such article that is for holding any medicinal product (within the meaning of the Medicines Act 1968) is excluded from this definition (s. 2(3)).

In relation to s. 2(1) 'the period of a designated sporting event' is provided by s. 9(4) of the Act which states that the period begins two hours before the start of the event or (if earlier) two hours before the time at which it is advertised to start and ending one hour after the end of the event.

In relation to subs. (1A) above, special provision is made by s. 5A(1) for private rooms from which the sporting event can be viewed.

A constable may, at any time during the period of a designated sporting event at any designated sports ground, enter any part of the ground for the purpose of enforcing the provisions of this Act, and search a person he/she has reasonable grounds to suspect is committing or has committed an offence under this Act (s. 7(1) and (2)).

Where a person is convicted of an offence under either s. 2(1) or (2) the court must consider imposing a banning order.

4.10.5.4   **Fireworks, Flares and Similar Objects at Sports Grounds and Events**

OFFENCE: **Having Fireworks, Flares etc.—*Sporting Events (Control of Alcohol***
etc.) Act 1985, s. 2A

> • Triable summarily • Three months' imprisonment and/or a fine

The Sporting Events (Control of Alcohol etc.) Act 1985, s. 2A states:

(1) A person is guilty of an offence if he has an article or substance to which this section applies in his possession—

    (a) at any time during the period of a designated sporting event when he is in any area of a designated sports ground from which the event may be directly viewed, or

    (b) while entering or trying to enter a designated sports ground at any time during the period of a designated sporting event at the ground.

(2) ...

(3) This section applies to any article or substance whose main purpose is the emission of a flare for purposes of illuminating or signalling (as opposed to igniting or heating) or the emission of smoke or a visible gas; and in particular it applies to distress flares, fog signals, and pellets and capsules intended to be used as fumigators or for testing pipes, but not to matches, cigarette lighters or heaters.

(4) This section also applies to any article which is a firework.

KEYNOTE

There is a defence under s. 2A(2) for the person to prove that he/she had possession of the article or substance with lawful authority. 'Possession' is quite a broad concept going beyond 'carrying'.

As with the offence under s. 2 (**see para. 4.10.5.3**), the powers of entry, search and arrest under s. 7 also apply to this offence as does the time period under s. 9(4).

4.10.6　Ticket Touts

OFFENCE: **Ticket Touts—*Criminal Justice and Public Order Act 1994, s. 166***

　　　• Triable summarily • Fine

The Criminal Justice and Public Order Act 1994, s. 166 states:

(1) It is an offence for an unauthorised person to—
　　(a) sell a ticket for a designated football match, or
　　(b) otherwise to dispose of such a ticket to another person.
(2) For this purpose—
　　(a) a person is 'unauthorised' unless he is authorised in writing to sell or otherwise dispose of tickets for the match by the organisers of the match;
　　(aa) a reference to selling a ticket includes a reference to—
　　　　(i) offering to sell a ticket;
　　　　(ii) exposing a ticket for sale;
　　　　(iii) making a ticket available for sale by another;
　　　　(iv) advertising that a ticket is available for purchase; and
　　　　(v) giving a ticket to a person who pays or agrees to pay for some other goods or services or offering to do so;
　　(b) a 'ticket' means anything which purports to be a ticket; and
　　(c) a 'designated football match' means a football match of a description, or a particular football match, for the time being designated for the purposes of this section by order made by the Secretary of State.

KEYNOTE

Section 32 of the Police and Criminal Evidence Act 1984 (search of persons and premises (including vehicles) upon arrest) shall have effect, in its application in relation to an offence under this section, as if the power conferred on a constable to enter and search any vehicle extended to any vehicle which the constable has reasonable grounds for believing was being used for any purpose connected with the offence (s. 166(5)).

The Breaching of Limits on Ticket Sales Regulations 2018 (SI 2018/735) provide a new summary offence of purchasing tickets for a recreational, sporting or cultural event using 'bots' (a web robot) in excess of conditions made by the event organiser that set a maximum number of tickets that a purchaser may buy. It is also an offence for a person to use software that is designed to enable or facilitate completion of any part of the process, with intent to obtain tickets in excess of the sales limit and with a view to any person obtaining financial gain. The offence is committed whether the offer of tickets is made, or anything is done, to obtain the tickets, in or outside the UK.

4.11 | Hatred and Harassment Offences

4.11.1 Introduction

The law in relation to offences involving hatred and harassment has been subject to considerable development in recent times. The result is a wide-ranging set of offences and powers that enable appropriate action to be taken in relation to such activity and, in certain circumstances, to protect against such activity occurring in the first place.

4.11.2 Offences Involving Racial, Religious or Sexual Orientation Hatred

Offences involving racial, religious or sexual orientation hatred are dealt with by the Public Order Act 1986. This section provides a summary of these offences which are aimed at addressing incidents specifically motivated by racial hatred, religious hatred or hatred on the grounds of sexual orientation.

For the purposes of the offences contrary to ss. 18 to 23 of the 1986 Act, 'racial hatred' means hatred against a group of persons defined by reference to colour, race, nationality (including citizenship) or ethnic or national origins (s. 17).

For the purposes of offences contrary to ss. 29B to 29G of the 1986 Act, 'religious hatred' means hatred against a group of persons defined by reference to religious belief or lack of religious belief (s. 29A).

Section 29AB of the 1986 Act defines 'hatred on the grounds of sexual orientation'. The definition covers hatred against a group of persons defined by reference to their sexual orientation, be they heterosexual, homosexual or bi-sexual.

4.11.2.1 Use of Words, Behaviour or Display of Written Material

OFFENCE: **Use of Words or Behaviour or Display of Written Material—*Public Order Act 1986, s. 18***

- Triable either way • Seven years' imprisonment and/or a fine on indictment
- Six months' imprisonment and/or a fine summarily

The Public Order Act 1986, s. 18 states:

(1) A person who uses threatening, abusive or insulting words or behaviour, or displays any written material which is threatening, abusive or insulting, is guilty of an offence if—
  (a) he intends thereby to stir up racial hatred, or
  (b) having regard to all the circumstances racial hatred is likely to be stirred up thereby.
(2) An offence under this section may be committed in a public or a private place, except that no offence is committed where the words or behaviour are used, or the written material is displayed, by a person inside a dwelling and are not heard or seen except by other persons in that or another dwelling.

KEYNOTE

This, and the other offences under ss. 19, 29B and 29C, may not be prosecuted without the consent of the Attorney-General (or Solicitor-General).

This offence does not apply to broadcasts in a programme (but **see para. 4.11.3**) and there are exemptions in the case of fair and accurate reports of parliamentary or court proceedings.

4.11.2.2   Defence

The Public Order Act 1986, s. 18 states:

> (4) In proceedings for an offence under this section it is a defence for the accused to prove that he was inside a dwelling and had no reason to believe that the words or behaviour used, or the written material displayed, would be heard or seen by a person outside that or any other dwelling.

4.11.2.3   Publishing or Distributing Written Material

OFFENCE: **Publishing or Distributing Written Material—*Public Order Act 1986, s. 19***

- • Triable either way • Seven years' imprisonment and/or a fine on indictment
- • Six months' imprisonment and/or a fine summarily

The Public Order Act 1986, s. 19 states:

> (1) A person who publishes or distributes written material which is threatening, abusive or insulting is guilty of an offence if—
>   (a) he intends thereby to stir up racial hatred, or
>   (b) having regard to all the circumstances racial hatred is likely to be stirred up thereby.
> (2) ...
> (3) References in this Part to the publication or distribution of written material are to its publication or distribution to the public or a section of the public.

4.11.2.4   Defence

The Public Order Act 1986, s. 19 states:

> (2) In proceedings for an offence under this section it is a defence for an accused who is not shown to have intended to stir up racial hatred to prove that he was not aware of the content of the material and did not suspect, and had no reason to suspect, that it was threatening, abusive or insulting.

4.11.2.5   Use of Words, Behaviour or Display of Written Material

OFFENCE: **Use of Words or Behaviour or Display of Written Material—*Public Order Act 1986, s. 29B***

- • Triable either way • Not exceeding seven years' imprisonment and/or a fine on indictment • Not exceeding six months' imprisonment and/or a fine summarily

The Public Order Act 1986, s. 29B states:

> (1) A person who uses threatening words or behaviour, or displays any written material which is threatening, is guilty of an offence if he intends thereby to stir up religious hatred or hatred on the grounds of sexual orientation.
> (2) An offence under this section is committed in a public or private place, except that no offence is committed where the words or behaviour are used, or the written material is displayed, by a

person inside a dwelling and are not heard or seen except by other persons in that or another dwelling.

KEYNOTE

The defences available to the offence under s. 18 apply to this particular section (no reason to believe the words or behaviour, etc., would be heard or seen outside the dwelling (s. 29B(4)), or where used solely for the purpose of being included in a programming service (s. 29B(5)).

Section 29J of the Act provides that the offences of stirring up religious hatred are not intended to limit or restrict discussion, criticism or expressions of antipathy, dislike, ridicule or insult or abuse of particular religions or belief systems or lack of religion or of the beliefs and practices of those who hold such beliefs or to apply to persons newly converted to a religious faith, evangelism or the seeking to convert people to a particular belief or to cease holding a belief.

In relation to the sexual orientation element of these offences the relevant act (namely, words, behaviour, written material or recordings or programme) must be threatening, and the offender must intend thereby to stir up hatred on the grounds of sexual orientation.

4.11.2.6   **Publishing or Distributing Material**

OFFENCE: **Publishing or Distributing Written Material—*Public Order Act 1986, s. 29C***

> • Triable either way • Not exceeding seven years' imprisonment and/or a fine on indictment • Not exceeding six months' imprisonment and/or a fine summarily

The Public Order Act 1986, s. 29C states:

(1) A person who publishes or distributes written material which is threatening is guilty of an offence if he intends thereby to stir up religious hatred or hatred on the grounds of sexual orientation.

(2) References in this Part to the publication or distribution of written material are to its publication or distribution to the public or a section of the public.

KEYNOTE

The offences under ss. 29B and 29C differ from the offences of stirring up racial hatred in part 3 of the 1986 Act, in two respects. First, the offences apply only to 'threatening' words or behaviour, rather than 'threatening, abusive or insulting' words or behaviour. Secondly, the offences apply only to words or behaviour if the accused 'intends' to stir up religious hatred or hatred on grounds of sexual orientation, rather than if hatred is either intentional or 'likely' to be stirred up.

4.11.3   **Harassment and Stalking**

There is a significant amount of material to examine in relation to the offences associated with harassment and stalking under the Protection from Harassment Act 1997. To aid understanding, the offences have been broken down into their component parts and follow the below order:

• Harassment contrary to ss. 1 and 2 of the Act (**see para. 4.11.4**). This section includes the law in relation to injunctions and restraining orders
• Putting people in fear of violence contrary to s. 4 of the Act (**see para. 4.11.5**)
• Stalking contrary to s. 2A of the Act and stalking involving fear of violence etc. contrary to s. 4A of the Act (**see para. 4.11.6**).

4.11.4　The Harassment Offences

OFFENCE: **Harassment—*Protection from Harassment Act 1997, ss. 1 and 2***
- Triable summarily • Six months' imprisonment and/or a fine

OFFENCE: **Racially or Religiously Aggravated Harassment—*Crime and Disorder Act 1998, s. 32(1)(a)***
- Triable either way • Two years' imprisonment and/or a fine on indictment
- Six months' imprisonment and/or a fine summarily

The Protection from Harassment Act 1997, ss. 1 and 2 state:

1.—(1) A person must not pursue a course of conduct—
　(a) which amounts to harassment of another, and
　(b) which he knows or ought to know amounts to harassment of the other.

(1A)　A person must not pursue a course of conduct—
　(a) which involves harassment of two or more persons, and
　(b) which he knows or ought to know involves harassment of those persons, and
　(c) by which he intends to persuade any person (whether or not one of those mentioned above)—
　　(i) not to do something that he is entitled or required to do, or
　　(ii) to do something that he is not under any obligation to do.
　　…

2.—(1) A person who pursues a course of conduct in breach of section 1(1) or (1A) is guilty of an offence.

4.11.4.1　'Person' and Companies

'Person' here does not include companies or corporate bodies and therefore they cannot be the victim of harassment or apply for injunctions under this part of the legislation. However, an individual employee or a clearly defined group of individuals could be such a victim (*DPP* v *Dziurzynski* [2002] EWHC 1380 (Admin)) and as such they can apply for injunctions (*Daiichi UK Ltd* v *(1) Stop Huntingdon Cruelty, and (2) Animal Liberation Front* [2003] EWHC 2337 (QB)). For injunctions relating to companies, **see para. 4.11.4.10.**

In *Majrowski* v *Guy's and St Thomas' NHS Trust* [2005] EWCA Civ 251, the Court of Appeal held that a company could be a 'person' capable of harassing 'another' within the meaning of the Act. This ruling could therefore have implications in relation to the self-employed, customers and suppliers of businesses and members of the public in general. Where it can be shown that the conduct was carried out in the course of employment the employer could be held to be vicariously liable for that conduct.

4.11.4.2　'Course of Conduct'

The 'course of conduct' by a person is defined under s. 7 of the Act which states:

(3)　A 'course of conduct' must involve—
　(a) in the case of conduct in relation to a single person (see s. 1(1)), conduct on at least two occasions in relation to that person, or
　(b) in the case of conduct in relation to two or more persons (see s. 1(1A)), conduct on at least one occasion in relation to each of those persons.

(3A) A person's conduct on any occasion shall be taken, if aided, abetted, counselled or procured by another—
　(a) to be conduct on that occasion of the other (as well as conduct of the person whose conduct it is); and
　(b) to be conduct in relation to which the other's knowledge and purpose, and what he ought to have known, are the same as they were in relation to what was contemplated or reasonably foreseeable at the time of the aiding, abetting, counselling or procuring.

(4) 'Conduct' includes speech.

(5) References to a person, in the context of the harassment of a person, are references to a person who is an individual.

KEYNOTE

The definition of a 'course of conduct' in s. 7 is an inclusive but not exhaustive list.

It appears that doing something remotely which has the desired effect on the victim, such as deliberately making a dog bark at someone, could form part of a 'course of conduct' for the purposes of an offence under the 1997 Act (*R (On the Application of Taffurelli) v DPP* [2004] EWHC 2791 (Admin)). However, simply *failing* to stop a dog barking is a different matter and one that the Divisional Court in *Taffurelli* did not resolve.

4.11.4.3   'Harassment'

'Harassment' includes alarming the person or causing him/her distress (s. 7(2) of the 1997 Act). The inclusion of harm and distress is significant as it has been held that a person, in this case a police officer, can be alarmed for the safety of another (*Lodge* v *DPP* [1989] COD 179). Although the words used in s. 7 are 'alarm *and* distress', the Divisional Court has held that they should be taken disjunctively and not conjunctively, that is, the court need only be satisfied that the behaviour involved one or the other; alarm *or* distress (*DPP* v *Ramsdale* [2001] EWHC Admin 106).

4.11.4.4   The s. 1(1A) Offence

The s. 1(1A) offence was introduced specifically to protect employees working for certain companies from harassment by animal rights protestors. Because of the courts' strict interpretation of the elements of the s. 1 offence (as discussed above) it was unclear how far such employees could be protected by this provision when they had not previously been harassed *individually* even where fellow employees had been. Section 1(1A) makes it an offence for a person to pursue a course of conduct involving the harassment of two or more people on separate occasions which the defendant knows or ought to know involves harassment. The purpose of such harassment is to persuade *any person* (not necessarily one of the people being harassed) not to do something he/she is entitled to do (such as going to work) or to do something he/she is not under any obligation to do (such as releasing animals or passing on confidential information).

The sort of behaviour envisaged by the offence would be the making of threats and intimidation which forces an individual or individuals to stop doing lawful business with another company or with another person. The subsection is not intended to outlaw peaceful protesting or lobbying. For instance, a person simply distributing leaflets outside a shop would not commit this offence unless they threatened or intimidated the people to whom they were handing their leaflets and that person felt harassed, alarmed or distressed. There would also need to be at least two separate incidents amounting to 'a course of conduct'.

KEYNOTE

Examples of 'course of conduct' in relation to s. 1(1A) are provided in Home Office Circular 34/2005 and include:

• Where an animal rights extremist sends a threatening letter on one occasion to an individual who works for a company and the same extremist sends a threatening email on another occasion to another individual who works for the same company, and his intention is to persuade the individuals that they should not work for that company because of the work that company does, or the contract that it has with other companies, he would commit an offence.

> • Where an animal rights extremist sends a threatening letter on one occasion to an individual who works for company A and the same extremist sends a threatening email on another occasion to another individual who works for company B, and his intention is to persuade the individuals that they should not work for these companies because both companies supply company C, or he intends by his actions to persuade companies A and B not to supply company C, he would commit an offence. In both these examples, if the letters or emails were sent by separate extremists, yet it could be proved that they were acting together, they both would be guilty of an offence. Additionally, under the new s. 3A both an individual employee or a company can apply for an injunction (see para. 4.11.4.10).

4.11.4.5 General Points

Not all courses of conduct will satisfy the offence of harassment. *Lau* v *DPP* [2000] 1 FLR 799 involved a battery (slapping across the face) against the complainant on one occasion, followed sometime later by a threat being made to the complainant's boyfriend in her presence. The court held that the evidence of a 'course of conduct' by the defendant was insufficient to convict. It stated that regard should be had to the number of incidents and the relative times when they took place; the fewer the incidents and the further apart in time that they took place, the less likely it was that a court would find that harassment had taken place.

There are some incidents that do not amount to harassment. Where a defendant approached the victim to strike up conversations and had sent her a gift, this was insufficient to constitute harassment. However, such incidents could provide a background to later behaviour that included covertly filming the victim and rummaging through her rubbish (*King* v *DPP* [2001] ACD 7).

On occasions the courts have accepted that two instances of behaviour by the defendant several months apart will suffice. Where a defendant wrote two threatening letters to a member of the Benefits Agency staff, he was convicted of harassment even though there had been four and a half months' interval between the two letters (*Baron* v *CPS* (2000) 13 June, unreported). The opposite course of conduct was found to amount to harassment where a defendant made several calls to the victim's mobile phone in the space of five minutes. In this case several abusive and threatening messages were left on the victim's voicemail facility and later replayed one after the other (*Kelly* v *DPP* [2002] EWHC 1428 (Admin)). The court held that it was enough that the victim was alarmed or distressed by the course of conduct as a whole rather than by each act making up the course of conduct. This is a different requirement from the more serious offence under s. 4 where the victim must be caused to fear violence on at least two occasions. In relation to that more serious offence, a magistrates' court has been allowed to regard a defendant's conduct on the second occasion as almost retrospectively affecting previous conduct on the first occasion.

There is no specific requirement that the activity making up the course of conduct be of the same nature. Therefore two distinctly different types of behaviour by the defendant (e.g. making a telephone call on one occasion and damaging the victim's property on another) may suffice. In a case involving the racially or religiously aggravated offence, the aggravating element will need to be proved in relation to both instances of the defendant's conduct.

Some behaviour will be sufficiently disturbing or alarming for two instances alone to suffice (e.g. the making of overt threats). Other behaviour, however, may not be sufficient to establish 'harassment' after only two occasions (e.g. the sending of flowers and gifts) and may require more than the bare statutory minimum of two occasions.

Although it may be helpful in terms of proving the occurrence of two or more acts amounting to 'a course of conduct', the practice in some police areas of issuing warnings and maintaining a register of the same (particularly in relation to their own officers) is not a specific requirement of the Act and may raise some issues of procedural fairness.

The repeated commission of other offences (say, public order offences or offences against property) involving the same victim may also amount to harassment. In such cases the advice of the CPS should be sought as to which charge(s) to prefer.

To recap the s. 1 offence, you must prove that:

- the 'person' pursued a 'course of conduct' and
- the 'course of conduct' amounted to 'harassment'.

The final element required to prove the offence is that the defendant knew, or ought to have known, that his/her conduct amounted to harassment.

To avoid the practical difficulties of proving the subjective intention of the defendant, the offence focuses on an *objective test*.

4.11.4.6 What a Reasonable Person Would Think Amounts to Harassment

In addition, s. 1 of the 1997 Act states:

> (2) For the purposes of this section, the person whose course of conduct is in question ought to know that it amounts to or involves harassment of another if a reasonable person in possession of the same information would think the course of conduct amounted to or involved harassment of the other.

KEYNOTE

Section 1(2) requires the jury/court to consider whether the defendant ought to have known that his/her conduct amounted to or involved harassment by the *objective* test of what a 'reasonable person' would think. Section 1(3)(c) also imposes an objective test as to whether that conduct was reasonable in the judgment of the jury/court. As a result, the Court of Appeal has held that no characteristics of the defendant can be attached to the word 'reasonable' (*R* v *Colohan* [2001] EWCA Crim 1251).

Although the defendant's mental illness may be relevant to sentence, the protective and preventive nature of the Act together with the objective nature of the tests above means that such illness does not provide a defence.

4.11.4.7 Aiding and Abetting

If someone aids, abets, counsels or procures another to commit an offence under the 1997 Act, the conduct of the 'primary' defendant will be taken to be the conduct of the aider, abettor, counsellor or procurer of the offence. This does not prevent the primary defendant's conduct from being relevant; what it does is to make the aider, abettor, etc. of the offence liable for the conduct which he/she has facilitated. The Act also makes provision for determining the knowledge and intention of aiders, abettors, etc. and although this is referred to as 'collective harassment', it overlaps with the concept of incomplete offences (**see *Crime*, chapter 1.3**) and the advice of the CPS should be sought in formulating appropriate charges.

4.11.4.8 Defences

If the person concerned in the course of conduct can show that he/she did so:

- for the purpose of preventing or detecting crime, or
- under any enactment or rule of law to comply with a particular condition or requirement, or
- in circumstances whereby the course of conduct was reasonable,

the offence under s. 1(1) and (1A) will not apply (s. 1(3)).

The burden of proving any of these features or circumstances lies with the defendant (on the balance of probabilities). Examples might be police or DSS surveillance teams, or court officers serving summonses.

Whether a course of conduct is 'reasonable' will be a question of fact for a court to decide in the light of all the circumstances. The wording of s. 1(2) suggests that such a test is an *objective* one (i.e. as a reasonable bystander) and not one based upon the particular belief or perception of the defendant, otherwise the main effect of the 1997 Act would be considerably diluted.

KEYNOTE

In *KD* v *Chief Constable of Hampshire* [2005] EWHC 2550 (QB) a police officer obtained from a female interviewee, over the course of several visits to her home, detailed explicit information about her sexual conduct. The interviewee was the mother of a complainant who had been allegedly raped and assaulted. The court held that the information obtained was not for the purpose of preventing or detecting crime under s. 1(3)(a) but to satisfy the officer's lewd interest.

4.11.4.9 **Injunctions and Restraining Orders**

The courts have two significant sources of power available to them to deal with harassment under the 1997 Act. These are injunctions and restraining orders. Injunctions are issued in the ordinary way of any civil injunction whereas restraining orders follow a *conviction* for an offence under ss. 2 or 4 (**see para 4.11.5**) of the Act.

4.11.4.10 **Injunctions**

Under ss. 3 and 3A of the Protection from Harassment Act 1997, the High Court or a county court may issue an injunction in respect of civil proceedings brought in respect of an actual or apprehended breach of s. 1(1) and (1A). The effect of this is that a defendant may be made the subject of an injunction even though his/her behaviour has not amounted to an offence under the 1997 Act.

Section 3 also states:

(3) Where—
    (a) in such proceedings the High Court or a county court grants an injunction for the purpose of restraining the defendant from pursuing any conduct which amounts to harassment, and
    (b) the plaintiff considers that the defendant has done anything which he is prohibited from doing by the injunction, the plaintiff may apply for the issue of a warrant for the arrest of the defendant.

The person who is the victim of the offence under s. 1(1A) or any person at whom the persuasion is aimed, may apply for an injunction. Therefore, where people who work for a life science or fur company are being harassed in order to persuade them not to work for that company, or in order to persuade the company not to supply another company, either the employees themselves or the company in question could apply for an injunction.

Section 3A states:

(1) This section applies where there is an actual or apprehended breach of section 1(1A) by any person ('the relevant person').
(2) In such a case—
    (a) any person who is or may be a victim of the course of conduct in question, or
    (b) any person who is or may be a person falling within section 1(1A)(c),
    may apply to the High Court or the county court for an injunction restraining the relevant person from pursuing any conduct which amounts to harassment in relation to any person or persons mentioned or described in the injunction.
(3) Sections 3(3) to (9) apply in relation to an injunction granted under subsection (2) above as they apply in relation to an injunction granted as mentioned in section 3(3)(a).

KEYNOTE

Anyone arrested under a warrant issued under s. 3(3)(b) may be dealt with by the court at the time of his/her appearance. Alternatively, the court may adjourn the proceedings and release the defendant, dealing with him/her within 14 days of his/her arrest provided the defendant is given not less than two days' notice of the adjourned hearing (Rules of the Supreme Court (Amendment) 1998 (SI 1998/1898) and the County Court (Amendment) Rules 1998 (SI 1998/1899)).

In a case involving an injunction restraining the actions of an anti-vivisection group, the Divisional Court held that the 1997 Act was not a means of preventing individuals from exercising their right to protest over issues of public interest. Such an extension of the law had clearly not been Parliament's intention and the courts would resist any attempts to interpret the Act widely (*Huntingdon Life Sciences Ltd* v *Curtin* (1997) *The Times*, 11 December).

The application for an injunction is essentially a private matter being pursued by an individual. The point at which the matter becomes of concern to policing is where the injunction is breached without reasonable excuse. The civil standard of proof (balance of probabilities) will apply to injunction applications (*Hipgrave* v *Jones* [2004] EWHC 2901 (QB)).

In harassment cases the High Court can grant a provisional injunction under s. 37(1) of the Senior Courts Act 1981. This injunction can restrain conduct which is not in itself tortious or unlawful but is reasonably necessary to protect the legitimate interests of others. This includes the power to impose an exclusion zone when granting a non-molestation injunction (*Burris* v *Azadani* [1995] 1 WLR 1372). However in *Hall* v *Save Newchurch Guinea Pigs (Campaign)* [2005] EWHC 372 (QB), the court held that a 200 km² exclusion zone was not reasonably necessary for the protection of the protected person's rights.

4.11.4.11   Breach of Injunctions

OFFENCE: **Breach of Injunction—*Protection from Harassment Act 1997, s. 3(6)***
- • Triable either way • Five years' imprisonment and/or a fine on indictment
- • Six months' imprisonment and/or a fine summarily

The Protection from Harassment Act 1997, s. 3 states:

(6) Where—
  (a) the High Court or a county court grants an injunction for the purpose mentioned in sub-section (3)(a), and
  (b) without reasonable ...
  he is guilty of an offence.

KEYNOTE

Civil injunctions generally will only involve the police where a power of an arrest has been attached (e.g. under s. 3(3) above). In these cases the role of the police will be to bring the defendant before the court in order that he/she can explain his/her behaviour. There is therefore no investigative or prosecuting function on the part of the officers. Section 3(6), however, creates a specific offence of breaching the terms of an injunction.

If a defendant breaches an injunction and commits the offence under s. 3(6), he/she will be dealt with in the way of any other prisoner brought into police detention and will face a prison sentence of five years.

4.11.4.12   Civil Claims for Harassment

Under s. 3(1) conduct or apprehended conduct falling within s. 1(1) and (1A) may be the subject of a civil claim by the victim/intended victim. This creates a 'statutory tort' of harassment in addition to the criminal offence.

4.11.4.13 Restraining Orders

The Protection from Harassment Act 1997, s. 5 states:

(2) The order may, for the purpose of protecting the victim or victims of the offence, or any other person mentioned in the order, from conduct which—
(a) amounts to harassment, or
(b) will cause a fear of violence,
prohibit the defendant from doing anything described in the order.

Section 5A of the Act enables the courts in England and Wales to impose a restraining order, when sentencing for any offence, for the purpose of protecting a person from conduct which amounts to harassment or will cause a fear of violence (**see para. 4.11.5**) by the defendant. The court will be able to make a restraining order on acquittal for any offence where it considers it necessary to protect a person from harassment. Any person mentioned in the restraining order has the right to make a representation if an application is made to vary or discharge the restraining order (equivalent powers are available in respect of Northern Ireland).

KEYNOTE

Unlike the injunction under s. 3(3), restraining orders can be made in a criminal court.

The order may be made for the protection of the victim or anyone else mentioned and it may run for a specified period or until a further order. Any order must identify by name the parties it is intended to protect (*R* v *Mann* (2000) 97(14) LSG 41).

In a case arising out of protests against fur retailers, the Divisional Court held that restraining orders under the 1997 Act did not generally breach the right to freedom of speech and association as protected by Articles 10 and 11 of the European Convention on Human Rights (*Silverton* v *Gravett* (2001) LTL 31 October).

The prosecutor, the defendant or anyone else mentioned in the order may apply to the court that made it to have the order varied or discharged (s. 5(4)). The courts have the power to vary an order made for a specified period of time so as to extend the expiry date of the order (*DPP* v *Hall* [2005] EWHC 2612 (Admin)). In *R* v *Debnath* [2005] EWCA Crim 3472 an order prohibiting an offender from publishing information indefinitely was held to be lawful and not in breach of Article 10 (Freedom of Expression) of the European Convention on Human Rights.

An example of how restraining orders can operate can be seen in *R* v *Evans (Dorothy)* [2004] EWCA 3102. In that case the appellant had been convicted of harassing her neighbours and a restraining order under s. 5(5) had been made by the court. Among other things, the order prohibited the appellant from 'using abusive words or actions' towards her neighbours. Some time into the life of the order, the neighbour called a plumber out to their house and he parked his van in the street. It was alleged that the appellant then moved her own car, which was also parked in the street, into such a position that it effectively blocked the plumber's van. The appellant was convicted of the offence of breaching the order and appealed, partly on the basis that her conduct could not properly be said to have amounted to 'abusive action'. The Court of Appeal held that such matters should be approached in the same way as specific legislation which outlaws abusive conduct, and that a jury was entitled to conclude that, as she had been motivated by spite, the appellant's actions could be 'abusive' for this purpose.

4.11.4.14 Breach of Restraining Order

OFFENCE: **Breach of Restraining Order—*Protection from Harassment Act 1997, s. 5(5)***

- Triable either way • Five years' imprisonment and/or a fine on indictment
- Six months' imprisonment and/or a fine summarily

The Protection from Harassment Act 1997, s. 5 states:

(5) If without reasonable excuse the defendant does anything which he is prohibited from doing by an order under this section, he is guilty of an offence.

KEYNOTE

The above offence is one of strict liability and therefore whether the defendant believed that the order was no longer in force is only relevant to the extent that he/she may have a reasonable excuse (*Barber* v *CPS* [2004] EWHC 2605 (Admin)). The prosecution needs simply to prove the existence and terms of the order (which it can do by an admission from the defendant in interview) and the doing of anything prohibited by it. Once that is done the offence is complete.

In the case of *R* v *Evans (Dorothy)* [2004] EWCA Crim 3102, the Court of Appeal held that harassment takes many forms and therefore the courts need to be able to prohibit conduct in fairly wide terms (e.g. in the wording of the order). It is, however, unclear just how far the defendant's subjective understanding of the terms of the order will be relevant. If a defendant honestly believed that his/her conduct did not breach the terms of the order, this would certainly be relevant when considering whether or not he/she had a 'reasonable excuse'.

Substituting or failing to include a charge under ss. 2 or 4 removes the court's powers to make a restraining order which may be the main remedy sought by a victim. In any cases of doubt the guidance of the CPS should be sought.

4.11.5 Putting People in Fear of Violence

OFFENCE: **Putting People in Fear of Violence—*Protection from Harassment Act 1997, s. 4***

- Triable either way • 10 years' imprisonment and/or a fine on indictment
- Six months' imprisonment and/or a fine summarily

OFFENCE: **Racially or Religiously Aggravated—*Crime and Disorder Act 1998, s. 32(1)(b)***

- Triable either way
- 14 years' imprisonment and/or a fine on indictment
- Six months' imprisonment and/or a fine summarily

The Protection from Harassment Act 1997, s. 4 states:

(1) A person whose course of conduct causes another to fear, on at least two occasions, that violence will be used against him is guilty of an offence if he knows or ought to know that his course of conduct will cause the other so to fear on each of those occasions.

KEYNOTE

'Course of conduct' is discussed above.

The defendant's course of conduct must cause the victim to fear that violence *will* (rather than might) be used against *him or her* (rather than someone else) so:

- showing that the conduct caused the victim to be seriously frightened of what *might happen* in the future is not enough (*R* v *Henley* [2000] Crim LR 582);
- causing a person to fear, on at least two occasions, that violence would be used against a member of their family is not enough (*Mohammed Ali Caurti* v *DPP* [2001] EWHC Admin 867).

The defendant must know, or ought to know that their conduct will cause the other person to fear violence. This may be shown by any previous conversations or communications between the defendant and the victim, together with the victim's response to the defendant's earlier behaviour (e.g. running away, calling the police, etc.).

The fear of violence being used against the victim must be present on both occasions. If it is present on one occasion but not the other, the offence under s. 2 above may be appropriate. This is not necessarily as straightforward as it may seem. What if the defendant's conduct on the first occasion (e.g. a threat to burn the victim's house down) did not cause the victim undue concern, but a second threat some time later to do the same thing *did* put the victim in fear of violence, partly because this was the second time the threat had been made? These were the circumstances in *R (On the Application of A)* v *DPP* [2004] EWHC 2454 (Admin), where the defendant argued that the victim had only been put in fear of violence by his threats to burn her house down on the second occasion and that therefore the offence had not been made out. The Divisional Court disagreed and held that the magistrates were entitled to find as a matter of fact that the two incidents had put the victim in fear of violence, notwithstanding her admission that, on the first occasion, she had not been too concerned.

Unlike some of the other racially or religiously aggravated offences, provisions are specifically made for alternative verdicts in relation to harassment (s. 32(6) of the Crime and Disorder Act 1998). Where the racially or religiously aggravated form of the offence is charged, the aggravating element of the defendant's conduct must be shown in relation to both instances.

As with the s. 2 offence, a single instance of behaviour may be enough to support a charge for another offence.

This offence is not one of *intent* but one which is subject to a test of reasonableness against the standard of an ordinary person in possession of the same information as the defendant.

For the powers of a court to issue a restraining order in relation to this offence, see para. 4.11.4.13.

The Protection from Harassment Act 1997, s. 4 goes on to state:

(2) For the purposes of this section, the person whose course of conduct is in question ought to know that it will cause another to fear that violence will be used against him on any occasion if a reasonable person in possession of the same information would think the course of conduct would cause the other so to fear on that occasion.

4.11.5.1 Defence

The Protection from Harassment Act 1997, s. 4 states:

(3) It is a defence for a person charged with an offence under this section to show that—
   (a) his course of conduct was pursued for the purpose of preventing or detecting crime,
   (b) his course of conduct was pursued under any enactment or rule of law or to comply with any condition or requirement imposed by any person under any enactment, or
   (c) the pursuit of his course of conduct was reasonable for the protection of himself or another or for the protection of his or another's property.

KEYNOTE

There is a slight difference in the wording of the defence when compared with that under s. 1(3) above. There, the defendant may show that his/her conduct was reasonable in the particular circumstances. In relation to the offence under s. 4, the defendant must show that his/her conduct was reasonable *for the protection of him/herself, another person or his/her own/another's property*. These are the only grounds on which the defendant may argue reasonableness in answer to a charge under s. 4. He/she could not therefore argue, say, that the pursuit of the course of conduct was 'reasonable' in order to enforce a debt or to communicate with the victim.

In addition, s. 12 allows for the Secretary of State to certify that the conduct was carried out by a 'specified person' on a 'specified occasion' related to:

• national security,
• the economic well-being of the United Kingdom, or
• the prevention or detection of serious crime,

on behalf of the Crown. If such a certification is made, the conduct of the specified person will not be an offence under the 1997 Act.

4.11.6   The Stalking Offences

The Protection of Freedoms Act 2012 created the specific offence of 'stalking' and inserted the below offences into the Protection from Harassment Act 1997.

4.11.6.1   The Offence of Stalking

OFFENCE: **Stalking—*Protection from Harassment Act 1997, s. 2A***

> • Triable summarily • Six months' imprisonment and/or a fine

OFFENCE: **Racially or Religiously Aggravated Stalking—*Crime and Disorder Act 1998, s. 32(1)(a)***

> • Triable either way • Two years' imprisonment and/or a fine on indictment
> • Six months' imprisonment and/or a fine summarily

The Protection from Harassment Act 1997, s. 2A states:

> (1) A person is guilty of an offence if—
>   (a) the person pursues a course of conduct in breach of s. 1(1), and
>   (b) the course of conduct amounts to stalking.

For the purposes of the offence under s. 2A (and also the following offence under s. 4A below), a course of conduct amounts to stalking of another person if:

- it amounts to harassment of that person (under s. 7(2) of the Protection from Harassment Act 1997, references to harassing a person include alarming the person or causing the person distress);
- the acts or omissions involved are ones associated with stalking; and
- the person whose course of conduct it is knows or ought to know that the course of conduct amounts to harassment of the other person.

KEYNOTE

What is 'Stalking'?

Section 2A(3) lists examples of behaviours associated with stalking. The list is not exhaustive but gives an indication of the types of behaviour that may be displayed in a stalking offence. The listed behaviours are:

- following a person;
- contacting, or attempting to contact, a person by any means;
- publishing any statement or other material (i) relating or purporting to relate to a person, or (ii) purporting to originate from a person;
- monitoring the use by a person of the internet, email or any other form of electronic communication;
- loitering in any place (whether public or private);
- interfering with any property in the possession of a person;
- watching or spying on a person.

Section 2A does not include a specific defence for stalking. However, because an offence of stalking can only be established where an offence of harassment has occurred, a person charged with an offence under s. 2A could rely on the defence to harassment under s. 1(3) (see para. 4.11.4.8).

Under s. 2B of the Act the police have a power of entry in relation to the s. 2A stalking offence. A constable can apply to a justice of the peace, who may issue a warrant authorising entry and search of premises providing there are reasonable grounds to believe the conditions in s. 2B are met. A constable may seize and retain anything for which a search was authorised, and may use reasonable force, if necessary, in the exercise of any power conferred by s. 2B.

Stalking Involving Fear of Violence or Serious Alarm or Distress

OFFENCE: **Stalking Involving Fear of Violence or Serious Alarm or Distress—**
Protection from Harassment Act 1997, s. 4A

- Triable either way • 10 years' imprisonment and/or an unlimited fine on indictment • Six months' imprisonment and/or a fine summarily

OFFENCE: **Racially or Religiously Aggravated Stalking Involving Fear of Violence or Serious Alarm or Distress—***Crime and Disorder Act 1998, s. 32(1)(b)*

- Triable either way • 14 years' imprisonment and/or a fine on indictment
- Six months' imprisonment and/or a fine summarily

The Protection from Harassment Act 1997, s. 4A states:

(1) A person ('A') whose course of conduct—
- (a) amounts to stalking, and
- (b) either—
  - (i) causes another ('B') to fear, on at least two occasions, that violence will be used against B, or
  - (ii) causes B serious alarm or distress which has a substantial adverse effect on B's usual day-to-day activities,

is guilty of an offence if A knows or ought to know that A's conduct will cause B so to fear on each of those occasions or (as the case may be) will cause such alarm or distress.

KEYNOTE

For the purposes of s. 4A(1)(b)(i) a person (A) ought to know that A's course of conduct will cause another (B) to fear that violence will be used against B on any occasion if a reasonable person in possession of the same information would think the course of conduct would cause B so to fear on that occasion.

The second arm of the offence prohibits a course of conduct which causes 'serious alarm or distress' which has a 'substantial adverse effect on the day-to-day activities of the victim'. It is designed to recognise the serious impact that stalking may have on victims, even where an explicit fear of violence is not created by each incident of stalking behaviour.

The phrase 'substantial adverse effect on the usual day-to-day activities' is not defined in s. 4A, and thus its construction will be a matter for the courts via judicial interpretation. However, the Home Office considers that evidence of a substantial adverse effect caused by the stalker may include:

- victims changing their routes to work, work patterns or employment;
- victims arranging for friends or family to pick up children from school (to avoid contact with the stalker);
- victims putting in place additional security measures in their home;
- victims moving home;
- physical or mental ill-health;
- victims' deterioration in performance at work due to stress;
- victims stopping or changing the way they socialise.

Although some victims try to continue their existing routines in defiance of a stalker, they may still be able to evidence substantial impact on their usual day-to-day activities, depending on the individual case.

For the purposes of s. 4A(1)(b)(ii), A ought to know that A's course of conduct will cause B serious alarm or distress which has a substantial adverse effect on B's usual day-to-day activities if a reasonable person in possession of the same information would think the course of conduct would cause B such alarm or distress.

Under s. 4A(4), there is a defence to the offence of stalking involving fear of violence or serious alarm or distress which is a mirror image of the defence to the offence under s.4 (see para. 4.11.5.1).

4.11.7 Police Direction to Prevent Intimidation or Harassment

In response to a number of campaigns against individuals believed to be involved in animal experiments, the Criminal Justice and Police Act 2001 gives the police specific powers to prevent the intimidation or harassment of people in their own or others' homes. Situations envisaged by the legislation typically arise where protestors gather outside a house where a particular individual is believed to be. Under such circumstances s. 42 provides the most senior ranking police officer at the scene with discretionary powers to give directions to people in the vicinity. The power arises where:

- the person is outside (or in the vicinity of) any premises that are used by any individual as his/her dwelling, and
- the constable *believes*, on reasonable grounds, that the person is there for the purpose of representing or persuading the resident (or anyone else)
- that he/she should not do something he/she is entitled or required to do, or
- that he/she should do something that he/she is under no obligation to do, and
- the constable also believes, on reasonable grounds, that the person's presence amounts to, or is likely to result in, the harassment of the resident or is likely to cause alarm or distress to the resident.

Although the premises involved may be in use by any 'individual' (e.g. *not* a company) and the purpose may be to persuade that or any other 'individual', the officer must believe that the ultimate effect will be harassment, alarm or distress of the *resident*. The requirement for reasonable grounds means that their existence or otherwise will be judged objectively and not simply from the personal standpoint of the officer using the power. Nevertheless, the officer is given a great deal of individual discretion in using this power.

A direction given under s. 42 requires the person(s) to do all such things as the officer specifies as being *necessary* to prevent the harassment, alarm or distress of the resident, including:

- a requirement to leave the vicinity of the premises in question, and
- a requirement to leave that vicinity and not to return to it within such period as the constable may specify, not being longer than three months,

and (in either case) the requirement to leave the vicinity may be to do so immediately or after a specified period of time (s. 42(4)).

The direction may be given orally and, where appropriate, may be given to a group of people together (s. 42(3)). There is no requirement that the officer giving the direction be in uniform.

The power under s. 42 cannot be used to direct someone to refrain from conduct made lawful under s. 220 of the Trade Union and Labour Relations (Consolidation) Act 1992 (Peaceful picketing).

4.11.7.1 Contravening a s. 42 Direction

OFFENCE: **Knowingly Contravening a s. 42 Direction—*Criminal Justice and Police Act 2001, s. 42(7)***

   • Triable summarily • Three months' imprisonment and/or a fine

The Criminal Justice and Police Act 2001, s. 42 states:

(7) Any person who knowingly fails to comply with a requirement in a direction given to him under this section (other than a requirement under subsection (4)(b)) shall be guilty of an offence.

KEYNOTE

You will need to show that the person acted 'knowingly' in failing to comply with a requirement in a direction and that it was 'given to them'. Generally the best proof of this will be to show that the person had received the direction (and the detail of its extent) personally and that he/she understood it. Therefore, although the section allows for directions to be given to groups, there may be practical benefits in giving personal directions where circumstances allow.

The reference to s. 42(4)(b) means a requirement to leave that vicinity and not to return to it within such period as the constable may specify, not being for a period longer than three months.

OFFENCE: **Unlawfully Returning to Vicinity—*Criminal Justice and Police Act 2001, s. 42(7A)***

> • Triable summarily • Imprisonment for a term not exceeding six months and/or a fine

The Criminal Justice and Police Act 2001, s. 42 states:

> (7A) Any person to whom a constable has given a direction including a requirement under subsection (4)(b) commits an offence if he—
>   (a) returns to the vicinity of the premises in question within the period specified in the direction beginning with the date on which the direction is given; and
>   (b) does so for the purpose described in subsection (1)(b).

KEYNOTE

The offence is committed where a person who is subject to a direction to leave the vicinity, returns within a period of up to three months (the precise length of time will be specified by the police officer) for the 'purposes' described at s. 42A(1)(b) (see para. 4.11.7.2)—representing to or persuading a person not to do something he/she is entitled to do, or to do something he/she is not obliged to do.

4.11.7.2 Harassment etc. of Person in their Home

OFFENCE: **Harassment of a Person in their Home—*Criminal Justice and Police Act 2001, s. 42A***

> • Triable summarily • Imprisonment for a term not exceeding six months and/or a fine

The Criminal Justice and Police Act 2001, s. 42A states:

> (1) A person commits an offence if—
>   (a) that person is present outside or in the vicinity of any premises that are used by any individual ('the resident') as his dwelling;
>   (b) that person is present there for the purpose (by his presence or otherwise) of representing to the resident or another individual (whether or not one who uses the premises as his dwelling), or of persuading the resident or such another individual—
>   (i) that he should not do something that he is entitled or required to do; or
>   (ii) that he should do something that he is not under any obligation to do;
>   (c) that person—
>   (i) intends his presence to amount to the harassment of, or to cause alarm or distress to, the resident; or
>   (ii) knows or ought to know that his presence is likely to result in the harassment of, or to cause alarm or distress to, the resident; and
>   (d) the presence of that person—
>   (i) amounts to the harassment of, or causes alarm or distress to, any person falling within subsection (2); or
>   (ii) is likely to result in the harassment of, or to cause alarm or distress to, any such person.

(2) A person falls within this subsection if he is—

    (a) the resident,

    (b) a person in the resident's dwelling, or

    (c) a person in another dwelling in the vicinity of the resident's dwelling.

KEYNOTE

This offence has a number of elements, each of which must be proved if a successful prosecution is to be brought. The ingredients include:

- Place—the defendant must be shown to have been in the relevant place (outside or in the vicinity of a 'dwelling'). 'Dwelling' means any structure or part of a structure occupied as a person's home or as other living accommodation (whether the occupation is separate or shared with others) but does not include any part not so occupied (s. 42A(7)).
- Purpose—the defendant's purpose in being there must be to represent to, or persuade the resident/ another individual that he/she should not do something he/she is entitled/required to do or that he/she should do something that he/she is not under any obligation to do.
- Intention/knowledge—you must prove that the defendant intended his/her presence to amount to harassment of, or to cause alarm or distress to, the resident or that he/she knew/ought to have known that his/her presence was likely to have that result.
- Consequences—you must show that the defendant's presence amounted to/was likely to result in the harassment of, or causing alarm or distress to, any resident, person in the resident's dwelling, or person in another dwelling in the vicinity of the resident's dwelling.

References in s. 42A(1)(c) and (d) to a person's presence are references either to his/her presence alone or together with that of any other people who are also present (s. 42A(3)).

For the purposes of this section a person ought to know that his/her presence is likely to result in the harassment of, or to cause alarm or distress to, a resident if a reasonable person in possession of the same information would think that it was likely to have that effect (s. 42A(4)).

4.12 Offences Involving Communications

4.12.1 Introduction

This chapter details offences regarding hoaxes, threats and other communications which are intended to cause alarm or anxiety. Such offences are sometimes committed via social media such as Facebook and Twitter, as in the case of *Chambers* v *DPP* [2012] EWHC 2157 (Admin) which examined a message interpreted as a bomb hoax at an airport.

4.12.2 Bomb Hoaxes

OFFENCE: **Bomb Hoaxes—*Criminal Law Act 1977, s. 51***
- Triable either way • Seven years' imprisonment on indictment
- Six months' imprisonment and/or a fine summarily

The Criminal Law Act 1977, s. 51 states:

(1) A person who—
   (a) places any article in any place whatever; or
   (b) dispatches any article by post, rail or any other means whatever of sending things from one place to another,
   with the intention (in either case) of inducing in some other person a belief that it is likely to explode or ignite and thereby cause personal injury or damage to property is guilty of an offence.
      In this subsection 'article' includes substance.

(2) A person who communicates any information which he knows or believes to be false to another person with the intention of inducing in him or any other person a false belief that a bomb or other thing liable to explode or ignite is present in any place or location whatever is guilty of an offence.

KEYNOTE

The Criminal Law Act 1977 offences relate specifically to bomb threats. The 'article' concerned in s. 51(1) can also be anything at all.

In *R* v *Webb* (1995) 92(27) LSG 31 the defendant admitted saying 'there is a bomb' whilst making a hoax bomb call (contrary to s. 51(2)). The defendant argued that the call he made did not specify any place or location and therefore the offence was incomplete. The trial judge rejected that submission. Webb appealed on the same grounds but the appeal was dismissed and the conviction upheld with the court ruling that the words 'in any place or location' meant 'somewhere'. The intention of the section did not require a specific place or location. The phrase 'there is a bomb' implied there was a bomb somewhere and that was sufficient to satisfy the wording of the offence.

The wording of the 1977 Act offence is in the *present* tense so a message threatening to place a bomb etc. some time in the *future* would not suffice.

The use of some form of code word is not a prerequisite of the offence but it does go towards proving the defendant's intention that the threat etc. be taken seriously; it may also be taken into account when passing sentence.

The 'communication' can be in any form (including the internet) and can be direct (e.g. to a railway station or department store where the bomb or device is alleged to be) or indirect (e.g. to a radio station switchboard).

There is no need for the person making the communication to have any particular person in mind at the time (s. 51(3)). The offences under s. 51(1) and (2) should be read as inducing the belief in a person anywhere in the world (for further explanation, see para. 4.12.3).

4.12.3 Hoaxes Involving Noxious Substances or Things

OFFENCE: **Hoaxes Involving Noxious Substances or Things—*Anti-terrorism, Crime and Security Act 2001, s. 114***

- Triable either way • Seven years' imprisonment on indictment
- Six months' imprisonment and/or a fine summarily

The Anti-terrorism, Crime and Security Act 2001, s. 114 states:

(1) A person is guilty of an offence if he—
   (a) places any substance or other thing in any place; or
   (b) sends any substance or other thing from one place to another (by post, rail or any other means whatever);

   with the intention of inducing in a person anywhere in the world a belief that it is likely to be (or contain) a noxious substance or other noxious thing and thereby endanger human life or create a serious risk to human health.

(2) A person is guilty of an offence if he communicates any information which he knows or believes to be false with the intention of inducing in a person anywhere in the world a belief that a noxious substance or other noxious thing is likely to be present (whether at the time the information is communicated or later) in any place and thereby endanger human life or create a serious risk to human health.

KEYNOTE

Section 51 of the Criminal Law Act 1977 (see para. 4.12.2) makes it an offence for someone to place or send any article intending to make another person believe that it is likely to explode or ignite and thereby cause personal injury or damage to property. It is also an offence for someone to communicate any information which he knows or believes to be false intending to make another person believe that a bomb is likely to explode or ignite—these offences only relate to hoax explosive devices meaning, other hoaxes, such as sending powders or liquids through the post and claiming that they are harmful, are not covered. The offences under s. 114 of the Anti-terror, Crime and Security Act 2001 were intended to fill that gap.

Therefore, as the offences under the Anti-terrorism, Crime and Security Act 2001 are committed when a person intends to induce a relevant belief in the mind of a person *anywhere in the world*, the offences under s. 51 of the 1977 Act should be construed in the same way—any other approach would be wholly inconsistent. For example, in *Webb* (see para. 4.12.2), the statement 'there is a bomb' made the defendant guilty of the s. 51(2) offence—if Webb had said 'there is a bomb in Paris' it would not make him any less guilty merely because he added a location outside the United Kingdom to his statement.

'Substance' for the 2001 Act offence includes any biological agent and any other natural or artificial substance (whatever its form, origin and method of production) (s. 115(1)). The Home Office guidance to the Anti-terrorism, Crime and Security Act 2001 offence gives examples of acts which, though at one time would not have been seen as threatening, would now amount to an offence under this section, for example scattering white powder in a public place or spraying water droplets around in an underground train, in each case with the requisite intent.

For a person to be guilty of an offence under s. 114, it is not necessary for him/her to have any particular person in mind as the person in whom he intends to induce the belief in question.

4.12.4   **Misuse and Obstruction of Postal Services**

OFFENCE: **Interfering with Mail**—*Postal Services Act 2000, s. 84*

> • Triable summarily • Six months' imprisonment and/or a fine

The Postal Services Act 2000, s. 84 states:

(1) A person commits an offence if, without reasonable excuse, he—
    (a) intentionally delays or opens a postal packet in the course of its transmission by post, or
    (b) intentionally opens a mail-bag

(2) ...

(3) A person commits an offence if, intending to act to a person's detriment and without reasonable excuse, he opens a postal packet which he knows or reasonably suspects has been incorrectly delivered to him.

KEYNOTE

The Postal Services Act 2000 creates two offences in relation to interfering with the mail, along with a further offence of opening someone else's mail that has been incorrectly delivered.

The first general offence, under s. 84(1), applies to anyone. You must show that the defendant acted without any reasonable excuse and that he/she also acted intentionally. The offence does not apply where the actions were carried out under a lawful warrant or statutory provision (e.g. the Regulation of Investigatory Powers Act 2000). Similarly, any action carried out in accordance with the terms and conditions of postage will not attract criminal liability here. Delays (but not the opening of mail) caused by industrial action also fall outside this offence.

The offence under s. 84(3) requires proof of a number of elements. First, it must be shown that the defendant opened a postal packet (as opposed to delaying it under s. 84(1)). It must also be shown that he/she did so intending 'to act to another person's detriment'; this can be any other person's detriment, not simply the addressee, but it is nevertheless a key feature of the offence. It must also be shown that the defendant knew or reasonably suspected that the postal packet had been incorrectly delivered to him/her. This means that the packet must have been 'delivered'; it would be difficult to show that someone reasonably suspected a packet that is still in transit to have been 'incorrectly delivered' to him/her. As with the general offence under s. 84(1), any opening of postal packets that is done properly in pursuance of a warrant, statutory authority or under the conditions of postage will not be an offence under s. 84(3).

There is a second offence (under s. 83) which specifically applies to postal workers and which is triable either way, carrying a maximum of two years' imprisonment. Under the second, more specific, offence, you have to prove the same elements as the offence under s. 84(1) but also need to show that the person was engaged in the business of a postal operator and that he/she was acting contrary to his/her duty.

4.12.4.1   **Sending Prohibited Article by Post**

OFFENCE: **Sending Prohibited Article by Post**—*Postal Services Act 2000, s. 85*

> • Triable either way • 12 months' imprisonment on indictment
> • Fine summarily

The Postal Services Act 2000, s. 85 states:

(1) A person commits an offence if he sends by post a postal packet which encloses any creature, article or thing of any kind which is likely to injure other postal packets in course of their transmission by post or any person engaged in the business of a postal operator.

(2) Subsection (1) does not apply to postal packets which enclose anything permitted (whether generally or specifically) by the postal operator concerned.

(3) A person commits an offence if he sends by post a postal packet which encloses—
    (a) any indecent or obscene print, painting, photograph, lithograph, engraving, cinematograph film or other record of a picture or pictures, book, card or written communication, or

(b) any other indecent or obscene article (whether or not of a similar kind to those mentioned in paragraph (a)).

(4) A person commits an offence if he sends by post a postal packet which has on the packet, or on the cover of the packet, any words, marks or designs which are of an indecent or obscene character.

KEYNOTE

The first offence addresses the sending of things that are likely to harm either other postal packets or postal workers. Evidence that any article is in the course of transmission by post, or has been accepted by a postal operator for transmission by post, will be enough to prove that it is in fact a 'postal packet' (s. 109). This offence will not apply to the sending of things that are permitted by the relevant postal operator.

The other offences under s. 85 apply irrespective of whether the offending packets are permitted by the postal operator and include indecent or obscene contents or packaging.

Whether an article is obscene etc. is a question of fact for the court to determine in each case. That test will not look at the particular views or frailties of the recipient but will be an objective test based on a reasonable bystander (*Kosmos Publications Ltd* v *DPP* [1975] Crim LR 345).

4.12.4.2   Obstruction of Postal Service

OFFENCE: **Obstruction—*Postal Services Act 2000, s. 88***

> • Triable summarily • Fine

The Postal Services Act 2000, s. 88 states:

(1) A person commits an offence if, without reasonable excuse, he—
   (a) obstructs a person engaged in the business of a universal service provider in the execution of his duty in connection with the provision of a universal postal service, or
   (b) obstructs, while in any universal postal service post office or related premises, the course of business of a universal service provider.

(2) ...

(3) A person commits an offence if without reasonable excuse, he fails to leave a universal postal service post office or related premises when required to do so by a person who—
   (a) is engaged in the business of a universal service provider, and
   (b) reasonably suspects him of committing an offence under subsection (1).

(4) A person who commits an offence under subsection (3)—
   (a) ...
   (b) may be removed by any person engaged in the business of a universal service provider.

KEYNOTE

The first offence involves the general obstruction, without reasonable excuse, of someone engaged in the business of a 'universal service provider'. These providers are broadly organisations empowered under the 2000 Act to carry on many of the services that were formerly provided by the Post Office.

The second offence relates to conduct in a post office or related premises. Such conduct must be shown to have obstructed, without reasonable excuse, *the course of business* of a universal service provider. Therefore, it is not a member of staff who has to be obstructed here, but rather the postal business itself.

Section 88(3) is of more immediate relevance to police officers. This offence is committed if a person fails without reasonable excuse to leave a post office or related premises when required to do so by someone engaged in the provider's business who reasonably suspects the other person of committing one of the obstruction offences under s. 88(1). Anyone failing to leave when properly required to do so under subs. (3) may be removed by the post office staff but also, subs. (5) provides that 'any constable shall on demand remove, or assist in removing, any such person'. This places a clear duty on, as opposed to just granting a power to, individual police officers to help in removing offenders under these circumstances.

'Related premises' are any premises belonging to a universal postal service post office or used together with any such post office (s. 88(6)).

4.12.5 Malicious Communications

OFFENCE: **Malicious Communications—*Malicious Communications Act 1988, s. 1(1)***

- Triable either way • Two years' imprisonment and/or a fine
- Six months' imprisonment and/or a fine summarily

The Malicious Communications Act 1988, s. 1 states:

(1) Any person who sends to another person—
    (a) a letter, electronic communication or article of any description which conveys—
        (i) a message which is indecent or grossly offensive;
        (ii) a threat; or
        (iii) information which is false and known or believed to be false by the sender; or
    (b) any article or electronic communication which is, in whole or part, of an indecent or grossly offensive nature,

is guilty of an offence if his purpose, or one of his purposes, in sending it is that it should, so far as falling within paragraph (a) or (b) above, cause distress or anxiety to the recipient or to any other person to whom he intends that it or its contents or nature should be communicated.

KEYNOTE

'Sending' will include transmitting (note that this offence is complete as soon as the communication is sent).

'Purposes' is simply another way of saying 'intention'.

Section 1(1)(b) covers occasions where the article itself is indecent or grossly offensive (such as putting dog faeces through someone's letter box).

The offence is not restricted to threatening or indecent communications and can include giving false information provided that *one* of the sender's purposes in so doing is to cause distress or anxiety. The relevant distress or anxiety may be intended towards the recipient or any other person.

In addition to letters, the above offence also covers *any* article; it also covers electronic communications which include any oral or other communication by means of an electronic communications network. This will extend to communications in electronic form such as emails, text messages, pager messages, social media, etc. (s. 1(2A)).

It is clear from s. 1(3) that the offence can be committed by using someone else to send, deliver or transmit a message. This would include occasions where a person falsely reports that someone has been a victim of a crime in order to cause anxiety or distress by the arrival of the police.

4.12.5.1 Defence Regarding Malicious Communications

Section 1 of the 1988 Act goes on to state:

(2) A person is not guilty of an offence by virtue of subsection (1)(a)(ii) above if he shows—
    (a) that the threat was used to reinforce a demand *made by him on reasonable grounds*; and
    (b) that he believed, *and had reasonable grounds for believing*, that the use of the threat was a proper means of reinforcing the demand.

KEYNOTE

The italicised words in the offence (author's emphasis) make the relevant test *objective*. It will not be enough that the person claiming the defence under s. 1(2) *subjectively* believed that he/she had reasonable grounds; the defendant will have to show:

- that there were *in fact* reasonable grounds for making the demand;
- that he/she believed that the accompanying threat was a proper means of enforcing the demand; and
- that *reasonable grounds existed* for that belief.

Given the decisions of the courts in similarly worded defences under the Theft Act 1968 (e.g. blackmail; see *Crime*, chapter 1.14), it is unlikely that any demand could be reasonable where agreement to it would amount to a crime.

The defence is intended to cover financial institutions and other commercial concerns which often need to send forceful letters to customers.

4.12.6 Public Communications

OFFENCE: **Improper Use of Public Electronic Communications Network—*Communications Act 2003, s. 127***

• Triable summarily • Six months' imprisonment and/or a fine

The Communications Act 2003, s. 127 states:

(1) A person is guilty of an offence if he—
    (a) sends by means of a public electronic communications network a message or other matter that is grossly offensive or of an indecent, obscene or menacing character; or
    (b) causes any such message or matter to be so sent.
(2) A person is guilty of an offence if, for the purpose of causing annoyance, inconvenience or needless anxiety to another, he—
    (a) sends by means of a public electronic communications network, a message that he knows to be false;
    (b) causes such a message to be sent; or
    (c) persistently makes use of a public electronic communications network.

If a message sent is grossly offensive, indecent, obscene, menacing or false it is irrelevant whether it was received. The offence is one of sending, so it is committed when the sending takes place.

KEYNOTE

These offences are designed to deal with 'nuisance' calls. They only apply to 'public' electronic communications networks. These are defined as an electronic communications network provided wholly or mainly for the purpose of making electronic communications services available to members of the public (s. 151) and would therefore not generally include internal calls in a workplace.

The wording would apply to the sending of messages via the internet (provided the system used comes within the definition under s. 151). They also take in public social media systems such as Twitter, as the case of *Chambers* v *DPP* [2012] EWHC 2157 (Admin) has held. This involved a man posting a joke on his Twitter account about a bomb hoax at an airport. He was arrested and charged under s. 127.

There is no need to show a particular 'purpose' (intention) on the part of the defendant for the first offence under s. 127(1) and that offence is complete if the message is, as a matter of fact, grossly offensive, indecent, obscene or menacing.

The offence also covers actions which cause others to send such a message.

Unlike the offence under s. 51(2) of the Criminal Law Act 1977 (see para. 4.12.3), there is no need for any information passed to be 'false'. In determining whether a message is 'grossly offensive', it is the message and not the content that is the basic ingredient of the offence. What constitutes 'grossly offensive' has to be judged by considering the reaction of reasonable people and the standards of an open and just multiracial society (*DPP* v *Collins* [2005] EWHC 1308 (Admin)).

The second offence, under s. 127(2), requires that you show the defendant acted with the purpose of causing annoyance, inconvenience or needless anxiety.

A person is to be treated as 'persistently misusing' a network or service in any case in which his/her misuse is repeated on a sufficient number of occasions for it to be clear that the misuse represents a pattern of behaviour or practice, or recklessness as to whether persons suffer annoyance, inconvenience or anxiety (s. 128(6)).

In assessing these points it is immaterial that the misuse was in relation to a 'network' on some occasions and in relation to a communications 'service' on others, that different networks or services were involved on different occasions or that the people likely to suffer annoyance, inconvenience or anxiety were different on different occasions (s. 128(7)).

This second offence is a 'penalty offence' for the purposes of s. 1 of the Criminal Justice and Police Act 2001.

Where a number of calls have been made to several different people within the community, the offence of public nuisance may also be considered.

4.12.6.1 False Alarms of Fire

OFFENCE: **Making False Alarm of Fire—*Fire and Rescue Services Act 2004, s. 49***
  • Triable summarily • Three months' imprisonment and/or a fine

The Fire and Rescue Services Act 2004, s. 49 states:

(1) A person commits an offence if he knowingly gives or causes to be given a false alarm of fire to a person acting on behalf of a fire and rescue authority.

KEYNOTE

The offence requires proof that the defendant acted 'knowingly' (as opposed to e.g. mistakenly). The offence clearly applies where someone makes a malicious call to a fire and rescue authority. However, the wording 'causes to be given' potentially covers the making of a false report to a body other than a fire and rescue authority, e.g. the police, if the person knew that this would result in the police passing that call to the relevant fire and rescue authority.

This offence is a 'penalty offence' for the purposes of s. 1 of the Criminal Justice and Police Act 2001.

Offences and Powers Relating to Information

4.13.1 Introduction

This chapter examines the provisions of the Freedom of Information Act 2000, Computer Misuse Act 1990, Data Protection Act 2018 and the Regulation of Investigatory Powers Act 2000.

Article 8 (Right to Respect for Private and Family Life, Home and Correspondence) of the European Convention on Human Rights has implications for the law in relation to all these areas, as well as other areas contained within this Manual.

4.13.2 Article 8—Right to Respect for Private and Family Life, Home and Correspondence

Article 8 of the Convention states:

1. Everyone has the right to respect for his private and family life, his home and his correspondence.
2. There shall be no interference by a public authority with the exercise of this right except such as is in accordance with the law and is necessary in a democratic society in the interests of national security, public safety or the economic well being of the country, for the prevention of disorder or crime, for the protection of health or morals, or for the protection of the rights and freedoms of others.

KEYNOTE

The provisions of Article 8 extend a right to respect for a person's private life, family life, home, and correspondence.

This Article protects these features of a person's life from arbitrary interference by 'public authorities' (*Kroon* v *Netherlands* (1995) 19 EHRR 263). 'Public authorities' include a court, tribunal or groups who are concerned solely with discharging functions of a public nature or those who have some public functions (s. 6 of the Human Rights Act 1998). However, the Convention does allow for individuals to raise issues of unjustified interference with their private lives and the courts have held that even celebrities have a basic right to privacy which will be protected by Article 8 (*Campbell* v *Mirror Group Newspapers* [2004] UKHL 22); similar arguments can be found in *Theakston* v *Mirror Group Newspapers* [2002] EWHC 137 (QB).

The State is under a duty not to interfere with a person's life except in accordance with Article 8(2). Many police activities such as entry onto premises, surveillance and the seizure of property, touch upon the features covered by Article 8.

Another reason why this Article is of importance to police services is that the State also has a positive obligation to prevent others from interfering with an individual's right to private life (*Stjerna* v *Finland* (1994) 24 EHRR 194). How far the police would have to go in order to discharge this obligation is unclear, but Article 8 will be relevant in many areas and in particular community safety.

It is here that the notion of balancing the rights and freedoms of individuals against each other and against those of the community at large can be seen most acutely.

4.13.3 Access to Information Held by Public Authorities

The Freedom of Information Act 2000, s. 1 provides for the general right of access to information held by public authorities, and states:

(1) Any person making a request for information to a public authority is entitled—
   (a) to be informed in writing by the public authority whether it holds information of the description specified in the request, and
   (b) if that is the case, to have that information communicated to him.

KEYNOTE

Public authorities for the purposes of this section include the police, the CPS and government departments, along with National Health Service bodies, schools and colleges (s. 3 and sch. 1). These public authorities are required to adopt and maintain a publication scheme and to publish information in accordance with it that sets out their specific plans for making certain types of information available (s. 19).

Requests for information must be in writing, state the name of the applicant and an address for correspondence, and describe the information requested (s. 8(1)). A request is to be treated as made in writing where the text of the request is transmitted by electronic means, is received in legible form, and is capable of being used for subsequent reference (s.8(2)). A fee may be charged for complying with the request (s. 9). Generally, a public authority must comply with a request for information promptly and in any event not later than the twentieth working day following the date of receipt (s. 10).

A number of exemptions and qualifications are imposed by the Act on the general 'right to know' and these usually arise due to the nature or the quantity of the material sought or the excessive costs involved in providing the information.

The Act creates the role of Information Commissioner (s. 18), and places a duty on the Commissioner to promote good practice by public authorities and promote the observance of the requirements of the Act and the Codes of Practice (s. 47).

4.13.4 Duty to Share Information

A number of public agencies have a duty to share information under the Multi-Agency Public Protection Arrangements (MAPPA). These are statutory arrangements to assess and manage the risk posed by certain sexual and violent offenders. They are established by virtue of ss. 325 to 327 of the Criminal Justice Act 2003 and bring together the police, probation and prison services into what is known as the 'MAPPA Responsible Authority' for each MAPPA Area.

4.13.5 Offences under the Computer Misuse Act 1990

The Computer Misuse Act 1990 Act ensures the United Kingdom's compliance with the European Union Framework Decision on Attacks Against Information Systems. This compliance requires that penalties relating to 'hacking' into computer systems, unauthorised access to computer material, the intentional serious hindering of a computer system and importing tools for cyber crime, reflect the seriousness of the criminal activities that can be involved in committing these offences.

4.13.5.1 Unauthorised Access to Computer Materials

OFFENCE: **Unauthorised Access to Computer Material ('Hacking')—*Computer Misuse Act 1990, s. 1***

- Triable either way • Two years' imprisonment and/or a fine on indictment
- Six months' imprisonment and/or a fine summarily

The Computer Misuse Act 1990, s. 1 states:

(1) A person is guilty of an offence if—
    (a) he causes a computer to perform any function with intent to secure access to any program or data held in any computer or to enable any such access to be secured;
    (b) the access he intends to secure, or enable to be secured, is unauthorised; and
    (c) he knows at the time when he causes the computer to perform the function that that is the case.
(2) The intent a person has to have to commit an offence under this section need not be directed at—
    (a) any particular program or data;
    (b) a program or data of any particular kind; or
    (c) a program or data held in any particular computer.

KEYNOTE

'Computer' is not defined and therefore must be given its ordinary meaning. Given the multiple functions of many electronic devices such as mobile phones, this could arguably bring them within the ambit of the Act.

This offence involves 'causing a computer to perform any function', which means more than simply looking at material on a screen or having any physical contact with computer hardware. In the latter case an offence of criminal damage may be appropriate. Any attempt to log on would involve getting the computer to perform a function (even if the function is to deny you access!).

Any access must be 'unauthorised'. If the defendant is authorised to *access* a computer, albeit for restricted purposes, then it was originally held that he/she did not commit this offence if he/she then *used* any information for some other unauthorised purpose (e.g. police officers using data from the Police National Computer (PNC) for private gain (*DPP* v *Bignell* [1998] 1 Cr App R 1)). However, in *R* v *Bow Street Metropolitan Stipendiary Magistrate, ex parte Government of the USA* [2000] 2 AC 216 it was held that where an employee accessed accounts that fell outside his normal scope of work and passed on the information, in this instance to credit card forgers, he was not authorised to access the specific data involved.

Essentially, the purpose of this section is to address unauthorised access as opposed to unauthorised use of data, and behaviour such as looking over a computer operator's shoulder to read what is on the screen would not be covered.

In order to prove the offence under s. 1 you must show that the defendant intended to secure access to the program or data. This is therefore an offence of 'specific intent' and lesser forms of *mens rea* such as recklessness will not do.

You must also show that the defendant knew the access was unauthorised.

In *R* v *Coltman* [2018] EWCA Crim 2059 an NHS employee used the computer of a colleague to access a file to which he had no authorised access. The material from that file was later passed by the defendant to a newspaper. The Court of Appeal rejected the defence that the material was disclosed in the public interest.

The Privacy and Electronic Communications (EC Directive) Regulations 2003 (SI 2003/2426) regulate the use of cookies and internet tracking devices, along with the use of unsolicited email and text messages. Guidance in their extent and practical effect is prepared by the Office of the Information Commissioner.

The powers of entry, search and seizure under the Police and Criminal Evidence Act 1984 apply to this offence.

4.13.5.2 Definition of Terms

The 1990 Act defines a number of its terms at s. 17 which states:

(2) A person secures access to any program or data held in a computer if by causing a computer to perform any function he—
    (a) alters or erases the program or data;
    (b) copies or moves it to any storage medium other than that in which it is held or to a different location in the storage medium in which it is held;
    (c) uses it; or

(d) has it output from the computer in which it is held (whether by having it displayed or in any other manner);

and references to access to a program or data (and to an intent to secure such access) shall be read accordingly.

(3) For the purposes of subsection (2)(c) above a person uses a program if the function he causes the computer to perform—

(a) causes the program to be executed; or

(b) is itself a function of the program.

(4) For the purposes of subsection (2)(d) above—

(a) a program is output if the instructions of which it consists are output; and

(b) the form in which any such instructions or any other data is output (and in particular whether or not it represents a form in which, in the case of instructions, they are capable of being executed or, in the case of data, it is capable of being processed by a computer) is immaterial.

(5) Access of any kind by any person to any program or data held in a computer is unauthorised if—

(a) he is not himself entitled to control access of the kind in question to the program or data; and

(b) he does not have consent to access by him of the kind in question to the program or data from any person who is so entitled,

but this subsection is subject to section 10.

(6) References to any program or data held in a computer include references to any program or data held in any removable storage medium which is for the time being in the computer; and a computer is to be regarded as containing any program or data held in any such medium.

…

(8) An act done in relation to a computer is unauthorised if the person doing the act (or causing it to be done)—

(a) is not himself a person who has responsibility for the computer and is entitled to determine whether the act may be done; and

(b) does not have consent to the act from any such person.

In this subsection 'act' includes a series of acts.

KEYNOTE

Securing access will therefore include:

- altering or erasing a program or data;
- copying or moving a program or data to a new storage medium;
- using data or having it displayed or 'output' in any form from the computer in which it is held.

Under s. 17(5) access is 'unauthorised' if the person is neither entitled to control that type of access to a program or data, nor does he/she have the consent of any person who is so entitled. The provision under s. 17(5)(a) was the basis for the decision in *Bow Street* (see para. **4.13.5.1**). This definition does not affect the powers available to any 'enforcement officers', i.e. police officers or other people charged with a duty of investigating offences (s. 10).

4.13.5.3 Unauthorised Access to Computers with Intent

OFFENCE: **Unauthorised Access with Intent to Commit Further Offences—**
Computer Misuse Act 1990, s. 2

- Triable either way • Five years' imprisonment and/or a fine on indictment
- Six months' imprisonment and/or a fine summarily

The Computer Misuse Act 1990, s. 2 states:

(1) A person is guilty of an offence under this section if he commits an offence under section 1 above ('the unauthorised access offence') with intent—

(a) to commit an offence to which this section applies; or

(b) to facilitate the commission of such an offence (whether by himself or by any other person); and the offence he intends to commit or facilitate is referred to below in this section as the further offence.

(2) This section applies to offences—
    (a) for which the sentence is fixed by law; or
    (b) for which a person of twenty-one years of age or over (not previously convicted) may be sentenced to imprisonment for a term of five years (or, in England and Wales, might be so sentenced but for the restrictions imposed by section 33 of the Magistrates' Courts Act 1980).
(3) It is immaterial for the purposes of this section whether the further offence is to be committed on the same occasion as the unauthorised access offence or on any future occasion.
(4) A person may be guilty of an offence under this section even though the facts are such that the commission of the further offence is impossible.

KEYNOTE

The defendant must be shown to have had the required intent at the time of the access or other *actus reus*.

The intended further offence does not have to be committed at the same time, but may be committed in future (e.g. where the data is used to commit an offence of blackmail or to secure the transfer of funds from a bank account).

The provision as to impossibility (s. 2(4)) means that a person would still commit the offence if he/she tried, say, to access the bank account of a person who did not in fact exist.

4.13.5.4   Unauthorised Acts with Intent to Impair Operation of Computer, etc.

OFFENCE: **Unauthorised Acts with Intent to Impair, or with Recklessness as to Impairing, Operation of Computer, etc.—*Computer Misuse Act 1990, s. 3***

- Triable either way • 10 years' imprisonment and/or a fine on indictment
- Six months' imprisonment and/or a fine summarily

The Computer Misuse Act 1990, s. 3 states:

(1) A person is guilty of an offence if—
    (a) he does any unauthorised act in relation to a computer;
    (b) at the time when he does the act he knows that it is unauthorised; and
    (c) either subsection (2) or subsection (3) below applies.
(2) This subsection applies if the person intends by doing the act—
    (a) to impair the operation of any computer;
    (b) to prevent or hinder access to any program or data held in any computer; or
    (c) to impair the operation of any such program or the reliability of any such data.
(3) This subsection applies if the person is reckless as to whether the act will do any of the things mentioned in paragraphs (a) to (c) of subsection (2) above.

KEYNOTE

This section is designed to ensure that adequate provision is made to criminalise all forms of denial of service attacks in which the attacker denies the victim(s) access to a particular resource, typically by preventing legitimate users of a service accessing that service. An example of this is where a former employee, acting on a grudge, impaired the operation of a company's computer by using a program to generate and send 5 million emails to the company (*DPP* v *Lennon* [2006] EWHC 1201 (Admin)).

The intention referred to in s. 3(2), or the recklessness referred to in s. 3(3), need not relate to any particular computer, any particular program or data, or a program or data of any particular kind (s. 3(4)). An 'unauthorised act' can include a series of acts, and a reference to impairing, preventing or hindering something includes a reference to doing so temporarily (s. 3(5)).

The 'hindering' provided by this section is intended to cover programs that generate denial of service attacks, or malicious code such as viruses.

Causing a computer to record that information came from one source when it in fact came from another clearly affects the reliability of that information for the purposes of s. 3(2)(c) (*Zezev* v *USA*; *Yarimaka* v *Governor of HM Prison Brixton* [2002] EWHC 589 (Admin)).

4.13.5.5 Unauthorised Acts Causing, or Creating Risk of, Serious Damage

OFFENCE: **Unauthorised Acts Causing, or Creating Risk of, Serious Damage—** ***Computer Misuse Act 1990, s. 3ZA***

- Triable on indictment • 14 years' imprisonment and/or a fine

The Computer Misuse Act 1990, s. 3ZA states:

(1) A person is guilty of an offence if—
   (a) the person does any unauthorised act in relation to a computer;
   (b) at the time of doing the act the person knows that it is unauthorised;
   (c) the act causes, or creates a significant risk of, serious damage of a material kind; and
   (d) the person intends by doing the act to cause serious damage of a material kind or is reckless as to whether such damage is caused.
(2) Damage is of a 'material kind' for the purposes of this section if it is—
   (a) damage to human welfare in any place;
   (b) damage to the environment of any place;
   (c) damage to the economy of any country; or
   (d) damage to the national security of any country.
(3) For the purposes of subsection (2)(a) an act causes damage to human welfare only if it causes—
   (a) loss to human life;
   (b) human illness or injury;
   (c) disruption of a supply of money, food, water, energy or fuel;
   (d) disruption of a system of communication;
   (e) disruption of facilities for transport; or
   (f) disruption of services relating to health.
(4) It is immaterial for the purposes of subsection (2) whether or not an act causing damage—
   (a) does so directly;
   (b) is the only or main cause of the damage.

KEYNOTE

Reference to doing an act includes a reference to causing an act to be done, and 'act' includes a series of acts. In reference to a country, this includes a reference to a territory, and to any place in, or part or region of, a country or territory (s. 3ZA(5)).

Where an offence under this section is committed as a result of an act causing or creating a significant risk of serious damage to human welfare of the kind mentioned in s. 3ZA(3)(a) or (b), or serious damage to national security, a person guilty of the offence is liable, on conviction on indictment, to imprisonment for life, or to a fine, or to both (s. 3ZA(7)).

Section 3ZA(1) sets out the elements of the offence. The *actus reus* (or conduct element) is that the accused undertakes an unauthorised act in relation to a computer (as in s. 3(1)(a) of the 1990 Act) and that act causes, or creates a significant risk of causing, serious damage of a material kind. The *mens rea* (namely the mental elements of the offence) is that the accused, at the time of committing the act, knows that it is unauthorised (as in s. 3(1)(b) of the 1990 Act) and intends the act to cause serious damage of a material kind or is reckless as to whether such damage is caused. An unauthorised act is defined in s. 17(8) of the 1990 Act as an act where the person doing the act does not have responsibility for the computer in question, which would thereby entitle him or her to determine whether the act is undertaken, and does not have the consent of the person responsible for the computer to commit the act.

4.13.5.6 **Making, Supplying or Obtaining Articles for Use in Offences under s. 1, 3 or 3ZA**

OFFENCE: **Making, Supplying or Obtaining Articles for Use in Offences under s. 1, 3 or 3ZA—*Computer Misuse Act 1990, s. 3A***

- Triable either way • Two years' imprisonment and/or a fine on indictment
- Six months' imprisonment and/or a fine summarily

The Computer Misuse Act 1990, s. 3A states:

(1) A person is guilty of an offence if he makes, adapts, supplies or offers to supply any article intending it to be used to commit, or to assist in the commission of, an offence under section 1, 3 or 3ZA.

(2) A person is guilty of an offence if he supplies or offers to supply any article believing that it is likely to be used to commit, or to assist in the commission of, an offence under section 1, 3 or 3ZA.

(3) A person is guilty of an offence if he obtains any article—

(a) intending to use it to commit, or to assist in the commission of, an offence under section 1, 3 or 3ZA, or

(b) with a view to its being supplied for use to commit, or to assist in the commission, of, an offence under section 1, 3 or 3ZA.

(4) In this section 'article' includes any program or data held in electronic form.

KEYNOTE

This section creates three offences designed to combat the market in electronic tools, such as 'hacker tools' which can be used for hacking into computer systems, and the increase in the use of such tools in connection with organised crime.

The Serious Crime Act 2015 amended s. 3A(3) of the 1990 Act to ensure that the offence provided for in s. 3A also applies to the making etc. of hacker tools intended to be used to commit the new s. 3ZA offence. Under the existing offence, the prosecution was required to show that the individual obtained the tool with a view to its being *supplied* for use to commit, or assist in the commission of an offence under s. 1 or 3 of the Act. Subsection (3) has been extended to include an offence of obtaining a tool for use to commit a Computer Misuse Act offence (including one under the new s. 3ZA) *regardless of an intention to supply* that tool.

4.13.6 **The Data Protection Act 2018**

The Data Protection Act 2018 replaces the Data Protection Act 1998 and is intended to provide a comprehensive legal framework for data protection in the UK. It sets new standards for protecting personal data, in accordance with the General Data Protection Regulation (EU) 2016/679 ('GDPR'). The GDPR forms part of the data protection regime alongside the 2018 Act. The Act and GDPR updates the rights provided for in the 1998 Act to make them easier to exercise and to ensure they continue to be relevant with the advent of more advanced data processing methods.

The four main matters provided for are general data processing, law enforcement data processing, data processing by the intelligence services, and regulatory oversight and enforcement.

The responsibility for compliance with the principles relating to processing of personal data rests on the shoulders of the 'controller', meaning an employer, public authority, agency or any other body which alone or jointly with others determines the purposes and means of the processing of personal data (Article 2(d) of the GDPR). The controller is required to notify the supervisory authority before starting to process data.

The supervisory authority with regulatory oversight of the GDPR in the UK is undertaken by the Information Commissioner who monitors the data protection level, gives advice to the government about administrative measures and regulations, and starts legal proceedings when the data protection regulation has been violated (Article 28). Individuals may lodge complaints about violations to the Information Commissioner.

4.13.6.1 Personal Data

The Data Protection Act 2018, s. 2 states:

(1) The GDPR, the applied GDPR and this Act protect individuals with regard to the processing of personal data, in particular by —

    (a) requiring personal data to be processed lawfully and fairly, on the basis of the data subject's consent or another specified basis,

    (b) conferring rights on the data subject to obtain information about the processing of personal data and to require inaccurate personal data to be rectified, and

    (c) conferring functions on the Commissioner, giving the holder of that office responsibility for monitoring and enforcing their provisions.

KEYNOTE

Personal data shall be processed lawfully, fairly and in a transparent manner in relation to the data subject (Article 6).

'Personal data' means any information relating to an identified or identifiable living individual.

'Identifiable living individual' means a living individual who can be identified, directly or indirectly, in particular by reference to—

(a) an identifier such as a name, an identification number, location data or an online identifier, or

(b) one or more factors specific to the physical, physiological, genetic, mental, economic, cultural or social identity of the individual.

(Article 2a of the GDPR.)

Data are 'personal data' when someone is able to link the information to a person, even if the person holding the data cannot make this link. Some examples of 'personal data' are: address, credit card number, bank statements, criminal record etc.

The GDPR covers the processing of personal data in two ways: personal data processed wholly or partly by automated means (i.e. information in electronic form); and personal data processed in a non-automated manner which forms part of, or is intended to form part of, a 'filing system' (i.e. manual information in a filing system). The notion processing means 'any operation or set of operations which is performed upon personal data, whether or not by automatic means, such as collection, recording, organization, storage, adaptation or alteration, retrieval, consultation, use, disclosure by transmission, dissemination or otherwise making available, alignment or combination, blocking, erasure or destruction' (Article 2(b)).

The data subject has the right to be informed when his/her personal data is being processed. The controller must provide his name and address, the purpose of processing, the recipients of the data and all other information required to ensure the processing is fair (Articles 10 and 11).

Data may be processed only if at least one of the following is true:

- when the data subject has given his/her consent (Article 7);
- when the processing is necessary for the performance of or the entering into a contract;
- when processing is necessary for compliance with a legal obligation;
- when processing is necessary in order to protect the vital interests of the data subject;
- processing is necessary for the performance of a task carried out in the public interest or in the exercise of official authority vested in the controller or in a third party to whom the data are disclosed;
- processing is necessary for the purposes of the legitimate interests pursued by the controller or by the third party or parties to whom the data are disclosed, except where such interests are overridden by the interests for fundamental rights and freedoms of the data subject. The data subject has the right to access all data processed about him/her. The data subject even has the right to demand the rectification, deletion

or blocking of data that is incomplete, inaccurate or not being processed in compliance with the data protection rules (Article 12).

In relation to Article 7, the data subject has the right to withdraw his or her consent at any time. The withdrawal of consent shall not affect the lawfulness of processing based on consent before its withdrawal.

Personal data may be processed only insofar as it is adequate, relevant and not excessive in relation to the purposes for which they are collected and/or further processed. The data must be accurate and, where necessary, kept up to date; every reasonable step must be taken to ensure that data which are inaccurate or incomplete, having regard to the purposes for which they were collected or for which they are further processed, are erased or rectified; the data should not be kept in a form which permits identification of data subjects for longer than is necessary for the purposes for which the data were collected or for which they are further processed. Appropriate safeguards may be adopted for personal data stored for longer periods for historical, statistical or scientific use (Article 6).

4.13.6.2 Sensitive Personal Data

Some of the personal data that may be processed can be more sensitive in nature and therefore requires a higher level of protection. The GDPR refers to the processing of this data as 'special categories of personal data'. This means personal data about an individual's:

- race;
- ethnic origin;
- political opinions;
- religious or philosophical beliefs;
- trade union membership;
- genetic data;
- biometric data (where this is used for identification purposes);
- health data;
- sex life; or
- sexual orientation.

KEYNOTE

There must still be a lawful basis for processing special category data under Article 6, in exactly the same way as for any other personal data.

This type of data could create more significant risks to a person's fundamental rights and freedoms, for example, by putting them at risk of unlawful discrimination. Additional specific conditions need to be satisfied in relation to this type of data (Article 9(2)).

The processing of the personal data of a child is lawful where the child is at least 16 years old. Where the child is below the age of 16 years, the consent or authorisation of the holder of parental responsibility is required (Article 8).

4.13.6.3 Data Protection Principles

The six data protection principles are central to GDPR compliance and all organisations are required to comply and demonstrate privacy by design.

The most significant addition to previous legislation is the accountability principle. The GDPR requires organisation to show how they comply with the principles, for example, by documenting the decisions you take about a processing activity.

The principles provided by Article 5 of the GDPR requires that personal data shall be:

1. processed lawfully, fairly and in a transparent manner in relation to individuals;

2. collected for specified, explicit and legitimate purposes and not further processed in a manner that is incompatible with those purposes; further processing for archiving purposes in the public interest, scientific or historical research purposes or statistical purposes shall not be considered to be incompatible with the initial purposes;
3. adequate, relevant and limited to what is necessary in relation to the purposes for which they are processed;
4. accurate and, where necessary, kept up to date; every reasonable step must be taken to ensure that personal data that are inaccurate, having regard to the purposes for which they are processed, are erased or rectified without delay;
5. kept in a form which permits identification of data subjects for no longer than is necessary for the purposes for which the personal data are processed; personal data may be stored for longer periods insofar as the personal data will be processed solely for archiving purposes in the public interest, scientific or historical research purposes or statistical purposes subject to implementation of the appropriate technical and organisational measures required by the GDPR in order to safeguard the rights and freedoms of individuals;
6. processed in a manner that ensures appropriate security of the personal data, including protection against unauthorised or unlawful processing and against accidental loss, destruction or damage, using appropriate technical or organisational measures.

KEYNOTE

In brief the six key principles of the GDPR are:

- Lawfulness, fairness and transparency
- Purpose limitation
- Data minimisation
- Accuracy
- Storage limitation
- Integrity and confidentiality (security)

4.13.6.4 Offences Relating to Personal Data

The 2018 Act creates a number of offences in relation to personal data, proceedings for which can only be instigated by the Commissioner, or with the consent of the Director of Public Prosecutions.

These offences include:

- Unlawful obtaining etc. of personal data (s. 170).
- Re-identification of de-identified personal data (s. 171).
- Alteration etc. of personal data to prevent disclosure to data subject (s. 173).

Specific defences are provided in relation to these offences including where it was necessary for the purposes of preventing or detecting crime.

All these offences are triable summarily and punishable by a fine.

4.13.7 The Regulation of Investigatory Powers Act 2000

The Regulation of Investigatory Powers Act 2000 (RIPA) is the Act governing the law in relation to the use of covert techniques by *public authorities* regarding the use of human intelligence sources and surveillance. It requires that when the police or other law enforcement bodies (e.g. the Serious Fraud Office or the National Crime Agency (NCA)), the security and intelligence services (MI5, MI6 and GCHQ), as well as a large number of other public bodies, including local government, need to use these covert techniques to obtain private information about a person, they do so in a way that is necessary, proportionate, and compatible with human rights. Surveillance measures necessarily involve some interference with private life but have the legitimate aim of protecting national security and economic well-being (*Kennedy* v *United Kingdom* (2011) 52 EHRR 4).

In a policing context, any breach of the Act's provisions, or the provisions contained in the Codes of Practice, issued by the Secretary of State under s. 71, can have three main consequences:

- any evidence obtained may be excluded by a court or tribunal as being unfair;
- proceedings may be taken under the relevant police conduct regulations; or
- a person may make a claim before the Investigatory Powers Tribunal.

4.13.7.1 Surveillance and Covert Human Intelligence Sources

Part II of the Regulation of Investigatory Powers Act 2000, s. 26 provides:

(1) This Part applies to the following conduct—
   (a) directed surveillance;
   (b) intrusive surveillance; and
   (c) the conduct and use of covert human intelligence sources.

KEYNOTE

Although only s. 26(1)(c) expressly uses the word 'covert' for the nature of the activity, it is relevant to *all three* of these areas. Part II is concerned with *covert* activity and so, as a general rule, if it is not covert, it is not covered.

Some law enforcement activities fall outside the scope of the Act, e.g. 'property interference' which is a very intrusive form of intelligence gathering such as attaching listening devices within people's homes. This type of activity is covered by part III of the Police Act 1997 and is beyond the scope of this Manual.

4.13.7.2 Covert Human Intelligence Sources (CHIS): Definition

The following, which relates to s. 26, is an extract from the Covert Human Intelligence Sources Revised Code of Practice (August 2018), Chapter 2, which states:

Definition of a covert human intelligence source (CHIS)

2.1 Under the 2000 Act, a person is a CHIS if:
- they establish or maintain a personal or other relationship with a person for the covert purpose of facilitating the doing of anything falling within paragraph 26(8)(b) or (c);
- they covertly use such a relationship to obtain information or to provide access to any information to another person; or
- they covertly disclose information obtained by the use of such a relationship or as a consequence of the existence of such a relationship.
   See section 26(8) of the 2000 Act.

2.2 A relationship is established or maintained for a covert purpose if and only if it is conducted in a manner that is calculated to ensure that one of the parties to the relationship is unaware of the purpose.
   See section 26(9)(b) of the 2000 Act for full definition.

2.3 A relationship is used covertly, and information obtained is disclosed covertly, if and only if the relationship is used or the information is disclosed in a manner that is calculated to ensure that one of the parties to the relationship is unaware of the use or disclosure in question.
   See section 26(9)(c) of the 2000 Act for full definition.

2.4 The Regulation of Investigatory Powers (Covert Human Intelligence Sources: Relevant Source) Order 2013 ('the 2013 Relevant Sources Order') further defines a particular type of CHIS as a 'relevant source'. This is a source holding an office, rank or position with the public authorities listed in the Order and Annex B to this code. Enhanced authorisation arrangements are in place for this type of CHIS as detailed in this code. Such sources will be referred to as a 'relevant source' throughout this code.

2.5 Any police officer deployed as a 'relevant source' in England and Wales will be required to comply with and uphold the principles and standards of professional behaviour set out in the College of Policing Code of Ethics.

KEYNOTE

Covert

A purpose is 'covert' here only if the relationship (and the subsequent disclosure of information) is conducted in a manner that is calculated to ensure that one of the parties is unaware of that purpose. Therefore the definition would not usually apply to members of the public generally supplying information to the police. Similarly, people who have come across information in the ordinary course of their jobs who suspect criminal activity (such as bank staff, local authority employees etc.) do not have a covert relationship with the police simply by passing on information.

Great care will be needed, however, if the person supplying the information is asked by the police to do something further in order to develop or enhance it. Any form of direction or tasking by the police in this way could make the person a CHIS and thereby attract all the statutory provisions and safeguards.

Use and Conduct

There are two areas to be considered when considering covert human intelligence sources: the 'use' of a CHIS and 'conduct' as a CHIS. Both areas are strictly controlled by the legislation and require the relevant authorisation if they are to be lawful.

The 'use' of a CHIS involves any action on behalf of a public authority to induce, ask or assist a person to engage in the conduct of a CHIS, or to obtain information by means of the conduct of a CHIS (s. 26(7)(b)).

The conduct of a CHIS is any conduct of a CHIS which falls within para. 2.1 above, that is, steps taken by the CHIS on behalf, or at the request, of a public authority (s. 26(7)(a)). Most CHIS authorisations will be for both use and conduct as public authorities usually task the CHIS to undertake covert action, and because the CHIS will be expected to take action in relation to the public authority, such as responding to particular tasking.

Generally, covertly recording conversations and other personal information about a particular person will amount to some form of 'surveillance' (and therefore will be governed by the strict rules regulating such operations). However, such use of a CHIS will not amount to 'surveillance' (s. 48(3)).

Note that, apart from the many other considerations of using a CHIS, the police owe a duty to take reasonable care to avoid unnecessary disclosure to the general public of information provided by a CHIS (*Swinney v Chief Constable of Northumbria (No. 2)* (1999) 11 Admin LR 811).

4.13.7.3   CHIS: General Rules on Authorisations

In relation to the authorisation of a CHIS by the police the Regulation of Investigatory Powers Act 2000, s. 29 states:

(1)   Subject to the following provisions of this Part, the persons designated for the purposes of this section shall each have power to grant authorisations for the conduct or the use of a covert human intelligence source.

(2)   A person shall not grant an authorisation for the conduct or the use of a covert human intelligence source unless he believes—

    (a) that the authorisation is necessary on grounds falling within subsection (3);

    (b) that the authorised conduct or use is proportionate to what is sought to be achieved by that conduct or use; and

    (c) that arrangements exist for the source's case that satisfy—

       (i)   the requirements of subsection (4A), in the case of a source of a relevant collaborative unit;

       (ii) …

       (iii) the requirements of subsection (5), in the case of any other source;

    and that satisfy such other requirements as may be imposed by order made by the Secretary of State.

(2A) For the meaning of 'relevant collaborative unit' in subsection (2)(c)(i), see section 29A.

(3) An authorisation is necessary on grounds falling within this subsection if it is necessary—

    (a) in the interests of national security;

    (b) for the purpose of preventing or detecting crime or of preventing disorder;

    (c) in the interests of the economic well-being of the United Kingdom;

    (d) in the interests of public safety;

    (e) for the purpose of protecting public health;

    (f) for the purpose of assessing or collecting any tax, duty, levy or other imposition, contribution or charge payable to a government department; or

    (g) for any purpose (not falling within paragraphs (a) to (f)) which is specified for the purposes of this subsection by an order made by the Secretary of State.

KEYNOTE

Note that in relation to s. 29(3)(b), preventing and detecting crime is defined in s. 81(5) and goes beyond the prosecution of offenders and includes actions taken to avert, end or disrupt the commission of criminal offences.

An authorisation under this section may not have the effect of authorising a covert human intelligence resource who is a person designated under s. 38 of the Police Reform Act 2002 to establish contact in person with another person (subs. (6A)). However, although a designated staff member or volunteer would not be able to work undercover face-to-face, they could do so online, for example as part of an online child sexual abuse investigation.

For the purposes of section 29(2)(c)(i), a 'relevant collaborative unit' is a unit that either consists of two or more police forces whose chief officers of police have made an agreement under s. 22A of the Police Act 1996 (s. 29A(2)) or it consists of one or more police forces and the National Crime Agency by virtue of an agreement made under s. 22A (s. 29A(3)).

The following extract from the Covert Human Intelligence Sources Code of Practice, Chapter 3, explains the terms 'necessary' and 'proportionate' contained within s. 29(2) and details the extent of authorisations:

Necessity and Proportionality

3.2 The 2000 Act stipulates that the authorising officer must believe that an authorisation for the use or conduct of a CHIS is necessary in the circumstances of the particular case for one or more of the statutory grounds listed in section 29(3) of the 2000 Act.

3.3 If the use or conduct of the CHIS is deemed necessary on one or more of the statutory grounds, the person granting the authorisation must also believe that it is proportionate to what is sought to be achieved by carrying it out. The degree of intrusiveness of the actions tasked on or undertaken by an authorised CHIS will vary from case to case, and therefore proportionality must be assessed on an individual basis. This involves balancing the seriousness of the intrusion into the private or family life of the subject of the operation (or any other person who may be affected) against the need for the activity in investigative and operational terms.

3.4 The authorisation will not be proportionate if it is excessive in the overall circumstances of the case. Each action authorised should bring an expected benefit to the investigation or operation and should not be disproportionate or arbitrary. The fact that a suspected offence may be serious will not alone render the use or conduct of a CHIS proportionate. Similarly, an offence may be so minor that any deployment of a CHIS would be disproportionate. No activity should be considered proportionate if the information, which is sought, could reasonably be obtained by other less intrusive means.

3.5 The following elements of proportionality should therefore be considered:

- balancing the size and scope of the proposed activity against the gravity and extent of the perceived crime or harm;

- explaining how and why the methods to be adopted will cause the least possible intrusion on the subject and others;

- whether the conduct to be authorised will have any implications for the privacy of others, and an explanation of why (if relevant) it is nevertheless proportionate to proceed with the operation;

- evidencing, as far as reasonably practicable, what other methods had been considered and why they were not implemented, or have been implemented unsuccessfully;

- considering whether the activity is an appropriate use of the legislation and a reasonable way, having considered all reasonable alternatives, of obtaining the information sought.

3.7 An authorisation under Part II of the 2000 Act for the use or conduct of a CHIS will provide lawful authority for any such activity that:
- involves the use or conduct of a CHIS as is specified or described in the authorisation;
- is carried out by or in relation to the person to whose actions as a CHIS the authorisation relates; and
- is carried out for the purposes of, or in connection with, the investigation or operation so described

3.8 In the above context, it is important that the CHIS is fully aware of the extent and limits of any conduct authorised, and that those involved in the use of a CHIS are fully aware of the extent and limits of the authorisation in question.

Authorising officers are also required to take into account collateral intrusion, namely, the risk of interference with the private and family life of persons who are not the intended subjects of the CHIS activity (Code of Practice, para. 3.9). They will also need to be aware of any particular sensitivities in the local community. Consideration should also be given to any adverse impact on community confidence or safety that may result from the use or conduct of a CHIS or use of information obtained from that CHIS (para. 3.17).

4.13.7.4 CHIS: Authorisation Procedures

The following extract from the Covert Human Intelligence Sources Code of Practice, Chapter 5, outlines authorisation procedures for the use or conduct of a CHIS:

Authorisation Procedures

5.4 Responsibility for authorising the use or conduct of a CHIS rests with the authorising officer and all authorisations require the personal authority of the authorising officer. The 2010 CHIS Order as amended by the 2013 Relevant Sources Order designates the authorising officer for each different public authority and the officers entitled to act only in urgent cases. In certain circumstances the Secretary of State will be the authorising officer (see section 30(2) of the 2000 Act).

5.5 The authorising officer must give authorisations in writing, except in urgent cases, where they may be given orally. In such cases, a statement that the authorising officer has expressly authorised the action should be recorded in writing by the applicant (or the person with whom the authorising officer spoke) as a priority. This statement need not contain the full detail of the application, which should however subsequently be recorded in writing when reasonably practicable (generally the next working day).

5.6 Other officers entitled to act in urgent cases may only give authorisation in writing e.g. written authorisation for directed surveillance given by a Superintendent.

5.7 A case is not normally to be regarded as urgent unless the time that would elapse before the authorising officer was available to grant the authorisation would, in the judgment of the person giving the authorisation, be likely to endanger life or jeopardise the operation or investigation for which the authorisation was being given. An authorisation is not to be regarded as urgent where the need for an authorisation has been neglected or the urgency is of the applicant's or authorising officer's own making.

KEYNOTE

Authorising CHIS

Authorising officers should, where possible, be independent of the investigation. However, it is recognised that this is not always possible, especially in the cases of small organisations, or where it is necessary to act urgently or for security reasons.

The Regulation of Investigatory Powers (Directed Surveillance and Covert Human Intelligence Sources) Order 2010 (SI 2010/521, as amended by SI 2013/2788), prescribes the ranks of those within the police service in England and Wales who can authorise a CHIS. The ranks, mode of authorisation and associated time frames are summarised below:

Type of Authorisation	→	Ordinary CHIS	Urgent CHIS
Minimum Rank	→	Superintendent or above	Inspector or above
Form	→	In Writing	Inspector—In Writing Superintendent—In Writing or Oral
Time Frame	→	12 months beginning on the day the authorisation is granted	72 hours beginning from the time authorisation is granted

The relevant rank of an authorising officer for a CHIS is a superintendent and above. However, in urgent cases, where it is not reasonably practicable to have the application considered by someone of that rank in the same organisation, an inspector may generally give the relevant authorisation (sch. 1, part 1 of the 2010 Order). Unless it is renewed, the authorisation given by a superintendent will ordinarily cease to have effect after 12 months beginning on the day it was granted (s. 43(3)(b)). If that authorisation was given orally by a superintendent in an urgent case, it will only last for 72 hours unless renewed, and where the case is urgent and the authority was given by an inspector, it will cease to have effect 72 hours later unless renewed (s. 43(3)(a)).

Authorisations may also be made on an application made by a member of another police force where such a police force is party to a collaborative agreement that provides for this (s. 33(3ZA)–(3ZC)).

Long-term authorisations (those exceeding 12 months) can only be given by a chief constable/commissioner and are subject to approval by a Judicial Commissioner.

A single authorisation can combine two or more different authorisations (e.g. the use of surveillance and the use of a CHIS) but they operate independently of each other (s. 43(2)). This means that when one authorisation lapses, any other authorisations made at the same time do not necessarily end as well.

Authorising 'Relevant Sources'

The ranks, mode of authorisation and associated time frames are summarised below:

Type of Authorisation	→	Ordinary 'Relevant Source'	Urgent 'Relevant Source'
Minimum Rank	→	ACC/Commander or above	Superintendent or above
Form	→	In Writing	In Writing
Time Frame	→	12 months beginning on the day the authorisation is granted	72 hours beginning from the time authorisation is granted

All deployments of undercover officers (referred to in the Order and Code as 'relevant sources') must be authorised by an assistant chief constable/commander or in urgent cases by a superintendent.

Authorisations lasting more than 12 months must be approved by a chief constable/commissioner and the Office of Surveillance Commissioners must give prior approval (sch. 1, part 1A to the 2010 Order). The CHIS Code of Practice states that all police officers deployed as a relevant source must comply with the College of Policing Code of Ethics.

Authorising Juvenile/Vulnerable CHIS

The ranks, mode of authorisation and associated time frames are summarised below:

Type of Authorisation	→	Juvenile/Vulnerable CHIS
Minimum Rank	→	ACC/Commander
Form	→	In Writing
Time Frame	→	Four months beginning on the day the authorisation is granted

Special safeguards apply in relation to juveniles and vulnerable individuals. Juveniles are those under 18 years of age. On no occasion should the use or conduct of a CHIS under 16 years of age be authorised to give information against his parents or any person who has parental responsibility for him. In other cases, authorisations should not be granted unless the special provisions contained within the Regulation of Investigatory Powers (Juveniles) (Amendment) Order 2018 (SI 2018/715) are satisfied.

A vulnerable individual is a person who is or may be in need of community care services by reason of mental or other disability, age or illness and who is or may be unable to take care of him/herself, or unable to protect him/herself against significant harm or exploitation.

The authorisation levels for juveniles and vulnerable individuals are assistant chief constable/commander where they are to be used as sources. Regular reviews of authorisations are required to assess whether it remains necessary and proportionate to use a CHIS and whether the authorisation remains justified. An authorisation must be cancelled if the use or conduct of the CHIS no longer satisfies the criteria for authorisation.

In *R (On the Application of Just for Kids Law)* v *Secretary of State for the Home Department* [2019] EWHC 1772 (Admin) the court held that the scheme relating to the use of a juvenile CHIS adequately protects children's welfare and their Article 8 rights.

An enhanced authorisation regime exists when, through the use or conduct of a CHIS, it is likely that knowledge of legally privileged material or other confidential information will be required (the Regulation of Investigatory Powers (Covert Human Intelligence Sources: Matters Subject to Legal Privilege) Order 2010 (SI 2010/521, as amended by SI 2013/2788)).

4.13.7.5 Covert Surveillance

The Covert Surveillance and Property Interference Revised Code of Practice (August 2018) provides:

2 Activity by public authorities to which this code applies

2.1 Part II of the 2000 Act provides for the *authorisation* of covert surveillance by *public authorities* listed at Schedule 1 of the 2000 Act where that surveillance is likely to result in the obtaining of *private information* about a person.

2.2 Surveillance, for the purpose of the 2000 Act, includes monitoring, observing or listening to persons, their movements, conversations or other activities and communications. It may be conducted with or without the assistance of a surveillance device and includes the recording of any information obtained.

    (See section 48(2) of the 2000 Act)

2.3 Surveillance is covert if, and only if, it is carried out in a manner calculated to ensure that any persons who are subject to the surveillance are unaware that it is or may be taking place.

    (As defined in section 26(9)(a) of the 2000 Act)

2.4 Specifically, covert surveillance may be authorised under the 2000 Act if it is either intrusive or directed:

- Directed surveillance is covert surveillance that is not intrusive but is carried out in relation to a specific investigation or operation in such a manner as is likely to result in the obtaining of *private information* about any person (other than by way of an immediate response to events or circumstances such that it is not reasonably practicable to seek *authorisation* under the 2000 Act);
- Intrusive surveillance is covert surveillance that is carried out in relation to anything taking place on residential premises or in any private vehicle (and that involves the presence of an individual on the premises or in the vehicle or is carried out by a means of a surveillance device).

KEYNOTE

Private Information

Private information includes any information relating to a person's private or family life (s. 26(10)). It should be taken generally to include any aspect of a person's private or personal relationship with others, including family. Family should be treated as extending beyond the formal relationships created by marriage or civil partnership and may include professional or business relationships. Private information may include personal data, such as names, telephone numbers and address details.

What DOES NOT Constitute Surveillance

Some surveillance activity does not constitute intrusive or directed surveillance for the purposes of part II of the 2000 Act and includes:

- covert surveillance by way of an immediate response to events, e.g. where police officers conceal themselves to observe suspicious persons that they come across in the course of a routine patrol;
- covert surveillance as part of general observation activities, e.g. where plain clothes police officers are on patrol to monitor a high street crime hot-spot or prevent and detect shoplifting;
- covert surveillance not relating to specified grounds, e.g. where a specific investigation or operation does not relate to the grounds specified at s. 28(3) of the 2000 Act;
- overt use of CCTV and ANPR systems, e.g. members of the public will be aware that such systems are in use, and their operation is covered by the Home Office Surveillance Camera Code of Practice (June 2013) pursuant to s. 30(1) of the Protection of Freedoms Act 2012 that sets out a framework of good practice that includes existing legal obligations, including the processing of personal data under the Data Protection Act 2018 and a public authority's duty to adhere to the Human Rights Act 1998. The overt use of ANPR systems to monitor traffic flows or detect motoring offences does not require an authorisation under the 2000 Act;
- overt use of facial recognition technology but this must show that it has balanced the individual's right to privacy and considered the risks with a Data Protection Impact Assessment. Otherwise, liability for infringement of Article 8 of the European Convention on Human Rights is possible and the public sector equality duty under s. 149 of the Equality Act 2010 (*R (On the Application of Bridges)* v *Chief Constable of South Wales Police* [2020] EWCA Civ 1058). The Surveillance Camera Commissioner's guidance, *The Police Use of Automated Facial Recognition Technology with Surveillance Cameras* (March 2019) provides best practice;
- certain other specific situations, e.g. the use of a recording device by a CHIS in respect of whom an appropriate use or conduct authorisation has been granted permitting him to record any information obtained in his presence (s. 48(3));
- the recording, whether overt or covert, of an interview with a member of the public where it is made clear that the interview is entirely voluntary and that the interviewer is a member of a public authority.

4.13.7.6 Directed and Intrusive Surveillance

Chapter 3 of the Code of Practice provides guidance on directed surveillance and states:

Directed surveillance

3.1 Surveillance is directed surveillance if the following are all true:
- it is covert, but not intrusive surveillance;
- it is conducted for the purposes of a specific investigation or operation;
- it is likely to result in the obtaining of *private information* about a person (whether or not one specifically identified for the purposes of the investigation or operation);
- it is conducted otherwise than by way of an immediate response to events or circumstances the nature of which is such that it would not be reasonably practicable for an *authorisation* under Part II of the 2000 Act to be sought.

3.2 Thus, the planned covert surveillance of a specific person, where not intrusive, would constitute directed surveillance if such surveillance is likely to result in the obtaining of *private information* about that, or any other person.

KEYNOTE

Where private information is acquired by means of covert surveillance of a person having a reasonable expectation of privacy, a directed surveillance authorisation is appropriate. The fact that a directed surveillance authorisation is available does not mean it is required. There may be other lawful means of obtaining personal data that do not involve directed surveillance.

While a person may have a reduced expectation of privacy when in a public place, covert surveillance of that person's activities in public may still result in the obtaining of private information. This is likely to be the case where that person has a reasonable expectation of privacy even though acting in public and where a record is being made by a public authority of that person's activities for future consideration or analysis. Note also that a person in police custody will have certain expectations of privacy.

Authorising of Directed Surveillance

An authorisation for directed surveillance should not be granted unless it is believed to be proportionate to what is sought to be achieved and necessary on the specified grounds (**see para. 4.13.7.3** in relation to 'necessary' and 'proportionate'). The specified grounds, contained in s. 28(3), are:

- in the interests of national security;
- for the purpose of preventing or detecting crime or of preventing disorder;
- in the interests of the economic well-being of the United Kingdom;
- in the interests of public safety;
- for the purpose of protecting public health;
- for the purpose of assessing or collecting any tax, duty, levy or other imposition, contribution or charge payable to a government department; or
- for any purpose (not falling within paras (a) to (f)) which is specified for the purposes of this subsection by an order made by the Secretary of State.

In *R* v *Bond* [2020] EWCA Crim 1596, where the authority to make a covert audio recording of two defendants speaking in the back of a police van was not necessary or proportionate under s. 28, the seriousness of the breach was mitigated by the fact that all the police officers concerned had acted in the genuine belief that the authority was necessary, proportionate and properly granted.

The Regulation of Investigatory Powers (Directed Surveillance and Covert Human Intelligence Sources) Order 2003 (SI 2003/3171), as amended, sets out the relevant roles and ranks for those who can authorise directed surveillance. The ranks, mode of authorisation and associated time frames are summarised below:

Type of Authorisation →	Ordinary Directed Surveillance	Urgent Directed Surveillance
Minimum Rank →	Superintendent or above	Inspector or above
Form →	In Writing	Inspector—In Writing Superintendent—In Writing or Oral
Time Frame →	Three months beginning on the day the authorisation is granted	72 hours beginning from the time authorisation is granted

In the case of the police the relevant rank will generally be at superintendent level and above, and the authorisation must be in writing except in urgent cases where oral authorisation may be given (s. 43(1)(a)). A written authorisation ceases to have effect after three months beginning on the day it was granted, and if given orally will only last 72 hours unless renewed (s. 43(3)). Where it is not reasonably practicable to have the application considered by a superintendent or above, having regard to the urgency of the case, then an inspector may give the relevant authorisation which will only last 72 hours unless renewed by a superintendent. For the NCA the authorising officer is a Senior Manager (Grade 2) and for urgent cases a Principal Officer (Grade 3).

In *Davies* v *British Transport Police* (2018) IPT/17/93/H it was held that an authorisation should have been obtained where a police officer covertly observed a man on a train suspected of sexual assaults and also took photographs of the suspect.

Authorisations may also be made on an application made by a member of another police force where such police forces are party to a collaborative agreement that provides for them (s. 33(3ZA)–(3ZC)).

As with a CHIS, the Codes of Practice provide additional procedural safeguards regarding where the material sought by the surveillance is subject to legal privilege, is confidential personal information or some journalistic material. It is of interest to note that the House of Lords has held that the 2000 Act permits covert surveillance of communications between lawyers and their clients even though these may be subject to legal professional privilege (*Re McE (Northern Ireland)* [2009] UKHL 15).

4.13.7.7 Intrusive Surveillance

Chapter 3 of the Code of Practice also provides guidance on intrusive surveillance and states:

Intrusive Surveillance

3.19 Intrusive surveillance is covert surveillance that is:
- carried out in relation to anything taking place on residential premises, or
- in any private vehicle, and
- involves the presence of an individual on the premises or in the vehicle, or
- is carried out by a means of a surveillance device.

3.21 The definition of surveillance as intrusive relates to the location of the surveillance, and not any other consideration of the nature of the information that is expected to be obtained, as it is assumed that intrusive surveillance will always be likely to result in the obtaining of private information. Accordingly, it is not necessary to consider whether or not intrusive surveillance is likely to result in the obtaining of private information.

KEYNOTE

Residential Premises

'Residential premises' are considered to be so much of any premises as is for the time being occupied or used by any person, however temporarily, for residential purposes or otherwise as living accommodation. This specifically includes hotel or prison accommodation that is so occupied or used (s. 48(1)). However, common areas (such as hotel dining areas) to which a person has access in connection with their use or occupation of accommodation are specifically excluded (s. 48(7)). The Act further states that the concept of premises should be taken to include any place whatsoever, including any vehicle or movable structure, whether or not occupied as land (s. 48(8)).

Private Vehicle

A 'private vehicle' is defined as any vehicle, including vessels, aircraft or hovercraft, which is used primarily for the private purposes of the person who owns it or a person otherwise having the right to use it. This would include, for example, a company car, owned by a leasing company and used for business and pleasure by the employee of a company (s. 48(1) and (7)).

In *R* v *Plunkett* [2013] EWCA Crim 261, in admitting evidence of statements and admissions by the accused in a police van which were covertly recorded, it was held that a police van is not a private vehicle for the purposes of s. 26(3) and that the authorisation given by a superintendent under s. 28 for directed surveillance was appropriate.

Surveillance is not intrusive if it is carried out by means only of a surveillance device designed or adapted principally for the purpose of providing information about the location of a vehicle (s. 25(4)(a)).

Consistent Quality

If the surveillance is carried out by means of a surveillance device in relation to anything taking place on the premises or private vehicle, but is carried out without that device being present on the premises or in the vehicle, it is not intrusive unless the device is such that it consistently provides information of the same quality and detail as might be expected to be obtained from a device actually present on the premises or in the vehicle (s. 25(5)).

Legal Consultations

The Regulation of Investigatory Powers (Extension of Authorisation Provisions: Legal Consultations) Order 2010 (SI 2010/461) provides that directed surveillance carried out in relation to anything taking place on any premises specified in the Order that are being used for the purpose of legal consultations shall be treated as 'intrusive surveillance'. The 'any premises' includes prisons, police stations, high security psychiatric hospitals, the place of business of any professional legal adviser; and any place used for the sittings and business of any court, tribunal, inquest or inquiry.

Authorising Intrusive Surveillance

As with the other authorisations under the Act, the authorising officer shall not grant an authorisation for the carrying out of intrusive surveillance unless he/she believes that the authorisation is necessary on the specified grounds and that the authorised surveillance is proportionate to what is sought to be achieved by carrying it out (s. 32(2)). The specified grounds, contained in s. 32(3) are:

- in the interests of national security;
- for the purpose of preventing or detecting serious crime;
- in the interests of the economic well-being of the United Kingdom.

In relation to 'national security' a senior authorising officer or designated deputy of a law enforcement agency shall not issue an authorisation for intrusive surveillance where the investigation or operation is within the responsibilities of one of the intelligence services and properly falls to be authorised by warrant issued by the Secretary of State.

'Serious crime' is defined in s. 81(2) and (3) as crime that comprises an offence for which a person who has attained the age of 21 and has no previous convictions could reasonably be expected to be sentenced to imprisonment for a term of three years or more, or which involves the use of violence, results in substantial financial gain or is conducted by a large number of persons in pursuit of a common purpose.

The ranks, mode of authorisation and associated time frames are summarised below:

Type of Authorisation →	Ordinary Intrusive Surveillance	Urgent Intrusive Surveillance
	↓	↓
Minimum Rank →	Chief Constable/Commissioner (or designated deputy)	Chief Constable/Commissioner (or designated deputy)
	↓	↓
Form →	In Writing	In Writing or Oral
	↓	↓
Time Frame →	Three months beginning when the Surveillance Commissioner approves the authorisation	72 hours beginning from the time authorised (provided notice is given to the Surveillance Commissioner)

Authorisations for intrusive surveillance will generally be granted by chief constables/commissioners and the Director General of the NCA (s. 32), or in some cases designated deputies.

A written authorisation will cease to have effect (unless renewed) at the end of a period of three months. Oral authorisations given in urgent cases will cease to have effect (unless renewed) at the end of the period of 72 hours beginning with the time when they took effect.

Except in urgent cases, authorisation granted for intrusive surveillance will not take effect until a Surveillance Commissioner has approved it and written notice of the Commissioner's decision has been given to the person who granted the authorisation. This means that the approval will not take effect until the notice has been received in the office of the person who granted the authorisation within the relevant force or organisation (s. 35(3)(a)). When the authorisation is urgent it will take effect from the time it is granted provided notice is given to the Surveillance Commissioner (s. 35(3)(b)).

Authorisations may also be made on an application made by a member of another police force where such police forces are party to a collaborative agreement that provides for them (s. 33(3ZA)–(3ZC)).

4.13.8 Interception of Communications and Unlawfully Obtaining Communications Data

The Investigatory Powers Act 2016 has repealed parts of the Regulation of Investigatory Powers Act 2000 and provided an updated framework for the use (by the security and intelligence agencies, law enforcement and other public authorities) of investigatory powers to obtain communications and communications data. These powers cover the interception of communications, the retention and acquisition of communications data, and equipment interference for obtaining communications and other data. Codes of Practice have been issued in relation to these provisions.

4.13.8.1 Offence of Unlawful Interception

OFFENCE: **Unlawful Interception—*Investigatory Powers Act 2016, s. 3(1)***
* Triable either way • 2 years' imprisonment and/or a fine on indictment
* Fine summarily

The Investigatory Powers Act 2016, s. 3 states:

(1) A person commits an offence if—
   (a) the person intentionally intercepts a communication in the course of its transmission by means of—
      (i) a public telecommunication system,
      (ii) a private telecommunication system, or
      (iii) a public postal service,
   (b) the interception is carried out in the United Kingdom, and
   (c) the person does not have lawful authority to carry out the interception.
(2) But it is not an offence under subsection (1) for a person to intercept a communication in the course of its transmission by means of a private telecommunication system if the person—
   (a) is a person with a right to control the operation or use of the system, or
   (b) has the express or implied consent of such a person to carry out the interception.

KEYNOTE

In relation to subs. (1)(a) above, the Interception of Communications Code of Practice (2018) states:

2.5 Section 261(11) of the Act defines 'telecommunications service' to mean any service that consists in the provision of access to, and of facilities for making use of, any telecommunication system (whether or not one provided by the person providing the service); and section 261(13) defines 'telecommunication system' to mean any system (including the apparatus comprised in it) which exists (whether wholly or partly in the United Kingdom or elsewhere) for the purpose of facilitating the transmission of communications by any means involving the use of electrical or electromagnetic energy. The definitions of 'telecommunications service' and 'telecommunication system' in the Act are intentionally broad so that they will remain relevant for new technologies.

2.6 The Act makes clear that any service which consists in or includes facilitating the creation, management or storage of communications transmitted, or that may be transmitted, by means of a telecommunication system is included within the meaning of 'telecommunications service'. Internet-based services such as web-based email, messaging applications and cloud-based services are, therefore, covered by this definition.

2.7 ...

2.8 ...

2.9 Section 262(7) of the Act defines 'postal service' to mean any service which consists in one or more of the collection, sorting, conveyance, distribution and delivery (whether in the United Kingdom or elsewhere) of postal items and which is offered or provided as a service the main purpose of which, or one of the main purposes of which, is to transmit postal items from place to place.

2.10 For the purposes of the Act a postal item includes letters, postcards and their equivalents as well as packets and parcels. It does not include freight items such as containers.

No proceedings for any offence under this section may be instituted except by or with the consent of the Director of Public Prosecutions (s. 3(7)).

4.13.8.2 Definition of Interception

The Investigatory Powers Act 2016, s. 4 states:

(1) For the purposes of this Act, a person intercepts a communication in the course of its transmission by means of a telecommunication system if, and only if—

    (a) the person does a relevant act in relation to the system, and

    (b) the effect of the relevant act is to make any content of the communication available, at a relevant time, to a person who is not the sender or intended recipient of the communication.

(2) In this section 'relevant act', in relation to a telecommunication system, means—

    (a) modifying, or interfering with, the system or its operation;

    (b) monitoring transmissions made by means of the system;

    (c) monitoring transmissions made by wireless telegraphy to or from apparatus that is part of the system.

(3) For the purposes of this section references to modifying a telecommunication system include references to attaching any apparatus to, or otherwise modifying or interfering with—

    (a) any part of the system, or

    (b) any wireless telegraphy apparatus used for making transmissions to or from apparatus that is part of the system.

KEYNOTE

The expression 'in the course of its transmission' is critical in applying the extent of the definition of interception. In a case where a listening device installed by the police in the defendant's car had recorded the defendant speaking on his mobile phone, the Court of Appeal held that this did not amount to 'interception', and mere eavesdropping on a conversation between one person at one end of a mobile phone or two people face-to-face could not constitute communication in the course of transmission (*R v Allsopp* [2005] EWCA Crim 703; see also *R v E (Admissibility: Covert Listening Device)* [2004] EWCA Crim 1243).

In relation to s. 4(1)(b), for the meaning of 'content' in relation to a communication, see s. 261(6).

In this section 'relevant time', in relation to a communication transmitted by means of a telecommunication system, means any time while the communication is being transmitted, and any time when the communication is stored in or by the system (whether before or after its transmission) (s. 4(4)). Email messages awaiting collection/access by the intended recipient are still 'being transmitted', as are unreceived or uncollected pager messages. This also includes a situation where a voicemail message has been saved by the recipient on the voicemail facility of a public telecommunications system (*R v Edmondson* [2013] EWCA Crim 1026).

Section 125(3) of the Postal Services Act 2000 explains that a postal packet is in the course of transmission from the time it is posted (i.e. delivered to a post office or letter box) to the time it is delivered to the person to whom it was addressed. The same rule applies in this Act (s. 4(7)).

The interception of a communication does not include references to the interception of any communication broadcast for general reception which covers broadcast such as television and radio (s. 5(1)). It also excludes certain conduct in relation to postal data attached to the communication, e.g. reading the address on the outside of a letter in order to ensure it is delivered to the appropriate location (s. 5(2)).

4.13.8.3 Lawful Authority

The Investigatory Powers Act 2016, s. 6 states:

(1) For the purposes of this Act, a person has lawful authority to carry out an interception if, and only if—

    (a) the interception is carried out in accordance with—

        (i) a targeted interception warrant or mutual assistance warrant under Chapter 1 of Part 2, or

        (ii) a bulk interception warrant under Chapter 1 of Part 6,

    (b) the interception is authorised by any of sections 44 to 52, or

(c) in the case of a communication stored in or by a telecommunication system, the interception—

    (i) is carried out in accordance with a targeted equipment interference warrant under Part 5 or a bulk equipment interference warrant under Chapter 3 of Part 6,

    (ii) is in the exercise of any statutory power that is exercised for the purpose of obtaining information or taking possession of any document or other property, or

    (iii) is carried out in accordance with a court order made for that purpose.

(2) Conduct which has lawful authority for the purposes of this Act by virtue of subsection (1)(a) or (b) is to be treated as lawful for all other purposes.

(3) Any other conduct which—

    (a) is carried out in accordance with a warrant under Chapter 1 of Part 2 or a bulk interception warrant, or

    (b) is authorised by any of sections 44 to 52,

is to be treated as lawful for all purposes.

KEYNOTE

This section sets out the circumstances in which a person has lawful authority to carry out interception, so the offence of unlawful interception is not committed.

There are three ways in which a person may have lawful authority to carry out interception:

- through a targeted or bulk warrant;
- through any of the other forms of lawful interception provided for in ss. 44 to 52 of the Act;
- in relation to stored communications, interception is lawful if authorised by an equipment interference warrant or if it is in exercise of any statutory power for the purpose of obtaining information or taking possession of any document or other property or in accordance with a court order.

There are three types of targeted warrant which can be issued under this chapter: a targeted interception warrant, a targeted examination warrant and a mutual assistance warrant (Part 2, Chapter 1 of the Act). A 'bulk interception warrant' is for the interception of overseas-related communications (Part 6, Chapter 1 of the Act).

Sections 44 to 52 list the other forms of lawful interception. These include interception with the consent of the sender or recipient, by providers of postal or telecommunications services, by businesses etc. for monitoring and record-keeping purposes, by postal services for enforcement purposes, by OFCOM in connection with wireless telegraphy, in prisons, in psychiatric hospitals etc., in immigration detention facilities, and in accordance with overseas requests.

For certain unlawful interceptions the Investigatory Powers Commissioner may serve a monetary penalty notice not exceeding £50,000 on a person if certain conditions are met (s. 7). These conditions are: the person has intercepted, in the United Kingdom, any communication in the course of its transmission by means of a public telecommunication system; the person did not have lawful authority to carry out the interception; the person was not, at the time of the interception, making an attempt to act in accordance with an interception warrant which might, in the opinion of the Commissioner, explain the interception; and the Commissioner does not consider that the person has committed an offence under section 3(1).

4.13.8.4   Unlawfully Obtaining Communications Data

OFFENCE: **Unlawfully Obtaining Communications Data—*Investigatory Powers Act 2016, s. 11***

    • Triable summarily • 12 months' imprisonment and/or a fine

The Investigatory Powers Act 2016, s. 11 states:

(1) A relevant person who, without lawful authority, knowingly or recklessly obtains communications data from a telecommunications operator or a postal operator is guilty of an offence.

(2) In this section 'relevant person' means a person who holds an office, rank or position with a relevant public authority (within the meaning of Part 3).

(3) Subsection (1) does not apply to a relevant person who shows that the person acted in the reasonable belief that the person had lawful authority to obtain the communications data.

KEYNOTE

This section creates the offence of knowingly or recklessly obtaining communications data from a telecommunications or postal operator without lawful authority.

The offence may be committed by a person within a public authority with powers to acquire communications data under Part 3 of the Act (restrictions on use or disclosure of material obtained under warrants etc.). It is a defence if a person in a public authority can show that they acted in the reasonable belief that they had lawful authority to obtain the communications data.

Offences Against the Administration of Justice and Public Interest

4.14.1 Introduction

This chapter deals with a wide range of offences against the administration of justice and also the public interest. The first group of offences involve some form of interference with the machinery of justice such as perjury and witness intimidation, while others have an indirect effect on the process.

4.14.2 Perjury

OFFENCE: **Perjury—*Perjury Act 1911, s. 1***
* Triable on indictment • Seven years' imprisonment

The Perjury Act 1911, s. 1 states:

(1) If any person lawfully sworn as a witness or as an interpreter in a judicial proceeding wilfully makes a statement material in that proceeding, which he knows to be false or does not believe to be true, he shall be guilty of perjury ...
(2) The expression 'judicial proceeding' includes a proceeding before any court, tribunal, or person having by law power to hear, receive, and examine evidence on oath.
(3) Where a statement made for the purposes of a judicial proceeding is not made before the tribunal itself, but is made on oath before a person authorised by law to administer an oath to the person who makes the statement, and to record or authenticate the statement, it shall, for the purposes of this section, be treated as having been made in a judicial proceeding.

KEYNOTE

To commit this offence a defendant must have been *lawfully sworn*; this will include a person who makes a solemn affirmation in place of an oath (Evidence Act 1851, s. 16). The statement made in a 'judicial proceeding' can be one given orally before the court or tribunal, or in the form of an affidavit (sworn statement). If a witness tenders a false statement used under s. 89 of the Criminal Justice Act 1967, he/she commits a separate, lesser offence (see para. 4.14.3). Evidence given by live TV link under the provisions of the Criminal Justice Act 1988, s. 32 is also subject to the offence of perjury.

'Wilful' means deliberate or intentional and it must be proved that any alleged perjury was not the result of a misunderstanding or an accidental slip of the tongue (*R v Millward* [1985] QB 519).

A 'statement material in that proceeding' means that the content of the evidence tendered in that case, although perhaps not crucial to the case, must have some importance to it and not just be of passing relevance. Whether something is material to a case is a question of law for a judge to decide. Whether a motorist had taken a drink between the time of having a road traffic accident and being breathalysed would be such a material issue, and to get a witness to provide false evidence about that matter would be a 'statement material in that proceeding' (*R v Lewins* (1979) 1 Cr App R (S) 246).

Evidence of an opinion provided by a witness who does not genuinely hold such an opinion may also be perjury.

Perjury may be proved by using a court transcript or the evidence of others who were present at the proceeding in question (Perjury Act 1911, s. 14).

Corroboration is required in cases of perjury (Perjury Act 1911, s. 13), solely in relation to the *falsity* of the defendant's statement. There is no requirement under s. 13 for corroboration of the fact that the defendant *actually made* the alleged statement, nor that he/she knew or believed it to be untrue. However, as that corroboration can be documentary and may even come from the defendant's earlier conduct (*R* v *Threlfall* (1914) 10 Cr App R 112) this requirement does not appear to present much of a hurdle to the prosecution.

4.14.2.1 Aiding and Abetting

OFFENCE: **Aiding and Abetting Perjury—*Perjury Act 1911, s. 7***
- If principal offence is contrary to s.1 triable on indictment • Seven years' imprisonment • Otherwise either way • Two years' imprisonment on indictment
- Six months' imprisonment and/or a fine summarily

The Perjury Act 1911, s. 7 states:

(1) Every person who aids, abets, counsels, procures, or suborns another person to commit an offence against this Act shall be liable to be proceeded against, indicted, tried and punished as if he were a principal offender.
(2) Every person who incites ... another person to commit an offence against this Act shall be guilty of a misdemeanour.

KEYNOTE

'Subornation' is the same as procuring.

4.14.3 Offences Similar to Perjury

OFFENCE: **False Statements in Criminal Proceedings—*Criminal Justice Act 1967, s. 89***
- Triable either way • Two years' imprisonment and/or a fine on indictment
- Six months' imprisonment and/or a fine summarily

The Criminal Justice Act 1967, s. 89 states:

(1) If any person in a written statement tendered in evidence in criminal proceedings by virtue of section 9 of this Act, wilfully makes a statement material in those proceedings which he knows to be false or does not believe to be true, he shall be liable ...
(2) The Perjury Act 1911 shall have effect as if this section were contained in that Act.

OFFENCE: **False Statements on Oath—*Perjury Act 1911, s. 2***
- Triable either way • Seven years' imprisonment and/or a fine on indictment
- Six months' imprisonment and/or a fine summarily

The Perjury Act 1911, s. 2 states:

If any person—

(1) being required or authorised by law to make any statement on oath for any purpose, and being lawfully sworn (otherwise than in a judicial proceeding) wilfully makes a statement which is material for that purpose and which he knows to be false or does not believe to be true; ...
he shall be [guilty of an offence].

KEYNOTE

The first offence covers witnesses who tender false statements in criminal proceedings. The second offence covers the making of false statements under an oath which is not sworn in connection with a judicial proceeding.

4.14.4 Perverting the Course of Justice

OFFENCE: **Perverting the Course of Justice—*Common Law***
 • Triable on indictment • Life imprisonment and/or a fine

It is an offence at common law to do an act tending and intended to pervert the course of public justice.

KEYNOTE

Although traditionally referred to as 'attempting' to pervert the course of justice, it is recognised that behaviour which is *aimed* at perverting the course of public justice does just that and the substantive offence should be charged (*R* v *Williams* (1991) 92 Cr App R 158).

'The course of public justice' includes the process of criminal investigation (*R* v *Rowell* (1978) 1 WLR 132).

Perverting the course of justice requires positive acts by the defendant, not merely standing by and allowing an injustice to take place, i.e. omissions. This offence can be committed in a wide variety of ways, including behaviour that could also be covered by other offences, e.g. intimidating witnesses (**see para. 4.14.5.1**). Such overlaps are not at all unusual in English law but, depending on the circumstances, it may be appropriate to charge with a more specific offence, e.g. perjury or witness intimidation.

One way in which this offence is commonly committed is where a prisoner uses a false identity when arrested. However, the Court of Appeal has held that, in many cases, the addition of such a charge is unnecessary and only serves to complicate the sentencing process (*R* v *Sookoo* [2002] EWCA Crim 800 where the defendant made an unsophisticated attempt to hide his/her identity and failed). If it was shown that there were serious aggravating features, for instance where a lot of police time and resources had been involved, a specific charge may be appropriate and could be justified.

Admitting to a crime to enable the true offender to avoid prosecution would fall under this offence (*R* v *Devito* [1975] Crim LR 175), as would abusing your authority as a police officer to excuse someone of a criminal charge (*R* v *Coxhead* [1986] RTR 411). Other examples include:

- making a false allegation of an offence (*R* v *Goodwin* (1989) 11 Cr App R (S) 194 (rape));
- giving another person's personal details when being reported for an offence (*R* v *Hurst* (1990–91) 12 Cr App R (S) 373);
- destroying and concealing evidence of a crime (*R* v *Kiffin* [1994] Crim LR 449).

Where a person makes a false allegation to the police justifying a criminal investigation with the possible consequences of detention, arrest, charge or prosecution and that person intends that the allegation be taken seriously, the offence of perverting the course of justice is *prima facie* made out, whether or not the allegation is capable of identifying specific individuals. This is clear from *R* v *Cotter* [2002] EWCA Crim 1033, a case involving the boyfriend of an Olympic athlete who claimed to have been attacked as part of a racist campaign.

It is important that the requisite intention is proved in every case as that intention cannot be implied, even from admitted facts (*R* v *Lalani* [1999] 1 Cr App R 481).

4.14.5 Considerations Affecting Witnesses, Jurors and Others

There are several areas of law to consider in relation to offences involving witnesses. The main legislative provisions are set out below.

The Serious Organised Crime and Police Act 2005 sets out provisions relating to witness protection arrangements. These arrangements stretch beyond witnesses and extend to a series of people involved in the criminal justice process, including people who are *or have been*:

- constables
- employees accredited under the Police Reform Act 2002
- jurors
- magistrates (or their equivalent outside the United Kingdom)
- holders of judicial office (whether in the United Kingdom or elsewhere)
- the DPP, criminal prosecutors and staff of the Crown Prosecution Service

(see the Serious Organised Crime and Police Act 2005, sch. 5).

Chapter 4 of the Act allows for the making of arrangements to protect these and other relevant people ordinarily resident in the United Kingdom where the 'protection provider' (usually the Chief Officer of Police or the Director General of the National Crime Agency) considers that the person's safety is at risk by virtue of being a witness, constable, juror etc. (s. 82(1)). A protection provider may vary or cancel any arrangements made by him/her under subs. (1) if the provider considers it appropriate to do so. Joint arrangements (e.g. between police forces) can be made where appropriate, and public authorities (other than courts and tribunals or parliament) are under a duty to take reasonable steps to assist protection providers where requested to do so (ss. 83 and 85).

4.14.5.1 Witnesses or Jurors in Investigation or Proceedings for an Offence

OFFENCE: **Intimidating Witnesses and Jurors—*Criminal Justice and Public Order Act 1994, s. 51***

> • Triable either way • Five years' imprisonment and/or a fine on indictment • Six months' imprisonment and/or a fine summarily

The Criminal Justice and Public Order Act 1994, s. 51 states:

(1) A person commits an offence if—
  (a) he does an act which intimidates, and is intended to intimidate, another person ('the victim'),
  (b) he does the act knowing or believing that the victim is assisting in the investigation of an offence or is a witness or potential witness or a juror or potential juror in proceedings for an offence, and
  (c) he does it intending thereby to cause the investigation or the course of justice to be obstructed, perverted or interfered with.
(2) A person commits an offence if—
  (a) he does an act which harms, and is intended to harm, another person or, intending to cause another person to fear harm, he threatens to do an act which would harm that other person,
  (b) he does or threatens to do the act knowing or believing that the person harmed or threatened to be harmed ('the victim'), or some other person, has assisted in an investigation into an offence or has given evidence or particular evidence in proceedings for an offence, or has acted as a juror or concurred in a particular verdict in proceedings for an offence, and
  (c) he does or threatens to do it because of that knowledge or belief.
(3) For the purposes of subsections (1) and (2) it is immaterial that the act is or would be done, or that the threat is made—
  (a) otherwise than in the presence of the victim, or
  (b) to a person other than the victim.
(4) The harm that may be done or threatened may be financial as well as physical (whether to the person or a person's property) and similarly as respects an intimidatory act which consists of threats.
(5) The intention required by subsection (1)(c) and the motive required by subsection (2)(c) above need not be the only or the predominating intention or motive with which the act is done or, in the case of subsection (2), threatened.

KEYNOTE

These offences are designed to exist alongside the common law offence of perverting the course of justice, and there will be circumstances which may fall under both the statutory and the common law offences.

Making a *threat* via a third person, knowing it will be passed on and that the ultimate recipient would be intimidated by it, amounts to an offence under s. 51(1) (*Attorney-General's Reference (No. 1 of 1999)* [2000] QB 365).

In a decision which appears to contradict the specific wording of the statute (s. 51(1)(a), 'he does an act which intimidates, and is intended to intimidate, another person') the Court of Appeal has confirmed that 'an act which intimidates' does not have to result in the victim *actually* being intimidated; so no intimidation 'result' from the defendant's actions is required even though the statute appears to require one. Therefore if a defendant seeks to deter a witness from giving evidence by means of intimidation, the offence could be made out even if the victim was not actually in fear.

In *R* v *Patrascu* [2004] EWCA Crim 2417, the court provided further detail with regard to interpretation of the term 'intimidation'. The court held that a person did an act which intimidated another within the meaning of s. 51(1) if he/she put that other person in fear, or sought by threat or violence to deter that person from some relevant action such as giving evidence. However, mere pressure which did not put the victim in fear or contained no element of threat or violence was insufficient. In other words, while not requiring an intimidation 'result', the defendant must do something more than just pressurising a victim to be guilty of the offence.

'Harm' for the purposes of s. 51(2) means physical harm and not simply an assault or battery. Therefore spitting at a person does not amount to 'harm' for these purposes (*R* v *Normanton* [1998] Crim LR 220).

Section 51(2) provides a similar offence for acts done or threatened in the knowledge or belief that the person, or *another person*, has so assisted or taken part in proceedings. Doing acts to third parties in order to intimidate or harm the relevant person is also covered by this offence (s. 51(3)). Making threats by telephone will amount to 'doing an act to another' (*DPP* v *Mills* [1997] QB 300).

The intention to obstruct, pervert or interfere with the course of justice need not be the only or even the main intention (s. 51(5)).

Section 51(8) creates a statutory presumption under certain circumstances that the defendant had the required motive at the time of the actions or threats.

4.14.5.2 Intimidation of Witnesses in Other Proceedings

OFFENCE: **Intimidation of Witnesses—*Criminal Justice and Police Act 2001, s. 39***

• Triable either way • Five years' imprisonment on indictment • Six months' imprisonment and/or a fine summarily

The Criminal Justice and Police Act 2001, s. 39 states:

(1) A person commits an offence if—
   (a) he does an act which intimidates, and is intended to intimidate, another person ('the victim');
   (b) he does the act—
      (i) knowing or believing that the victim is or may be a witness in any relevant proceedings; and
      (ii) intending, by his act, to cause the course of justice to be obstructed, perverted or interfered with; and
   (c) the act is done after the commencement of those proceedings.
(2) For the purposes of subsection (1) it is immaterial:
   (a) whether or not the act that is done is done in the presence of the victim;
   (b) whether that act is done to the victim himself or to another person; and
   (c) whether or not the intention to cause the course of justice to be obstructed, perverted or interfered with is the predominating intention of the person doing the action in question.

KEYNOTE

In proceedings against a person for this offence, if you can prove that the defendant:

- did any act that intimidated, and was intended to intimidate, another person, and
- that the defendant did that act knowing or believing that that other person was or might be a 'witness' in any relevant proceedings that had already commenced,

there will be a presumption that the defendant did the act with the intention of causing the course of justice to be obstructed, perverted or interfered with (s. 39(3)). This presumption is rebuttable.

'Witness' here extends to anyone who provides, or is able to provide, any information, document or other thing which might be used in evidence in those proceedings (see s. 39(5)).

References to doing an act include threats against people and/or their property and the making of any other statement (s. 39(6)).

This offence is concerned with protecting people who are in some way connected with 'relevant proceedings' which are '*any proceedings in or before the Court of Appeal, the High Court, the Crown Court or any county or magistrates' court which are not proceedings for an offence*' (s. 41(1)). This means that the offence will be relevant if the proceedings involved are civil proceedings in the higher courts or the county court or if they are non-offence proceedings in the Crown Court or magistrates' court (e.g. a hearing to deal with a breach of a community order). You must show that the relevant proceedings had already commenced by the time of the offence.

Inquests or police conduct hearings are not covered by the above offences.

4.14.6 Harming Witnesses

OFFENCE: **Harming Witnesses—*Criminal Justice and Police Act 2001, s. 40***
> • Triable either way • Five years' imprisonment on indictment • Six months' imprisonment and/or a fine summarily

The Criminal Justice and Police Act 2001, s. 40 states:

(1) A person commits an offence if in circumstances falling within subsection (2)—
    (a) he does an act which harms, and is intended to harm, another person; or
    (b) intending to cause another person to fear harm, he threatens to do an act which would harm that other person.
(2) The circumstances fall within this subsection if—
    (a) the person doing or threatening to do the act does so knowing or believing that some person (whether or not the person harmed or threatened or the person against whom harm is threatened) has been a witness in relevant proceedings; and
    (b) he does or threatens to do that act because of that knowledge or belief.

KEYNOTE

This offence is aimed at the general protection of people who have been (or are believed to have been) a witness in 'relevant proceedings' (for 'witness' and 'relevant proceedings', **see para. 4.14.5.2**). The harm caused or threatened does not have to be directed towards the witness him/herself; the key element is the motivation of the defendant. In relation to that motivation, the Act creates a presumption that if you can prove that, between the start of the proceedings and one year after they are concluded, the defendant:

- did an act which harmed, and was intended to harm, another person, or
- threatened to do an act which would harm another person intending to cause that person to fear harm

with the knowledge or belief required by s. 40(2)(a), the defendant will be presumed to have acted because of that knowledge or belief (s. 40(3)). Again, this is rebuttable. It is immaterial whether the act or threat is made (or would be carried out) in the presence of the person who is or would be harmed, or of the person threatened or whether the motive mentioned in s. 40(2)(b) is the main motive. The harm done or threatened can be physical or financial and can be made to a person or property (s. 40(4)).

4.14.7 Assisting Offenders

OFFENCE: **Assisting Offenders—*Criminal Law Act 1967, s. 4***

- Triable on indictment; either way if original offence is either way • Where sentence for original offence is fixed by law, 10 years' imprisonment and/or a fine on indictment; six months' imprisonment and/or a fine summarily • Where sentence for original offence is 14 years' imprisonment, seven years' imprisonment and/or a fine on indictment; six months' imprisonment and/or a fine summarily • Where sentence for original offence is 10 years' imprisonment, five years' imprisonment and/or a fine on indictment; six months' imprisonment and/or a fine summarily • Otherwise three years' imprisonment and/or a fine on indictment; six months' imprisonment and/or a fine summarily

The Criminal Law Act 1967, s. 4 states:

(1) Where a person has committed a relevant offence, any other person who, knowing or believing him to be guilty of the offence or of some other relevant offence, does without lawful authority or reasonable excuse any act with intent to impede his apprehension or prosecution shall be guilty of an offence.

(1A) In this section and section 5 below, 'relevant offence' means—

    (a) an offence for which the sentence is fixed by law,

    (b) an offence for which a person of 18 years or over (not previously convicted) may be sentenced to imprisonment for a term of five years (or might be so sentenced but for the restrictions imposed by section 33 of the Magistrates' Courts Act 1980).

KEYNOTE

For there to be an offence under s. 4 there must first have been a relevant offence committed by someone. That relevant offence must, in the case of the above offence, have been committed by the 'assisted' person.

It must be shown that the defendant knew or believed the person to be guilty of that *or some other* relevant offence. Mere *suspicion*, however strong, that the 'assisted' person had committed a relevant offence will not be enough. Therefore, if the defendant believed that the 'assisted' person had committed a robbery when in fact he/she had committed a theft, that mistaken part of the defendant's belief will not prevent a conviction for this offence.

The defendant can commit the offence before the person assisted is convicted of committing the relevant offence.

This offence must involve some positive act by the defendant; doing or saying nothing will not suffice.

Although there is no duty on people to assist the police in their investigations generally, this offence and the one below create a negative duty not to interfere with investigations after an offence has taken place.

This offence requires the consent of the DPP before a prosecution is brought (s. 4(4)).

This offence cannot be 'attempted' (Criminal Attempts Act 1981, s. 1(4)).

4.14.8 Concealing Relevant Offences

OFFENCE: **Concealing Relevant Offences—*Criminal Law Act 1967, s. 5***

- Triable on indictment; either way if original offence is triable either way
- Two years' imprisonment on indictment
- Six months' imprisonment and/or a fine summarily

The Criminal Law Act 1967, s. 5 states:

(1) Where a person has committed a relevant offence, any other person who, knowing or believing that the offence or some other relevant offence has been committed, and that he has information which might be of material assistance in securing the prosecution or conviction of an offender for it, accepts or agrees to accept for not disclosing that information any consideration

other than the making good of loss or injury caused by the offence, or the making of reasonable compensation for that loss or injury, shall be liable....

KEYNOTE

Again, someone must have committed a relevant offence before this particular offence can be committed. This offence requires proof, not only of the defendant's knowledge or belief that a relevant offence had been committed, but also that the defendant has information that might be of material assistance in securing the *prosecution or conviction* of *an offender* for it.

The main focus of this offence is:

- the acceptance of, or agreement to accept 'consideration' (i.e. anything of value)
- beyond reasonable compensation for loss/injury *caused by the relevant offence*
- in exchange for not disclosing material information.

'Disclosure' does not appear to be confined to information passed to the police. It would probably extend to other agencies with a duty to investigate offences but is perhaps even wider than that.

This offence requires the consent of the DPP before a prosecution can be brought (s. 5(3)) and cannot be attempted (Criminal Attempts Act 1981, s. 1(4)).

4.14.9   Miscellaneous Offences Relating to Offenders

OFFENCE: **Escaping—*Common Law***
- Triable on indictment • Unlimited punishment

KEYNOTE

A person who, being in lawful custody either in prison or elsewhere on a criminal charge, escapes without the use of force commits the common law offence of Escape.

The 'custody' from which a person escapes must be shown to have been lawful. The offence applies to police custody or police detention (see the Police and Criminal Evidence Act 1984, s. 118) or custody following conviction. D is not lawfully confined if he/she has been mistakenly kept in prison after his/her proper release date (*R* v *O'Connor* [2010] EWCA Crim 2842) but note that it is irrelevant if he/she is guilty of the crime for which he/she was imprisoned.

Whether a person was 'in custody' is a question of fact and the word 'custody' is to be given its ordinary and natural meaning (*E* v *DPP* [2002] EWHC 433 (Admin) and *Richards* v *DPP* [1988] QB 701). In proving that a person was in custody at a particular time it should be shown that his/her liberty was restricted in a way that meant that he/she was confined by another and that his/her freedom of movement was controlled; it is not necessary, however, to show that the person's actual ability to move around was physically impeded, e.g. in secure accommodation (*E* v *DPP*).

People may be in lawful custody even if not directly in the custody of a sworn police officer, for example those people who are being dealt with by an investigating officer or escort officers under sch. 4 to the Police Reform Act 2002.

People detained under the Mental Health Act 1983, s. 136, are also in lawful custody.

If a defendant uses force to *break out* of a prison or a police station, he/she commits an offence of prison breach, again at common law and attracting the same punishment and mode of trial as escaping.

Under the Prisoners (Return to Custody) Act 1995, s. 1, a person who has been temporarily released under the Prison Act 1952 commits a summary offence if he/she remains unlawfully at large or fails to respond to an order of recall to prison.

Escort officers designated under sch. 4 to the Police Reform Act 2002 have a duty to prevent the escape of people in their charge whom they are escorting in accordance with their statutory powers (Police Reform Act 2002, sch. 4, part 4, para. 35).

OFFENCE: **Assisting Escape—*Prison Act 1952, s. 39***

- Triable on indictment • 10 years' imprisonment

The Prison Act 1952, s. 39 states:

(1) Any person who
- (a) assists a prisoner in escaping or attempting to escape from a prison, or
- (b) intending to facilitate the escape of a prisoner—
  - (i) brings, throws or otherwise conveys anything into prison,
  - (ii) causes another person to bring, throw or otherwise convey anything into prison, or
  - (iii) gives anything to a prisoner or leaves anything in any place (whether inside or outside a prison),

  is guilty of an offence.

KEYNOTE

Assisting escape can take many different forms. In *R* v *Williams* (1992) 13 Cr App R (S) 236, the offender committed the offence by changing places with a prisoner in an open prison for one night to allow the prisoner to spend the night at home. In *R* v *Walker* (1990–91) 12 Cr App R (S) 65 the offence was committed by an offender who aided a prisoner to escape by meeting him outside the prison and giving him a lift in his car.

The offence under s. 39 applies where the escape is from a prison, remand centre or young offender institution.

The offence under s. 39 does not apply to a prisoner who escapes while in transit to or from prison (*R* v *Moss and Harte* (1986) 82 Cr App R 116).

OFFENCE: **Harbouring Offenders—*Criminal Justice Act 1961, s. 22(2)***

- Triable either way • 10 years' imprisonment and/or a fine on indictment • Six months' imprisonment and/or a fine summarily

The Criminal Justice Act 1961, s. 22 states:

(2) If any person knowingly harbours a person who has escaped from a prison or other institution to which the said section thirty-nine applies, or who, having been sentenced in any part of the United Kingdom or in any of the Channel Islands or the Isle of Man to imprisonment or detention, is otherwise unlawfully at large, or gives to any such person any assistance with intent to prevent, hinder or interfere with his being taken into custody, he shall be liable ...

KEYNOTE

The offence under s. 22(2) applies where the escape is from a prison, remand centre or young offender institution.

The offence under s. 22 does not apply to a prisoner who escapes while in transit to or from prison (*Moss*).

4.14.10 Wasting Police Time

OFFENCE: **Wasting Police Time—*Criminal Law Act 1967, s. 5(2)***

- Triable summarily • Six months' imprisonment and/or a fine

The Criminal Law Act 1967, s. 5 states:

(2) Where a person causes any wasteful employment of the police by knowingly making to any person a false report tending to show that an offence has been committed, or to give rise to apprehension for the safety of any persons or property, or tending to show that he has information material to any police inquiry, he shall be liable ...

KEYNOTE

It is widely thought that there is a minimum number of hours which must be wasted before a prosecution can be brought for this offence. There is no reliable authority on this point.

No proceedings for this offence may be instituted except by or with the consent of the DPP (s. 5(3)). Under the Penalties for Disorderly Behaviour (Amount of Penalty) Order 2002 (SI 2002/1837), the offence under s. 5(2) is a penalty offence and the amount payable is £90.

4.15 Terrorism and Associated Offences

4.15.1 Introduction

The law on terrorism contained in this chapter relates to the Terrorism Act 2000, Anti-terrorism, Crime and Security Act 2001, Terrorism Act 2006 and the Counter-Terrorism and Border Act 2019.

4.15.2 Terrorism Defined

Terrorism is defined in the Terrorism Act 2000, s. 1 as:

(1) ... the use or threat of action where—
    (a) the action falls within subsection (2),
    (b) the use or threat is designed to influence the government or an international governmental organisation, or to intimidate the public or a section of the public, and
    (c) the use or threat is made for the purpose of advancing a political, religious, racial or ideological cause.
(2) Action falls within this subsection if it—
    (a) involves serious violence against a person,
    (b) involves serious damage to property,
    (c) endangers a person's life, other than that of the person committing the action,
    (d) creates a serious risk to the health or safety of the public or a section of the public, or
    (e) is designed seriously to interfere with or seriously to disrupt an electronic system.
(3) The use or threat of action falling within subsection (2) which involves the use of firearms or explosives is terrorism whether or not subsection (1)(b) is satisfied.

KEYNOTE

This definition includes domestic terrorism, and should be considered when dealing with other, more familiar offences such as blackmail, contamination of goods and threats to kill.

The definition recognises that terrorist activity may be motivated by religious, racial or fundamental reasons rather than simply political ones. It also encompasses broad activities (including threats) which, though potentially devastating in their impact on society, may not be overtly violent. Examples of such activity might be interference with domestic water and power supplies or serious disruption of computer networks.

The provision at s. 1(3) means that, where the relevant criminal activity involves the use of firearms or explosives, there is no further need to show that the behaviour was designed to influence the government or to intimidate the public or a section of the public. An example of such activity might be the shooting of a senior military or political figure. A 'firearm' for this purpose includes air weapons (s. 121).

The reference to 'action' here includes action outside the United Kingdom. Similarly, references to people, property, the public and governments apply to all those features whether in the United Kingdom or elsewhere (s. 1(4)).

4.15.2.1 Membership of a Proscribed Organisation

OFFENCE: **Membership of a Proscribed Organisation—*Terrorism Act 2000, s. 11***
    • Triable either way • 10 years' imprisonment and/or a fine on indictment
    • Six months' imprisonment and/or a fine summarily

The Terrorism Act 2000, s. 11 states:

(1) A person commits an offence if he belongs or professes to belong to a proscribed organisation.
(2) It is a defence for a person charged with an offence under subsection (1) to prove—
    (a) that the organisation was not proscribed on the last (or only) occasion on which he became a member or began to profess to be a member, and
    (b) that he has not taken part in the activities of the organisation at any time while it was proscribed.

KEYNOTE

Specific organisations are proscribed by the Secretary of State and include some of the most active and widely known terrorist groups across the world, including Al-Qa'ida (sch. 2 to the Act). What amounts to membership is likely to depend on the nature of an organisation, e.g. membership of a loose and unstructured organisation may not need any formal steps or express process by which a person becomes a member (*R* v *Ahmed* [2011] EWCA Crim 184).

The reverse burden of proof contained in s. 11(2) has been held as imposing an evidential, as opposed to a persuasive, burden of proof (*Attorney-General's Reference (No. 4 of 2002), Sheldrake* v *DPP* [2004] UKHL 43).

Other offences relating to proscribed organisations are provided by s. 12 and include: inviting support; arranging or managing (or assisting in doing so) a meeting of three or more people in public or private, to support, further the activities or be addressed by a person belonging to a proscribed organisation; or addressing a meeting to encourage support or further the activities of the organisation. The Counter-Terrorism and Border Security Act 2019 extends this section by adding that the offence may be committed by expressing an opinion or belief supportive of a proscribed organisation whilst being reckless as to whether a person to whom the expression is directed will be encouraged to support a proscribed organisation (s. 12(1A)).

The Act also created a summary offence of wearing an item of clothing, or wearing, carrying or displaying an article in such a way or in such circumstances as to arouse reasonable suspicion that the defendant is a member or supporter of a proscribed organisation (s. 13). In *Pwr* v *DPP* [2020] EWHC 798 (Admin) it was held that s. 13(1) was a strict liability offence and, although Article 10 of the European Convention on Human Rights (freedom of expression) was engaged, s. 13(1) was a proportionate response. The Counter-Terrorism and Border Security Act 2019 extended this section whereby the offence can be committed by publishing an image of an item of clothing or other article in such a way or in such circumstances as to arouse 'reasonable suspicion' that the writer is a member of or supports a proscribed organisation (s. 13(1A)). Reference to an image is a reference to a still or moving image (produced by any means) (s. 13(1B)).

4.15.3 Terrorism Act 2000: Financial Measures

The main financial measures under the Terrorism Act 2000 relate to terrorist fundraising, possession of property and funding arrangements, and include:

- *inviting* another to provide money or other property (s. 15(1));
- *providing* money or other property (s. 15(3));
- *receiving* money or other property (s. 15(2));
- *possessing* money or other property (s. 16(2));
- *arranging* for money or other property to be made available (s. 17);

in each case intending that, or having reasonable cause to suspect that, it may be used for the purposes of terrorism (ss. 15, 16(2) and 17);

- *using* money or other property for the purposes of terrorism (s. 16(1));
- *concealing, moving or transferring* any terrorist property (s. 18).

Each of these offences is punishable by a maximum of 14 years' imprisonment on indictment (s. 22).

In relation to ss. 15, 16(2) and 17, 'having reasonable cause to suspect' does not mean that the accused must actually suspect that money may be used for the purpose of terrorism but from the information available to the accused, a reasonable person *would* (not might or could) suspect that the money might be used for terrorism (*R v Lane* [2018] UKSC 36).

4.15.4 Terrorism Act 2000: Duty of Disclosure and Tipping Off

The 2000 Act creates a number of offences in relation to the unlawful disclosure of information and provides where disclosure is permissible.

4.15.4.1 Disclosure of Information

OFFENCE: **Disclosure of Information—*Terrorism Act 2000, s. 19***
- Triable either way • Five years' imprisonment and/or a fine on indictment
- Six months' imprisonment and/or a fine summarily

The Terrorism Act 2000, s. 19 states:

(1) This section applies where a person—
   (a) believes or suspects that another person has committed an offence under any of sections 15 to 18, and
   (b) bases his belief or suspicion on information which comes to his attention—
      (i) in the course of a trade, profession or business, or
      (ii) in the course of his employment (whether or not in the course of a trade, profession or business).
(1A) But this section does not apply if the information came to the person in the course of a business in the regulated sector.
(2) The person commits an offence if he does not disclose to a constable as soon as is reasonably practicable—
   (a) his belief or suspicion, and
   (b) the information on which it is based.

KEYNOTE

In relation to s. 19(2), a constable includes an authorised member of staff of the National Crime Agency (s. 19(7B)).

This section requires businesses to report any suspicions they may have that someone is laundering terrorist money or committing any of the other terrorist property offences in ss. 15 to 18. Section 19(1)(b) ensures the offence is focused on suspicions which arise at work.

'Employment' means any employment (paid or unpaid) including work under a contract for services or as an office holder, work experience provided pursuant to a training course or programme or in the course of training for employment, and voluntary work (s. 22A).

It is a defence for a person to prove that he/she had a reasonable excuse for not making the disclosure (s. 19(3)), or that the matters specified were disclosed in accordance with an established procedure for the making of disclosures (s. 19(4)). Disclosure by a professional legal adviser is not required if the information was obtained in privileged circumstances (s. 19(5)).

The Act also provides for offences of failure to disclose information by businesses in the 'regulated sector', i.e. accountancy firms, investment companies, etc. (s. 21A) and tipping-off by businesses in the regulated sector (s. 21D). Businesses in the regulated sector are described in sch. 3A to the Act.

4.15.4.2 Disclosure of Information: Permission

The Terrorism Act 2000, s. 20 states:

(1) A person may disclose to a constable—
   (a) a suspicion or belief that any money or other property is terrorist property or is derived from terrorist property;
   (b) any matter on which the suspicion or belief is based.
(2) A person may make a disclosure to a constable in the circumstances mentioned in section 19(1) and (2).
(3) Subsections (1) and (2) shall have effect notwithstanding any restriction on the disclosure of information imposed by statute or otherwise.
(4) Where—
   (a) a person is in employment, and
   (b) his employer has established a procedure for the making of disclosures of the kinds mentioned in subsection (1) and section 19(2),
   subsections (1) and (2) shall have effect in relation to that person as if any reference to disclosure to a constable included a reference to disclosure in accordance with the procedure.

KEYNOTE

Section 20 ensures that businesses can disclose information to the police without fear of breaching legal restrictions.

4.15.4.3 Information about Acts of Terrorism

OFFENCE: **Information about Acts of Terrorism—*Terrorism Act 2000, s. 38B***
   - Triable either way • 10 years' imprisonment and/or a fine on indictment
   - Six months' imprisonment and/or a fine summarily

The Terrorism Act 2000, s. 38B states:

(1) This section applies where a person has information which he knows or believes might be of material assistance—
   (a) in preventing the commission by another person of an act of terrorism, or
   (b) in securing the apprehension, prosecution or conviction of another person, in the United Kingdom, for an offence involving the commission, preparation or instigation of an act of terrorism.
(2) The person commits an offence if he does not disclose the information as soon as reasonably practicable in accordance with subsection (3).
(3) Disclosure is in accordance with this subsection if it is made—
   (a) in England and Wales, to a constable ...

KEYNOTE

This offence relates to any person who has information that he/she knows or believes might help prevent an act of terrorism or help bring terrorists to justice.

A person resident in the United Kingdom could be charged with this offence notwithstanding that he/she was outside the country when he/she became aware of the information (s. 38B(6)).

It is a defence for a person charged to prove that he/she had a reasonable excuse for not making the disclosure (s. 38B(4)).

4.15.4.4 Disclosure of and Interference with Information Offences

OFFENCE: **Disclosure of Information etc.—*Terrorism Act 2000, s. 39***
   - Triable either way • Five years' imprisonment and/or a fine on indictment
   - Six months' imprisonment and/or a fine summarily

The Terrorism Act 2000, s. 39 states:

(1) Subsection (2) applies where a person knows or has reasonable cause to suspect that a constable is conducting or proposes to conduct a terrorist investigation.
(2) The person commits an offence if he—
  (a) discloses to another anything which is likely to prejudice the investigation, or
  (b) interferes with material which is likely to be relevant to the investigation.
(3) Subsection (4) applies where a person knows or has reasonable cause to suspect that a disclosure has been or will be made under any of sections 19 to 21B or 38B.
(4) The person commits an offence if he—
  (a) discloses to another anything which is likely to prejudice an investigation resulting from the disclosure under that section, or
  (b) interferes with material which is likely to be relevant to an investigation resulting from the disclosure under that section.

KEYNOTE

The offences within this section, including that at s. 39(2)(a), which is sometimes called 'tipping off', are essential to the disclosure regime and have a powerful deterrent effect. The defence at s. 39(5)(a) is listed in s. 118(5) and therefore imposes an evidential burden only on the defendant.

It is a defence for a person charged with an offence under s. 39(2) or (4) to prove that he/she did not know and had no reasonable cause to suspect that the disclosure or interference was likely to affect a terrorist investigation, or that he/she had a reasonable excuse for the disclosure or interference. The evidential burden of proof lies on the defendant.

Section 21D of the Act also provides for a similar offence of 'tipping off' in the regulated sector.

4.15.5 Terrorism Act 2006: Offences

For the purposes of the 2006 Act the offences are grouped into three specific areas; encouragement etc. of terrorism; preparation of terrorist acts and terrorist training; offences involving radioactive devices and materials and nuclear facilities and sites. The offences relating to preparation of terrorist acts and offences involving radioactive devices are beyond the scope of this Manual.

4.15.5.1 Encouragement etc. of Terrorism

The offences within this group are:

- publishes a statement to encourage the commission, preparation or instigation of acts of terrorism or Convention offences (s. 1(2));
- engages in the dissemination of terrorist publications (s. 2(1)).

For the purpose of both these sections it is necessary to prove that the published statement(s) glorifies the act of terrorism and that a reasonable person would understand the statement as an encouragement or inducement to them to commit, prepare or instigate an act of terrorism. This 'reasonable person test' was introduced by the Counter-Terrorism and Border Security Act 2019.

'Glorification' includes any form of praise or celebration, and similar expressions are to be construed accordingly (s. 20(2)). The 'Convention offences' mentioned in s. 1(2) are those offences listed in sch. 1 to the Act and include offences in relation to explosives, biological weapons, chemical weapons, nuclear weapons, hostage-taking, hijacking, terrorist funds, etc.

In relation to an offence under s. 2 of the Act it was held that videos uploaded onto the internet of scenes showing attacks on soldiers of the Coalition forces in Iraq and Afghanistan by insurgents were depicting scenes of terrorism within the definition of s. 1

of the 2000 Act (*R v Gul* [2013] UKSC 64). Under this section, although the accused is free to argue that the prosecution constituted an unacceptable interference with the applicant's right to freedom of speech at common law, this defence is always a matter to be determined by the jury (*R v Brown* [2011] EWCA Crim 2751). In *Faraz v R* [2012] EWCA Crim 2820, it was held that evidence of possession of a publication cannot prove by itself that a person was encouraged by it to commit or instigate terrorist offences. This section does not prevent a person from holding offensive views or personally supporting a terrorist cause or communicating the fact that he or she supports such a cause. What this section prohibits is the intentional or reckless dissemination of a terrorist publication where the effect of an offender's conduct is a direct or indirect encouragement to the commission, preparation or instigation of acts of terrorism (*R v Ali (Humza)* [2018] EWCA Crim 547).

Section 3(1) provides that the offences under ss. 1 and 2 can be committed by publishing a statement electronically, i.e. via the internet. In *Iqbal v R* [2014] EWCA Crim 2650 the defendant posted and shared videos, articles and lectures that amounted to the glorification or encouragement of terrorism. 'Statement' includes a communication of any description, including a communication without words consisting of sounds or images or both (s. 20(6)). Section 3(3) provides for a notice to be served by a constable on the person electronically publishing the statement declaring that it is, in the constable's opinion, unlawfully terrorism-related and requiring its removal or modification (s. 3(3)). The methods for giving such a notice are provided in s. 4 of the Act. The offences under ss. 1 and 2 are punishable on indictment by a term of imprisonment not exceeding fifteen years or a fine or both, and summarily by a term of imprisonment not exceeding six months or a fine or both.

4.15.6 Terrorism Act 2000: Police Powers

The Terrorism Act 2000 (Codes of Practice for the Exercise of Stop and Search Powers) Order 2012 (SI 2012/1794) sets out the basic principles for the use of powers by police officers.

4.15.6.1 Arrest without Warrant

The Terrorism Act 2000, s. 41 states:

(1) A constable may arrest without a warrant a person whom he reasonably suspects to be a terrorist.

> **KEYNOTE**
>
> The definition of a terrorist is broadly a person who has committed one of the main terrorism offences under the Act (including ss. 11, 12, 15 to 18, 54 and 56 to 63), or is or has been concerned in the commission, preparation or instigation of acts of terrorism (s. 40).
>
> A magistrates' warrant may be obtained authorising any constable to enter and search the specified premises for the purpose of arresting the person to whom s. 41 applies (s. 42).

4.15.6.2 Search of Persons

The Terrorism Act 2000, s. 43 states:

(1) A constable may stop and search a person whom he reasonably suspects to be a terrorist to discover whether he has in his possession anything which may constitute evidence that he is a terrorist.
(2) A constable may search a person arrested under section 41 to discover whether he has in his possession anything which may constitute evidence that he is a terrorist.
(3) ...

(4) A constable may seize and retain anything which he discovers in the course of a search of a person under subsection (1) or (2) and which he reasonably suspects may constitute evidence that the person is a terrorist.

(4A) Subsection (4B) applies if a constable, in exercising the power under subsection (1) to stop a person whom the constable reasonably suspects to be a terrorist, stops a vehicle (see section 116(2)).

KEYNOTE

Where a vehicle is stopped the constable may search the vehicle, and anything in or on it, to discover whether there is anything which may constitute evidence that the person concerned is a terrorist, and may seize and retain anything which the constable discovers in the course of such a search, and reasonably suspects may constitute evidence that the person is a terrorist (s. 43(4B)). Nothing in s. 43(4B) confers a power to search any person but the power to search in that subsection is in addition to the power in subsection (1) to search a person whom the constable reasonably suspects to be a terrorist (s. 43(4C)).

In relation to s. 43(4A), s. 116(2) provides that the power to stop a person includes the power to stop a vehicle (other than an aircraft which is airborne).

4.15.6.3 Search of Vehicles

The Terrorism Act 2000, s. 43A states:

(1) Subsection (2) applies if a constable reasonably suspects that a vehicle is being used for the purposes of terrorism.

(2) The constable may stop and search—
   (a) the vehicle;
   (b) the driver of the vehicle;
   (c) a passenger in the vehicle;
   (d) anything in or on the vehicle or carried by the driver or a passenger;
   to discover whether there is anything which may constitute evidence that the vehicle is being used for the purposes of terrorism.

KEYNOTE

A constable may seize and retain anything which the constable discovers in the course of a search under this section, and reasonably suspects may constitute evidence that the vehicle is being used for the purposes of terrorism (s. 43A(3)).

'Driver' in relation to an aircraft, hovercraft or vessel, means the captain, pilot or other person with control of the aircraft, hovercraft or vessel or any member of its crew and, in relation to a train, includes any member of its crew (s. 43A(5)).

4.15.6.4 Stop and Search in Specified Locations

The Terrorism Act 2000, s. 47A states:

(1) A senior police officer may give an authorisation under subsection (2) or (3) in relation to a specified area or place if the officer—
   (a) reasonably suspects that an act of terrorism will take place; and
   (b) reasonably considers that—
      (i) the authorisation is necessary to prevent such an act;
      (ii) the specified area or place is no greater than is necessary to prevent such an act; and
      (iii) the duration of the authorisation is no longer than is necessary to prevent such an act.

(2) An authorisation under this subsection authorises any constable in uniform to stop a vehicle in the specified area or place and to search—
   (a) the vehicle;
   (b) the driver of the vehicle;

(c) a passenger in the vehicle;

(d) anything in or on the vehicle or carried by the driver or a passenger.

(3) An authorisation under this subsection authorises any constable in uniform to stop a pedestrian in the specified area or place and to search—

(a) the pedestrian;

(b) anything carried by the pedestrian.

KEYNOTE

A constable in uniform may exercise the power conferred by an authorisation only for the purpose of discovering whether there is anything which may constitute evidence that the vehicle concerned is being used for the purposes of terrorism or (as the case may be) that the person concerned is a terrorist within the meaning of s. 40 (s. 47A(4)). However, the power conferred by such an authorisation may be exercised whether or not the constable reasonably suspects that there is such evidence (s. 47A(5)).

A constable may seize and retain anything which the constable discovers in the course of a search if he/she reasonably suspects that it may constitute evidence that the vehicle concerned is being used for the purposes of terrorism or (as the case may be) that the person is a terrorist (s. 47A(6)).

A 'senior police officer' who may give an authorisation is a police officer for the area who is of at least the rank of assistant chief constable (or commander) (sch. 6B).

Authorisation may also be given to prohibit or restrict parking on a specified road where it is considered expedient for the prevention of acts of terrorism (s. 48(1) and (2)). The power may be exercised by a constable placing a traffic sign on the road concerned (s. 49(1)).

4.15.7 Cordons

The 2000 Act gives the police the power, for a limited period, to designate or demarcate a specific area as a cordoned area for the purposes of a terrorist investigation, for instance, in the wake of a bomb.

4.15.7.1 Cordoned Areas

The Terrorism Act 2000, s. 33 states:

(1) An area is a cordoned area for the purposes of this Act if it is designated under this section.

(2) A designation may be made only if the person making it considers it expedient for the purposes of a terrorist investigation.

(3) If a designation is made orally, the person making it shall confirm it in writing as soon as is reasonably practicable.

KEYNOTE

Section 32 provides the meaning of 'terrorist investigation' as an investigation of:

- the commission, preparation or instigation of acts of terrorism;
- an act which appears to have been done for the purposes of terrorism;
- the resources of a proscribed organisation;
- the commission, preparation or instigation of an offence under this Act or under part 1 of the Terrorism Act 2006 other than an offence under s. 1 or 2 of that Act.

The person making a designation shall arrange for the demarcation of the cordoned area, so far as is reasonably practicable, by means of tape marked with the word 'police', or in such other manner as a constable considers appropriate (s. 33(4)).

4.15.7.2 Power to Designate

The Terrorism Act 2000, s. 34 states:

(1) Subject to subsections (1A), (1B) and (2), a designation under section 33 may only be made—
  (a) where the area is outside Northern Ireland and is wholly or partly within a police area, by an officer for the police area who is of at least the rank of superintendent, and
  (b) ...

(1A) ...

(1B) ...

(1C) ...

(2) A constable who is not of the rank required by subsection (1) may make a designation if he considers it necessary by reason of urgency.

(3) Where a constable makes a designation in reliance on subsection (2) he shall as soon as is reasonably practicable—
  (a) make a written record of the time at which the designation was made, and
  (b) ensure that a police officer of at least the rank of superintendent is informed.

(4) An officer who is informed of a designation in accordance with subsection (3)(b)—
  (a) shall confirm the designation or cancel it with effect from such time as he may direct, and
  (b) shall, if he cancels the designation, make a written record of the cancellation and the reason for it.

KEYNOTE

This power is designated to be investigatory in its nature.

Subsections (1A), (1B) and (1C) provide powers to designate to the Ministry of Defence and British Transport Police in relation to specified areas under their jurisdiction.

The period of designation begins at the time the order is made and ends on the date specified in the order. The initial designation cannot extend beyond 14 days (s. 35(2)). However, the period during which a designation has effect may be extended in writing from time to time by the person who made it, or an officer of at least superintendent rank (s. 35(3)). There is a time limit of 28 days on extended designations and this appears to mean an overall time limit of 28 days beginning with the day on which the order is made (s. 35(5)).

4.15.7.3 Police Powers

The Terrorism Act 2000, s. 36 states:

(1) A constable in uniform may—
  (a) order a person in a cordoned area to leave it immediately,
  (b) order a person immediately to leave premises which are wholly or partly in or adjacent to a cordoned area,
  (c) order the driver or person in charge of a vehicle in a cordoned area to move it from the area immediately,
  (d) arrange for the removal of a vehicle from a cordoned area,
  (e) arrange for the movement of a vehicle within a cordoned area,
  (f) prohibit or restrict access to a cordoned area by pedestrians or vehicles.

KEYNOTE

The officer giving the order or making the arrangements and prohibitions set out here must be in uniform. Therefore detectives or other plain clothes officers involved in the terrorist investigation will not have these powers available to them.

The powers under s. 36 are among those that can be conferred on a Police Community Support Officer designated under sch. 4 to the Police Reform Act 2002.

Failing to comply with an order, prohibition or restriction under this section is a summary offence punishable by three months' imprisonment and/or a fine (s. 36(2) and (4)).

This wording will presumably cover refusal. There is a defence if the person can show that he/she had a reasonable excuse for the failure.

A superintendent or above may request passenger, service and crew information from an owner or agent of a ship or aircraft which is arriving, or expected to arrive, at any place in the United Kingdom or is leaving, or expected to leave, from any place in the United Kingdom (Immigration, Asylum and Nationality Act 2006, s. 32(2)). There is a similar power to request freight information from the owners or agents of a ship or aircraft, and in the case of a vehicle, the owner or hirer (s. 33(2) and (3)).

It is an offence if without reasonable excuse a person fails to comply with a requirement imposed under ss. 32(2) or 33(2). The request must be for a police purpose, i.e. the prevention, detection, investigation or prosecution of criminal offences; safeguarding national security; and such other purposes as may be specified (s. 33(5)).

4.15.8 Offences Involving Explosive Substances

OFFENCE: **Causing Explosion Likely to Endanger Life or Property—*Explosive Substances Act 1883, s. 2***

- Triable on indictment • Life imprisonment

The Explosive Substances Act 1883, s. 2 states:

(1) A person who in the United Kingdom or (being a citizen of the United Kingdom and Colonies) in the Republic of Ireland unlawfully and maliciously causes by any explosive substance an explosion of a nature likely to endanger life or to cause serious injury to property shall, whether any injury to person or property has been actually caused or not, be guilty of an offence ...

KEYNOTE

The consent of the Attorney-General (or Solicitor-General) is required before prosecuting this offence (s. 7(1) of the 1883 Act).

'Explosive substance' includes any materials for making any explosive substance; any implement or apparatus used, or intended or adapted to be used for causing or aiding any explosion (s. 9(1)).

The definition of 'explosive' under the Explosives Act 1875 also applies to this offence (*R* v *Wheatley* [1979] 1 WLR 144). Therefore fireworks and petrol bombs will be covered (*R* v *Bouch* [1983] QB 246).

Articles which have been held to amount to 'explosive substances' include:

- shotguns (*R* v *Downey* [1971] NI 224);
- electronic timers (*R* v *Berry (No. 3)* [1995] 1 WLR 7; *R* v *G* [2009] UKHL 13);
- gelignite with a fuse and detonator (*R* v *McCarthy* [1964] 1 WLR 196).

You must prove that the act was carried out 'maliciously'.

Sections 73 to 75 of the Explosives Act 1875 provide powers to search for explosives in connection with the offences under ss. 2, 3 and 4.

OFFENCE: **Attempting to Cause Explosion or Keeping Explosive with Intent—*Explosive Substances Act 1883, s. 3***

- Triable on indictment • Life imprisonment

The Explosive Substances Act 1883, s. 3 states:

(1) A person who in the United Kingdom or a dependency or (being a citizen of the United Kingdom and Colonies) elsewhere unlawfully and maliciously—
   (a) does any act with intent to cause, or conspires to cause, by an explosive substance an explosion of a nature likely to endanger life, or cause serious injury to property, whether in the United Kingdom or elsewhere, or

(b) makes or has in his possession or under his control an explosive substance with intent by means thereof to endanger life, or cause serious injury to property, whether in the United Kingdom or elsewhere, or to enable any other person so to do

shall, whether any explosion does or does not take place, and whether any injury to person or property is actually caused or not, be guilty of an offence ...

OFFENCE: Making or Possessing Explosive under Suspicious Circumstances—*Explosive Substances Act 1883, s. 4*

- Triable on indictment • 14 years' imprisonment

The Explosive Substances Act 1883, s. 4 states:

(1) Any person who makes or knowingly has in his possession or under his control any explosive substance under such circumstances as to give rise to a reasonable suspicion that he is not making it or does not have it in his possession or under his control for a lawful object, shall, unless he can show that he made it or had it in his possession or under his control for a lawful object, be guilty of [an offence] ...

KEYNOTE

The offence under s. 3 is one of specific intent.

Both of the offences under ss. 3 and 4 require the consent of the Attorney-General (or Solicitor-General) before a prosecution can be brought.

In cases of 'possession' the wording of these offences requires the prosecution to prove that a defendant *had* the relevant article in his/her possession and that he/she knew the nature of it (*R v Hallam* [1957] 1 QB 569). This should be contrasted with the usual approach to offences involving 'possession' where the second part (knowledge of the 'quality' of an item) does not need to be shown. However, the concept of 'in your possession' or 'under your control' is a wide one, as illustrated in a case where the defendant had moved out of his property and left homemade bombs and other articles in some boxes with a friend. New tenants in the property had discovered the boxes which later turned up on a rubbish tip. The defendant went to the police station after learning that he was a suspect and he claimed that he had collected the articles many years previously when he was too young to appreciate how dangerous they were. Although he had left the boxes with his friend he was nevertheless convicted of the offence under s. 4(1) as he still had the explosives under his control when he left the property (*R v Campbell* [2004] EWCA Crim 2309).

'Reasonable suspicion' in this case will be assessed *objectively*, that is, you must prove that the circumstances of the possession or making of the explosive substance would give rise to suspicion in a reasonable and objective bystander (*R v Fegan* (1971) 78 Cr App R 189; *R v G* [2009] UKHL 13).

Whether a person's purpose in having the items prohibited by these offences is a 'lawful object' will need to be determined in each case (*Fegan*). In *R v Riding* [2009] EWCA Crim 892, the defendant alleged he had made a pipe bomb out of mere curiosity, using explosives drained from a number of fireworks. The defence contended that 'lawful object' meant the absence of a criminal purpose rather than a positive object that was lawful. However, the court was satisfied it meant the latter and mere curiosity could not be a 'lawful object' in making a lethal pipe bomb. However, in *R v Copeland* [2020] UKSC 8 it was held that personal experimentation or self-education could be regarded as a 'lawful object'. In a further case considering the lawful object defence, it was held that given the obvious risks with using explosive substances, any experimentation involving them which gives rise to a risk of harm to other people or their property, or other unlawfulness such as causing a public nuisance, will not be capable of coming within the scope of the defence (*R v Flint* [2020] EWCA Crim 1266).

There is no need to show any criminal intent or an unlawful purpose on the part of the defendant (see *Campbell*).

4.16.1 Introduction

The Equality Act 2010 provides a framework of protection against direct and indirect discrimination, harassment and victimisation in services and public functions; premises; work; education; associations; and transport.

This chapter briefly sets out the key features of the 2010 Act together with Article 14 of the European Convention on Human Rights in relation to the 'prohibition of discrimination'.

4.16.2 Article 14—Prohibition of Discrimination

Article 14 of the European Convention on Human Rights states:

> The enjoyment of the rights and freedoms set forth in this Convention shall be secured without discrimination on any ground such as sex, race, colour, language, religion, political or other opinion, national or social origin, association with a national minority, property, birth or other status.

KEYNOTE

Article 14 simply provides a guarantee that access to the Convention's other provisions must be enjoyed equally by everyone under the jurisdiction of the particular State. The list set out in the Article is not exhaustive and other categories of people or grounds of discrimination may be added by the courts (and have been added by the European Court of Human Rights). A person claiming a breach of Article 14 must show that his/her own individual circumstances are similar to those of another person who has been treated differently in relation to the enjoyment of Convention rights.

The open-ended wording of Article 14 means that a wide range of categories of people who can be grouped by reference to their status may be protected. It makes express provision for *indirect* discrimination (see para. 4.16.4.7) and the Divisional Court has expressed considerable doubt as to whether Article 14 provides protection against indirect, as opposed to direct, discrimination (*R (On the Application of Barber)* v *Secretary of State for Work and Pensions* [2002] EWHC 1915 (Admin)).

4.16.3 Protected Characteristics

The protected characteristics covered by the Act are:

- Age
- Disability
- Gender reassignment
- Marriage and civil partnerships
- Race
- Religion or belief
- Sex
- Sexual Orientation

KEYNOTE

Although Pregnancy and Maternity are also protected characteristics they are dealt with separately in the Act (see para. 4.16.4.6).

The Police and Criminal Evidence Act 1984, Code of Practice, Code B, para. 1.3A provides that the Equality Act 2010 makes it unlawful for police officers to discriminate against, harass or victimise any person on the grounds of the 'protected characteristics' of age, disability, gender reassignment, race, religion or belief, sex or sexual orientation, marriage or civil partnership, pregnancy and maternity, when using their powers.

4.16.3.1 Age

The Equality Act 2010, s. 5 states:

(1) In relation to the protected characteristic of age—
  (a) a reference to a person who has a particular protected characteristic is a reference to a person of a particular age group;
  (b) a reference to persons who share a protected characteristic is a reference to persons of the same age group.
(2) A reference to an age group is a reference to a group of persons defined by reference to age, whether by reference to a particular age or to a range of ages.

KEYNOTE

Where people fall in the same age group they share the protected characteristic of age, for example, an age group would include 'over fifties' or 21-year-olds.

The Equality Act 2010 (Age Exceptions) Order 2012 (SI 2012/2466) details situations where age discrimination is permitted. Discrimination may take place in areas such as financial services, age-based state allowances and benefits, private clubs or associations catering for a particular age group, positive action measures, and objective justification. Persons aged 18 and under do not benefit from the protections in relation to goods, services, and public functions.

4.16.3.2 Disability

The Equality Act 2010, s. 6 states:

(1) A person (P) has a disability if—
  (a) P has a physical or mental impairment, and
  (b) the impairment has a substantial and long-term adverse effect on P's ability to carry out normal day-to-day activities.
(2) A reference to a disabled person is a reference to a person who has a disability.
(3) In relation to the protected characteristic of disability—
  (a) a reference to a person who has a particular protected characteristic is a reference to a person who has a particular disability;
  (b) a reference to persons who share a protected characteristic is a reference to persons who have the same disability.

KEYNOTE

Only people who have a disability, or have had a disability in the past, are protected against discrimination.

Schedule 9 to the Act and regulations made under the 2010 Act clarify the definition of disability. Physical or mental impairment includes sensory impairments such as sight and hearing, or mental impairments such as Asperger's Syndrome, autism, dyslexia, and mental health issues. Cancer, HIV infection and multiple sclerosis are each a disability. The focus of the Act is on the effect of impairment where there is evidence of a substantial long-term adverse effect. The effect of an impairment is long term if it has lasted for at least

12 months, it is likely to last for at least 12 months, or it is likely to last for the rest of the life of the person affected.

The Equality Act (Disability) Regulations 2010 (SI 2010/2128) contain provisions regarding who is to be considered as having the protected characteristic of disability and is a disabled person for the purposes of the Act.

In relation to s. 6(1)(b) 'ability to carry out normal day-to-day activities', in *Chief Constable of Dumfries and Galloway Constabulary* v *Adams* [2009] ICR 1034 it was held that normal day-to-day activities for a police officer included working nights. Confrontational duties were also considered a 'normal day-to-day activity' (*Hart* v *Chief Constable of Derbyshire Constabulary* [2008] EWCA Civ 929).

4.16.3.3 Gender Reassignment

The Equality Act 2010, s. 7 states:

(1) A person has the protected characteristic of gender reassignment if the person is proposing to undergo, is undergoing or has undergone a process (or part of a process) for the purpose of re-assigning the person's sex by changing physiological or other attributes of sex.

(2) A reference to a transsexual person is a reference to a person who has the protected characteristic of gender reassignment.

(3) In relation to the protected characteristic of gender reassignment—

(a) a reference to a person who has a particular protected characteristic is a reference to a transsexual person;

(b) a reference to persons who share a protected characteristic is a reference to transsexual persons.

KEYNOTE

A woman making the transition to being a man and a man making the transition to being a woman both share the characteristic of gender reassignment, as does a person who has only just started out on the process of changing his/her sex and a person who has completed the process.

The established legal principle in law is that gender is set at birth. If you are born male you remain male and vice versa (*Corbett* v *Corbett* [1970] 2 WLR 1306). However, in *A* v *Chief Constable of West Yorkshire and the Secretary of State for Work and Pensions* [2004] UKHL 21 it was held that it was no longer possible in the context of employment to regard a transsexual as being his/her birth gender. But public interest considerations in relation to the police service may determine that a gender-reassigned applicant is not offered employment.

4.16.3.4 Marriage and Civil Partnerships

The Equality Act 2010, s. 8 states:

(1) A person has the protected characteristic of marriage and civil partnership if the person is married or is a civil partner.

(2) In relation to the protected characteristic of marriage and civil partnership—

(a) a reference to a person who has a particular protected characteristic is a reference to a person who is married or is a civil partner;

(b) a reference to persons who share a protected characteristic is a reference to persons who are married or are civil partners.

KEYNOTE

People who are not married or civil partners do not have this characteristic.

The Marriage (Same Sex Couples) Act 2013 extended marriage to same-sex couples and the Civil Partnership (Opposite-sex Couples) Regulations 2019 extended civil partnership to opposite sex couples.

4.16.3.5 Race

The Equality Act 2010, s. 9 states:

(1) Race includes—
    (a) colour;
    (b) nationality;
    (c) ethnic or national origins.
(2) In relation to the protected characteristic of race—
    (a) a reference to a person who has a particular protected characteristic is a reference to a person of a particular racial group;
    (b) a reference to persons who share a protected characteristic is a reference to persons of the same racial group.
(3) A racial group is a group of persons defined by reference to race; and a reference to a person's racial group is a reference to a racial group into which the person falls.
(4) The fact that a racial group comprises two or more distinct racial groups does not prevent it from constituting a particular racial group.

KEYNOTE

People who have or share characteristics of colour, nationality or ethnic or national origins can be described as belonging to a particular racial group. A racial group can be made up of two or more different racial groups.

'Nationality' has been held to include citizenship acquired by birth, and in *Souster* v *BBC Scotland* [2001] IRLR 150, it was held that an English applicant can be discriminated against by a Scottish employer.

'Ethnic group' may include any group with a shared culture or history (*Mandla* v *Dowell Lee* [1983] 2 AC 548). Sikhs (*Mandla* v *Dowell Lee* [1983] 2 AC 548), Jews (*Seide* v *Gillette Industries Ltd* [1980] IRLR 427), Romany Gypsies (*Commission for Racial Equality* v *Dutton* [1989] QB 783), and Irish Travellers (*O'Leary* v *Allied Domecq Inns Ltd* (CL 950275 July 2000, Central London County Court), have all been held to be ethnic groups, but Scots, Welsh and English are however not an ethnic group (*Dawkins* v *Department of the Environment* [1993] IRLR 284).

'National origins' may overlap with nationality but the two concepts can be distinguished since 'nationality' is concerned with membership of a particular nation, and 'national origins' describes a person's connection by birth with a nation (*Ealing London Borough Council* v *Race Relations Board* [1972] AC 342).

'Racial group' includes a group of people who have or share a colour, ethnic, or national origin or nationality.

A Minister of the Crown may amend the Act so as to add 'caste' to the current definition of 'race' (s. 9(5)). The term 'caste' denotes a hereditary, endogamous (marrying within the group) community associated with a traditional occupation and ranked accordingly on a perceived scale of ritual purity, e.g. the four classes (varnas) of Hindu tradition (the Brahmin, Kshatriya, Vaishya and Shudra communities). In *Chandhok* v *Tirkey* [2014] UKEAT 0190/14/1912 it was considered that 'caste' might come within s. 9(1)(c) since 'ethnic origins' had a wide and flexible ambit, including characteristics determined by 'descent'.

4.16.3.6 Religion or Belief

The Equality Act 2010, s. 10 states:

(1) Religion means any religion and a reference to religion includes a reference to a lack of religion.
(2) Belief means any religious or philosophical belief and a reference to belief includes a reference to a lack of belief.
(3) In relation to the protected characteristic of religion or belief—
    (a) a reference to a person who has a particular protected characteristic is a reference to a person of a particular religion or belief;
    (b) a reference to persons who share a protected characteristic is a reference to persons who are of the same religion or belief.

KEYNOTE

The section provides a definition in line with the freedom of thought, conscience and religion guaranteed by Article 9 of the European Convention on Human Rights. The main limitation is that the religion must have a clear structure and belief system. Denominations or sects within a religion can be considered to be a religion or belief, such as Protestants and Catholics within Christianity.

In *Eweida* v *United Kingdom* (2013) 57 EHRR 8 it was held that prohibiting a woman from visibly wearing a cross at work amounted to an interference with her right to manifest her Christian religion and this was in breach of the positive obligation under Article 9 of the European Convention on Human Rights (Right to freedom of thought, conscience and religion). However, in three other applications in the same case, which related to practising Christians, there was held to be no breach of either Article 9 or Article 14. (The rights and freedoms set forth in the Convention shall be secured without discrimination on any ground such as religion.) These applications included: a nurse wearing a cross where the discrimination was based on health and safety rather than religious grounds; a registrar of births, deaths and marriages who believed that same-sex civil partnerships are contrary to God's law and refused to carry out civil partnerships; a Relate counsellor who refused to work with couples on same-sex sexual practices.

Religious belief can vary from individual to individual within the same religion. Jewish people believe men should wear the Kippah (skull cap) at all times; and some Muslims believe women should cover their entire body and face with the Jilbab and Burqa (*R (On the Application of Begum)* v *Governors of Denbigh High School* [2006] UKHL 15). In *Power* v *Greater Manchester Police Authority* [2011] Eq LR 16 where a person was dismissed on grounds of his beliefs, it was not the belief itself but the expression of those beliefs which was in part the cause of his dismissal.

The criteria for determining what is a 'philosophical belief' are that it must be genuinely held; be a belief and not an opinion or viewpoint based on the present state of information available; be a belief as to a weighty and substantial aspect of human life and behaviour; attain a certain level of cogency, seriousness, cohesion and importance; and be worthy of respect in a democratic society, compatible with human dignity and not conflict with the fundamental rights of others. For example, a belief in 'climate change' affecting how a person lived his/her life is protected by the Act (*Grainger plc* v *Nicholson* [2010] 2 All ER 253). Also, in *Cassamitjana* v *League Against Cruel Sports* [2020] UKET 3331129/2018 (21 January 2020) an employment tribunal judge ruled that ethical veganism was a philosophical belief.

4.16.3.7 Sex

The Equality Act 2010, s. 11 states:

> In relation to the protected characteristic of sex—
> (a) a reference to a person who has a particular protected characteristic is a reference to a man or to a woman;
> (b) a reference to persons who share a protected characteristic is a reference to persons of the same sex.

KEYNOTE

This provision explains that references in the Act to people having the protected characteristic of sex are to mean being a man or a woman, and that men share this characteristic with other men, and women with other women.

The Act contains provisions (ss. 66 to 70) designed to achieve equality between men and women in pay and other terms of employment where the work of an employee and his/her comparator, a person of the opposite sex, is equal. It does so by providing for a sex equality clause to be read into the employee's contract of employment. This is designed to ensure parity of terms between the employee and his/her comparator.

For work to be equal, a claimant must establish that he/she is doing like work, work rated as equivalent or work of equal value to a comparator's work (s. 65). For example, in *Blackburn* v *West Midlands Police* [2008] EWCA Civ 1208 it was held that where police officers needed to work hours compatible with their child care responsibilities they were not entitled to special payments received by officers working 24/7 shift patterns.

The Equality Act 2010, s. 12 states:

(1) Sexual orientation means a person's sexual orientation towards—
    (a) persons of the same sex,
    (b) persons of the opposite sex, or
    (c) persons of either sex.
(2) In relation to the protected characteristic of sexual orientation—
    (a) a reference to a person who has a particular protected characteristic is a reference to a person who is of a particular sexual orientation;
    (b) a reference to persons who share a protected characteristic is a reference to persons who are of the same sexual orientation.

KEYNOTE

This section defines the protected characteristic of sexual orientation as being a person's sexual orientation towards: people of the same sex as him/her (the person is a gay man or a lesbian); people of the opposite sex from him/her (the person is heterosexual); people of both sexes (the person is bisexual).

4.16.4   Discrimination

The Equality Act 2010 provides for the following six different types of discrimination which are discussed within this section:

- **Direct discrimination**: discrimination because of a protected characteristic.
- **Associative discrimination**: direct discrimination against someone because he/she is associated with another person with a protected characteristic.
- **Indirect discrimination**: a rule or policy that applies to everyone but disadvantages a person with a protected characteristic.
- **Harassment**: behaviour deemed offensive by the recipient.
- **Victimisation**: discrimination against someone because he/she made or supported a complaint under Equality Act legislation.
- **Discrimination by perception**: direct discrimination against someone because others think he/she has a protected characteristic.

KEYNOTE

In proceedings relating to contraventions of the Act (save offences), the burden of proof rests initially with the complainant. Once the complainant establishes facts from which it might be presumed that there had been discrimination, the burden of proof shifts to the respondent to prove no breach of the principle of equal treatment (s. 136).

4.16.4.1   Direct Discrimination

The Equality Act 2010, s. 13 states:

(1) A person (A) discriminates against another (B) if, because of a protected characteristic, A treats B less favourably than A treats or would treat others.
(2) If the protected characteristic is age, A does not discriminate against B if A can show A's treatment of B to be a proportionate means of achieving a legitimate aim.
(3) If the protected characteristic is disability, and B is not a disabled person, A does not discriminate against B only because A treats or would treat disabled persons more favourably than A treats B.

(4) If the protected characteristic is marriage and civil partnership, this section applies to a contravention of Part 5 (work) only if the treatment is because it is B who is married or a civil partner.

(5) If the protected characteristic is race, less favourable treatment includes segregating B from others.

(6) If the protected characteristic is sex—

    (a) less favourable treatment of a woman includes less favourable treatment of her because she is breast-feeding;

    (b) in a case where B is a man, no account is to be taken of special treatment afforded to a woman in connection with pregnancy or childbirth.

KEYNOTE

To constitute direct discrimination the treatment experienced by B must be different from that of another person. This difference is often referred to as a 'comparator'. The treatment of B must be less favourable than the treatment afforded a comparator. The comparator can be hypothetical where B can establish direct discrimination by showing that if there was another person in similar circumstances, but without B's protected characteristic, that person would be treated more favourably (for an explanation of hypothetical comparators see *Shamoon* v *Chief Constable of the Royal Ulster Constabulary* [2003] UKHL 11).

Less favourable treatment is a broad concept and any disadvantage to which B has been subject will constitute such treatment. B need not have suffered a tangible or material loss (*Chief Constable of West Yorkshire Police* v *Khan* [2001] UKHL 48) but it is not enough merely to show unreasonable treatment (*Bahl* v *The Law Society* [2004] IRLR 799).

The test of whether less favourable treatment was 'because of' a protected characteristic is an objective test of causation. The words 'because of' have the same meaning as the words 'on the grounds of' which were used in the previous legislation. This change in wording does not alter the legal meaning of the definition, but rather, is designed to make it more accessible to the ordinary user of the Act.

Less favourable treatment of a person because that person is associated with a protected characteristic, e.g. because the person has a friend or partner with a particular protected characteristic, or carries out work related to a protected characteristic, is within the scope of this section. This might include carers of disabled people and elderly relatives, who can claim they were treated unfairly because of duties that they had to carry out at home relating to their care work. For example, the non-disabled mother of a disabled child can be discriminated against because of the child's disability (*Coleman* v *Attridge Law* (Case C-303/06) [2008] IRLR 722). It also covers discrimination against someone because, for example, his/her partner is from another country. This is known as 'associative discrimination'.

The use of the words 'because of' are also wide enough to allow claims for direct discrimination where less favourable treatment is based on the claimant's perceived protected characteristics, i.e. where others think he/she has a protected characteristic (even if he/she does not). This is known as 'discrimination by perception'. For example, in *English* v *Thomas Sanderson Ltd* [2008] EWCA Civ 1421 it was held that homophobic banter amounts to unlawful harassment even when the victim's tormentors know the person is not gay.

4.16.4.2 Discrimination Arising from Disability

The Equality Act 2010, s. 15 states:

(1) A person (A) discriminates against a disabled person (B) if—

    (a) A treats B unfavourably because of something arising in consequence of B's disability, and

    (b) A cannot show that the treatment is a proportionate means of achieving a legitimate aim.

(2) Subsection (1) does not apply if A shows that A did not know, and could not reasonably have been expected to know, that B had the disability.

KEYNOTE

This section provides that it is discrimination to treat a disabled person unfavourably not because of the person's disability itself but because of something arising from, or in consequence of, that disability, such as the need to take a period of disability-related absence. It is, however, possible to justify such treatment if it can be shown to be a proportionate means of achieving a legitimate aim. In *Buchanan* v *The Commissioner of Police of the Metropolis* [2016] UKEAT 0112/16/RN, where a seriously injured police motor cyclist was subject to the 'Unsatisfactory Performance Procedure' it was held that he had received unfavourable treatment arising from a disability. The tribunal was required to consider whether the *treatment* was justified, as it was not sufficient to ask whether the underlying procedure was justified.

For this type of discrimination to occur, the employer or other person must know, or reasonably be expected to know, that the disabled person has a disability.

In the judgment of *Lewisham London Borough Council* v *Malcolm* [2008] UKHL 43, it was held that the previous legislative provisions no longer provided the degree of protection from disability-related discrimination that is intended for disabled people. This section is aimed at re-establishing an appropriate balance between enabling a disabled person to make out a case of experiencing a detriment which arises because of his/her disability, and providing an opportunity for an employer or other person to defend the treatment.

4.16.4.3 Adjustments for Disabled Persons

The duty to make reasonable adjustments is a key element of a range of measures intended to eliminate barriers to access and participation for disabled people.

The Equality Act 2010, s. 20 states:

(1) Where this Act imposes a duty to make reasonable adjustments on a person, this section, sections 21 and 22 and the applicable Schedule apply; and for those purposes, a person on whom the duty is imposed is referred to as A.

(2) The duty comprises the following three requirements.

(3) The first requirement is a requirement, where a provision, criterion or practice of A's puts a disabled person at a substantial disadvantage in relation to a relevant matter in comparison with persons who are not disabled, to take such steps as it is reasonable to have to take to avoid the disadvantage.

(4) The second requirement is a requirement, where a physical feature puts a disabled person at a substantial disadvantage in relation to a relevant matter in comparison with persons who are not disabled, to take such steps as it is reasonable to have to take to avoid the disadvantage.

(5) The third requirement is a requirement, where a disabled person would, but for the provision of an auxiliary aid, be put at a substantial disadvantage in relation to a relevant matter in comparison with persons who are not disabled, to take such steps as it is reasonable to have to take to provide the auxiliary aid.

KEYNOTE

The duty to make reasonable adjustments comprises three requirements which apply where a disabled person is placed at a substantial disadvantage in comparison with non-disabled people.

The first requirement covers changing the way things are done (such as changing a practice), the second covers making changes to the built environment (such as providing access to a building), and the third covers providing auxiliary aids and services (such as providing special computer software or providing a different service). A claimant had a disability which caused her to suffer from migraines caused by computer software. The respondent unsuccessfully tried to address this by use of screen magnification software and eventually moved the claimant to a paper-based role. Although there was an unreasonable delay in making these adjustments, it was held that the respondent had complied with this section (*Department of Work and Pensions* v *Robinson* [2019] UKEAT 0021/19/2307).

Under the second requirement, taking steps to avoid the disadvantage will include removing, altering or providing a reasonable means of avoiding the physical feature, where it would be reasonable to do so (s. 209). Where the first or third requirements involve the way in which information is provided, a reasonable step includes providing that information in an accessible format (s. 20(6)). It also makes clear that, except where the Act states otherwise, it would never be reasonable for a person bound by the duty to pass on the costs of complying with it to an individual disabled person (s. 20(7)).

The section contains only one threshold for the reasonable adjustment duty, that of 'substantial disadvantage'. Section 212(1) defines 'substantial' as more than minor or trivial.

Section 21 provides that a failure to comply with any one of the reasonable adjustment requirements amounts to discrimination against a disabled person to whom the duty is owed. It also provides that, apart from under this Act, no other action can be taken for failure to comply with the duty. The test of reasonableness is an objective one (*Collins* v *Royal National Theatre Board Ltd* [2004] IRLR 395), and will always depend on the particular circumstances in an individual case (*Archibald* v *Fife County Council* [2004] IRLR 651).

Although accepting the difficult role the police are often called upon to play, in *ZH* v *Commissioner of Police for the Metropolis* [2012] EWHC 604 (QB) it was held that the police dealing with a person who was severely autistic had a duty to make reasonable adjustments in *dealing* with that person irrespective of the fact that they acted in a well-intentioned but misguided manner.

In *Chief Constable of South Yorkshire* v *Jelic* [2010] IRLR 744 it was determined that the force had not acted 'reasonably' when it failed to allow an officer suffering from chronic anxiety syndrome to swap jobs with another officer. Also, in *Hinsley* v *Chief Constable of West Mercia Constabulary* [2010] UKEAT 0200/10/0911, it was decided that there was a breach of duty to make reasonable adjustments where there was a failure to reinstate a probationary police officer who had resigned while depressed. However, where an officer was perceived to have a dangerous mental condition, the adjustments made to ensure he did not present a danger to colleagues or to the public were considered reasonable (*Aitken* v *Commissioner of Police of the Metropolis* [2011] EWCA Civ 582). In *Cordell* v *Foreign and Commonwealth Office* [2012] ICR 280 a tribunal dismissed claims of direct discrimination and discrimination by way of failure to make reasonable adjustments where the costs of providing an English-speaking lip-speaker support for a deaf employee were about £230,000 a year.

It was held that police officers lawfully searching the home of a man whom they knew to be profoundly deaf did not have any effect on the ability of the man and the officers to communicate with each other effectively without a British Sign Language interpreter being present. Officers who had had previous dealings with the man were satisfied on the basis of these dealings that they could achieve a basic level of communication with him without the benefit of an interpreter (*Finnegan* v *Chief Constable of Northumbria* [2013] EWCA Civ 1191).

4.16.4.4 Gender Reassignment Discrimination: Cases of Absence from Work

The Equality Act 2010, s. 16 states:

(1) This section has effect for the purposes of the application of Part 5 (work) to the protected characteristic of gender reassignment.
(2) A person (A) discriminates against a transsexual person (B) if, in relation to an absence of B's that is because of gender reassignment, A treats B less favourably than A would treat B if—
   (a) B's absence was because of sickness or injury, or
   (b) B's absence was for some other reason and it is not reasonable for B to be treated less favourably.
(3) A person's absence is because of gender reassignment if it is because the person is proposing to undergo, is undergoing or has undergone the process (or part of the process) mentioned in section 7(1).

KEYNOTE

A person's absence is 'because of gender reassignment' if it is because the person is proposing to undergo, is undergoing, or has undergone gender reassignment. For example, where a female to male transsexual person takes time off work to receive hormone treatment as part of his gender reassignment, his employer cannot discriminate against him because of his absence from work for this purpose.

4.16.4.5 Pregnancy and Maternity Discrimination: Non-work Cases

The Equality Act 2010, s. 17 states:

(1) This section has effect for the purposes of the application to the protected characteristic of pregnancy and maternity of—
 (a) Part 3 (services and public functions);
 (b) Part 4 (premises);
 (c) Part 6 (education);
 (d) Part 7 (associations).

(2) A person (A) discriminates against a woman if A treats her unfavourably because of a pregnancy of hers.

(3) A person (A) discriminates against a woman if, in the period of 26 weeks beginning with the day on which she gives birth, A treats her unfavourably because she has given birth.

(4) The reference in subsection (3) to treating a woman unfavourably because she has given birth includes, in particular, a reference to treating her unfavourably because she is breast-feeding.

(5) For the purposes of this section, the day on which a woman gives birth is the day on which—
 (a) she gives birth to a living child, or
 (b) she gives birth to a dead child (more than 24 weeks of the pregnancy having passed).

KEYNOTE

Note that pregnancy and maternity are 'protected characteristics' even though they are not grouped with the other protected characteristics in the Act.

Pregnancy and maternity discrimination is excluded from the definition of direct sex discrimination (s. 17(6)) and is dealt with under this separate provision and s. 18 (work situations, see para. 4.16.4.6).

4.16.4.6 Pregnancy and Maternity Discrimination: Work Cases

The Equality Act 2010, s. 18 states:

(1) This section has effect for the purposes of the application of Part 5 (work) to the protected characteristic of pregnancy and maternity.

(2) A person (A) discriminates against a woman if, in the protected period in relation to a pregnancy of hers, A treats her unfavourably—
 (a) because of the pregnancy, or
 (b) because of illness suffered by her as a result of it.

(3) A person (A) discriminates against a woman if A treats her unfavourably because she is on compulsory maternity leave.

(4) A person (A) discriminates against a woman if A treats her unfavourably because she is exercising or seeking to exercise, or has exercised or sought to exercise, the right to ordinary or additional maternity leave.

KEYNOTE

In relation to s. 18(2), if the treatment of a woman is in implementation of a decision taken in the protected period, the treatment is to be regarded as occurring in that period (even if the implementation is not until after the end of that period (s. 18(5)).

The duration of the protected period depends on the statutory maternity leave entitlements as set out in the Employment Rights Act 1996 which defines the right to compulsory, ordinary and additional maternity leave. The protected period starts when a woman becomes pregnant and ends either:

- if she has the right to ordinary and additional maternity leave, at the end of the additional maternity leave period or (if earlier) when she returns to work after the pregnancy; or
- if she does not have that right, at the end of the period of two weeks beginning with the end of the pregnancy.

As with s. 17 of the 2010 Act, sex discrimination does not apply to treatment of a woman in so far as it is in the protected period, or it is for a reason mentioned in s. 18(3) or (4).

Unfavourable treatment suffered because of an association with a pregnant woman or because of being perceived to be pregnant are not covered by this section, though such treatment might constitute direct discrimination under s. 13.

In *Maksymiuk* v *Bar Roma Partnership* [2012] Eq LR 917 an employee who was the only one of a number of bar staff who was selected for dismissal by reason of purported redundancy only a matter of days after she had announced that she was pregnant, had her claim of discrimination on the ground of pregnancy or sickness related to pregnancy dismissed.

In *The Commissioner of the City of London Police* v *Geldart* [2019] UKEAT 0032/19/2911, it was held to be direct sex discrimination where an officer on maternity leave was not given payment or partial payment of what is known as the London Allowance during her absence from duty.

4.16.4.7 Indirect Discrimination

The Equality Act 2010, s. 19 states:

(1) A person (A) discriminates against another (B) if A applies to B a provision, criterion or practice which is discriminatory in relation to a relevant protected characteristic of B's.

(2) For the purposes of subsection (1), a provision, criterion or practice is discriminatory in relation to a relevant protected characteristic of B's if—

(a) A applies, or would apply, it to persons with whom B does not share the characteristic,

(b) it puts, or would put, persons with whom B shares the characteristic at a particular disadvantage when compared with persons with whom B does not share it,

(c) it puts, or would put, B at that disadvantage, and

(d) A cannot show it to be a proportionate means of achieving a legitimate aim.

KEYNOTE

Apart from pregnancy and maternity, indirect discrimination applies to all the protected characteristics.

Indirect discrimination occurs when a policy which applies in the same way for everybody has an effect which particularly disadvantages people with a protected characteristic. Where a particular group is disadvantaged in this way, a person in that group is indirectly discriminated against if he/she is put at that disadvantage, unless the person applying the policy can justify it.

When a policy would put a person at a disadvantage if it were applied, e.g. where a person is deterred from applying for a job or taking up an offer of service because a policy which would be applied would result in his/her disadvantage, this may also be indirect discrimination. Examples of indirect discrimination have included: requiring all employees to work within 'normal office hours' (*Bhudi* v *IMI Refiners* [1994] IRLR 204); requiring all workers to have short hair thereby making it difficult for some groups such as Sikhs to comply (*Mandla* v *Dowell Lee* [1983] 2 AC 548); where 100 per cent of males could comply with a policy relating to rostering of duties, but only 95.2 per cent of women were able to do so, the policy discriminated indirectly against females (*London Underground Ltd* v *Edwards (No. 2)* [1998] IRLR 364).

4.16.4.8 Harassment

The Equality Act 2010, s. 26 states:

(1) A person (A) harasses another (B) if—

(a) A engages in unwanted conduct related to a relevant protected characteristic, and

(b) the conduct has the purpose or effect of—

(i) violating B's dignity, or

(ii) creating an intimidating, hostile, degrading, humiliating or offensive environment for B.

(2) A also harasses B if—

(a) A engages in unwanted conduct of a sexual nature, and

(b) the conduct has the purpose or effect referred to in subsection (1)(b).

(3) A also harasses B if—
  (a) A or another person engages in unwanted conduct of a sexual nature or that is related to gender reassignment or sex,
  (b) the conduct has the purpose or effect referred to in subsection (1)(b), and
  (c) because of B's rejection of or submission to the conduct, A treats B less favourably than A would treat B if B had not rejected or submitted to the conduct.

KEYNOTE

This section defines three types of harassment.

The first type, which applies to the protected characteristics apart from pregnancy and maternity, and marriage and civil partnership, involves unwanted conduct which is related to a relevant characteristic and has the purpose or effect of creating an intimidating, hostile, degrading, humiliating or offensive environment for the complainant or of violating the complainant's dignity. In deciding whether conduct has the effect referred to in s. 26(1)(b), the perception of B, the other circumstances of the case, and whether it is reasonable for the conduct to have that effect, must be taken into account (s. 26(4)).

The second type is sexual harassment which is unwanted conduct of a sexual nature where this has the same purpose or effect as the first type of harassment. In *Wadman* v *Carpenter Farrer Partnership* [1993] IRLR 374 sexual harassment was described as conduct of a sexual nature or other conduct based on sex affecting the dignity of women and men at work. This could include verbal remarks, written comments and physical contact.

The third type is treating someone less favourably because he/she has either submitted to or rejected sexual harassment, or harassment related to sex or gender reassignment. Note that harassment related to sexual orientation and religion and belief is not unlawful outside a work context.

4.16.4.9 Employees and Applicants: Harassment

The Equality Act 2010, s. 40 states:

(1) An employer (A) must not, in relation to employment by A, harass a person (B)—
  (a) who is an employee of A's;
  (b) who has applied to A for employment.

KEYNOTE

The liability of employers for third party harassment of employees (s. 40(2)–(4)) was removed by s. 65 of the Enterprise and Regulatory Reform Act 2013.

Apart from marriage and civil partnerships and pregnancy and maternity, this section extends to the other protected characteristics including the employer's liability for sexual harassment. This can include behaviour such as requests for sexual favours, lewd jokes, promises, and threats concerning a person's employment conditions in return for sexual favours.

In *Urso* v *Department for Work and Pensions* [2017] UKEAT 0045/16/DA, it was held that this section prohibits harassment at every stage of employment (before, during and after employment) and a submission that a dismissal may not be an affront to an employee's dignity was rejected.

4.16.4.10 Victimisation

The Equality Act 2010, s. 27 states:

(1) A person (A) victimises another person (B) if A subjects B to a detriment because—
  (a) B does a protected act, or
  (b) A believes that B has done, or may do, a protected act.
(2) Each of the following is a protected act—
  (a) bringing proceedings under this Act;
  (b) giving evidence or information in connection with proceedings under this Act;

(c) doing any other thing for the purposes of or in connection with this Act;

(d) making an allegation (whether or not express) that A or another person has contravened this Act.

(3) Giving false evidence or information, or making a false allegation, is not a protected act if the evidence or information is given, or the allegation is made, in bad faith.

KEYNOTE

Victimisation takes place where one person treats another badly because he/she in good faith has done a 'protected act', e.g. taken or supported any action taken for the purpose of the Act, including in relation to any alleged breach of its provisions. In *Chief Constable of West Yorkshire Police* v *B & C* [2016] UKEAT 0306/15/RN, two former undercover police officers were found to have been subjected to detriments for making protected disclosures that related to the inadequate supervision and support of undercover operatives. Both officers had been removed from undercover duties and assigned civilian roles.

The test to be applied in assessing whether or not victimisation has taken place is, 'was the real reason for the victim's treatment the fact that they had carried out a protected act' (*Chief Constable of West Yorkshire Police* v *Khan* [2001] UKHL 48). In *Bayode* v *Chief Constable of Derbyshire* [2008] UKEAT 0499/07/2205 it was held that a police constable, who was black African and Nigerian by national origin, had not been victimised where his colleagues recorded any problems they encountered with him in their PNBs for fear of a race discrimination claim at some future date.

Only an individual can bring a claim for victimisation, and a person is not protected from victimisation where he/she maliciously makes or supports an untrue complaint.

4.16.5 Police Officers

The 2010 Act prohibits discrimination, victimisation and harassment in other non-employment work relationships and this specifically includes police officers.

The Equality Act 2010, s. 42 states:

(1) For the purposes of this Part, holding the office of constable is to be treated as employment—

(a) by the chief officer, in respect of any act done by the chief officer in relation to a constable or appointment to the office of constable;

(b) by the responsible authority, in respect of any act done by the authority in relation to a constable or appointment to the office of constable.

KEYNOTE

This section provides that police constables (and police cadets (s. 42(2))) are treated as employees. The relevant employer is either the chief officer (or, in Scotland, the chief constable) or the responsible authority (s. 43), depending on who commits the act in question. For example, if a chief officer refused to allocate protective equipment to female constables he/she would be treated as the employer in a direct discrimination claim.

Constables serving with the Civil Nuclear Constabulary are treated as employees of the Civil Nuclear Police Authority (s. 55(2) of the Energy Act 2004). A constable seconded to the National Crime Agency (NCA) is treated as employed by the NCA.

4.16.6 Employees and Applicants

The Equality Act 2010, s. 39 makes it unlawful for an employer to discriminate against or victimise employees and people seeking work. It applies where the employer is making arrangements to fill a job, and in respect of anything done in the course of a person's employment.

KEYNOTE

Examples of direct discrimination in relation to work have included: rescinding an officer's posting on the grounds of force policy that spouses should not work in the same Division because neither officer would be compellable as a witness against the other (*Graham* v *Chief Constable of Bedfordshire Constabulary* [2002] IRLR 239); treating a police officer of one racial group, who was under investigation for disciplinary matters, differently from another officer under such investigation belonging to a different racial group (*Virdi* v *Commissioner of Police for the Metropolis* (2000) LTL 5 February); acceding to a request by a customer not to be served by someone of a particular colour (*Eldridge & Barbican Car Hire Ltd* v *Zhang* (2001) LTL 10 May).

There are a number of exceptions and defences to the provisions of the Act but two of the more relevant defences in relation to discrimination or victimisation in employment are 'genuine occupational requirement' and 'positive action'.

The principle behind 'genuine occupational requirement' is that, in certain jobs and roles, there may well be a legitimate reason that an employee is of a particular sex or belongs to a particular racial group (sch. 1, part 1, para. 1(1)(a)). In reality there are far more potential exceptions to discrimination on the grounds of sex and sexual orientation than for reasons of the other protected characteristics.

'Positive action' refers to measures to alleviate disadvantage experienced by people who share a protected characteristic, reduce their under-representation in relation to particular activities, and meet their particular needs (s. 158). It allows for measures to be targeted to particular groups, including training to enable them to gain employment, but any such measures must be a proportionate way of achieving the relevant aim.

An employer may also take a protected characteristic into consideration when deciding whom to recruit or promote, where people having the protected characteristic are at a disadvantage or are under-represented (s. 159). This can be done only where the candidates are as qualified as each other. The aim is to help employers achieve a more diverse workforce by giving them the option, when faced with candidates of equal merit, to choose a candidate from an under-represented group.

4.16.7 Liability for Discrimination in Employment

The Equality Act 2010, s. 109 states:

(1) Anything done by a person (A) in the course of A's employment must be treated as also done by the employer.
(2) …
(3) It does not matter whether that thing is done with the employer's or principal's knowledge or approval.

KEYNOTE

This section makes employers and principals liable for acts of discrimination, harassment and victimisation carried out by their employees in the course of employment. It does not matter whether or not the employer or principal knows about or approves of those acts. For example, where police officers engage in inappropriate sexual behaviour towards a colleague at a work-related function, the chief officer may be liable for the acts of his/her officers at that function (*Chief Constable of Lincolnshire* v *Stubbs* [1999] IRLR 81).

Employers who can show that they took all reasonable steps to prevent their employees from acting unlawfully will not be held liable (s. 109(4)). An employer could not rely on this defence where training was stale and no longer effective to prevent harassment, and that there were further reasonable steps by way of refresher training that the employer should have taken (*Allay (UK) Ltd* v *Gehlen (Race Discrimination)* [2021] UKEAT 0031 20 0402).

An employee is also personally liable for unlawful acts committed in the course of employment where, because of s. 109, the employer is also liable (s. 110).

4.16.8 Public Sector Equality Duty

The Equality Act 2010, s. 149 states:

(1) A public authority must, in the exercise of its functions, have due regard to the need to—
  (a) eliminate discrimination, harassment, victimisation and any other conduct that is prohibited by or under this Act;
  (b) advance equality of opportunity between persons who share a relevant protected characteristic and persons who do not share it;
  (c) foster good relations between persons who share a relevant protected characteristic and persons who do not share it.

KEYNOTE

Public authorities are required, in carrying out their functions, to have due regard to the need to achieve the objectives set out under s. 149.

The following extract from PACE Code C relates to the public sector equality duty and states:

1 General

1.0 The powers and procedures in this Code must be used fairly, responsibly, with respect for the people to whom they apply and without unlawful discrimination. Under the Equality Act 2010, section 149 (Public sector Equality Duty), police forces must, in carrying out their functions, have due regard to the need to eliminate unlawful discrimination, harassment, victimisation and any other conduct which is prohibited by that Act, to advance equality of opportunity between people who share a relevant protected characteristic and people who do not share it, and to foster good relations between those persons. The Equality Act *also* makes it unlawful for police officers to discriminate against, harass or victimise any person on the grounds of the 'protected characteristics' of age, disability, gender reassignment, race, religion or belief, sex and sexual orientation, marriage and civil partnership, pregnancy and maternity, when using their powers.

Notes for Guidance

1AA In paragraph 1.0, under the Equality Act 2010, section 149, the 'relevant protected characteristics' are age, disability, gender reassignment, pregnancy and maternity, race, religion/belief and sex and sexual orientation.

4.17 Complaints and Misconduct

4.17.1 Introduction

Police complaints and misconduct have always been a complex area of police law and procedure, and they have evolved considerably. One of the key points to emerge from the 2005 Taylor Review of police officer disciplinary arrangements was the need to shift the emphasis and culture in lower-level police misconduct matters towards an environment focused on development and improvement as opposed to one focused on blame and punishment. Additionally, the report stressed the importance of carrying out a full assessment of the alleged conduct at an early stage with a view to then implementing a proportionate and non-bureaucratic response.

There have been numerous changes to the police conduct regime in just the past five years, culminating in new regulations governing complaints and conduct, which took effect from 1 February 2020.

The Policing and Crime Act 2017 had already changed the former Independent Police Complaints Commission into a new and refocused Independent Office for Police Conduct (IOPC) from 8 January 2018. The IOPC, like the IPCC before it, investigates the most serious and sensitive complaints and recordable conduct matters involving the police, including deaths and serious injuries as well as matters such as allegations of serious corruption. It oversees the complaints system in England and Wales and sets the standards by which police forces should handle complaints.

Further developments in the area of police conduct have also settled in. The Police Barred List and Police Advisory List Regulations 2017 require the College of Policing to maintain a publicly searchable Police Barred List, to prevent forces and policing bodies from employing officers, staff and special constables who have been dismissed for conduct or performance matters. A separate Police Advisory List contains the names of officers, staff or special constables who resign or retire from the service while under investigation for conduct matters only, as well as designated volunteers whose status is withdrawn. As no finding has been made against an individual, the Police Advisory List is not publicly available.

The recently enacted Police (Conduct) Regulations 2020 change the definition of misconduct and the available misconduct sanctions and introduce an entirely new process called the Reflective Practice Review, for addressing low-level misconduct as a performance issue.

Misconduct is now defined as a breach of the Standards of Professional Behaviour that is so serious as to justify disciplinary action (**see para. 4.17.2**). The lowest misconduct sanction now available is a written warning—so that misconduct is a breach of the Standards sufficiently serious to justify a written warning. If the level of misconduct is lower than this, it must be addressed in the Reflective Practice Review process (**see para. 4.17.9.10**). Gross misconduct remains a breach of the Standards of Professional Behaviour that is so serious as to justify dismissal. Unsatisfactory performance or unsatisfactory attendance remains an inability or failure of a police officer to perform the duties of the role or rank they are currently undertaking to a satisfactory standard or level.

Where officers had retired or resigned, the Police (Conduct, Complaints and Misconduct and Appeal Tribunal) (Amendment) Regulations 2017 enabled disciplinary proceedings still to be taken against them. This is now transferred to the Police (Conduct) Regulations 2020, which permits investigations and proceedings in respect of former officers.

The Police (Complaints and Conduct) Regulations 2013 (SI 2013/281) strengthened the role and powers of the IOPC, particularly with regard to compelling officers to attend interviews. The amended Standards of Professional Behaviour, as stated below, also now require officers positively to cooperate with investigations.

Primary legislation, a series of statutory instruments and statutory guidance provide the performance and misconduct framework:

- The Police Reform Act 2002 (PRA) sets out the definitions for complaints, conduct matters and the procedures for the investigation of complaints and recordable conduct matters. The consideration of each and every complaint or conduct matter starts with a PRA assessment.
- The Police (Performance) Regulations 2020 (SI 2020/3) set out the procedures for dealing with cases of unsatisfactory performance or attendance of police officers.
- The Police (Conduct) Regulations 2020 (SI 2020/4) set out the procedures for investigating non-recordable conduct matters and the hearing of all misconduct proceedings. They contain the 'Standards of Professional Behaviour', to which all police officers are required to adhere.
- The Police (Complaints and Misconduct) Regulations 2020 (SI 2020/2) augment the provisions in sch. 3 to the PRA for the assessment of complaints and conduct matters and for the investigation of complaints and recordable (but not non-recordable) conduct matters.
- The Police Appeals Tribunals Rules 2020 (SI 2020/1) set out the procedures for an appeal to a Police Appeals Tribunal and the grounds on which a police officer or special constable can appeal against a finding and/or a particular outcome from a misconduct hearing or a third stage performance meeting.
- The Home Office Statutory Guidance on Professional Standards, Performance and Integrity in Policing augments the Police (Conduct) Regulations.
- The IOPC Statutory Guidance on the police complaints system augments the PRA and Police (Complaints and Misconduct) Regulations.
- The College of Policing Code of Ethics explains, illustrates and augments the Standards of Professional Behaviour.
- The College of Policing Guidance on Outcomes in Police Misconduct Proceedings outlines the general framework for assessing the seriousness of conduct, including factors which may be taken into account, when deciding upon the appropriate disciplinary outcome.

4.17.2   The Standards of Professional Behaviour

The Standards of Professional Behaviour provide the yardstick by which the conduct of police officers is judged. They apply to police officers of all ranks, special constables, and to those subject to suspension. They are not intended to describe every situation but rather to set a framework which enables everybody to know what type of conduct by a police officer is acceptable and what is unacceptable.

The Police (Conduct) Regulations 2020 change the standard relating to Duties and Responsibilities. This now provides that police officers have a responsibility to cooperate in investigations when identified as a witness. This has no effect on the right to silence of an officer who is under investigation.

The standards are:

- **Honesty and Integrity**: Police officers are honest, act with integrity and do not compromise or abuse their position.
- **Authority, Respect and Courtesy**: Police officers act with self-control and tolerance, treating members of the public and colleagues with respect and courtesy. Police officers do not abuse their powers or authority and respect the rights of all individuals.

- **Equality and Diversity:** Police officers act with fairness and impartiality. They do not discriminate unlawfully or unfairly.
- **Use of Force:** Police officers only use force to the extent that it is necessary, proportionate and reasonable in all the circumstances.
- **Orders and Instructions:** Police officers only give and carry out lawful orders and instructions. Police officers abide by police regulations, force policies and lawful orders.
- **Duties and Responsibilities:** Police officers are diligent in the exercise of their duties and responsibilities. Police officers have a responsibility to give appropriate cooperation during investigations, inquiries and formal proceedings, participating openly and professionally in line with the expectations of a police officer when identified as a witness.
- **Confidentiality:** Police officers treat information with respect and access or disclose it only in the proper course of police duties.
- **Fitness for Duty:** Police officers when on duty or presenting themselves for duty are fit to carry out their duties and responsibilities.
- **Discreditable Conduct:** Police officers behave in a manner which does not discredit the police service or undermine public confidence, whether on or off duty. Police officers report any action taken against them for a criminal offence, conditions imposed by a court or the receipt of any penalty notice.
- **Challenging and Reporting Improper Conduct:** Police officers report, challenge or take action against the conduct of colleagues which has fallen below the standards of professional behaviour.

4.17.3 The Role of the Police Friend

At all stages of the misconduct or performance proceedings (including any interview during an investigation into misconduct), police officers have the right to consult with and be accompanied by a police friend.

The police friend can be a police officer, a police staff member, or a person nominated by the police officer's staff association. A person asked to be a police friend is entitled to refuse and cannot be appointed to act if they had any involvement in that particular case. The police friend can:

- advise the police officer concerned throughout the proceedings under the Police (Conduct) Regulations 2020, Police (Complaints and Misconduct) Regulations 2020 or Police (Performance) Regulations 2020;
- represent the police officer concerned at misconduct proceedings including an accelerated misconduct hearing or appeal meeting, performance proceedings, including an appeal meeting, or at a Police Appeals Tribunal unless the officer has the right to be legally represented and has chosen to be so represented;
- make representations to the appropriate authority concerning any aspect of the proceedings under the Police (Conduct) Regulations 2020 or Police (Performance) Regulations 2020;
- accompany the police officer concerned to any interview, meeting or hearing which forms part of any proceedings under the Police (Conduct) Regulations 2020, Police (Complaints and Misconduct) Regulations 2020 or Police (Performance) Regulations 2020.

The appropriate authority for matters concerning the chief officer or acting chief officer of police is the local policing body (the Police and Crime Commissioner). For every other officer, the appropriate authority is the chief officer of police under whose direction the officer was serving at the relevant time. The chief officer of police may delegate any of their functions under the Police (Conduct) Regulations 2020 to a police officer of at least the rank of inspector or a police staff member who the chief officer considers to be of at least a similar level of seniority to an inspector.

A police friend who has agreed to accompany a police officer is entitled to take a reasonable amount of duty time to fulfil those responsibilities and is considered to be on duty when attending interviews, meetings or hearings.

Subject to any timescales set out in the Police (Conduct) Regulations 2020 or Police (Performance) Regulations 2020, at any stage of a case, up to and including a misconduct meeting or hearing or an unsatisfactory performance meeting, the police officer concerned or their police friend may submit that there are insufficient grounds upon which to base the case and/or that the correct procedures have not been followed, clearly setting out the reasons and submitting any supporting evidence. It will be for the person responsible for the relevant stage of the case to consider any such submission and determine how best to respond to it, bearing in mind the need to ensure fairness to the police officer concerned.

At a misconduct meeting, hearing or accelerated misconduct hearing under the Police (Conduct) Regulations 2020 or Police (Performance) Regulations 2020 where the police friend attends, they may:

(a) put the police officer concerned's case;
(b) sum up that case;
(c) respond on the police officer concerned's behalf to any view expressed at the meeting;
(d) make representations concerning any aspect of the proceedings;
(e) confer with the police officer concerned;
(f) in a misconduct meeting or hearing, ask questions of any witness, subject to the discretion of the person(s) conducting that hearing.

A police officer is entitled to be legally represented at a misconduct hearing or accelerated misconduct hearing (in cases that fall to be dealt with under the Police (Conduct) Regulations 2020) or a third stage performance meeting for dealing with an issue of gross incompetence under the Police (Performance) Regulations 2020). Where they decide to be so represented, the police friend can also attend and may consult with the police officer concerned, but will not carry out functions (a)–(d) and (f) described above. A police officer may not be legally represented in any meetings held as part of the Reflective Practice Review process or at a standard third stage performance or absence meeting.

Where a police officer is arrested or interviewed in connection with a criminal offence committed while off duty and that has no connection with their role as a serving police officer, the police friend has no right to attend the criminal interview.

4.17.4 Death or Serious Injury Matters

A death or serious injury (DSI) matter is defined in s. 12 of the Police Reform Act 2002. Where there is an investigation into a DSI case and there is no complaint or indication of any conduct matter, the investigation will focus on the circumstances of the incident. However, where during the course of the investigation into the DSI matter there is an indication that a person serving with the police may have committed a criminal offence or behaved in a manner that would justify the bringing of disciplinary proceedings, the DSI matter will be reclassified as a recordable conduct matter (or complaint if appropriate) and dealt with accordingly.

4.17.5 Misconduct Procedures

The procedures are intended to provide a fair, open and proportionate method of dealing with alleged misconduct and to encourage a culture of learning and development.

Where the conduct is linked to a complaint, recordable conduct matter or DSI matter the appropriate authority is required to follow the provisions in the Police Reform Act 2002, the accompanying Police (Complaints and Misconduct) Regulations 2020 and the IOPC Statutory Guidance, which set out how complaints by members of the public are to be dealt with.

Probationer constables are not subject to the procedures for dealing with unsatisfactory performance, since there are separately established procedures for dealing with the performance of student police officers. However, they are subject to the misconduct procedures. The chief officer has discretion whether to use the misconduct procedures or the procedures set out at reg. 13 of the Police Regulations 2003 (Discharge of Probationer) as the most appropriate means of dealing with a misconduct matter. In exercising this discretion regard should be had to whether the officer admits the conduct or not. Where the misconduct in question is not admitted then in most, if not all, cases the matter will fall to be determined under the misconduct procedures. If the reg. 13 procedure is used, the student police officer should be given a fair hearing (i.e. an opportunity to comment and present mitigation) under that procedure.

4.17.5.1 Suspension or Change of Duty

Suspension is not a formal misconduct outcome and does not suggest any prejudgement. The period of suspension should be as short as possible and any investigation into the conduct of a suspended police officer should be made a priority. The decision to suspend a police officer may be taken only where there is an allegation of misconduct/gross misconduct and where:

- an effective investigation may be prejudiced unless the police officer is suspended; or
- the public interest, having regard to the nature of the allegation and any other relevant considerations, requires that the police officer be suspended; and
- a temporary move to a new location or role has been considered but is not appropriate in the circumstances.

A temporary move to a new location or role must always be considered first as an alternative to suspension. While suspended, a police officer ceases to hold the office of constable and, in the case of a member of a police force, ceases to be a member of a police force, save for the purposes of the misconduct proceedings.

The police officer or their police friend may make representations against the initial decision to suspend (within seven working days beginning with the first working day after being suspended) and at any time during the course of the suspension if they believe the circumstances have changed and that the suspension is no longer appropriate.

The police officer should be told exactly why they are being suspended or being moved to other duties and this should be confirmed in writing. If suspension is on public interest grounds, it should be clearly explained, so far as possible, what those grounds are. The use of suspension must be reviewed at least every four weeks, and sooner where facts have become known which suggest that suspension is no longer appropriate. In cases where the suspension has been reviewed and a decision has been made to continue that suspension, the police officer must be informed in writing of the reasons why. Suspension must be authorised by a senior officer (which is an officer holding a rank above that of chief superintendent) although the decision can be communicated to the police officer by an appropriate manager.

In cases where the IOPC is supervising, managing or independently investigating a matter, the appropriate authority will consult with the IOPC before making a decision on whether or not to suspend, although the decision remains that of the appropriate authority. The appropriate authority must also consult the IOPC before making the decision to allow a police officer to resume their duties following suspension (unless the suspension ends because there will be no misconduct or accelerated misconduct proceedings or because these have concluded) in cases where the IOPC is supervising, managing or independently investigating a case involving that police officer.

The Standards of Professional Behaviour continue to apply to police officers who are suspended from duty. The appropriate authority can impose such conditions or restrictions on the police officer concerned as are reasonable in the circumstances, e.g. restricting access to police premises or police social functions.

4.17.5.2 Assessment of Misconduct

The appropriate authority must initially consider whether an allegation against an officer is a complaint or conduct matter.

If the matter is a complaint and is made to a chief officer, the chief officer must decide whether to record it and consider whether it involves death or serious injury, an allegation which if proved might amount to a criminal offence or justify the bringing of misconduct proceedings or a breach of Article 2 or 3 of the European Convention on Human Rights. In addition, the chief officer must consider whether there is an indication that the complaint involves a serious assault, a serious sexual offence, serious corruption, including abuse of position for a sexual purpose or pursuing an improper emotional relationship, a criminal offence or behaviour which amounts to misconduct only but which is aggravated by discrimination on a protected ground, or a relevant offence. If so the chief officer must handle it pursuant to the PRA and consider whether it is necessary or appropriate to refer the matter to the IOPC.

If the matter is a conduct matter, then the appropriate authority must consider whether it is a recordable conduct matter—which is where the alleged conduct appears to have resulted in death or serious injury, a member of the public has been adversely affected or where it indicates a serious assault, a serious sexual offence, serious corruption, including abuse of position for a sexual purpose or pursuing an improper emotional relationship, a criminal offence or behaviour which amounts to misconduct only but which is aggravated by discrimination on a protected ground, a relevant offence or conduct whose gravity or exceptional circumstances make it appropriate to record the matter. If so, the appropriate authority must decide whether it is necessary or appropriate to refer the matter to the IOPC.

Where it is decided that there be a misconduct investigation into a complaint or a recordable conduct matter, the IOPC or the appropriate authority, as the case may be, must appoint an investigator. In an IOPC independent or directed investigation, the Director General performs an initial severity assessment according to reg. 16 of the Police (Complaints and Misconduct) Regulations 2020. In an investigation by the appropriate authority, the investigator performs the initial severity assessment according to reg. 16 of the Police (Complaints and Misconduct) Regulations 2020, after consulting with the appropriate authority. Where the allegation is neither a complaint nor a recordable conduct matter, it is a non-recordable conduct matter. The appropriate authority performs the initial severity assessment according to reg. 14 of the Police (Conduct) Regulations 2020 and then appoints an investigator.

The PRA assessment and a decision on whether to record or refer a matter to the IOPC must be taken before any initial severity assessment. The person who performs the initial severity assessment will depend therefore upon whether the matter is a complaint, recordable conduct or non-recordable conduct matter. Where it is a complaint or recordable conduct matter, it will further depend upon whether the investigation is conducted or directed by the IOPC or the appropriate authority.

Where it is not possible for the appropriate authority or the IOPC to make an immediate PRA assessment, a scoping process should be conducted but only to the extent that it is necessary to understand the nature of the allegation, whether it amounts to a complaint, conduct matter or neither and, if it is either a complaint or a conduct matter, to determine which procedure should be used. It is perfectly acceptable to ask questions to seek to establish which police officers may have been involved in a particular incident and therefore to eliminate those police officers who are not involved.

The person performing the initial severity assessment must consider whether, if proved, the behaviour of the officer would amount to misconduct, gross misconduct or neither. The assessment will also determine whether, if the matter was referred to misconduct proceedings, those proceedings would be likely to be a misconduct meeting (for cases of misconduct) or a misconduct hearing (for cases of gross misconduct or if the police officer concerned has a live final written warning at the time of the assessment and there is a further allegation of misconduct). If new evidence emerges or there is a change of circumstances or considerations, a fresh assessment can be made and the matter may be moved up to a level of gross misconduct or down to a level of misconduct.

Where the persons performing the above assessments decide that the matter falls below the level of misconduct, they must consider whether there are any developmental or organisational issues which may need to be addressed through the Reflective Practice Review process.

4.17.5.3 Written Notification to Officer

Written notification will be given to the police officer concerned by the investigator appointed to investigate the case, advising the officer that their conduct is under investigation—either under reg. 17 of the Police (Conduct) Regulations 2020 or Police (Complaints and Misconduct) Regulations 2020.

The written notice will:

- inform the police officer that there is to be an investigation of their potential breach of the Standards of Professional Behaviour;
- state the identity of the investigator;
- describe the conduct that is the subject of the investigation and how that conduct is alleged to have fallen below the Standards of Professional Behaviour;
- inform the police officer concerned of the result of the severity assessment, namely whether the conduct alleged, if proved, would amount to misconduct or gross misconduct;
- inform the police officer of whether, if the case were to be referred to misconduct proceedings, those would be likely to be a misconduct meeting or misconduct hearing;
- inform the police officer that if the likely form of any misconduct proceedings changes, the police officer will be notified of this together with the reasons for that change;
- inform the police officer of their right to seek advice from their staff association or any other body, and whom the police officer may choose to act as their police friend;
- inform the police officer that if their case is referred to a misconduct hearing or accelerated misconduct hearing, they have the right to be legally represented by a relevant lawyer. If the police officer elects not to be so represented, they may be represented by a police friend. The notice will also make clear that if they elect not to be legally represented they may be dismissed or receive any other disciplinary outcome without being so represented;
- inform the officer that if they are dismissed, their name and a description of the conduct which led to their dismissal will be added to the Police Barred List and may be subject to publication for up to five years;
- inform the police officer that within 10 working days of receipt of the notice (unless this period is extended by the investigator), they may provide a written or oral statement, including any document, relating to any matter under investigation to the investigator within this time;
- inform the police officer that while they do not have to say anything, it may harm their case if they do not mention when interviewed or when providing any information within the relevant time limits something which they later rely on in any misconduct proceedings or accelerated misconduct hearing or at an appeal meeting or Police Appeals Tribunal.

The written notification may be given to the officer in person, left with a person at or sent by recorded delivery to the officer's last known address, given to the officer in person by his police friend where the police friend has agreed to this or given to the officer in any manner agreed with the officer. The responsibility for ensuring that the notice is served rests with the person who is required to give it.

4.17.5.4 Investigation

The purpose of an investigation is to:

- gather evidence to establish the facts and circumstances of the alleged misconduct;
- assist the appropriate authority or IOPC to establish whether there is a case to answer in respect of either misconduct or gross misconduct or that there is no case to answer;
- identify any learning opportunities for the individual or the organisation.

In cases which are not being managed or dealt with by the IOPC, the appropriate authority should ensure that a proportionate and balanced investigation is carried out as soon as possible after any alleged misconduct comes to the appropriate authority's attention and that the investigation is carried out as quickly as possible allowing for the complexity of the case. It is therefore crucial that any investigation is kept proportionate to ensure that an overly lengthy investigation does not lead to grounds for challenge. Where the investigation identifies that the issue is one of performance rather than misconduct, the police officer should be informed as soon as possible that the matter is now being treated as a performance issue.

The investigator is required to notify the police officer of the progress of the investigation at least every four weeks from the start of the investigation.

The investigator has a duty to consider the suggestions submitted to them in response to the reg. 17 notice. The investigator should consider and document reasons for following or not following any submissions made by the police officer or their police friend with a view to ensuring that the investigation is as fair as possible. The suggestions may involve a further suggested line of investigation or further examination of a particular witness. The purpose is to enable a fair and balanced investigation report to be prepared and, where appropriate, made available for consideration at a misconduct meeting/hearing.

An investigation by the appropriate authority should be completed within 12 months of the date on which the allegation first came to its attention. Where it is not completed within this time, the appropriate authority must inform the local policing body, and the IOPC in the case of a recordable conduct matter or complaint, of the investigation's progress, an estimate of when it will be concluded and a report submitted, the reason for the time taken and a summary of the planned steps to bring it to a conclusion. Where the investigation is conducted by the IOPC, whether independent or directed, it must provide the same information in writing to the local policing body and the chief officer of the investigated officer.

4.17.5.5 Interviews during Investigation

It will not always be necessary to conduct a formal interview with the police officer subject to the investigation. In some cases, particularly involving low level misconduct cases, it may be more appropriate, proportionate and timely to request a written account from the police officer. In an investigation for gross misconduct, however, an interview may be an essential protection to enable the officer to give an early account and to inform the investigator as to further lines of inquiry. The police officer must attend the interview when required to do so and it may be a further misconduct matter to fail to attend.

If the police officer concerned or their police friend is not available at the date or time specified by the investigator, the police officer may propose an alternative time. Provided that the alternative time is reasonable and falls within a period of five working days beginning with the first working day after that proposed by the investigator the interview must be postponed to that time.

Where a police officer is on certificated sick leave, the investigator should seek to establish when the police officer will be fit for interview. It may be that the police officer is not fit for ordinary police duty but is capable of being interviewed. Alternatively, the police officer concerned may be invited to provide a written response to the allegations within a specified period and may be sent the questions that the investigator wishes to be answered.

Where a police officer is alleged to have committed a criminal offence, a normal criminal investigation will take place, with the police officer being cautioned in accordance with the PACE Code of Practice. Where the matter to be investigated involves both criminal and misconduct allegations, it should be made clear to the police officer concerned at the start of the interview whether they are being interviewed in respect of the criminal or misconduct allegations. This may be achieved by conducting two separate interviews, although this does not prevent the responses given in respect of the criminal interview being used in the misconduct investigation and, therefore, a separate misconduct interview may not be required.

Care should be taken when conducting a misconduct interview where the police officer is also the subject of a criminal investigation in respect of the same behaviour, as anything said by the police officer concerned in the misconduct interview when not under criminal caution and then used in the criminal investigation could be subject to an inadmissibility ruling by the court at any subsequent trial. At the beginning of a misconduct interview or when asking a police officer to provide a written response to an allegation, the police officer shall be reminded of the warning contained in reg. 17 of the Police (Conduct) Regulations 2020 or Police (Complaints and Misconduct) Regulations 2020.

Prior to an interview with a police officer who is the subject of a misconduct investigation, the investigator must ensure that the police officer is provided with sufficient information and time to prepare for the interview. The information provided should always include full details of the allegations made against the police officer, including the relevant dates and places of the alleged misconduct if known. The investigator should consider whether there are good reasons for withholding certain evidence obtained prior to the interview and if there are no such reasons, the police officer should normally be provided with all the relevant evidence obtained. The police officer will then have the opportunity to provide their version of the events together with any supporting evidence that they may wish to provide. The police officer will be reminded that a failure to provide any account or response to any questions at this stage of the investigation may lead to an adverse inference being drawn at a later stage.

Interviews do not have to be electronically recorded but if they are the person being interviewed shall be given a copy upon request. If the interview is not electronically recorded a written record or summary of the discussion must be given to the person being interviewed. The police officer concerned should be given the opportunity to check and sign that they agree with the summary as an accurate record of what was said and should sign and return a copy to the investigator. Where a police officer refuses or fails to exercise their right to agree and sign a copy, this will be noted by the investigator. The police officer may make a note of the changes that they want to make to the record and a copy of this will be given to the persons conducting the hearing/meeting along with the investigator's account of the record.

Other than for a joint criminal/misconduct investigation interview, it will not be necessary for criminal-style witness statements to be taken. In misconduct investigations an agreed and signed written record of the information supplied will be sufficient.

4.17.5.6 Investigation Report and Supporting Documents

At the conclusion of the investigation the investigator must as soon as practicable submit their report of the investigation, setting out an accurate summary of the evidence that has been gathered. Where the investigation is by the appropriate authority, the report must indicate the investigator's opinion as to whether there is a case to answer in respect of misconduct or gross misconduct or neither. Where it is neither, the report must indicate the investigator's opinion as to whether the matter should be dealt with in the Reflective Practice Review process or in performance proceedings under the Police (Performance) Regulations 2020.

Where the investigation is by the appropriate authority, the appropriate authority must, as soon as practicable, determine whether the officer has a case to answer in respect of misconduct or gross misconduct or, if neither, whether the case amounts to practice requiring improvement to be dealt with in the Reflective Practice Review, it should be dealt with under the Police (Performance) Regulations 2020 or that no action should be taken: reg. 23 of the Police (Conduct) Regulations 2020.

In respect of an IOPC-directed investigation, the IOPC must make its own determination or may seek the views of the appropriate authority on this.

In matters involving a complaint or recordable conduct matter, the decision of the appropriate authority may be subject to an appeal by the complainant to the IOPC. Similarly in such cases, the IOPC has the power to make recommendations and give directions as to whether there is a case to answer and/or the types of misconduct proceedings that should be undertaken. If no further action is to be taken then it is good practice that the investigation report or part of the investigation report that is relevant to the police officer should be given, subject to the harm test, to the police officer on request.

4.17.5.7 Action Prior to Misconduct Meetings/Hearings

Where the appropriate authority consider that there is a case to answer in respect of misconduct/gross misconduct, a misconduct meeting/hearing should be arranged and the police officer shall, subject to the harm test, be given a copy of the investigation report (or the part of the report which is relevant to them), any other relevant documents gathered during the course of the investigation and a copy of their statement to the investigator.

In determining which documents are relevant, the test to be applied will be that under the Criminal Procedure and Investigations Act 1996, namely whether any document or other material undermines the case against the police officer concerned or would assist the police officer's case. The Act does not, however, directly apply.

Where a case is referred to misconduct proceedings, the appropriate authority must provide the police officer with a written notice of the referral, the particulars of the behaviour that is alleged to amount to misconduct/gross misconduct, the name of the person conducting or chairing the proceedings and confirmation that they have been selected on a fair and transparent basis: reg. 30(1)(a) of the Police (Conduct) Regulations 2020.

It is important to note that in cases where the misconduct to be considered was identified as a direct result of a complaint, any decision by the appropriate authority to hold or not to hold a particular misconduct proceeding may be subject to an appeal by the complainant. The appropriate authority, having made its decision on the outcome of the investigation into the complaint and whether there is a case to answer in respect of misconduct or gross misconduct, will notify the complainant of its determination and inform the complainant of their right of appeal. The police officer who is the subject of the investigation should be informed both of the determination of the appropriate authority and that this could be subject to an appeal to the IOPC. The appropriate authority should then wait for a period of 28 days plus 2 days, being the time in which the complainant may appeal, before serving the written notice described above, confirming how the proceedings are to be dealt with.

There is no requirement to wait where the appropriate authority determines that the case should be dealt with at a misconduct hearing or an accelerated misconduct hearing.

No final decision can be taken by the appropriate authority in the case of a complaint or recordable conduct matter where the IOPC is considering whether to recommend or direct that an appropriate authority take particular misconduct proceedings unless the appropriate authority intends to refer the matter to a misconduct hearing or an accelerated misconduct hearing.

Within 15 working days (unless this period is extended by the person conducting the misconduct meeting/hearing for exceptional circumstances) beginning with the first working day after being supplied with the investigator's report and relevant documents and written notice, the police officer will be required to submit in writing:

- whether or not they accept that the behaviour described in the particulars amounts to misconduct or gross misconduct as the case may be;
- where they accept that their conduct amounts to misconduct or gross misconduct, as the case may be, any written submission they wish to make in mitigation;
- where they do not accept that their conduct amounts to misconduct or gross misconduct, as the case may be, or they dispute part of the case, written notice of the particulars of the allegations that they dispute, their account of the relevant events and any arguments on points of law they wish the person conducting the meeting or hearing to consider.

The police officer concerned must also (within the same time limit) provide the appropriate authority and the person conducting the misconduct proceedings with a copy of any document that they intend to rely on at the misconduct proceedings.

The police officer shall be informed of the name of the person holding the misconduct proceedings with the name of any person appointed to advise them as soon as reasonably practicable after they have been appointed. The police officer may object to any person hearing or advising at a misconduct meeting or hearing within three working days starting with the first working day after they are notified of the person's name.

If the police officer concerned submits a compelling reason why such a person should not be involved in the proceedings, which will usually have to relate to some form of bias, a replacement should be found and the police officer will be notified of the name of the replacement. Although there is no statutory right to object to any replacement, standards of public law fairness will require the appropriate authority to consider any further such objections. The police officer concerned may object to a person conducting a misconduct meeting or hearing or advising at such proceedings if, for example, the person has been involved in the case in a way that would make it difficult to make an objective and impartial assessment of the facts of the case.

Where the IOPC has decided to present the case, the officer must provide the above documents to the IOPC.

4.17.5.8 Documents for the Meeting/Hearing

The person conducting the misconduct meeting/hearing shall be supplied with:

- a copy of the notice supplied to the police officer that sets out the fact that the case was to be referred to a misconduct meeting/hearing and details of the alleged misconduct etc.;
- a copy of the investigator's report or such parts of the report as relate to the police officer concerned, any other relevant documents gathered during the course of the investigation and a copy of any statement made by the officer;
- the notice provided by the police officer setting out whether or not the police officer accepts that their conduct amounts to misconduct or gross misconduct, any submission they wish to make in mitigation where the conduct is accepted and, where they do not

accept that the alleged conduct amounts to misconduct or gross misconduct or they dispute part of the case, the allegations they dispute and their account of the relevant events;

- any arguments on points of law submitted by the police officer concerned as well as any documents on which they intend to rely at the meeting/hearing, submitted under reg. 31 of the Police (Conduct) Regulations 2020;
- where the police officer concerned does not accept that the alleged conduct amounts to misconduct or gross misconduct as the case may be or where they dispute any part of the case, any other documents that in the opinion of the appropriate authority should be considered at the meeting/hearing;
- any other documents that the persons conducting the meeting/hearing request that are relevant to the case.

4.17.5.9 Witnesses

A witness will be required to attend a misconduct meeting/hearing where it is necessary to resolve a disputed matter of fact either in their evidence or in relation to the evidence of another person.

The appropriate authority and the officer concerned shall inform each other of any witnesses they wish to attend, including brief details of the evidence those persons can provide and their addresses. They should attempt to agree which witnesses are necessary to deal with the issues in dispute.

The appropriate authority shall supply the person conducting the proceedings with a list of the witnesses agreed between the parties or, where there is no agreement, the lists provided by both the officer and the appropriate authority. The person conducting a misconduct meeting or the chair of a misconduct hearing will decide whether to allow such witnesses. They may also decide that a witness other than one on such lists should be required to attend.

In an accelerated misconduct hearing, only the officer concerned may give live evidence. Where there is a material, evidential dispute, the matter will not qualify as one to be heard in an accelerated misconduct hearing and must be heard in a standard misconduct hearing.

4.17.5.10 Pre-hearings

A person chairing a misconduct hearing (but not a misconduct meeting) may decide to hold a misconduct pre-hearing under reg. 33 of the Police (Conduct) Regulations 2020. It is held in private, can be held by video or telephone and does not have to be recorded. The officer, the officer's police friend, the officer's counsel and counsel representing the appropriate authority (or the IOPC if it is the presenting authority) are entitled to attend.

Where a chair decides to hold a pre-hearing, they must inform the appropriate authority and the officer of this within 15 days after the first working day on which they receive the case documents under reg. 32 of the Police (Conduct) Regulations 2020. At the hearing, the chair must decide the date, time and duration of the misconduct hearing, consider the list of witnesses and decide which, if any, should attend the hearing, any preliminary points of law, any points of disclosure and the imposition of any conditions for the misconduct hearing.

4.17.6 Misconduct Proceedings

There are two types of misconduct proceedings:

- A misconduct meeting for cases where there is a case to answer in respect of misconduct and where the highest level of outcome is a final written warning.

- A misconduct hearing for cases where there is a case to answer in respect of gross misconduct or where the police officer has a live final written warning and there is a case to answer in respect of a further act of misconduct. The highest level of outcome at this hearing is dismissal from the police service without notice. An outcome of dismissal without notice will result in the officer's name and the detail of the misconduct being added to the Barred List.

It is important that misconduct hearings are only used for those matters where the police officer has a live final written warning and has potentially committed a further act of misconduct that warrants misconduct proceedings or where the misconduct alleged is so serious that, if proven or admitted, dismissal from the police service would be justified.

4.17.6.1 Timing for Holding Meetings/Hearings

A misconduct meeting shall take place not later than 20 working days beginning with the first working day after the date on which the documents and material for the meeting have been supplied to the police officer under reg. 30 of the Police (Conduct) Regulations 2020.

Misconduct hearings must commence within 100 working days beginning with the first working day after service of the misconduct notice under reg. 30 of the Police (Conduct) Regulations 2020. The person conducting or chairing the misconduct proceedings may extend the time limit where they consider that this would be in the interests of justice.

In order to maintain confidence in the misconduct procedures it is important that the misconduct meetings/hearings are held as soon as practicable and that extensions to the timescales are an exception rather than the rule.

4.17.6.2 Purpose of Misconduct Meeting/Hearing

The purpose of a formal misconduct meeting/hearing is to:

- give the police officer a fair opportunity to make their case, having considered the investigation report, including supporting documents, and to put forward any factors the police officer wishes to be considered in mitigation;
- decide on the balance of probabilities if the conduct of the police officer fell below the standards set out in the Standards of Professional Behaviour, having regard to all of the evidence and circumstances;
- consider what the outcome should be imposed if misconduct/gross misconduct is proven or admitted. Consideration will be given to any live written warnings or final written warnings (and any previous disciplinary outcomes that have not expired), the officer's culpability, the harm caused, and aggravating and mitigating factors.

4.17.6.3 Misconduct Meeting/Hearing—Non-senior Officers

A misconduct meeting for non-senior officers (police officers up to and including the rank of chief superintendent) will be heard by a member of a police force of at least one rank above the police officer concerned. A misconduct meeting for a special constable will be heard by a member of a police force of the rank of sergeant or above (regardless of the internal grade or 'rank' that the special constable holds) or a senior human resources professional. Alternatively, a police staff member who, in the opinion of the appropriate authority, is a grade above that of the police officer or special constable concerned can be appointed, but not if the case substantially involves operational policing matters.

A misconduct hearing for non-senior officers will consist of a three-person panel, chaired by a legally qualified person and assisted by an officer of at least the rank of superintendent and an independent member.

4.17.6.4 Misconduct Hearings in Public

Misconduct hearings, including accelerated misconduct hearings, are held in public, subject to any decision by the legally qualified chair to hold part or all of it in private.

4.17.6.5 Joint Meetings/Hearings

Cases may arise where two or more police officers are to appear before a misconduct meeting or hearing in relation to apparent failures to meet the standards set out in the Standards of Professional Behaviour stemming from the same incident. In such cases, each police officer may have played a different part and any alleged misconduct may be different for each police officer involved. It will normally be considered necessary to deal with all the matters together in order to disentangle the various strands of action, and therefore a single meeting/hearing will normally be appropriate.

A police officer may request a separate meeting/hearing if they can demonstrate that there would be a real risk of unfairness to that police officer if their case was dealt with in a joint meeting/hearing. It is for the person conducting the proceedings to decide if a separate meeting or hearing is appropriate.

4.17.6.6 Meeting/Hearing in Absence of Officer Concerned

It is in the interests of fairness to ensure that the misconduct meeting/hearing is held as soon as possible. Thus a meeting/hearing may take place if the police officer fails to attend. In cases where the police officer is absent (e.g. through illness or injury) a short delay may be reasonable to allow them to attend. If this is not possible or any delay is considered not appropriate in the circumstances the persons conducting the meeting/hearing may allow the police officer to participate by telephone or video link. In these circumstances a police friend will always be permitted to attend the meeting/hearing to represent the police officer in the normal way (and in the case of a misconduct hearing the police officer's legal representative where appointed).

If a police officer is detained in prison or other institution by order of a court, there is no requirement on the appropriate authority to have the officer concerned produced for the purposes of the misconduct meeting/hearing. Fairness may require that they are able to attend by way of video link.

4.17.6.7 Conduct of Misconduct Meeting/Hearing

It will be for the persons conducting the meeting/hearing to determine the course of the meeting/hearing in accordance with the principles of procedural fairness. They will have read the investigator's report together with any account given by the police officer concerned during the investigation or when submitting their response under reg. 31 of the Police (Conduct) Regulations 2020. They will also have had the opportunity to read any relevant documents attached to the investigator's report.

Any document or other material that was not submitted in advance of the meeting/hearing by the appropriate authority or the police officer concerned may still be considered at the meeting/hearing at the discretion of the persons conducting the meeting/hearing. Where any such document or other material is permitted to be considered, a short adjournment may be necessary to enable the appropriate authority or police officer concerned, as the case may be, to read or consider the document or other material and consider its implications.

Where there is evidence at the meeting or hearing that the police officer concerned, at any time after being given written notice under reg. 17 of the Police (Conduct) Regulations 2020 or Police (Complaints and Misconduct) Regulations 2020, failed to mention when interviewed or when making representations to the investigator or under reg. 30 of the Police (Conduct) Regulations 2020, any fact relied on in their defence at the meeting/hearing, being a fact which in the circumstances existing at the time the police officer concerned could reasonably have been expected to mention when questioned or providing a written response, the persons conducting the meeting/hearing may draw such inferences from this failure as appear appropriate.

The persons conducting the misconduct meeting/hearing will consider the facts of the case and decide on the balance of probabilities whether the police officer's conduct amounted to misconduct, gross misconduct (in the case of a misconduct hearing) or neither. Where proceedings are conducted by a panel, any decision shall be based on a majority.

4.17.6.8 Standard of Proof

In deciding matters of fact misconduct meetings/hearings must apply the standard of proof required in civil cases, that is, the balance of probabilities. Conduct will be proved on the balance of probabilities if the persons conducting the meeting/hearing are satisfied that it is more likely than not that the conduct occurred.

4.17.6.9 Outcomes of Meetings/Hearings

If the persons conducting the misconduct meeting/hearing find that the police officer's conduct has failed to meet the Standards of Professional Behaviour, they must determine the most appropriate disciplinary outcome. In considering the question of outcome, the persons conducting the meeting/hearing should consider the College of Policing Guidance on Outcomes in Police Misconduct Proceedings. This requires the panel to assess the seriousness of the conduct, to keep in mind the purpose for imposing outcomes in police misconduct proceedings and then to choose the outcome which most appropriately fulfils that purpose.

The seriousness of conduct is assessed by reference to the officer's culpability for the misconduct, the harm caused by it, the existence of any aggravating factors and the existence of any mitigating factors. The purpose of imposing outcomes is threefold—to maintain public confidence in and the reputation of the police service, to uphold high standards in policing and deter misconduct and to protect the public.

The meeting/hearing will need to take into account any previous written warnings imposed under the Police (Conduct) Regulations 2020 or 2012 that were live at the time of the initial assessment of the conduct in question and have regard to the police officer's record of service, including any previous disciplinary outcomes that have not been expunged in accordance with reg. 15 of the Police Regulations 2003. The persons conducting the meeting/hearing may (only if deemed necessary and at their discretion) receive evidence from any witness whose evidence would assist them in this regard.

The persons conducting the meeting/hearing are also entitled to take account of any early admission of the conduct on behalf of the police officer concerned and attach whatever weight to this he, she or they consider appropriate in the circumstances of the case, insofar as this demonstrates an officer's insight into their behaviour and the consequent lowering of any prospect of their misconducting themselves again.

The appropriate authority (or the IOPC if it is presenting the misconduct proceedings) has the opportunity to make representations as to the most appropriate outcome. Where a misconduct hearing considers the outcome of a reduction in rank, the appropriate authority must be given the opportunity to make representations on this. The police officer concerned and their police friend (or where appropriate legal representative) must also be given the opportunity to make representations.

4.17.6.10   Outcomes Available at Misconduct Meetings/Hearings

The meeting/hearing may record a finding that the conduct of the police officer concerned amounted to misconduct and take no further action or impose one of the following outcomes:

- **Written warning**—The police officer will be told the reason for the warning, that they have a right to appeal, the name of the person to whom the appeal should be sent and that the warning will be put on their personal file and remain live for 18 months from the date that the warning is given. This means that any misconduct in the following 18 months is likely to lead to (at least) a final written warning.
- **Final written warning**—The police officer will be told the reason for the warning, that any future misconduct may result in dismissal, that they have a right to appeal, the name of the person to whom the appeal should be sent and that the final written warning will be put on their personal file. A misconduct hearing may impose a final written warning for between two and five years and it will remain live for this period from the date that the warning is given. This means that only in exceptional circumstances will further misconduct (that justifies more than management advice) not result in dismissal.

Where a misconduct hearing finds that the conduct of an officer amounts to misconduct (but not gross misconduct), in addition to the two outcomes above, the persons conducting the hearing will also have available the outcomes of:

- **Reduction in rank**—This is available where there was a final written warning in force at the date of the initial severity assessment and the misconduct hearing finds that the officer's misconduct arises from more than one incident and where those incidents are not closely factually connected.
- **Dismissal without notice**—Dismissal without notice will mean that the police officer is dismissed from the police service with immediate effect.

Where a police officer appears before a misconduct hearing for an alleged act of gross misconduct, and the persons conducting the hearing find that the conduct amounts to misconduct rather than gross misconduct, then (unless the police officer already has a live final written warning) the disciplinary outcomes available to the panel are those that are available at a misconduct meeting only.

Where a misconduct hearing finds that the conduct of an officer amounts to gross misconduct, the persons conducting the hearing will have available the outcomes of:

- **Final written warning**.
- **Reduction in rank**, without the conditions stated above.
- **Dismissal without notice**.

4.17.6.11   Notification of the Outcome

In all cases the police officer will be informed in writing of the outcome of the misconduct meeting/hearing. This will be done as soon as practicable and in any case within five working days beginning with the first working day after the conclusion of the misconduct meeting/hearing. The notification in the case of a misconduct meeting will include notification to the police officer concerned of their right to appeal against the finding and/or outcome and the name of the person to whom any appeal should be sent. In the case of a police officer who has attended a misconduct hearing, the notification will include their right of appeal to a Police Appeals Tribunal against any finding and/or outcome imposed. In cases involving a complainant, where the complaint was the subject of a local or supervised investigation the appropriate authority will be responsible for informing the complainant of the outcome. In cases investigated by the IOPC, whether independent or directed, the

IOPC will be responsible for informing the complainant of the outcome. Police forces have five days to inform the College of Policing of dismissals, for inclusion on the Police Barred List. Names placed on the Police Barred List, which is a publicly searchable database, will remain there for a period of five years from the date of publication.

4.17.6.12 Expiry of Warnings

Notification of written warnings issued, including the date issued and expiry date, will be recorded on the police officer's personal record, along with a copy of the written notification of the outcome and a summary of the matter. Where a police officer has a live written warning and transfers from one force to another, the live warning will transfer with the police officer and will remain live until the expiry of the warning and should be referred to as part of any reference before the police officer transfers.

Where a police officer who has a live written warning or final written warning takes a career break in accordance with Police Regulations, any time on such a break will not count towards the period for which the written warning or final written warning is live.

4.17.6.13 Attendance of Complainant or Interested Person at Misconduct Proceedings

Where a misconduct meeting is being held as a result of a public complaint or a recordable conduct matter, the complainant or interested person will have the right to attend it as an observer. This is subject to the right of the person conducting the meeting to exclude or impose conditions on the complainant's or interested party's attendance to facilitate the proper conduct of proceedings and to exclude them while evidence is being given where disclosure to the complainant or interested party would be contrary to the harm test. They may be accompanied by one other person and, if they have a special need, one further person to accommodate that need (e.g. an interpreter, sign language expert etc.).

Misconduct hearings are held in public, such that all members of the public may remain throughout the entirety of it.

4.17.6.14 IOPC Direction, Attendance and Presentation at Meetings/Hearings

Where the IOPC exercises its power (under para. 27 of sch. 3 to the 2002 Act) to direct an appropriate authority to hold misconduct proceedings, this will also include a direction as to whether the proceedings will be a misconduct meeting or hearing. In making such a direction the IOPC will have regard to the severity assessment that has been made in the case and notified to the police officer concerned.

Where a misconduct meeting/hearing is to be held following:

- an investigation independently investigated or directed by the IOPC; or
- a local investigation where the IOPC has made a recommendation under para. 27(3) of sch. 3 to the Police Reform Act 2002 that misconduct proceedings should be taken and the recommendation has been accepted by the appropriate authority; or
- the IOPC has given a direction under para. 27(4) of that schedule that misconduct proceedings shall be taken,

the IOPC may attend the misconduct meeting/hearing to make representations. Such representations may be an explanation why the IOPC has directed particular misconduct proceedings to be brought or to comment on the investigation. Where the IOPC is to attend a misconduct hearing, it may instruct a relevant lawyer to represent it.

The IOPC may decide to present a case referred to a misconduct hearing or accelerated misconduct hearing where it has expressed a different view from the appropriate authority on whether there was a case to answer, where the appropriate authority did not accept a recommendation in respect of there being a case to answer, where the appropriate authority agrees that it should do so or where the IOPC considers that there is a compelling public interest for it to do so.

4.17.7 Right of Appeal

A police officer has a right of appeal against the finding and/or the outcome imposed at a misconduct meeting. The appeal is commenced by the police officer concerned giving written notice of appeal to the appropriate authority, clearly setting out the grounds for the appeal within seven working days beginning with the first working day after the receipt of the notification of the outcome of the misconduct meeting (unless this period is extended by the appropriate authority for exceptional circumstances). The police officer has the right to be accompanied by a police friend.

The police officer concerned may only appeal on the grounds that:

- the finding or disciplinary action imposed was unreasonable;
- there is evidence that could not reasonably have been considered at the misconduct meeting which could have materially affected the finding or decision on disciplinary action; or
- there was a serious breach of the procedures set out in the Regulations or other unfairness which could have materially affected the finding or decision on disciplinary action.

4.17.7.1 Appeal following Misconduct Meeting—Non-senior Officers

An appeal against the finding and/or the outcome of a misconduct meeting will be heard by a member of the police service of a higher rank or, unless the case substantially involves operational policing matters, a police staff manager who is considered to be more senior than the person who conducted the misconduct meeting. A police officer or police staff member may be present to advise the person conducting the appeal on procedural matters. The person determining the appeal will be provided with the following documents:

- the notice of appeal from the police officer concerned setting out their grounds of appeal;
- the record of the original misconduct meeting;
- the documents that were given to the person who held the original misconduct meeting;
- any evidence that the police officer concerned wishes to submit in support of their appeal that was not considered at the misconduct meeting.

The person appointed to deal with the appeal must first decide whether the notice of appeal sets out arguable grounds of appeal. If they determine that there are no arguable grounds they must dismiss the appeal and inform the police officer concerned accordingly, setting out their reasons. Where the person appointed to hear the appeal determines that there are arguable grounds of appeal and the police officer concerned has requested to be present at the appeal meeting, the person appointed to conduct the proceedings must hold a meeting with the police officer concerned. Where the police officer fails to attend the meeting, the person conducting the appeal may proceed in their absence.

The person conducting the appeal may consider:

- whether the finding of the original misconduct meeting was unreasonable having regard to all the evidence considered or if the finding could now be in doubt due to evidence which has emerged since the meeting;
- any outcome imposed by the misconduct meeting which may be considered as unreasonable, having regard to all the circumstances of the case;

- whether the finding or outcome could be unsafe due to procedural unfairness. The person conducting the appeal must consider whether there was unfairness and, if so, whether it could have materially influenced the outcome).

The person determining the appeal may confirm or reverse the decision appealed against. Where the person determining the appeal decides that the original disciplinary action imposed was too lenient, they may increase the outcome up to a maximum of a final written warning. An appeal is not a rehearing of the misconduct meeting. It is to examine a particular part of the misconduct case or procedural issue which is under question and which may have affected the finding or the outcome.

The appeal will normally be heard within five working days beginning with the working day after the determination that the officer concerned has arguable grounds of appeal. The officer concerned can object to the person appointed to conduct the appeal in the same way as they could for the original misconduct meeting (**see para. 4.17.5.7**).

4.17.7.2 Appeal Following Misconduct Hearing

Where a police officer has appeared before a misconduct hearing, any appeal against the finding or outcome is to the Police Appeals Tribunal (**see paras 4.17.9 to 4.17.9.9**). The police officer should be informed that the Police Appeals Tribunal can increase any outcome imposed as well as reduce or overturn the decision of the misconduct hearing or accelerated misconduct hearing.

Senior officers have the right to appeal against the finding and/or outcome of a misconduct meeting or hearing. The appeal in both cases will be made to the Police Appeals Tribunal. The police officer should be informed that the Police Appeals Tribunal can increase any outcome imposed as well as reduce or overturn the decision of the misconduct hearing or accelerated misconduct hearing.

4.17.8 Accelerated Misconduct Cases

The operation of the accelerated misconduct procedures is set out in part 5 of the Police (Conduct) Regulations 2020. They can be used if the appropriate authority certifies the case as one where the 'special conditions' are satisfied or if the IOPC has given a direction under para. 20A of sch. 3 to the Police Reform Act 2002.

The 'special conditions' are that there is sufficient evidence, in the form of written statements or other documents, without the need for further evidence, whether written or oral, to establish on the balance of probabilities that the conduct of the police officer concerned constitutes gross misconduct, and it is in the public interest for the police officer concerned to cease to be a police officer without delay. The first condition will be satisfied only where there is no material, evidential dispute.

These procedures are, therefore, designed to deal with cases where the evidence is incontrovertible in the form of statements, documents or other material (e.g. CCTV, DNA), such that this is sufficient to prove gross misconduct, and it is in the public interest if the case is found or admitted for the police officer to cease to be a member of the police service forthwith. Even where the criteria for a special case are met, there may be circumstances where it would not be appropriate to certify it, for instance, where to do so might prematurely alert others (police officers or non-police officers) who are, or may be, the subject of an investigation.

In the case of non-senior officers, the case will be heard by the police officer's chief constable (assistant commissioner in the Metropolitan Police) or in cases where the chief constable is an interested party or is unavailable, another chief constable or an assistant commissioner. Insofar as a deputy chief constable may exercise all the powers of a chief constable during any period when they are unable to exercise functions or at any other time with their consent, a deputy chief constable may conduct an accelerated misconduct hearing. The police officer will have a right of appeal under reg. 63 of the Police (Conduct) Regulations 2020 to a Police Appeals Tribunal against any finding of gross misconduct and/or the disciplinary action imposed.

An accelerated misconduct hearing is held in public. There is no live witness evidence, other than from the police officer concerned.

The hearing may proceed in the absence of the police officer concerned, but the persons conducting the hearing should ensure that the police officer concerned has been informed of their right to be legally represented at the hearing or to be represented by a police friend where the police officer chooses not to be legally represented.

4.17.8.1 Accelerated Misconduct Process

Where the appropriate authority determines that the special conditions are satisfied and unless it considers that the circumstances are such as to make it inappropriate to do so, it shall certify the case as one where the special conditions are satisfied and refer it to an accelerated misconduct hearing.

If, after certifying the case, the appropriate authority decides that the special case conditions are no longer satisfied, it must refer the case back to the investigator if further investigation is required or to misconduct proceedings under the standard procedures. If the appropriate authority decides to refer the matter to an accelerated hearing, it will sign a special conditions certificate and will provide to the police officer concerned notice giving particulars of the conduct that is alleged to constitute gross misconduct and copies of:

- the special conditions certificate;
- any statement the police officer may have made to the investigator during the course of the investigation;
- subject to the harm test:
  - the investigator's report (if any) or such parts of that report as relate to the police officer concerned, together with any documents attached to that report; and
  - any relevant statement or documents gathered during the course of the investigation.

The police officer concerned will also be told the date, time and place of the hearing and of their right to legal representation and to advice from a police friend. The date of the accelerated misconduct hearing will be not less than 10 working days and not more than 15 working days from the date the special conditions certificate and other documents are provided to the police officer concerned.

Within seven working days of the first working day after the day on which the written notice and documents are supplied to the police officer concerned, the police officer shall provide a written notice to the appropriate authority of:

- whether or not they accept that their conduct constituted gross misconduct;
- where they accept that the conduct constituted gross misconduct, any submission they wish to make in mitigation;
- where they do not accept that the conduct constituted gross misconduct;
  - the allegations they dispute and their version of the relevant events; and
  - any arguments on points of law they wish to be considered by the person or persons conducting the meeting.

At the same time the police officer must provide the appropriate authority with copies of any documents they intend to rely on at the hearing. Where the IOPC has decided to present the hearing, the documents must be provided to it instead of the appropriate authority.

4.17.8.2 Outcome of Accelerated Misconduct Hearing

Where the person conducting the accelerated misconduct hearing finds that the conduct of the police officer concerned constituted gross misconduct, they shall impose disciplinary action, which may be a final written warning (unless a final written warning was in force at the date of the initial severity assessment), reduction in rank or dismissal without notice.

Where the person conducting the hearing determines that the conduct does not amount to gross misconduct, they may dismiss the case. Alternatively, they may return the case to the appropriate authority to be dealt with at a misconduct meeting or hearing (where there is a live final written warning) under the standard procedures. This may be because the person conducting the hearing consider that the conduct is misconduct rather than gross misconduct. There is power under reg. 50 of the Police (Conduct) Regulations 2020 for the appropriate authority to remit the case to be dealt with under the standard procedures at any time prior to the start of the accelerated misconduct hearing, if it considers that the special conditions are no longer satisfied.

Where the police officer admits the allegation or the person conducting the hearing finds it proved on the balance of probabilities, then the person conducting the hearing:

- shall have regard to the record of police service of the police officer concerned as shown on their personal record;
- may consider such documentary evidence as would, in their opinion, assist them in determining the question; and
- shall give the police officer concerned, and their police friend or relevant lawyer, an opportunity to make oral or written representations.

The police officer concerned shall be informed of the finding and any disciplinary action imposed or a decision to dismiss the case or revert it back to be dealt with under the standard procedures as soon as practicable and in any event shall be provided with written notice of these matters and a summary of the reasons within five working days beginning with the first working day after the conclusion of the hearing.

4.17.9 Appeals to the Police Appeals Tribunal

The Police Appeals Tribunal Rules 2020 govern the composition and operation of the Police Appeals Tribunal.

A police officer has a right of appeal to a Police Appeals Tribunal against any disciplinary finding and/or disciplinary outcome imposed at a misconduct hearing or accelerated misconduct hearing held under the Police (Conduct) Regulations 2020. Senior police officers, in addition, have the right to appeal to a Police Appeals Tribunal against any disciplinary finding and/or outcome imposed at a misconduct meeting. A police officer may not appeal to a tribunal against a finding of misconduct or gross misconduct where that finding was made following acceptance by the officer that their conduct amounted to that. A police officer of a rank up to and including chief superintendent has a right of appeal to a Police Appeals Tribunal against the finding and/or the following outcomes imposed following a third stage meeting under the Police (Performance) Regulations 2020 to dismiss or reduce in rank. In addition, if the case has been dealt with at a stage three meeting, without having progressed through stages one and two, the police officer may appeal against redeployment to alternative duties, the issue of a final written improvement notice, or the issue of a written improvement notice.

4.17.9.1 Composition and Timing of Police Appeals Tribunals

Where the appeal is made by a person who was, at the time of their dismissal, a non-senior officer or former officer and/or a special constable or former special constable the Police Appeals Tribunal will consist of:

- a legally qualified chair drawn from a list maintained by the Home Office;
- a serving senior officer;
- a lay person.

4.17.9.2 Grounds of Appeal

A Police Appeals Tribunal is not a re-hearing of the original matter; rather its role is to consider an appeal based on specific grounds.

In the case of matters dealt with under the Police (Conduct) Regulations 2020, the grounds for appeal are:

- the finding or disciplinary action imposed was unreasonable; or
- there is evidence that could not reasonably have been considered at the misconduct meeting (in the case of senior police officers), the misconduct hearing or accelerated misconduct hearing (as the case may be); or
- there was a breach of the procedures set out in the Police (Conduct) Regulations 2020, the Police (Complaints and Misconduct) Regulations 2020, sch. 3 to the Police Reform Act 2002 or other unfairness which could have materially affected the finding or decision on disciplinary action.

In the case of matters dealt with under the Police (Performance) Regulations 2020 the grounds for appeal are:

- the finding of unsatisfactory performance or attendance or gross incompetence, or the outcome imposed, was unreasonable; or
- there is evidence that could not reasonably have been considered at the third stage meeting which could have materially affected the finding or decision on the outcome; or
- there was a breach of the procedures set out in the Police (Performance) Regulations 2020 or other unfairness which could have materially affected the finding or decision on the outcome; or
- where the police officer was required to attend a third stage meeting following a first and second stage meeting, the police officer concerned should not have been required to attend that meeting as their unsatisfactory performance or attendance was not similar to or connected with the unsatisfactory performance or attendance referred to in their final written improvement notice.

4.17.9.3 Notice of Appeal

Where a police officer wishes to appeal, they will need to give notice of their appeal in writing to the 'relevant local policing body'. The notice of appeal must be given within 10 working days, beginning with the first working day after the police officer is supplied with a written copy of the decision that they are appealing against. In cases where the police officer fails to submit their notice of appeal within the 10-working-day period, they may, within a reasonable time after the end of that period, submit a notice of appeal accompanied by the reasons why it was not submitted within that period and the reasons for the officer's view that it was served within a reasonable time after that period. The tribunal chair must then determine whether the appeal could have reasonably and practicably been submitted within the time limit.

4.17.9.4   Procedure on Notice of Appeal

As soon as reasonably practicable after receipt of a copy of the notice of appeal and in any case within 15 working days (beginning with the first working day following the day of such receipt) the respondent to the appeal must provide to the relevant local policing body:

- a copy of the decision appealed against (namely the written judgment of the original panel/person);
- any documents that were available to the panel/person conducting the original hearing; and
- the transcript or part of the transcript of the proceedings at the original hearing requested by the appellant (a copy of the transcript (if applicable) shall also at the same time be sent to the appellant).

The appellant, within 20 working days beginning with the first working day following the day on which they are supplied with a copy of the transcript or, where no transcript is requested, within 35 working days (beginning with the first working day following the day on which the appellant gave notice of their appeal), shall provide to the relevant local policing body:

- a notice setting out the finding, disciplinary action or outcome appealed against and of their grounds for the appeal;
- any supporting documents;
- where the appellant is allowed to call witnesses (for appeals made only on the ground of there being evidence that could not reasonably have been considered at the original hearing and which could have materially affected the finding or outcome):
  - a list of any proposed witnesses; and
  - a witness statement from each of the proposed witnesses;
- if they consent to the appeal being determined without a hearing (that is, on the basis of the papers alone), notice in writing that they so consent.

In relation to the appellant, a 'proposed witness' is a person whom the appellant wishes to call to give evidence at the hearing, whose evidence was not and could not reasonably have been considered at the hearing and whose evidence could have materially affected the decision being appealed against.

4.17.9.5   Determination of an Appeal

Where the tribunal chair allows the appeal to go forward to a hearing, the local policing body will be responsible for making the administrative arrangements prior to and at the tribunal and for ensuring that the members of the tribunal appointed to deal with the appeal are sent the papers together with a schedule of the documents that each of the members should have.

The tribunal chair who made the determination as to whether to allow the notice of appeal to proceed to a tribunal need not necessarily be the same tribunal chair who hears the subsequent appeal. However, the chair who makes the decision as to whether the appeal should be dealt with at a hearing or on the papers should be the chair appointed to hear the appeal itself.

Where an appeal has not been dismissed at the review stage, the tribunal chair shall determine whether the appeal should be dealt with at a hearing. It is expected that this decision will be made by the tribunal chair within ten working days of receiving the papers. If the appellant has not consented to an appeal being dealt with on the papers then a hearing shall be held. If the appellant has consented, the tribunal chair may determine that the appeal shall be dealt with without a hearing. If the appeal is to be dealt with at a hearing, the chair shall give the appellant and the respondent their name and contact address.

4.17.9.6 Legal and Other Representation

The appellant can be represented at a hearing by a relevant lawyer or a police friend. Where the appellant is represented by a lawyer the appellant's police friend may also attend.

4.17.9.7 Procedure at Hearing

Where the case is to be heard at a tribunal hearing, the chair of the tribunal shall cause the appellant and the respondent to be given written notice of the time, date and place of the hearing, at least 20 working days or such shorter period as may with the agreement of both parties be determined, before the hearing begins.

The tribunal chair will determine in advance of the tribunal whether to allow any witness that the appellant or respondent proposes to call to give evidence at the tribunal. Witnesses will only be permitted where the ground for appeal is that there is evidence that could not reasonably have been considered at the original hearing which could have materially affected the finding or decision on outcome. No witnesses shall give evidence at the hearing unless the chair reasonably believes that it is necessary for the witness to do so. Any witness that does attend the tribunal may be subject to questioning and cross questioning. It is for the tribunal to decide on the admissibility of any evidence, or to determine whether or not any question should or should not be put to a witness. A verbatim record of the evidence given at the hearing shall be taken; and the relevant local policing body shall keep such record for a period of not less than two years from the date of the end of the hearing.

The tribunal has discretion to proceed with the hearing in the absence of either party, whether represented or not, if it appears to be just and proper to do so. Where it is decided to proceed in the absence of either party the tribunal should record its reasons for doing so. The tribunal may adjourn the appeal as necessary.

The hearing is held in public.

4.17.9.8 Attendance of Other Persons

Where the matter to be dealt with at the appeal is related directly to a complaint made against the appellant or a conduct matter involving an interested party, the chair of the tribunal shall cause the complainant or interested party to be given notice of the time, date and place of the tribunal.

4.17.9.9 Determination and Outcome of Appeal

A tribunal need not be unanimous in its determination of the appeal or of any other decision before it and may reach a decision based on a majority. Where a tribunal finds itself divided equally, the tribunal chair will have the casting vote.

A tribunal, when determining any disciplinary or unsatisfactory performance outcome imposed, may impose any outcome that the original panel/person could have imposed. The tribunal has the power to increase as well as reduce the outcome imposed by the original panel/person. The decision of the tribunal will normally be made on the day of the tribunal hearing.

The tribunal chair shall, within three working days of the tribunal determining the appeal, give written notice to the appellant of the tribunal's decision.

A police officer ordered to be reinstated in their former force or rank will be deemed to have served in their force and/or rank continuously from the date of the original decision to the date of reinstatement. Reinstatement means that the officer is put back in the role in which they would have been if not dismissed or reduced in rank.

4.17.9.10 Reflective Practice Review Process

The Reflective Practice Review process is entirely new and replaces the previous options of management action and management advice, which the Police (Conduct) Regulations 2008 had introduced. It comprises three stages: a fact-finding stage, a discussion stage and then a production of a reflective review development report and monitoring of the officer in line with this.

The reviewer who conducts the process must be the line manager of or a police officer or staff member who is more senior to the officer. Where the reviewer considers that the officer is failing to engage with the process, they may refer the matter back to the appropriate authority for a renewed severity assessment.

The Reflective Practice Review process is considered to be a performance rather than a disciplinary process, so that an officer participating in it may continue to apply for and obtain promotion. Similarly, an officer may not be represented during it—whether by a lawyer or a police friend and such persons may make no representations to the appropriate authority about any aspect of the process.

Where a matter is referred to the Reflective Practice Review process, the reviewer must provide the officer with details of the matter and invite them to provide their account of it. The officer must provide their account within five working days after the first working day on which the invitation is received, unless this is extended. The reviewer must then make inquiries which are reasonable, proportionate and relevant to establish the facts of the matter.

If evidence becomes available which was not available to the appropriate authority when it referred the matter, the reviewer must refer it back for a renewed severity assessment. If the matter is then referred to a misconduct investigation, any account that the officer has given is not admissible in subsequent disciplinary proceedings, unless it relates to something not referred.

Otherwise, or where the Reflective Practice Review process continues, following the fact-finding stage the reviewer must invite the officer to a Reflective Practice Review discussion. This must include a discussion both of the practice requiring improvement and related circumstances and the identification of any key lessons to be learnt by the officer, their line management or their police force, to address the matter and prevent a reoccurrence of it.

After the discussion has ended, the reviewer must produce a reflective review development report containing a summary of the issue and background circumstances, a summary of the discussion, the key actions to be taken within a specified period, the lessons identified for the officer, line management and/or police force and the period of time for reviewing the report and the actions to be taken. The reviewer will send a copy of the report to the appropriate authority, which must ensure that any lessons for line management or the force are addressed. The report and the review notes must then be discussed as part of the officer's PDR (performance and development review) during the 12-month period following the report.

4.18 Unsatisfactory Performance and Attendance

4.18.1 Introduction

The formal procedures to deal with unsatisfactory performance and attendance are set out in the Police (Performance) Regulations 2020. These are referred to as 'UPPs' (and are referred to by that abbreviation in this chapter).

The aim of the procedures is to provide a fair, open and proportionate method of dealing with performance and attendance issues, encouraging a culture of learning and development for individuals and the organisation. Early intervention via management action should achieve the desired effect of improving and maintaining a police officer's performance or attendance to an acceptable level; however, in some cases it will be appropriate for managers to take formal action under the procedures. The procedures in the UPPs are largely the same whether applied to unsatisfactory performance or attendance (the differences that do exist are set out below). However, the issues that arise in attendance cases may be different from those in performance cases.

Where a police officer's absence or poor performance is due to an underlying medical condition, which may amount to a disability for the purposes of the Equality Act 2010, consideration should be given as to whether the officer requires a referral to occupational health, the benefit of reasonable adjustments and/or if they are medically unfit for performing the ordinary duties of a member of the police force, for the purposes of the Police Pensions Regulations 1987, 2006 or 2015. If they are medically unfit and there are no reasonable adjustments that can be made to mitigate the disparate impact of their disability then the officer should be progressed through the ill-health retirement process and not the Police (Performance) Regulations 2020. Otherwise, such action may amount to unlawful disability discrimination.

4.18.2 Applicability

The procedures apply to police officers up to and including the rank of chief superintendent, including special constables. However, given the nature of special constables as unpaid volunteers, initiation of such cases may be limited to those where the special constable either contests that his/her performance or attendance is unsatisfactory or agrees that it is unsatisfactory but expresses a desire to continue with his/her special constable duties. In other cases the special constable may choose to resign from his/her role as a special constable. In setting meeting dates and establishing panels, regard should be had to the nature of special constables as volunteers.

> **KEYNOTE**
>
> The procedures *do not apply* to student police officers during their probationary period. The procedures governing performance and attendance issues in respect of police students are determined locally by each force. These procedures are underpinned by reg. 13 of the Police Regulations 2003.

4.18.3 Ongoing Performance Assessment and Review

Every police officer should have some form of performance appraisal, commonly referred to as a 'performance and development review' (PDR). The PDR should be the principal method by which the police officer's performance and attendance are monitored and assessed. The activities and behaviours expected of a police officer in order to achieve his/her objectives should be in accordance with the relevant national framework which will form the basis of the police officer's role profile.

4.18.4 Sources of Information

Unsatisfactory performance or attendance will often be identified by the immediate line manager of the police officer as part of his/her normal management responsibilities. Where the police officer currently works to a manager who has no line management responsibility for him/her, it is the responsibility of that manager to inform the police officer's line manager of any performance or attendance issues he/she has identified. It is possible that line managers may be alerted to unsatisfactory performance or attendance on the part of one of their police officers as a result of information or complaint from a member of the public. Such cases must be dealt with in accordance with the established procedures for the handling of complaints.

The outcome of an investigation into a complaint alleging misconduct may identify an issue of unsatisfactory performance or attendance. Consequently, the appropriate authority may determine that there is no case to answer in respect of misconduct or gross misconduct but it may be appropriate to take action under the UPPs.

While the unsatisfactory performance and attendance procedures are internal management procedures, it may be necessary at times to inform public complainants of action taken with respect to the police officer to whom the complaint relates.

4.18.5 Informal Intervention Before Formal Proceedings

Managers should try to address poor performance informally before initiating formal performance action proceedings:

- the line manager should discuss any shortcoming(s) or concern(s) with the individual at the earliest possible opportunity. It would be wrong for the line manager to accumulate a list of concerns about the performance or attendance of an individual and delay telling him/her about them until the occasion of the police officer's annual or mid-term PDR meetings;
- the reason for dissatisfaction must be made clear to the individual as soon as possible and there must be a factual basis for discussing the issues, i.e. the discussion must relate to specific incidents or omissions that have occurred;
- line managers should seek to establish whether there are any underlying reasons for the unsatisfactory performance or attendance;
- consideration should be given as to whether there is any health or welfare issue that is or may be affecting performance or attendance;
- in cases where the difficulty appears to stem from a personality clash with a colleague or line manager, or where for other reasons a change of duties might be appropriate, the police officer's line management may, in consultation with the appropriate human resources adviser, consider redeployment if this provides an opportunity for the police officer to improve his/her performance or attendance. Where a police officer is redeployed

in this way, the police officer and his/her new line management should be informed of the reasons for the move and of the assessment of his/her performance or attendance in the previous role;

- the line manager must make it clear to the police officer that he/she is available to give further advice and guidance if needed;
- depending on the circumstances, it may be appropriate to indicate to the police officer that if there is no, or insufficient, improvement, then the matter will be dealt with under the UPPs;
- line managers are expected to gather relevant evidence and keep a contemporaneous note of interactions with the police officer;
- challenging unsatisfactory performance or attendance in an appropriate manner does not constitute bullying.

The above principles cover the position when a line manager first becomes aware of some unsatisfactory aspect of the police officer's performance or attendance and is dealing with the issue as part of normal line management responsibilities.

Such management action should be put on record. Particularly, the line manager should record the nature of the performance or attendance issue, the advice given, and steps taken to address the problems identified. Such action ensures continuity in circumstances where one or more members of the management chain may move on to other duties or the police officer concerned moves to new duties.

Ideally performance or attendance will improve and continue to an acceptable level. Where there is insufficient or unsustained improvement, it will then be appropriate to use the UPPs. The period of time agreed or determined by the line manager for the police officer concerned to improve his/her performance or attendance prior to using the UPPs must be sufficient to provide a reasonable opportunity for the desired improvement or attendance to take place and must be time limited.

4.18.6 Performance Issues

Police officers should know what standard of performance is required of them and be given appropriate support to attain that standard and managers should let a police officer know when he/she is doing well or, if the circumstances arise, when there are the first signs that there is a need for improvement in his/her performance.

KEYNOTE

Unsatisfactory performance (or attendance) is defined in reg. 4 of the UPPs as 'an inability or failure of a police officer to perform the duties of the role or rank he [or she] is currently undertaking to a satisfactory standard or level'.

There is no formula for determining the point at which a concern about a police officer's performance should lead to formal procedures under the UPPs being taken. Each case must be considered on its merits. However, the following points need to be emphasised:

- the intention of performance management, including formal action under the UPPs is to improve performance;
- occasional lapses should be dealt with in the course of normal management activity and should not involve the application of the UPPs, which are designed to cover repeated failures to meet such standards or more serious cases of unsatisfactory performance;
- managers should be able to demonstrate that they have considered whether management action is appropriate before using the UPPs.

4.18.7 Attendance Issues

Where the UPPs are used in relation to attendance matters, they will normally relate to periods of sickness absence such that the ability of the police officer to perform his/her duties is compromised. Other forms of absence unrelated to genuine sickness would normally be dealt with under the misconduct procedures, e.g. where a police officer's absence is unauthorised. Except where a police officer fails to cooperate, appropriate supportive action must be taken before formal action is taken under the UPPs. A failure by a police officer to cooperate will not prevent formal action being taken or continued. If supportive action is taken, the police officer cooperates and the attendance improves and is maintained at a satisfactory level, there will be no need to take formal action under the UPPs. Where police officers are injured or ill they should be treated fairly and compassionately. Managers should be able to demonstrate that they have acted reasonably in all actions taken at all stages of the attendance management process, including any action under the UPPs.

4.18.7.1 Monitoring Attendance

Line managers, in conjunction with the force's human resources department if necessary, are responsible for monitoring a police officer's attendance. A formal record of a police officer's period of illness will be kept in accordance with reg. 15 of the Police Regulations 2003. The force Occupational Health Service is an essential part of effective attendance management and should be involved as soon as any concerns about a police officer's attendance are identified. Where action is taken under the UPPs in respect of a police officer's attendance, the police officer may be referred to the Occupational Health Service for up-to-date information and advice at any stage within the procedure in accordance with force policy. This should enable the force to make an informed decision about a police officer's attendance. Where police officers do not attend appointments or otherwise fail to co-operate with the force's Occupational Health Service, an assessment will be made on the information available.

4.18.7.2 Action Under the UPPs

Formal action under the UPPs may be taken in cases of both unacceptable levels of persistent short-term absences and long-term absences due to sickness and/or injury. In deciding whether to take action under the procedures, managers must consider all of the facts available to them, including:

- the nature of the illness, injury or condition;
- the likelihood of the illness, injury or condition (or some other related illness, injury or condition) recurring;
- the pattern and length of absence(s) and the period of good health between them;
- the need for the work to be done, i.e. what impact on the force's performance and workload the absence is having;
- the extent to which a police officer has cooperated with supportive management action;
- whether the police officer was made aware, in the earlier supportive action, that unless an improvement was made, action under the UPPs might be used;
- whether the selected medical practitioner (SMP) has been asked to consider the issue of permanent disablement and/or the police force is considering medical retirement;
- the impact of the Equality Act 2010 and the public sector equality duty.

Where an officer may be disabled pursuant to the Equality Act 2010, they should be referred to occupational health, who should be asked what reasonable adjustments could be made. Where the officer is medically unfit for performing the ordinary duties of a member of the police force, this should be addressed through the ill-health retirement process before any consideration of proceedings under the Police (Performance) Regulations 2020.

4.18.8 Multiple Instances of Unsatisfactory Performance

A police officer can move to a later stage of the UPPs only in relation to unsatisfactory performance or attendance that is similar to or connected with the unsatisfactory performance or attendance referred to in any previous written improvement notice. Where failings relate to different forms of unsatisfactory performance or attendance it will be necessary to commence the UPPs at the first stage (unless the failing constitutes gross incompetence). If more than one UPP is commenced, then, given that the procedures will relate to different failings and will have been identified at different times, the finding and outcome of each should be without prejudice to the others.

There may be circumstances where procedures have been initiated for a particular failing and an additional failing comes to light prior to the first stage meeting. In such circumstances it is possible to consolidate the two issues at the first stage meeting provided that there is sufficient time prior to the meeting to comply with the notification requirements explained in more detail below.

4.18.9 The First Stage

Where a line manager decides that the UPPs are the most appropriate way of addressing the performance or attendance matter, he/she will notify the police officer in writing that he/she is required to attend a first stage meeting and include in that notification the following details:

- details of the procedures for determining the date and time of the meeting;
- a summary of the reasons why the line manager considers the police officer's performance or attendance unsatisfactory;
- the possible outcomes of a first stage, second stage and third stage meeting;
- that a human resources professional or a police officer (who should have experience of UPPs and be independent from the line management chain) may attend the meeting to advise the line manager on the proceedings;
- that if the police officer agrees, any other person specified in the notice may attend the meeting;
- that prior to the meeting the police officer must provide the line manager with any documentation he/she intends to rely on in the meeting; and
- the police officer's rights, i.e. his/her right to seek advice from a representative of his/her staff association and to be accompanied and represented at the meeting by a police friend.

KEYNOTE

The notice shall be accompanied by copies of related documentation relied upon by the line manager in support of the view that the police officer's performance or attendance is unsatisfactory. In advance of the meeting, the police officer shall provide the line manager with any documents on which he/she intends to rely in support of his/her case. Any document or other material that was not submitted in advance of the meeting may be considered at the meeting at the discretion of the line manager, ensuring fairness to all parties. However the presumption should be that such documents or material will not be permitted unless it can be shown that they were not previously available to be submitted in advance. Where such a document or other material is permitted to be considered, a short adjournment may be necessary to enable the line manager or the police officer, as the case may be, to read or consider the document or other material and consider its implications. The length of the adjournment will depend upon the case.

Wherever possible, the meeting date and time should be agreed between the line manager and the police officer. However, where agreement cannot be reached the line manager must specify a time and date. If the police officer or his/her police friend is not available at the date or time specified by the line manager, the police officer may propose an alternative time. Provided that the alternative time is reasonable and falls within a period of five working days beginning with the first working day after that specified by the line manager, the meeting must be postponed to that time. Once the date for the meeting is fixed, the line manager should send to the police officer a notice in writing of the date, time and place of the first stage meeting.

4.18.9.1 First Stage Meeting

The meeting can take place in the absence of the officer, where they fail to attend. At the first stage meeting the line manager will:

- explain to the police officer the reasons why the line manager considers that the performance or attendance of the police officer is unsatisfactory;
- provide the police officer with the opportunity to make representations in response;
- provide his/her police friend (if he/she has one) with an opportunity to make representations;
- listen to what the police officer (and/or his/her police friend) has to say, ask questions and comment as appropriate.

Where the line manager finds that the performance or attendance of the police officer has been satisfactory during the period in question, he/she will inform the police officer that no further action will be taken. Where having considered any representations by either the police officer and/or his/her police friend, the line manager finds that the performance or attendance of the police officer has been unsatisfactory he/she shall:

- inform the police officer in what respects his/her performance or attendance is considered unsatisfactory;
- inform him/her of the improvement that is required in his/her performance or attendance;
- inform the police officer that, if a sufficient improvement is not made within the period specified by the line manager, he/she may be required to attend a second stage meeting;
- inform the police officer that he/she will receive a written improvement notice;
- inform the police officer that if the sufficient improvement in his/her performance or attendance is not maintained during the validity period of such notice he/she may be required to attend a second stage meeting.

4.18.9.2 Procedure Following the First Stage Meeting

As soon as reasonably practicable, following the meeting, the line manager shall cause to be prepared a written record of the meeting and, where he/she found at the meeting that the performance or attendance of the police officer was unsatisfactory, a written *improvement notice*. The written record and any improvement notice shall be sent to the officer as soon as reasonably practicable after they have been prepared, whether or not the officer attended the meeting.

KEYNOTE

Improvement notices require a police officer to improve his/her performance or attendance and must state:

- in what respect the police officer's performance or attendance is considered unsatisfactory;
- the improvement in performance or attendance required to bring the police officer to an acceptable standard;
- a 'specified period' within which improvement is expected to be made; and
- the 'validity period' of the written improvement notice.

Specified Period

The 'specified period' of an improvement notice is a period specified by the manager conducting the meeting (having considered any representations made by or on behalf of the police officer) within which the police officer must improve his/her performance or attendance. It is expected that the specified period for improvement would not normally exceed *three months*. On the application of the police officer or otherwise (e.g. on the application of his/her line manager), the appropriate authority may extend the specified period; if it considers it appropriate to do so. In setting an extension to the specified period, consideration should be given to any known periods of extended absence from the police officer's normal role, e.g. if the police officer is going to be on long periods of pre-planned holiday leave, study leave, or is due to undergo an operation. The extension should not lead to the improvement period exceeding *12 months* unless the appropriate authority is satisfied that there are exceptional circumstances making this appropriate.

Validity Period

The 'validity period' of an improvement notice describes the period of 12 months from the date of the notice within which performance or attendance must be maintained (assuming improvement is made during the specified period). If the improvement is not maintained within this period the next stage of the procedures may be used. The period for improvement under an improvement notice and the validity period of an improvement notice do not include any time that the police officer is taking as a career break.

The written record supplied to the police officer should comprise a summary of the proceedings at that meeting. Any improvement notice must be accompanied by a notice informing the police officer of his/her right to appeal and the name of the person to whom the appeal should be sent. The notice must also inform the police officer of his/her right to submit written comments on the written record of the meeting and of the procedure for doing so.

The police officer may submit written comments on the written record not later than the end of seven working days after the date that he/she received it (unless an extension has been granted by his/her line manager). However, if the police officer has exercised his/her right to appeal against the finding or outcome of the first stage meeting, the police officer may not submit comments on the written record. It is the responsibility of the line manager to ensure that the written record, written improvement notice and any written comments of the police officer regarding the written record are retained together and filed in accordance with force policies.

KEYNOTE

Action Plan

An improvement notice would normally be followed by an action plan which should:

- identify any weaknesses which may be the cause of unsatisfactory performance or attendance;
- describe what steps the police officer must take to improve performance and/or attendance and what support is available from the organisation, e.g. training;
- specify a period within which actions identified should be followed up; and
- set a date for a staged review of the police officer's performance or attendance.

The action plan will set out the actions which should assist the police officer to perform his/her duties to an acceptable standard. This may be agreed at the UPP meeting or at a later time specified by the line manager. It is expected that the police officer will cooperate with implementation of the action plan and take responsibility for his/her own development or improvement. Equally, the police officer's managers must ensure that any actions to support the police officer to improve are implemented.

4.18.9.3 Assessment of Performance or Attendance

It is expected that the police officer's performance or attendance will be actively monitored against the improvement notice and, where applicable, the action plan by the line manager throughout the specified period of the improvement notice. The line manager should discuss with the police officer any concerns that the line manager has during this period as regards his/her performance or attendance and offer advice and guidance where appropriate.

As soon as possible after the improvement notice period comes to an end, the line manager must formally assess the performance or attendance of the police officer during that period. If the line manager considers that the police officer's performance or attendance is satisfactory, the line manager should notify the police officer in writing of this. The notification should also inform the police officer that while the performance or attendance of the police officer is now satisfactory, the improvement notice is valid for a period of 12 months from the date printed on the notice so that it is possible for the second stage of the procedures to be initiated if the performance or attendance of the police officer falls below an acceptable level within the remaining period.

If the line manager considers that the police officer's performance or attendance is still unsatisfactory, the line manager should notify the police officer in writing of this. The line manager must also notify the police officer that he/she is required to attend a second stage meeting to consider these ongoing performance or attendance issues.

If the police officer has improved his/her performance or attendance to an acceptable standard within the specified improvement period, but then fails to maintain that standard within the 12-month validity period, it is open to the line manager to initiate stage two of the procedures. In such circumstances the line manager must notify the police officer in writing of his/her view that the police officer's performance or attendance is unsatisfactory as the police officer has failed to maintain the improvement and that as a consequence the police officer is required to attend a second stage meeting to discuss his/her failure to maintain a satisfactory standard of performance or attendance.

4.18.9.4 First Stage Appeals

A police officer has a right of appeal. However, any outcome of this first stage meeting will continue to apply up to the date that the appeal is determined. Therefore, where the police officer contests the finding or outcome, he/she should continue to follow the terms of the improvement notice and any accompanying action plan pending the determination of the appeal. The notice of appeal must clearly set out the grounds and evidence for the appeal.

The grounds for appeal are:

- the finding of unsatisfactory performance or attendance is unreasonable;
- any of the terms of the improvement notice are unreasonable;
- there is evidence that could not reasonably have been considered at the first stage meeting which could have materially affected the finding of unsatisfactory performance or attendance or any of the terms of the written improvement notice;
- there was a breach of the procedures set out in the UPPs or other unfairness which could have materially affected the finding of unsatisfactory performance or attendance or the terms of the improvement notice.

On the basis of the above grounds of appeal, the police officer may appeal against the finding of unsatisfactory performance or attendance or the terms of the written improvement notice, those being:

- the respect in which the police officer's performance or attendance is considered unsatisfactory;
- the improvement which is required of the police officer; and/or
- the length of the period specified for improvement by the line manager at the first stage meeting.

KEYNOTE

At the first stage appeal meeting the second line manager will provide the police officer with the opportunity to make representations and provide his/her police friend (if he/she has one) with an opportunity to make representations. Having considered any representations by either the police officer and/or his/her police friend, the second line manager may confirm or reverse the finding of unsatisfactory performance or attendance or endorse or vary the terms of the improvement notice appealed against.

The second line manager may deal with the police officer in any manner in which the line manager could have dealt with him/her at the first stage meeting. Where the second line manager has reversed the finding of unsatisfactory performance or attendance he/she must also revoke the written improvement notice.

Within three working days of the day following the conclusion of the appeal meeting, the police officer will be given written notice of the second line manager's decision. If the second line manager is in a position to send a written summary of the reasons for that decision, this may also accompany the written notice of the decision. Any decision made that changes the finding or outcome of the first stage meeting will take effect by way of substitution for the finding or terms appealed against and as from the date of the first stage meeting.

4.18.10 The Second Stage

Initiation of the second stage *must* be for matters similar to or connected with the unsatisfactory performance or attendance referred to in the improvement notice issued at the first stage. Where, at the end of the period specified in an improvement notice, the line manager finds that the police officer's performance or attendance has not improved to an acceptable standard during that period or that the police officer has not maintained an acceptable level of performance or attendance during the validity period of the notice, the second line manager will notify the police officer in writing that he/she is required to attend a second stage meeting. The notification will state:

- the details of the procedures for determining the date and time of the meeting;
- a summary of the reasons why the line manager considers the police officer's performance or attendance unsatisfactory;
- the possible outcomes of a second stage and third stage meeting;
- that the line manager may attend the meeting;
- that a human resources professional or a police officer (who should have experience of UPPs and be independent from the line management chain) may attend the meeting to advise the second line manager on the proceedings;
- that if the police officer agrees, any other person specified in the notice may attend the meeting;
- that prior to the meeting the police officer must provide the second line manager with any documentation he/she intends to rely on in the meeting; and
- the police officer's rights, i.e. his/her right to seek advice from a representative of his/her staff association (in the case of a member of the police force) and to be accompanied and represented at the meeting by a police friend.

KEYNOTE

The notice must also include copies of related documentation relied upon by the line manager in support of the view that the police officer's performance or attendance continues to be unsatisfactory.

In advance of the meeting, the police officer shall provide the second line manager with any documents on which he/she intends to rely on in support of his/her case. Any document or other material that was not submitted in advance of the meeting may be considered at the meeting at the discretion of the second line manager, ensuring fairness to all parties. However, the presumption should be that such documents or other material will not be permitted unless it can be shown that they were not previously available to be submitted in advance.

The second line manager should explain that there is potentially a further stage to the procedures and that the maximum outcome of stage two is a final improvement notice. The second line manager will also explain that if the procedure is followed to the final stage, possible outcomes include dismissal, a reduction in rank (in the case of a member of a police force and in performance cases only), redeployment to alternative duties or an extended improvement notice (in exceptional circumstances).

4.18.10.1 Second Stage Meeting

At the second stage meeting the second line manager will:

- explain to the police officer the reasons why he/she has been required to attend a second stage meeting;
- provide the police officer with the opportunity to make representations in response;
- provide the police officer's police friend (if he/she has one) with an opportunity to make representations;
- listen to what the police officer (and/or his/her police friend) has to say, ask questions and comment as appropriate.

The second line manager may adjourn the meeting at any time if he/she considers it is necessary or expedient to do so. Where, having considered any representations by either the police officer and/or his/her police friend, the second line manager finds that the performance or attendance of the police officer has been unsatisfactory (either during the period specified in the written improvement notice or during the validity period of the written improvement notice) he/she shall:

- inform the police officer in what respect(s) his/her performance or attendance is considered unsatisfactory;
- inform the police officer of the improvement that is required in his/her performance or attendance;
- inform the police officer that, if a sufficient improvement is not made within the period specified by the second line manager, he/she may be required to attend a third stage meeting;
- inform the police officer that he/she will receive a final written improvement notice; and
- inform the police officer that if the sufficient improvement in his/her performance or attendance is not maintained during the validity period of such notice, he/she may be required to attend a third stage meeting.

A performance matter can be referred to a second stage meeting without a first stage meeting where, following a formal conduct investigation and a decision that there is no case to answer, the appropriate authority:

(a) considers that there are reasonable grounds based on the evidence from the investigation, to conclude that the officer concerned has demonstrated a serious inability or serious failure to perform the duties of their rank or role, where they are otherwise undertaking it to a satisfactory standard;

(b) has consulted the officer, their line manager or second line manager, and is satisfied that the officer has been given a reasonable opportunity to address their inability or failure to perform but has failed to make a sufficient improvement.

A performance matter can also be referred to such a second stage meeting where the IOPC makes a recommendation to this effect, following the investigation of a complaint or recordable conduct matter.

4.18.10.2 Procedure Following the Second Stage Meeting

A written record of the meeting and any improvement notice shall be sent to the officer as soon as reasonably practicable after they have been prepared.

Any improvement notice must be accompanied by a notice informing the police officer of his/her right to appeal and the name of the person to whom the appeal should be sent. The notice must also inform the police officer of his/her right to submit written comments on the written record of the meeting and of the procedure for doing so.

The police officer may submit written comments on the written record not later than the end of seven working days after the date that he/she received it (unless an extension has been granted by the second line manager following an application by the police officer).

4.18.10.3 Second Stage Appeals

A police officer has a right of appeal against the finding and the terms of the improvement notice imposed at stage two of the UPPs and against the decision to require him/her to attend the meeting. However, any finding and outcome of this second stage meeting will continue to apply up to the date that the appeal is determined. Therefore, where the police officer contests the finding or outcome, he/she should continue to follow the terms of the improvement notice and any accompanying action plan pending the determination of the appeal. Any appeal should be made in writing to the senior manager within seven working days following the day of the receipt of the improvement notice. The notice of appeal must clearly set out the grounds and evidence for the appeal. The grounds for appeal are as follows:

- the finding of unsatisfactory performance or attendance is unreasonable;
- any of the terms of the improvement notice are unreasonable;
- there is evidence that could not reasonably have been considered at the second stage meeting which could have materially affected the finding of unsatisfactory performance or attendance or any of the terms of the improvement notice;
- there was a breach of the procedures set out in the Police (Performance) Regulations or other unfairness which could have materially affected the finding of unsatisfactory performance or attendance or the terms of the written improvement notice;
- the police officer should not have been required to attend the second stage meeting as the meeting did not concern unsatisfactory performance or attendance which was similar to or connected with the unsatisfactory performance or attendance referred to in the written improvement notice that followed the first stage meeting.

On the basis of the above grounds of appeal, the police officer may appeal against the finding of unsatisfactory performance or attendance, the decision to require him/her to attend the second stage meeting or the terms of the written improvement notice, those being:

- the respect in which the police officer's performance or attendance is considered unsatisfactory;
- the improvement which is required of the police officer;
- the length of the period specified for improvement by the second line manager at the second stage meeting.

KEYNOTE

The police officer has the right to be accompanied and represented by a police friend at the second stage appeal meeting.

Once a date for the meeting is fixed, the senior manager should send to the police officer a notice in writing of the date, time and place of the second stage appeal meeting together with the information required to be provided under reg. 24 of the Performance Regulations.

At the second stage appeal meeting the senior manager will provide the police officer with the opportunity to make representations and provide his/her police friend (if he/she has one) with an opportunity to make representations. Having considered any representations by either the police officer and/or his/her police friend, the senior manager may make a finding that the officer should not have been required to attend the second stage meeting, and reverse the finding made at that meeting, confirm or reverse the finding of unsatisfactory performance or attendance or endorse or vary the terms of the improvement notice.

Any decision made that changes the finding or outcome of the second stage meeting will take effect by way of substitution for the finding or terms appealed against and as from the date of the second stage meeting.

4.18.11   The Third Stage

Where, at the end of the period specified in the final written improvement notice, the line manager finds that the police officer's performance or attendance has not improved to an acceptable standard during that period or that the police officer has not maintained an acceptable level of performance or attendance during the validity period of the notice, the line manager must notify the police officer in writing that he/she is required to attend a third stage meeting to discuss these issues. As soon as reasonably practicable thereafter, the senior manager must give a notice to the officer informing him/her:

- that the meeting will be with a panel appointed by the appropriate authority;
- the procedures for determining the date and time of the meeting;
- a summary of the reasons why the police officer's performance or attendance is considered unsatisfactory;
- the possible outcomes of a third stage meeting;
- if the outcome is dismissal, the officer's name and a description of the conduct which led to their dismissal will be added to the barred list;
- that a human resources professional or a police officer (who should have experience of UPPs and be independent from the line management chain) may attend to advise the panel on the proceedings;
- that counsel or a solicitor may attend the meeting to advise the panel on the proceedings and on any question of law that may arise at the meeting;
- where the police officer is a special constable, inform him/her that a member of the special constabulary will attend the meeting to advise the panel;
- that if the police officer agrees, any other person specified in the notice may attend, e.g. a person attending for development reasons; and
- the police officer's rights, i.e. his/her right to seek advice from a representative of his/her staff association (in the case of a member of the police force) and to be accompanied and represented at the meeting by a police friend.

The notice must also include copies of related documentation relied upon by the line manager in support of the view that the police officer's performance or attendance continues to be unsatisfactory. It is important to note that a third stage meeting may not take place unless the officer has been notified of his/her right to representation by a police friend. The notice does not at this stage need to give the names of the panel members as these may not be known at the time of issue. However, as soon as the panel has been appointed by the appropriate authority, the appropriate authority should notify the police officer of the members' names.

The purpose of the meeting is for the panel to hear the evidence of the unsatisfactory performance or attendance and to give the police officer the opportunity to put forward his/her views. It will also be an opportunity to hear of any factors that are continuing to affect the police officer's performance or attendance and what the police officer considers can be done to address them.

Where the police officer has reached stage three following stages one and two (i.e. not a gross incompetence meeting), the possible outcomes of this stage three meeting are as follows:

- redeployment;
- reduction in rank (in the case of a member of a police force and for performance cases only);
- dismissal (with a minimum of 28 days' notice); or
- extension of a final improvement notice (in exceptional circumstances).

Where the panel grants an extension to the final improvement notice, it will specify a new period within which improvement to performance or attendance must be made. The 12-month validity period of the extended final improvement notice will apply in full from the date of extension. The panel may also vary any of the terms in the notice.

4.18.11.1 Stage Three Gross Incompetence Meetings

There may be circumstances where the appropriate authority considers the performance (not attendance) of the police officer to be so unsatisfactory as to warrant the procedures being initiated at the third stage. This would be as a result of a single incident of 'gross incompetence'. It is not envisaged that an appropriate authority would initiate the procedures at the third stage in respect of a series of acts over a period of time.

KEYNOTE

'Gross incompetence' is defined in the Police (Performance) Regulations 2020 as 'a serious inability or serious failure of a police officer to perform the duties of the officer's rank or the role the officer is currently undertaking to a satisfactory standard or level, without taking into account the officer's attendance, to the extent that dismissal would be justified and "grossly incompetent" is to be construed accordingly'.

Where the appropriate authority determines it is appropriate to initiate the procedures at this stage, then the police officer must be informed in writing that he/she is required to attend a third stage meeting to discuss his/her performance. Where the appropriate authority has informed the police officer that he/she is to attend a third stage only meeting, it must, as soon as reasonably practicable, send the police officer a notice in writing which will include the following details:

- that the meeting will be with a panel appointed by the appropriate authority;
- the procedure for determining the date and time of the meeting;
- a summary of the reasons why the police officer's performance is considered to constitute gross incompetence;
- the possible outcomes of a third stage only meeting;
- if the outcome is dismissal, the officer's name and a description of the conduct which led to their dismissal will be added to the barred list;
- that a human resources professional and a police officer (who should have experience of UPPs and be independent from the line management chain) may attend to advise the panel on the proceedings;
- that counsel or a solicitor may attend the meeting to advise the panel on the proceedings and on any question of law that may arise at the meeting;

- where the police officer is a special constable, inform him/her that a member of the special constabulary will attend the meeting to advise the panel;
- if the police officer agrees, any other person specified in the notice may attend, e.g. a person attending for development reasons; and
- the police officer's rights, i.e. his/her right to seek advice from a representative of his/her staff association (in the case of a member of the police force) and to be accompanied at the meeting by a police friend.

The purpose of the meeting is for the panel to hear the evidence of the gross incompetence and to give the police officer and his/her representative the opportunity to make representations on the matter.

The appropriate authority will explain that the police officer is required to attend the third stage meeting and that the possible outcomes of the stage three meeting are:

- redeployment to alternative duties;
- the issue of a final written improvement notice;
- reduction in rank (with immediate effect);
- dismissal (with immediate effect); or
- the issue of a written improvement notice (if the panel considers that there has been unsatisfactory performance and not gross incompetence).

4.18.11.2 **Panel Membership and Procedure**

The panel will comprise a panel chair and two other members and be appointed by the appropriate authority of the force in which the police officer is a member. At least one of the three panel members must be a police officer and one should be a human resources professional. Membership will be as follows:

- First panel member (chair): Senior police officer (holding a rank above that of chief superintendent) or senior human resources professional.
- Second panel member: Police officer of at least the rank of superintendent or human resources professional who in the opinion of the appropriate authority is at least equivalent to that rank.
- Third panel member: Police officer of at least the rank of superintendent or police staff member who in the opinion of the appropriate authority is at least equivalent to that rank.

KEYNOTE

Panel Membership

None of the panel members should be junior in rank to the police officer concerned. For the purposes of chairing a third stage meeting, the UPPs define a 'senior human resources professional' as 'a human resources professional who, in the opinion of the appropriate authority, has sufficient seniority, skills and experience to be a panel chair'. The panel chair should be senior in rank (or, in the opinion of the appropriate authority, is senior in rank) to the police officer concerned.

The appropriate authority may appoint police officers or police staff managers from another police force to be members of a panel. No panel member should be an interested party, i.e. a person whose appointment could reasonably give rise to a concern as to whether he/she could act impartially under the procedures.

As soon as the appropriate authority has appointed a third stage panel, it should arrange for copies of all relevant documentation to be sent to those members. In particular, any document:

- that was available to the line manager in relation to any first stage meeting;
- that was available to the second line manager in relation to any second stage meeting;
- that was prepared or submitted in advance of the third stage meeting;

- that was prepared or submitted following those meetings, i.e. improvement notices, action plans and meeting notes;
- relating to any appeal.

As soon as the appropriate authority has appointed a third stage panel, it must send the police officer written confirmation of the names of panel members. The police officer has the right to object to any panel members appointed by the appropriate authority and any such objection must be made in writing to the appropriate authority no later than three working days after receipt of the notification of the names of the panel members. The police officer must include the ground of his/her objection to any panel member in that submission. The appropriate authority must inform the police officer in writing whether it upholds or rejects an objection to a panel member. If the appropriate authority upholds the objection, a new panel member will be appointed as a replacement. As soon as practicable after any such appointment, the police officer will be informed in writing of the name of the new panel member. The appropriate authority must ensure that the requirements for the composition of the panel are met. The police officer may object to the newly appointed panel member in the same way whereupon the appropriate authority must follow the same procedure again.

4.18.11.3   Special Constables and Third Stage Meetings

In cases where the police officer is a special constable, as indicated above (**see para. 4.18.11**), the force will appoint a member of the special constabulary to attend the meeting to advise the panel (this is for the purpose of fairness). The special constable advising the panel must have sufficient seniority and experience of the special constabulary to be able to advise the panel. The special constable advising the panel can be a police officer serving in a different force. The special constable adviser will not form part of the panel and will not have a role in determining whether or not the police officer's performance or attendance is unsatisfactory. In arranging a third stage meeting involving special constables, due consideration should be given to the fact that special constables are unpaid volunteers and may therefore have full-time employment or other personal commitments.

4.18.11.4   Third Stage Meeting Dates and Timeframes

Any third stage meeting should take place no later than 30 working days after the date that the notification has been sent to the police officer. Within that timeframe, wherever possible, the meeting date and time should be agreed between the panel chair and the police officer. However, where agreement cannot be reached the panel chair must specify a time and date. If the police officer or his/her police friend is not available at the date or time specified by the panel chair, the police officer may propose an alternative time. Provided that the alternative time is reasonable and falls within a period of five working days beginning with the first working day after that specified by the panel chair, the meeting must be postponed to that time. If the panel chair considers it to be in the interests of fairness to do so, he/she may extend the 30-working-day period within which the meeting should take place and the reasons for any such extension must be notified in writing to both the appropriate authority and the police officer. As soon as a date for the meeting is fixed, the panel chair should send to the police officer a notice in writing of the date, time and place of the third stage meeting.

4.18.11.5   Procedure on Receipt of Notice of Third Stage Meeting

Within 14 working days of the date on which a notice has been sent to the police officer (unless this period is extended by the panel chair for exceptional circumstances), the police officer must provide to the appropriate authority:

- a written notice of whether or not he/she accepts that his/her performance or attendance has been unsatisfactory or that he/she has been grossly incompetent, as the case may be;

- where he/she accepts that his/her performance or attendance has been unsatisfactory or that he/she has been grossly incompetent, any written submission he/she wishes to make in mitigation.

Where the police officer does not accept that his/her performance or attendance has been unsatisfactory or that he/she has been grossly incompetent or where he/she disputes part of the matters referred to in the notice that he/she has received, he/she shall provide the appropriate authority with a written notice of:

- the matters he/she disputes and his/her account of the relevant events; and
- any arguments on points of law he/she wishes to be considered by the panel.

The police officer shall provide the appropriate authority and the panel with a copy of any document he/she intends to rely on at the third stage meeting.

Before the end of three working days following the officer's compliance the senior manager and the officer shall each supply a list of proposed witnesses or give notice that they do not have any witnesses. Where witnesses are proposed, this must be accompanied by brief details of their evidence and their address. The officer should try to agree a list of witnesses with the senior manager. Where agreement has not been reached, the officer shall send to the appropriate authority his/her list of witnesses. As soon as reasonably practicable after any list of witnesses has been agreed or, in the case where no agreement could be reached, supplied to the appropriate authority, the appropriate authority must send the lists to the panel chair together with, in the latter case, a list of its proposed witnesses. The panel chair will consider the list of proposed witnesses and will determine which, if any, witnesses should attend the third stage meeting.

The panel chair can determine that persons not named in the list should attend as witnesses. No witnesses will give evidence at a third stage meeting unless the panel chair reasonably believes that it is necessary in the interests of fairness for the witness to do so, in which case he/she will:

- in the case of a police officer, cause him/her to be ordered to attend the third stage meeting;
- in any other case, cause him/her to be given notice that his/her attendance at the third stage meeting is necessary.

Such notices will include the date, time and place of the meeting.

Where a witness attends to give evidence then any questions to that witness should be made through the panel chair. This would not prevent the panel chair allowing questions to be asked directly if he/she feels that this is appropriate.

The documents or other material to be relied upon at the meeting are required to be submitted in advance. Any document or other material that was not submitted in advance of the meeting may be considered at the meeting at the discretion of the panel chair. However, the presumption should be that such documents or other material will not be permitted unless it can be shown that they were not previously available to be submitted in advance or that they relate to mitigation following a finding of unsatisfactory performance or attendance that was contested by the police officer.

4.18.11.6 At the Third Stage Meeting

At the third stage meeting the panel chair will conduct the meeting and will explain to the police officer the reasons why he/she has been required to attend a third stage meeting and provide the police officer with the opportunity to make representations in response. Where the case is one of gross incompetence and the police officer has opted for legal representation, the chair will provide the police officer's legal representative with the opportunity to make representations. If the officer has chosen not to be legally represented, they will provide the police officer's police friend (if they have one) with an opportunity to make representations. The panel chair has a duty to listen to what the police officer and/or police friend has to say and to ask questions as appropriate.

Having considered any representations by either the police officer and/or his/her police friend or (where applicable) the police officer's legal representative, the panel will come to a finding as to whether or not the performance or attendance of the police officer has been unsatisfactory or whether or not his/her behaviour constitutes gross incompetence, as the case may be. If there is a difference of view between the three panel members, the finding or decision will be based on a simple majority vote, but it will not be indicated whether it was taken unanimously or by a majority.

The panel must prepare (or cause to be prepared) its decision in writing which shall also state the finding. Where the panel has found that the police officer's performance or attendance has been unsatisfactory or that he/she has been grossly incompetent, the decision must also state the panel's reasons and any outcome which it orders.

As soon as reasonably practicable after the conclusion of the meeting, the panel chair shall send a copy of the decision to the police officer and the line manager. However, the police officer must be given written notice of the finding of the panel within three working days of the conclusion of the meeting. Where the panel has made a finding of unsatisfactory performance or attendance or gross incompetence the copy of the decision sent to the police officer must also be accompanied by a notice informing him/her of the circumstances in which and the timeframe within which he/she may appeal to a Police Appeals Tribunal. A verbatim record of the meeting should be taken. The police officer must, on request, be supplied with a copy of the record.

4.18.11.7 Postponement and Adjournment of a Third Stage Meeting

If the panel chair considers it necessary or expedient, he/she may direct that the third stage meeting should take place at a different time from that originally notified to the police officer. The panel chair's alternative time may fall after the period of 30 working days. In the event that the panel chair postpones a third stage meeting he/she should notify the following relevant parties in writing of his/her reasons and the revised time and place for the meeting:

- the police officer;
- other panel members; and
- the appropriate authority.

KEYNOTE

Video Link

If the police officer informs the panel chair in advance that he/she is unable to attend the third stage meeting on grounds which the panel chair considers reasonable, the panel chair may allow the police officer to participate in the meeting by video link or other means. In cases where the police officer is absent (e.g. through illness or injury) a short delay may be reasonable to allow him/her to attend. If this is not possible or any delay is considered not appropriate in the circumstances then the persons conducting the meeting/hearing may allow the police officer to participate by telephone or video link. In these circumstances a police friend will always be permitted to attend the meeting/hearing to represent the police officer in the normal way (and, in the case of a gross incompetence meeting, the police officer's legal representative where appointed).

4.18.11.8 Assessment of Final and Extended Final Improvement Notices Issued at the Third Stage

Where the police officer has been issued with a final improvement notice or, in exceptional cases, the panel has extended a final improvement notice period, it is expected that the police officer's performance or attendance will be actively monitored by the line manager throughout the specified period of the final/extended final improvement notice. The line manager should discuss with the police officer any concerns that the line manager has during this period as regards his/her performance or attendance and offer advice and guidance where appropriate.

As soon as reasonably practicable after the specified period of the final/extended final improvement notice comes to an end, the panel will assess the performance or attendance of the police officer during that period. The panel chair must then inform the police officer in writing of the panel's conclusion following assessment, i.e. whether there has been sufficient improvement in his/her performance or attendance during the specified period. If the panel considers that there has been insufficient improvement the panel chair shall also notify the officer that he/she is required to attend another third stage meeting.

If, at the end of the validity period of the final/extended final improvement notice, the panel considers that sufficient improvement to the police officer's performance or attendance has not been made or maintained during this period, the panel chair will inform the police officer of the panel's assessment. Any such notification to the police officer must also include notification that he/she is required to attend a further third stage meeting. Where an officer is required to attend a further third stage meeting, the UPPs shall apply as if he/she were required to attend that meeting for the first time and following a second stage meeting.

As with the initiation of stages one and two for unsatisfactory performance or attendance, a further third stage meeting must relate to matters similar to or connected with the unsatisfactory performance or attendance or gross incompetence referred to in the final improvement notice extended or issued by the panel. The panel should (where possible) be composed of the same persons who conducted the previous third stage meeting. However, there may be cases where reconstitution of the panel is either inappropriate or not possible. In such circumstances the appropriate authority may substitute members as it sees fit subject to the requirements in **para. 4.18.11.2**. As soon as reasonably practicable after the appointment of any new panel members, the police officer should be notified in writing of the changes in panel membership. The police officer will have the opportunity to object to any new panel members.

A police officer may only be given an extension to a final improvement notice on one occasion. Therefore where the police officer is required to attend a reconvened third stage meeting and the panel finds that the police officer's performance or attendance continues to be unsatisfactory, the only outcomes available to the panel are redeployment, reduction in rank (only for a member of a police force and in performance cases) or dismissal (with notice).

In cases where a police officer was issued with an improvement notice (as opposed to a final improvement notice) for unsatisfactory performance at a gross incompetence third stage meeting, that written improvement notice will be equivalent to a written improvement notice issued at a first stage meeting. In that case the procedure for assessing the performance of the police officer will be the same as that following the first stage.

4.18.11.9 Third Stage Appeals

Following a third stage meeting, a police officer may be able to appeal to a Police Appeals Tribunal. However, any finding and outcome of the third stage meeting will continue to apply up to the date that the appeal is determined.

4.18.12 Attendance at Each Stage of the Procedures and Ill-health

Attendance at any stage meeting is not subject to the same considerations as reporting for duty and the provisions of reg. 33 (sick leave) of the Police Regulations 2003 *do not apply*.

An illness or disability may render a police officer unfit for duty without affecting his/her ability to attend a meeting. However, if the police officer is incapacitated, the meeting may be deferred until he/she is sufficiently improved to attend. A meeting will not be deferred indefinitely because the police officer is unable to attend, although every effort should be made to make it possible for the police officer to attend if he/she wishes to be present. For example:

- the acute phase of a serious physical illness is usually fairly short-lived, and the meeting may be deferred until the police officer is well enough to attend;
- if the police officer suffers from a physical injury (for instance a broken leg) it may be possible to hold the meeting at a location convenient to him/her.

Where such circumstances apply at a stage three meeting, the force may wish to consider the use of video, telephone or other conferencing technology. Where, despite such efforts having been made and/or the meeting having been deferred, the police officer either persists in failing to attend the meeting or maintains his/her inability to attend, the person conducting the meeting will need to decide whether to continue to defer the meeting or whether to proceed with it, if necessary in the absence of the police officer. The person conducting the meeting must judge the most appropriate course of action. Nothing in this paragraph should be taken to suggest that, where a police officer's medical condition is found to be such that he/she would normally be retired on medical grounds, the UPPs should prevent or delay retirement.

4.18.13 The Use of Records under UPPs

Records of any part of the UPPs should not be taken into account after an improvement notice has ceased to be valid. Equally, where a police officer appeals and that appeal is successful, the record of that procedure should not be taken into consideration in any future proceedings or for any other purpose.

4.18.14 Misconduct, Performance and Attendance Issues for Seconded Officers

The procedures set out in the UPPs cannot be applied by the organisation to which the police officer is seconded under s. 97 of the Police Act 1996. However, the procedures set out in the Regulations can be applied by the parent force in respect of conduct, performance or attendance while on secondment. Those responsible for managing police officers on secondment are expected to manage any issue of unsatisfactory performance or attendance or minor misconduct in a proportionate, fair and timely manner without returning an officer to his/her parent force. Only if it is necessary to institute the formal procedures should an officer be returned to force, in accordance with the principles and procedures expressed below.

Where an officer is on secondment under the Police (Overseas Service) Act 1945, with the Police Ombudsman for Northern Ireland or with the Police Service of Northern Ireland, then he/she can be dealt with by the receiving organisation under its disciplinary arrangements. However, on return to his/her force, he/she can still be dealt with under the disciplinary arrangements in respect of the same matters.

It is important that police officers on secondment are clear about who has line management responsibility for them. The line managers for such police officers must ensure that the police officer continues to have a PDR and is made aware of these arrangements for dealing with issues of misconduct or unsatisfactory performance or attendance.

Where there is no or insufficient improvement in the performance or attendance of the police officer, the seconded police officer's line manager should prepare a written report which details the nature of the unsatisfactory performance or attendance together with the remedial and other measures taken, and send this report to the head of the organisation to which the police officer is seconded (or his/her nominated representative). The head of the organisation (or nominated representative), in conjunction with the appropriate authority for the police officer concerned, will decide whether it is appropriate that the police officer concerned should be returned to his/her parent force or whether the unsatisfactory performance or attendance can be addressed with the police officer remaining on secondment. Where a police officer who has been returned to his/her parent force under this procedure continues to demonstrate the same pattern of unsatisfactory performance or attendance, the details of the unsatisfactory performance or attendance while on secondment may be used to inform the decision whether it is appropriate to use the UPPs.

In alleged cases of misconduct by a secondee, the organisation to which the police officer has been seconded will need to make an initial assessment of the allegation of misconduct. If that assessment determines that the matter can be dealt with by management action, the seconded officer's manager is expected to deal with the matter in this way. As part of this decision making process, it may be necessary for the line manager to contact the appropriate authority for the seconded officer to assist in determining the nature of the conduct and whether it should be investigated. In this regard, the appropriate authority will need to consider its obligations under the Police Reform Act 2002 and any requirement to refer a matter to the Independent Office for Police Conduct (IOPC).

However, where the line manager considers that an alleged breach of the Standards of Professional Behaviour is more serious and indicates that the police officer concerned may have committed a criminal offence, or behaved in a manner that would justify the bringing of disciplinary proceedings, the head of the organisation to which the police officer is seconded (or his/her nominated representative) will liaise with the appropriate authority from which the police officer concerned is seconded to assess whether the officer should be returned to the force while a preliminary assessment into the matter is conducted by the parent force. If, as a result of that preliminary assessment, the parent force or the IOPC considers it appropriate to issue a notice according to reg. 17 of the Police (Conduct) Regulations 2020 or Police (Complaints and Misconduct) Regulations 2020 in relation to the matter, the officer must be returned to force.

Where it is determined by the appropriate authority for the seconded officer and the organisation to which he/she is seconded, that the conduct, if proved or admitted, would not justify the bringing of disciplinary proceedings, management action may still be taken where appropriate. At the conclusion of any disciplinary proceedings, where the police officer has been returned to the parent force, that force together with the organisation to which the police officer concerned was seconded will decide if it is appropriate for the police officer to be able to resume his/her secondment.

4.18.15 Vicarious Liability of Chief Officers

Section 88 of the Police Act 1996 originally provided that a chief officer will be vicariously liable for the 'torts' (civil wrongs) of his/her officers committed in the performance (or purported performance) of their duties. This meant that the chief officer was responsible for the payment of any damages arising out of a civil claim in respect of such a tort. The extent of this vicarious liability was wider than that imposed on employers generally (*Weir* v *Chief Constable of Merseyside Police* [2003] EWCA Civ 111).

However, despite the fact that the vicarious liability of chief officers was broader than that of any ordinary employer, its limitation to strictly actionable civil wrongs was felt to have led to some inequities, denying remedies to individuals while failing to impose full accountability on the relevant chief officers. The Police Reform Act 2002 clarified the position and amended s. 88 to provide that chief officers will be liable for the 'unlawful conduct' (as opposed to purely civil wrongs) of their officers and employees when acting as such (s. 102).

4.18.16 Other Regulations

In addition to the specific provisions for conduct, complaints and efficiency, there are several other sources of regulation that govern the employment and deployment of police officers.

4.18.16.1 Restrictions on Private Lives

The Police Regulations 2003 impose restrictions on the private lives of officers. Regulation 6 provides that the restrictions contained in sch. 1 shall apply to all members of a police force. It also provides that no restrictions other than those designed to secure the proper exercise of the functions of a constable shall be imposed by the chief officer of police on the private lives of members of a police force except such as may temporarily be necessary or such as may be approved by the Secretary of State after consultation with the Police Advisory Board for England and Wales.

Schedule 1

Schedule 1 provides that a member of a police force:

- shall at all times abstain from any activity which is likely to interfere with the impartial discharge of his/her duties or which is likely to give rise to the impression among members of the public that it may so interfere;
- shall in particular:
  - not take any active part in politics;
  - not belong to any organisation specified or described in a determination of the Secretary of State.

For this purpose the Secretary of State has determined that no member of a police force may be a member of the British National Party (BNP), Combat 18 or the National Front.

- shall not reside at premises which are not for the time being approved by the chief officer of police;
- shall not, without the previous consent of the chief officer of police, receive a lodger in a house or quarters with which he/she is provided, or sub-let any part of the house or quarters;
- shall not, unless he/she has previously given written notice to the chief officer of police, receive a lodger in a house in which he/she resides and in respect of which he/she receives an allowance under sch. 3, or sub-let any part of such a house;
- shall not wilfully refuse or neglect to discharge any lawful debt.

4.18.16.2 Business Interests

Some business interests preclude people from applying to be a police constable (reg. 7 of the Police Regulations 2003).

Regulation 8 provides that, if a member of a police force or a relative included in his/her family proposes to have, or has, a 'business interest', the member shall forthwith give written notice of that interest to the chief officer of police unless that business interest was disclosed at the time of the officer's appointment as a member of the force.

On receipt of such a notice, the chief officer shall determine whether or not the interest in question is compatible with the member concerned remaining a member of the force and shall notify the member in writing of his/her decision within 28 days.

If a business interest is felt to be incompatible, the chief officer may dispense with the member's services after giving him/her an opportunity to make representations. Regulation 7(2) provides that a member of a police force or relative has a business interest if:

- the member holds any office or employment for hire or gain or carries on any business;
- the member or a relative of the member has a pecuniary interest in any licence or permit granted in relation to alcohol licensing, refreshment houses or betting and gaming or regulating places of entertainment in the area of the police force in question.

'Relative' means a spouse or civil partner who is not separated from the member, a person living with the member as if they were their spouse or civil partner, or a parent, son, daughter, brother or sister who is included in the member's family.

A police officer must notify his/her chief officer of any changes in a business interest.

4.18.17 Offences

The following criminal offences relate to the general abuse of public office and specific offences relating to police officers or impersonation of officers or officials.

4.18.17.1 Misconduct in a Public Office

OFFENCE: **Misconduct in a Public Office—*Common Law***
  - Triable on indictment • Imprisonment at large

It is a misdemeanour at common law for the holder of a public office to do anything that amounts to a malfeasance or a 'culpable' misfeasance (*R v Wyat* (1705) 1 Salk 380).

Where there is clear evidence of one or more statutory offences, they should usually form the basis of the case, with the 'public office' element being put forward as an aggravating factor for sentencing purposes.

The use of the common law offence should therefore be limited to the following situations:

- where there is no relevant statutory offence, but the behaviour or the circumstances are such that they should nevertheless be treated as criminal;
- where there is a statutory offence but it would be difficult or inappropriate to use it. This might arise because of evidential difficulties in proving the statutory offence in the particular circumstances;
- because the maximum sentence for the statutory offence would be entirely insufficient for the seriousness of the misconduct.

KEYNOTE

This offence has also been described as 'A man accepting an office of trust concerning the public is answerable criminally to the King for misbehaviour in his office ... by whomsoever and in whatever way the officer is appointed' (*R v Bembridge* (1783) 3 Dougl 327).

Such offences can only be tried on indictment and the court has a power of sentence 'at large', that is, there is no limit on the sentence that can be passed. This ancient common law oddity is both a civil wrong (tort) giving rise to an action for damages in the county and High Court, and a criminal offence which is triable on indictment and punishable by an unlimited term of imprisonment.

Given the wide scope of the 'offence' element, it can cover a multitude of transgressions by police officers, from mistreating prisoners to the improper use of criminal intelligence. The conduct can be separated into occasions of *mal*feasance and *mis*feasance. The first requires some degree of wrongful motive or intention on the part of the officer while the second is more likely to apply where there has been some form of wilful neglect of duty: both are difficult to prove.

The essence of both is generally an abuse of public power in bad faith (*Thomas* v *Secretary of State for the Home Office* [2000] Prison LR 188). There must at least be some real connection between the alleged misconduct and the public office, for instance where a man employed by a local council as a maintenance manager dishonestly caused his employees to carry out works on his girlfriend's premises (*R* v *Bowden* [1996] 1 WLR 98). Therefore, simply behaving badly while off duty would not of itself make a public office holder (such as a police officer) guilty of this offence (*Elliott* v *Chief Constable of Wiltshire* (1996) *The Times*, 5 December—disclosure of previous convictions from PNC to a newspaper capable of amounting to misfeasance). It may, however, make the relevant *chief officer* vicariously liable under other heads of law if the off-duty officer was purporting to rely on his/her status as a constable (*Weir* v *Chief Constable of Merseyside* [2003] EWCA Civ 111).

The key elements of the offence so far as it applies to public office holders (such as police officers) were set out by the Court of Appeal in *Attorney-General's Reference (No. 3 of 2003)* [2004] EWCA Crim 868. That case arose out of a death in police custody and the officers were charged with manslaughter by gross negligence, along with the alternative offence of misconduct in a public office. It was argued that misconduct in a public office is a 'conduct' crime, i.e. one where the acts (or omissions) themselves were the real consideration and not the consequences which those acts/omissions brought about (see *Crime*, chapter 1.2). Although reluctant to try to give an exhaustive definition of the offence, the Court of Appeal identified the elements of conduct and state of mind that must be proved in order to convict an officer of misfeasance, holding the main ingredients to be:

- Conduct (or omission) which involved the public office holder *acting as such*. In other words, this would need to arise from the actions (or omissions) of a police officer while acting in his/her capacity as a constable. A purely personal matter arising while the officer was off duty would not normally meet this first criterion.
- Evidence of wilful neglect and/or wilful misconduct. Simple inadvertence or accidental action/omission without more will not be enough.
- The degree of wilful neglect/misconduct must be such as to amount to an abuse of the public's trust in the office holder.
- Proof that the officer acted/omitted to act without any reasonable excuse or justification.

In the civil setting, even though there might be circumstances where officers could be criticised for failures, including incompetence, excess of zeal and even serious negligence, the absence of bad faith or deliberate misuse of power would generally mean that there is not enough to support an allegation of misfeasance (*Ashley* v *Chief Constable of Sussex* [2005] EWHC 415 (QB)).

The ingredients of the civil wrong are fully set out in *Three Rivers District Council* v *Governor and Company of the Bank of England (No. 3)* [2003] 2 AC 1. Their application, especially in the case of police officers, was discussed at length in *Cornelius* v *London Borough of Hackney* [2002] EWCA Civ 1073. In *Three Rivers*, Lord Steyn confirmed that the civil and criminal wrongs bore some resemblance. Although many of the earlier cases involved an element of corruption, this is not a requirement for the offence (*R* v *Dytham* [1979] QB 722). This offence might be committed where a police officer wilfully neglects to prevent a criminal assault (as in *Dytham*), or possibly where a supervisory officer fails to intervene in a situation where one of his/her officers is carrying out an unlawful act.

From the many authorities (especially *Bowden*) it is arguable that this offence could be extended in appropriate circumstances to misconduct of non-sworn employees such as those designated (or perhaps even those accredited) under the Police Reform Act 2002.

The Court of Appeal has held that, where the police wrote to the registered keepers of vehicles believed to have been stolen in another country, informing those keepers that they may not be the legal owners, the person who imported and sold the vehicles *might* be able to bring a claim for misfeasance—much would depend on the state of mind and intentions of the relevant individual in acting as they did (*R Cruickshank Ltd* v *Chief Constable of Kent* [2002] EWCA Civ 1840).

4.18.17.2 Offences Relating to Impersonation

OFFENCE: **Impersonating a Police Officer—*Police Act 1996, s. 90(1)***

> • Triable summarily • Six months' imprisonment

The Police Act 1996, s. 90 states:

> (1) Any person who with intent to deceive impersonates a member of a police force or special constable, or makes any statement or does any act calculated falsely to suggest that he is such a member or constable, shall be guilty of an offence and liable ...

OFFENCE: **Wearing or Possessing Uniform—*Police Act 1996, s. 90(2) and (3)***

> • Triable summarily • Fine *(No specific power of arrest)*

The Police Act 1996, s. 90 states:

> (2) Any person who, not being a constable, wears any article of police uniform in circumstances where it gives him an appearance so nearly resembling that of a member of a police force as to be calculated to deceive shall be guilty of an offence ...
>
> (3) Any person who, not being a member of a police force or special constable, has in his possession any article of police uniform shall, unless he proves that he obtained possession of that article lawfully and has possession of it for a lawful purpose, be guilty of an offence ...

KEYNOTE

'Article of police uniform' means:

- any article of uniform, or
- any distinctive badge or mark, or
- any document of identification

usually issued to members of police forces or special constables (s. 90(4)).

OFFENCE: **Impersonating Designated or Accredited Person—*Police Reform Act 2002, s. 46(3)***

> • Triable summarily • Six months' imprisonment and/or a fine *(No specific power of arrest)*

The Police Reform Act 2002, s. 46 states:

> (3) Any person who, with intent to deceive—
> (a) impersonates a designated person, an accredited person or an accredited inspector,
> (b) makes any statement or does any act calculated falsely to suggest that he is a designated person, that he is an accredited person or that he is an accredited inspector, or
> (c) makes any statement or does any act calculated falsely to suggest that he has powers as a designated or accredited person or as an accredited inspector that exceed the powers he actually has,
>
> is guilty of an offence.

KEYNOTE

These offences are based on the corresponding offences for police officers.

4.18.17.3 Causing Disaffection Among the Police

OFFENCE: **Causing Disaffection—*Police Act 1996, s. 91(1)***

> • Triable either way • Two years' imprisonment on indictment • Six months' imprisonment and/or a fine summarily *(No specific power of arrest)*

The Police Act 1996, s. 91 states:

(1) Any person who causes, or attempts to cause, or does any act calculated to cause, disaffection amongst the members of any police force, or induces or attempts to induce, or does any act calculated to induce, any member of a police force to withhold his services, shall be guilty of an offence ...

4.18.17.4 Corrupt or Other Improper Exercise of Police Powers and Privileges

Section 26 of the Criminal Justice and Courts Act 2015 makes it an offence for a police officer and certain other persons to improperly exercise the powers and privileges of the office of constable. It supplements and expands upon the existing common law offence of misconduct in public office.

The definition of a constable includes a constable of a Home Office police force in England and Wales as well as the British Transport Police, a special constable of a police force or the British Transport Police, and National Crime Agency officers designated with the powers and privileges of a constable.

Subsection (1) provides that a police constable commits an offence if he or she exercises the powers and privileges of a constable improperly and the officer knows or ought to know that it is improper. A person guilty of the offence is liable on conviction on indictment to a sentence of imprisonment for 14 years or a fine, or both.

Subsection (4) provides that a police constable exercises the powers and privileges of a constable improperly if the exercise of a power or privilege is for the purpose of achieving a benefit to the officer, or a benefit or detriment for another person, and that a reasonable person would not expect the power or privilege to be exercised for the purpose of achieving that benefit or detriment. Subsection (9) defines 'benefit' or 'detriment' as meaning any benefit or detriment, whether or not in money and whether or not permanent.

The improper exercise of a power or privilege for the purpose of the offence can refer to cases in which there is a failure to exercise a power or privilege, or there is a threat to exercise a power or privilege or to fail to do so, in each case for the purpose of achieving a benefit or detriment and in any of these cases a reasonable person would not expect the power or privilege to be exercised for the purpose of achieving that benefit or detriment.

This new offence does not affect what constitutes the common law offence of misconduct in public office in England and Wales or Northern Ireland.

4.18.18 Health and Safety

Because police officers are not 'employees' (they are holders of the office of constable), many of the statutory provisions regulating the workplace do not apply directly to them. The health and safety regime created by the Health and Safety at Work etc. Act 1974 applies principally to 'employees' and therefore did not cover police officers (though it clearly covers their non-sworn support colleagues who *are* employees). However, the Police (Health and Safety) Act 1997 made changes to the legislation by treating police officers for certain purposes relating to health and safety as if they were employees. Briefly, these areas include:

• the application of part 1 of the 1974 Act to the police;
• the right of police officers not to be subjected to a detriment in relation to health and safety issues, e.g. not to be punished for raising appropriate health and safety issues or undertaking duties as health and safety representatives (s. 49A of the Employment Rights Act 1996);
• the right of police officers not to be unfairly dismissed in relation to health and safety issues (s. 134A of the Employment Rights Act 1996).

Under the Health and Safety at Work etc. Act 1974, any prosecution of a chief officer of police for an offence under that Act will be brought against the office of chief constable rather than against the individual him/herself. This change to the law (brought in by the Serious Organised Crime and Police Act 2005) brings the position of a chief officer into line with that of police authorities and their liability for breaches of health and safety legislation in respect of police staff (who are their employees). However, a chief officer may also be prosecuted in a personal capacity if it can be shown that he/she personally consented to the commission of an offence or personally connived in its commission or was personally negligent.

Appendix 4.1

PACE Code of Practice for the Exercise by Police Officers of Statutory Powers of Stop and Search; Police Officers and Police Staff of Requirements to Record Public Encounters (Code A), Annexes A–C

A thick grey line down the margin denotes text that is an extract of the PACE Code itself. This material is examinable for both Sergeants and Inspectors.

ANNEX A—SUMMARY OF MAIN STOP AND SEARCH POWERS

THIS TABLE RELATES TO STOP AND SEARCH POWERS ONLY. INDIVIDUAL STATUTES BELOW MAY CONTAIN OTHER POLICE POWERS OF ENTRY, SEARCH AND SEIZURE

Power	Object of Search	Extent of Search	Where Exercisable
Unlawful articles general			
1. Public Stores Act 1875, s. 6.	HM Stores stolen or unlawfully obtained.	Persons, vehicles and vessels.	Anywhere where the constabulary powers are exercisable.
2. Firearms Act 1968, s. 47.	Firearms.	Persons and vehicles.	A public place, or anywhere in the case of reasonable suspicion of offences of carrying firearms with criminal intent or trespassing with firearms.
3. Misuse of Drugs Act 1971, s. 23.	Controlled drugs.	Persons and vehicles.	Anywhere.
4. Customs and Excise Management Act 1979, s. 163.	Goods: (a) on which duty has not been paid; (b) being unlawfully removed, imported or exported; (c) otherwise liable to forfeiture to HM Revenue and Customs.	Vehicles and vessels only.	Anywhere.

Power	Object of Search	Extent of Search	Where Exercisable
5. Aviation Security Act 1982, s. 24B. *Note: This power applies throughout the UK but the provisions of this Code will apply only when the power is exercised at an aerodrome situation in England and Wales.*	Stolen articles or articles made, adapted or intended for use in the course of/in connection with conduct which constitutes an offence in the part of the UK where the aerodrome is situated or would so do, if it occurred there.	Persons, vehicles and aircraft. Anything in or on a vehicle or aircraft.	Any part of an aerodrome.
6. Police and Criminal Evidence Act 1984, s. 1.	Stolen goods.	Persons and vehicles.	Where there is public access.
	Articles made, adapted or intended for use in the course of or in connection with, certain offences under the Theft Act 1968, Fraud Act 2006 and Criminal Damage Act 1971;	Persons and vehicles.	Where there is public access.
	Offensive weapons, Bladed or sharply-pointed articles (except folding pocket knives with a bladed cutting edge not exceeding 3 inches);	Persons and vehicles.	Where there is public access.
	Fireworks: Category 4 (display grade) fireworks if possession prohibited, Adult fireworks in possession of a person under 18 in a public place.	Persons and vehicles.	Where there is public access.
7. Sporting events (Control of Alcohol etc.) Act 1985, s. 7.	Intoxicating liquor.	Persons, coaches and trains.	Designated sports grounds or coaches and trains travelling to or from a designated sporting event.
8. Crossbows Act 1987, s. 4.	Crossbows or parts of crossbows (except crossbows with a draw weight of less than 1.4 kilograms).	Persons and vehicles.	Anywhere except dwellings.
9. Criminal Justice Act 1988 s. 139B.	Offensive weapons, bladed or sharply pointed article.	Persons.	School premises.

Evidence of game and wildlife offences

Power	Object of Search	Extent of Search	Where Exercisable
10. Poaching Prevention Act 1862, s. 2.	Game or poaching equipment.	Persons and vehicles.	A public place.
11. Deer Act 1991, s. 12.	Evidence of offences under the Act.	Persons and vehicles.	Anywhere except dwellings.

Power	Object of Search	Extent of Search	Where Exercisable
12. Conservation of Seals Act 1970, s. 4.	Seals or hunting equipment.	Vehicles only.	Anywhere.
13. Protection of Badgers Act 1992, s. 11.	Evidence of offences under the Act.	Persons and vehicles.	Anywhere.
14. Wildlife and Countryside Act 1981, s. 19.	Evidence of wildlife offences.	Persons and vehicles.	Anywhere except dwellings.
Other			
15. Paragraphs 6 & 8 of Schedule 5 to the Terrorism Prevention and Investigation Measures Act 2011.	Anything that contravenes measures specified in a TPIM notice.	Persons in respect of whom a TPIM notice is being served or is in force.	Anywhere.
16. Paragraph 10 of Schedule 5 to the Terrorism Prevention and Investigation Measures Act 2011.	Anything that could be used to threaten or harm any person.	Persons in respect of whom a TPIM notice is in force.	Anywhere.
17. *Not used*			
18. *Not used*			
19. Section 60 Criminal Justice and Public Order Act 1994.	Offensive weapons or dangerous instruments to prevent incidents of serious violence or to deal with the carrying of such items or find such items which have been used in incidents of serious violence.	Persons and vehicles.	Anywhere within a locality authorised under subsection (1).

ANNEX B—SELF-DEFINED ETHNIC CLASSIFICATION CATEGORIES

White	**W**
A. White–British	W1
B. White–Irish	W2
C. Any other White background	W9
Mixed	**M**
D. White and Black Caribbean	M1
E. White and Black African	M2
F. White and Asian	M3
G. Any other Mixed Background	M9
Asian/Asian–British	**A**
H. Asian–Indian	A1
I. Asian–Pakistani	A2
J. Asian–Bangladeshi	A3
K. Any other Asian background	A9

Black/Black-British	B
L. Black–Caribbean	B1
M. Black African	B2
N. Any other Black background	B9
Other	**O**
O. Chinese	O1
P. Any other	O9
Not Stated	NS

ANNEX C—SUMMARY OF POWERS OF COMMUNITY SUPPORT OFFICERS TO SEARCH AND SEIZE

The following is a summary of the search and seizure powers that may be exercised by a community support officer (CSO) who has been designated with the relevant powers in accordance with Part 4 of the Police Reform Act 2002.

When exercising any of these powers, a CSO must have regard to any relevant provisions of this Code, including section 3 governing the conduct of searches and the steps to be taken prior to a search.

1. *Not used*

2. Powers to search requiring the consent of the person and seizure

A CSO may detain a person using reasonable force where necessary as set out in Part 1 of Schedule 4 to the Police Reform Act 2002. If the person has been lawfully detained, the CSO may search the person provided that person gives consent to such a search in relation to the following:

Designation	Powers conferred	Object of Search	Extent of Search	Where Exercisable
Police Reform Act 2002, Schedule 4, paragraphs 7 and 7A.	(a) Criminal Justice and Police Act 2001, s. 12(2).	(a) Alcohol or a container for alcohol.	(a) Persons.	(a) Designated public place.
	(b) Confiscation of Alcohol (Young Persons) Act 1997, s. 1.	(b) Alcohol.	(b) Persons under 18 years old.	(b) Public place.
	(c) Children and Young Persons Act 1933, s. 7(3).	(c) Tobacco or cigarette papers.	(c) Persons under 16 years old found smoking.	(c) Public place.

3. Powers to search not requiring the consent of the person and seizure

A CSO may detain a person using reasonable force where necessary as set out in Part 1 of Schedule 4 to the Police Reform Act 2002. If the person has been lawfully detained, the CSO may search the person without the need for that person's consent in relation to the following:

Designation	Power conferred	Object of Search	Extent of Search	Where Exercisable
Police Reform Act 2002, Schedule 4, paragraph 2A.	Police and Criminal Evidence Act 1984, s. 32.	(a) Objects that might be used to cause physical injury to the person or the CSO. (b) Items that might be used to assist escape.	Persons made subject to a requirement to wait.	Any place where the requirement to wait has been made.

4. Powers to seize without consent

This power applies when drugs are found in the course of any search mentioned above.

Designation	Power conferred	Object of Search	Where Exercisable
Police Reform Act 2002, Schedule 4, paragraph 7B.	Police Reform Act 2002, Schedule 4, paragraph 7B.	Controlled drugs in a person's possession.	Any place where the person is in possession of the drug.

Index

Terms are indexed to paragraph numbers.

C

P

PACE Codes
  Code A *see* **Statutory Powers of Stop and Search and Requirements to Record Public Encounters by Police Officers and Police Staff (PACE Code A)**
  Code B *see* **Searches of Premises by Police Officers and the Seizure of Property Found by Police Officers on Persons or Premises (PACE Code B)**
  Code G *see* **Statutory Power of Arrest by Police Officers (PACE Code G)**
Parades *see* **Processions and assemblies**
Parenting orders 4.7.8–4.7.8.1
  binding over of parents or guardians 4.7.8.2
  parenting orders 4.7.8.1
Penalty offences 4.6.8, 4.6.9, 4.9.8
Performance and development reviews 4.18.3
Performance, unsatisfactory *see* **Unsatisfactory performance**
Perjury
  aiding and abetting 4.14.2.1
  similar offences 4.14.3
  statutory provisions 4.14.2
Persons lacking capacity *see* **Mentally disordered persons**
Perverting the course of justice
  assisting offenders 4.14.7
  common law offence 4.14.4
  concealing relevant offences 4.14.8
  criminal proceedings 4.14.5.1
  other proceedings 4.14.5.2
  statutory provisions 4.14.5
  escaping from custody 4.14.9
  harming witnesses 4.14.6
  intimidating witnesses or jurors 4.14.5.1
  wasting police time 4.14.10
'Place of safety': definition 4.4.2
Police Advisory List 4.17.1
Police Appeals Tribunal
  attendance of complainants or interested persons 4.17.9.8
  composition and timing of appeals 4.17.9.1
  determination and outcome of appeals 4.17.9.5, 4.17.9.9
  grounds of appeal 4.17.9.2
  legal and other representation 4.17.9.6
  notice of appeal 4.17.9.3
  Police Barred List 4.17.1, 4.17.6.11
  Police body cameras 4.4.6
  procedure 4.17.9.4, 4.17.9.7
  reflective practice review process 4.17.9.10
  right of appeal to 4.17.9
Police community support officers *see* **Community support officers**
Police friends: role in disciplinary proceedings 4.17.3
Police officers
  chief officers *see* **Chief officers**
  community support officers *see* **Community support officers**
  criminal allegations against *see* **Offences by police officers**
  designated persons *see* **Designated persons**
  disciplinary proceedings against *see* **Disciplinary proceedings**
  employment restrictions
    business interests 4.18.16.2
    private lives 4.18.16.1

  employment rights
    health and safety rights 4.18.18
    protection from discrimination *see* **Discrimination**
  employment status 4.16.5, 4.18.18
  escort officers 4.3.12
  impersonation 4.18.17.2
  misconduct *see* **Misconduct**
  'officer in charge of the search': definition 4.2.3, 4.2.3.1
  probationer constables, disciplinary proceedings 4.17.5
  seconded officers, unsatisfactory performance 4.18.14
  special constables, unsatisfactory performance 4.17.2, 4.18.2, 4.18.11.3
  unsatisfactory performance *see* **Unsatisfactory performance**
  wasting police time 4.14.10
Police powers
  anticipatory powers *see* **Anticipatory police powers**
  arrest *see* **Arrest; Statutory Power of Arrest by Police Officers (PACE Code G)**
  communications-based investigations *see* **Communications**
  covert surveillance *see* **Covert surveillance**
  entry, search and seizure *see* **Entry, search and seizure; Searches of Premises by Police Officers and the Seizure of Property Found by Police Officers on Persons or Premises (PACE Code B)**
  improper exercise 4.18.17.4
  stop and search *see* **Statutory Powers of Stop and Search and Requirements to Record Public Encounters by Police Officers and Police Staff (PACE Code A); Stop and search**
  terrorist investigations *see* **Terrorism: terrorist investigations**
  towards mentally disordered persons *see* **Mentally disordered persons**
  use of force *see* **Use of force**
Police stations
  designated stations 4.3.12
  'places of safety' for mentally disordered persons 4.4.2
Postal services: misuse *see* **Communications: offences**
Pregnancy and maternity: discrimination 4.16.4.5–4.16.4.6 *see also* **Discrimination**
Premises
  covert surveillance of *see* **Covert surveillance**
  definition 4.2.3, 4.2.3.4
  'dwelling': definition 4.2.3, 4.2.3.4
  'enclosed' premises: definition 4.5.6
  licensed premises *see* **Licensed premises**
  NHS premises, causing nuisance or disturbance on 4.5.7
  powers of entry and search *see* **Entry, search and seizure; Searches of Premises by Police Officers and the Seizure of Property Found by Police Officers on Persons or Premises (PACE Code B)**
  premises licences 4.6.4.1 *see also* **Licensing**
  'residential premises': definition 4.13.7.7

  schools *see* **Schools**
  trespass *see* **Trespass** *see also* **Houses**
Privacy, right to 4.1.4.6, 4.13.2 *see also* **Communications; Data protection**
Privileged material 4.2.3.8, 4.2.3.10, 4.2.8, 4.2.8.7, 4.2.8.11
Probationer constables: disciplinary proceedings 4.17.5
Processions and assemblies
  advance notice of public processions 4.8.4.1
  'assembly': definition 4.8.4.5
  breach of conditions 4.8.4.2, 4.8.4.4
  grounds for prohibiting 4.8.4.3, 4.8.4.5
  holding prohibited procession or assembly 4.8.4.3, 4.8.4.5
  human rights 4.8.1, 4.8.2, 4.8.3, 4.8.4.4
  power to impose conditions 4.8.4.2, 4.8.4.4
  trespass *see* **Trespass**
  trying to break up public meetings 4.8.5
  see also **Breach of the peace; Public disorder**
Production orders: application procedure 4.2.4, 4.2.4.1 *see also* **Search warrants**
Properties *see* **Premises**
Proscribed organisations: membership 4.15.2.1
Protected disclosures, victimisation for 4.16.4.10
Protests *see* **Processions and assemblies**
Psychoactive substances 4.7.2
Public authorities
  data protection duties *see* **Data protection**
  freedom of information duties 4.13.3
  sharing of information under Multi-Agency Public Protection Arrangements (MAPPA) 4.13.4
  see also **Local authorities**
Public confidence 4.1.4.3
Public disorder
  human rights defences 4.8.2, 4.8.3, 4.9.8.1
  offences
    acting, or inciting others to act, in a disorderly fashion at elections 4.8.5
    affray 4.9.5
    causing nuisance or disturbance on NHS premises 4.5.7
    fear or provocation of violence 4.9.6
    harassment, alarm or distress 4.9.8 *see also* **Harassment offences**
    intentionally causing harassment, alarm or distress 4.9.7 *see also* **Harassment offences**
    riot 4.9.3
    trespass offences *see* **Trespass**
    trying to break up public meetings 4.8.5
    unlawful violence 4.9.3.1
    violent disorder 4.9.4
  see also **Anti-social behaviour; Breach of the peace; Processions and assemblies**
Public entertainments requiring licences 4.6.6
Public gatherings
  trying to break up public meetings 4.8.5
  see also **Processions and assemblies**
Public sector equality duty 4.1.3, 4.1.4.3, 4.2.2, 4.3.4, 4.16.8 *see also* **Discrimination; Human rights**
Pubs and bars *see* **Licensed premises**